T0274955

TRIAL BY THEATRE

REPORTS ON CZECH DRAMA

BARBARA DAY

UNIVERZITA KARLOVA
NAKLADATELSTVÍ KAROLINUM 2019

DRAMATICA

KAROLINUM PRESS is a publishing department of Charles University
Ovocný trh 560/5, 116 36 Prague 1, Czech Republic
www.karolinum.cz

Cover and Design by Jan Šerých
Photography by Barbara Day; Miroslav Hák; Jaroslav Kořán; Jaroslav Krejčí;
Petr Mazanec; Vilém Sochůrek; Jaromír Svoboda
Images courtesy of: the Arts and Theatre Institute; the City of Brno Archives;
the Czech News Agency; the Museum of Czech Literature; the Theatre on a String
archives; Wikimedia Commons
The cover photograph is of Otomar Krejča's production of *Romeo and Juliet*
at the National Theatre, 1963. Photo by Jaromír Svoboda (courtesy of the photographer)
Frontispiece photograph is of Peter Scherhaufer's production of Chameleon, 1984.
Photo by Jaroslav Krejčí (courtesy of the photographer)
Set and printed in the Czech Republic by Karolinum Press
First edition

Cataloging-in-Publication Data is available from the National Library
of the Czech Republic

Peer reviewed by Veronika Ambros (Slavic Languages and Literatures, University
of Toronto) and Martin Pšenička (Theatre Studies, Charles University)

ISBN 978-80-246-3953-6
ISBN 978-80-246-3922-2 (pdf)
ISBN 978-80-246-4068-6 (epub)
ISBN 978-80-246-4069-3 (mobi)

CONTENTS

LIST OF ILLUSTRATIONS

PREFACE

In the country now called the Czech Republic, the 1960s are known nostalgically as the *Zlatá šedesátá*, the "Golden Sixties." For a quarter of a century, Czechoslovakia had been shrouded in Nazi and Stalinist totalitarianism, but seemed in that decade to be emerging into a time of freedom. Czechs were looking forward to speaking and behaving as they wished, without fear of betrayal. The political hopes of the period, summed up in the phrase "Socialism with a human face," proved an illusion. But the Prague Spring itself was not; the decade of the sixties really was a time when literature and the arts flourished. Freedom of speech culminated in the summer of '68, when censorship was abolished.

I was fortunate enough to be there. Intrigued by meetings with young Slovaks and Czechs in Italy and France,* I found a way to cross the Iron Curtain by means of the bilateral cultural exchange programme administered by the British Council. In October 1965 I registered in the Drama Faculty of the Academy of Performing Arts (DAMU). I was overwhelmed—by the beauty of Prague, by the eagerness of new acquaintances to introduce me to their culture. Everyone went to the theatre, it seemed, and moreover had connections to someone working in it. My most important discovery was the Theatre on the Balustrade (*Divadlo Na zábradlí*); at first Ladislav Fialka's mime company, whose production *Fools* (1965) had a poetry and intensity I had never experienced in the British theatre. Then I met the drama company, led by the theatre director Jan Grossman with his close colleague, the playwright Václav

* This was in 1963 and 1964, when travel restrictions began to ease; students from the Bratislava Academy of Performing Arts (*Vysoká škola múzických umení*, VŠMU) brought Pavel Kohout's musical version of *Around the World in 80 Days* to Parma's 11th Festival Internazionale del Teatro Universitario. The student group included the future stars of Czechoslovak theatre, Emília Vášáryová and Marián Labuda.

Havel—Czechoslovakia's future president. Within weeks I had seen Havel's first plays in their original productions,* as well as Jan Grossman's iconic *Ubu Roi* (1964). In May 1966 I was watching the rehearsals for Grossman's dramatisation of Kafka's *The Trial*.

As a fresh graduate from Manchester University's department of drama, I was accustomed to the hierarchy of English theatre. But in my discovery of the Czech theatre, I found myself running neck and neck with luminaries of the British theatre: Peter Brook, Martin Esslin, Kenneth Tynan, Peter Daubeny... In the spring of 1967 and 1968, the Theatre on the Balustrade was a highlight of London's World Theatre Season; I was there, employed in an undefined role backstage. In June 1968 I returned to Prague hoping to negotiate a more defined role—until we were woken before dawn one August morning by the thunder of Soviet aircraft.†

Over the next few years I watched from a distance the gradual demolition of the society that had so engaged me. The country entered its third phase of totalitarianism. The lowest point came in 1979, with the imprisonment of the playwright who, in 1966, had lent me the first English translations of his plays: Václav Havel. I realised that not only had the whole world of the 1960s disappeared and its playwrights, directors, and dramaturges been dismissed, expelled, or otherwise silenced, but that the period could not be written about *at all*, that its names and activities were being erased from history. In an unserious moment I observed that the ban could not apply to me; I was beyond the jurisdiction of President Husák's "Normalisation." The observation was taken seriously by the scholar and expert in Russian theatre, Edward Braun; in 1980 I was accepted for postgraduate study at Bristol University, researching the history of the Theatre on the Balustrade and the small stages of the 1960s.

On my return to Prague in 1982, I was registered in the Department of Theatre Studies of the Arts Faculty of Charles University. A remorseless purge had been operating in the faculty throughout the 1970s; a process that had involved not simply the abolition of departments and the dismissals of academic staff, but long drawn-out appeals, examinations, justifications, and assessments followed by constant checks, in an effort to ensure the faculty's loyalty to the regime.‡ In retrospect, I appreciate all the more the assistance I was given by my ironical consultant, the theatre historian Milan Lukeš, and

* *The Garden Party* (1963) and *The Memorandum* (1965).

† AN-12s carrying tanks.

‡ In the early part of this century, this operation was the subject of research project *KSČ na FF UK 1969–1989* (The Communist Party of Czechoslovakia at the Arts Faculty of Charles University 1969–1989) funded by Charles University, the Academy of Sciences, and the Czech Science Foundation. The resulting literature can be found in the Bibliography.

by those he suggested I should met. At the same time, I sought out my old contacts; knowing now what humiliations these practitioners and scholars had suffered and the risks they still ran, I look back with amazement at the willingness with which archives and memories were opened. I remember a visit to a windowless archive where the theatre historian Jindřich Černý introduced me to the daughter of the philosopher Jan Patočka; the lilac-scented, crumbling Sova Mills on Kampa Island, where I interviewed the theatre historian Vladimír Just; an enigmatic summons from the head of the Theatre Institute, Eva Soukupová; and long conversations with Jan Grossman in his apartment on the Vltava embankment. Later, I brought copies of articles I had written for the British press to Karel Král in the documentation department of the Theatre Institute; and met Anna Freimanová, who was secretly working on the samizdat journal *O divadle*, in the corridors of the National Museum's theatre department, where she was officially employed. Then, as I went around Prague one day in spring 1984, I was quietly informed by three different people that Havel had been taken from prison to hospital. I became increasingly aware of solidarity in theatre circles, and a network of connections functioning below the surface.

Not all my research was on the decade of the 1960s. I became fascinated by Czech theatre history, especially the nineteenth-century National Awakening and the interwar avant-garde. Above all, I discovered that theatre under "Normalisation" was not the barren land it seemed from a distance, but was full of fresh growth that subtly camouflaged itself to avoid attention from the authorities. Most dynamic of all, commended to me immediately on my arrival by Jan Grossman and by Milan Lukeš, was the Brno Theatre on a String (*Divadlo na provázku*). Its impact was similar to that of the Balustrade Theatre twenty years earlier, but this time my role was to bring the theatre to England. With the cooperation of Bristol University and many others, in a festival held during one of the low points of the Cold War (1985), audiences were cheering not only Theatre on a String but also the dance theatre Chorea Bohemica, the jazz musician Jiří Stivín, and other high points of Czech culture. Through the dramaturge Petr Oslzlý, the driving force behind Theatre on a String, I became involved with the "underground seminars"; that is another story, told in *The Velvet Philosophers* (1999), but I thank Roger Scruton, my colleague then, for his encouragement with the present book.

Over the years I have many people to thank: for the original dissertation, Edward Braun and Bristol University, and the British Academy, which helped to fund my research; also the bilateral exchange programme administered by the British Council, which made longer visits to Czechoslovakia possible; and my examiners, J. P. Stern of Cambridge and Robert Porter of Bristol. Robert Pynsent and David Short of London University and James Naughton of Oxford University were generous with their time and knowledge. Simon Trussler published a long essay in *New Theatre Quarterly* (August 1986), following which Nick Hern commissioned *Czech Plays* (Nick Hern Books, 1991).

Among my Czech teachers and friends, I remember with especial gratitude Karel Brušák of Cambridge University and Jan Grossman. Jitka Martin, Petr Oslzlý, and Richard Weber were also immensely important. Close behind came Oldřich Černý, Lída Engelová, Jiří Hanák, Antonín Jelínek, Karel Král, Zuzana Kočová, and Zdenka Kratochvílová. Those who gave much help when I was researching the original dissertation included Jan Burian, František Černý, Jindřich Černý, Drahomíra Fialková, Jarmila Gabrielová, Vladimír Just, Jakub Korčák, Otomar Krejča, Milan Lukeš, Lída Myšáková-Paulová, Bořivoj Srba, Jiří Suchý, Milena Tomíšková, and Ivan Vyskočil. I also interviewed or corresponded with Jiří Daněk, Jan Dušek, Ladislav Fialka, Václav Havel, Miroslav Horníček, Václav Hudeček, Jan Hyvnar, Karel Jernek, Jaromír Kazda, Jan Kopecký, Karel Kraus, Ivan Kyncl, Oldřich Lipský, Harry Macourek, Miloš Macourek, Luboš Malinovský, Zdeněk Míka, Jiří Nesvadba, Petr Pavlovský, Karel Pech, Boleslav Polívka, Zdeněk Potužil, Jan Přeučil, Petr Scherhaufer, Evald Schorm, Otakar Roubínek, Zdeněk Šikola, Josef Škvorecký, Ladislav Smoček, Zdeněk Svěrák, Ctibor Turba, Milan Uhde, Nina Vangeli, Radim Vašinka, Vladimír Vodička, and Stanislav Vyskočil. The help of the Theatre Institute has been invaluable throughout. More recently, my thanks go to Veronika Ambros, Marie Boková, Jan Dvořák, Anna Freimanová, Vlasta Gallerová, Jaroslav Krejčí (photographer), Julek Neumann, Jana Patočková, Ladislava Petišková, Jitka Sloupová, and Eva Šormová. Finally, I want to thank Martin Pšenička for his encouragement and perseverance in seeing this project through from 2014.

I am grateful to the students on the Arts and Social Change program of SIT Study Abroad, Czech Republic, and Academic Director Sarah Brock, and to the students on the international programme at DAMU, Dean Doubravka Svobodová and Vice Dean Marek Bečka, for giving me the chance to relive this story of Czech theatre. At the final stage, I turn again to the Department of Theatre Studies of the Arts Faculty of Charles University Prague and the Karolinum Press, and thank them for enabling this publication.

Barbara Day June 2018

INTRODUCTION

The past is never far away in Central Europe, and this book is for those interested in the ethical and cultural resistance to the destructive ideologies of the twentieth century. ***Trial by Theatre: Reports on Czech Drama*** is not concerned with theatre alone; nor is it intended as a comprehensive history of the Czech theatre. It is rather an exploration of why the theatre is central to the social and political history of the Czech lands (Bohemia and Moravia). Czech theatre, described by the historian Jarka Burian as the "Reflector and Conscience of a Nation," is neither peripheral nor elitist, but an essential part of daily culture. Historically, it is identified with the spirit of the nation, and with the revival of its language. It is about the power of the creative spirit and its engagement with the deadly forces of totalitarianism.

Trial by Theatre is a revision and completion of my dissertation *The Theatre on the Balustrade of Prague and the Small Stage Tradition in Czechoslovakia* (1986). I worked on this during the years of "Normalisation," to keep alive the memory of the small stages that had played a critical role in the society and politics of the 1960s. I followed threads leading back to the Czech "National Awakening" in the Habsburg Empire. In the Bohemian lands, the theatre's status and reputation enabled its practitioners to develop visual, linguistic, and dramatic features that they used to promote national objectives. The pressures of history led to their constant reinvention and redeployment at times of social and political crisis. Between the wars, the Prague Structuralists created a laboratory for the analysis of theatre. During the Nazi occupation, theatre became a refuge. The intense theatrical creativity of the 1960s was partly due to the ideological barriers that forced intellectuals out of literature and academia. Similarly, the theatre of the 1980s owed much of its vitality to the influence of personalities banned from public life after the Soviet invasion of 1968. It was, as it turned out in 1989, the theatre that shaped the Velvet Revolution. The historical examples I have chosen often come from the "poor theatre" (in Jerzy Grotowski's sense) rather than from the classic stage. The deeper I went, the more I realised how much more there is to discover. I do not consider this book to be a definitive text, but a handbook for further exploration.

The prologue reports on a debate organised by the journal *Divadlo* (Theatre) in November 1968, three months after the Soviet invasion. The theatre directors, playwrights, dramaturges, and critics involved were aware of how the theatre could influence the emotions and behaviour of the public, and of their own responsibility in this context. Conscious that they were standing at a historic moment, they reflected on the emotional power of history, and on how it had been used and misused. Since they invoked the National Awakening, I have made this the starting point of my narrative. In the nineteenth and first part of the twentieth century, two theatre cultures ran side by side: the mainstream German-language theatre and its makeshift country cousin, the Czech-language theatre, always translating, improvising, complaining, shouldering its way onto the stage. The roots of theatre in the Bohemian Crown Lands, however, reach deeper. Maybe they took hold in the first century AD when the Celtic Boii settled at the crossroads of Europe, or perhaps five centuries later with the arrival of the Slavs. Surrounded on three sides by Germanic tribes, the Czechs took possession of a bowl of the most fertile and picturesque territory in Europe. Among the legends later dramatised are those of Princess Libuše, prophet of the greatness of Prague. The martyrdom of Jan Hus in 1415 established him as a national hero, while the military defeat of 1620 (the Battle of the White Mountain) was followed by the executions of the Czech aristocracy and the emigration of the Protestant intelligentsia. The next three hundred years, controversially denoted an "age of darkness," were marked by re-catholicisation and the dominance of German as the language of education and administration. This formed a historical context in which an emotional yet practical and articulate resistance developed on several levels.

In this environment, theatre became a tool for survival in the hands of a nation that felt existentially threatened. This was when the "myth of the National Theatre" emerged—the "Golden Chapel" built out of the contributions of ordinary people. Even if one allows that most of the funding came from state sources, the myth has its own validity, and its impact on the popular attitude to theatre is recognisable today. In the nineteenth century the theatre was an essential element of Czech identity; in the twentieth it asked increasingly difficult questions, instinctively analysing and subverting any ideological programme. In its role as the conscience of the land, the theatre has been educational without being didactic, ethical without being self-righteous. Although often intensely political, it did not condemn or endorse, but invited theatregoers to decide for themselves. That is not to say it did not know right from wrong; rather, it asked theatregoers to look at right and wrong from different angles, and maybe to revise their conclusions. The audience took the questions home, or debated them there and then in the theatre foyer.

In this "theatre on the move" (*divadlo na pohybu*)* every performance was different and thus "always at a beginning." It drew inspiration (but not convention) from the past. It relied on the paradox that an event in history can happen only once, yet in the theatre that one time is "here and now". With censorship on its heels, it learnt to express itself through simile and metaphor, through juxtaposition, allegory and allusion, requiring the full engagement of the theatregoer. This kind of theatre was at home on the "small stages" (*malé scény*) that originated in the 1960s, in the "*auteur théâtre*" (*autorské divadlo*)† of the 1970s and in the "studio-type theatres" (*divadla studiového typu*) of the 1980s, when its practitioners, taking responsibility for an otherwise "normalised" nation, pressed for change.

In *Trial by Theatre: Reports on Czech Drama*, I try to tell the story of a national theatre whose history parallels that of society, using particular themes and personalities to follow it from one generation to another. I have summarised or omitted (maybe unfairly) some aspects of theatre history which deserved a fuller treatment, but which did not illuminate the story of "theatre that is always at a beginning." Conversely, I have sometimes highlighted minor figures or incidents to emphasise a particular relevance. The continuity of the Czech theatre community makes it possible for this to work organically. More tangibly, the Czechs have been (and still are) exceptionally diligent in recording and analysing their own theatre history.

The Cabinet for the Study of Czech Theatre (*Kabinet pro studium českého divadla*) was founded in 1956 as part of the Institute of Czech Literature of the Czechoslovak Academy of Sciences. Its researchers were engaged in long-term projects such as the four-volume *Dějiny českého divadla* (*The History of the Czech Theatre*; 1968, 1969, 1977, 1983). Notoriously, the history never advanced onto the delicate ground beyond 1945. It would be a major work of scholarship were it not for its ideological bias—for which I do not blame the researchers, most of whom would have wished things otherwise. Under Communism, the Cabinet was not only the workplace of ideologists, but also

---

* Theatre on the Move is the name of a festival held by Theatre (Goose) on a String (see p. 236–241) in Brno in 1973 and subsequently at unpredictable intervals, but always at a critical moment in the life of the theatre.

† In the sense that the author is one or more members of the company, cf. Josef Kovalčuk, *Autorské divadlo 70. let* (1982).

a refuge for banned teachers and dramaturges, much of whose research remained unpublished until after 1989. When, in the early 1990s, the budget of the Academy of Sciences was radically cut, the Cabinet was rescued by the Theatre Institute (*Divadelní ústav*). A team of researchers still produces scholarly encyclopedias and histories such as *Česká divadla: Encyklopedie divadelních souborů* (*Czech Theatres: Encyclopedia of Theatre Companies*).

The Theatre Institute itself—now the Arts and Theatre Institute (*Institut umění - Divadelní ústav*)—was founded in 1959 by the Ministry of Culture bureaucrat who had been responsible for the hugely successful Czechoslovak exhibit at Expo 58 in Brussels. It became an essential part of the Czechoslovak theatre scene and in the 1990s adapted to the electronic age, not only through a comprehensive website, but also through networking all theatres and associated institutions.* It organises conferences and exhibitions (including the Prague Quadrennial), is an initial point of contact for foreigners, collates information from theatres and teaching institutes countrywide, operates an accessible library and documentation department, and publishes a range of books on theatre.

One feature of Czech theatre that intrigues foreigners is the lack of unemployment; under Communism this was manipulated by the Plan—the number of students selected by the teaching institutions corresponded to the number of personnel required for the countrywide theatre network. They were prepared at the academies, the universities, and the Prague Conservatoire (musicians and dancers). The Academy of Performing Arts (*Akademie múzických umění*) in Prague† and the Janáček Academy of Music and Performing Arts (*Janáčkova akademie múzických umění*) in Brno‡ are prestigious, university-level institutions on the international network. They prepare students for practical roles in the theatre, including acting, directing, puppetry, arts management, and stage design. Dramaturgy, which straddles the practical and academic fields, can be studied either in the performing arts academies or in one of the university departments for theatre studies at Charles University in Prague, Masaryk University in Brno, or Palacký University in Olomouc. The university departments became independent more gradually than the Academies, which were established in the energetic postwar years. In Brno and Olomouc they emerged as fully fledged departments only after 1989; while the department in Prague barely survived the purges of the Normalisation period, in the process being merged with the department of music. These organisations and their publications are important for any researcher of Czech

* The Theatre Institute director responsible (from 1996–2007) was Ondřej Černý, son of the theatre historian Jindřich Černý. He then became director of the National Theatre (2007–2012).

† Opened in 1946, it has three faculties: Music/Dance, Drama, and Film/TV.

‡ Opened in 1947, it has two faculties: Music and Drama.

theatre, as is the Clementinum Library, the Baroque complex of buildings in the Old Town of Prague.* The British Library in London also has impressive holdings of material on Czech theatre. However, there was very little available in English in the 1980s, and the situation has not improved as much as one would hope. Two well-researched but contrasting books *Czech Drama Since World War II* by Paul Trensky (1978) and *The Silenced Theatre* by Marketa Goetz-Stankiewicz (1979) emerged at the end of the 1970s.† A number of articles have appeared in specialised theatre journals; the best of them are by Jarka Burian, who subsequently shaped some of them into *Leading Creators of Twentieth-Century Czech Theatre* (2002), as well as publishing *Modern Czech Theatre: Reflector and Conscience of a Nation* (2000). I recommend the latter as the best available introduction to Czech theatre. Since 1989, two histories of the Czech theatre have been translated and published by the Drama Faculty of the Academy of Performing Arts (DAMU): Jaromír Kazda's *Czech Theatre* (1994) and Jan Císař's *The History of the Czech Theatre* (2010). The first is clear and factual, but very brief; the second is thorough and erudite, but complex for a newcomer to the subject.‡

Czechoslovakia briefly caught the attention of the West by its success at Expo 58 in Brussels, which also launched the international career of the stage designer Josef Svoboda. However, Svoboda's ascent, although fuelled by half a century of Czech scenographic experiment, was largely solo, and its specifically Czech features were uncredited abroad. His work is described in Helena Albertová's *Josef Svoboda: Scenographer*, and that of his predecessors Vlastislav Hofman and František Tröster in the monographs *Vlastislav Hofman* and *František Tröster: Artist of Light and Space* (theatre designers are more fortunate than theatre directors in having their work made accessible to the international public; puppetry is likewise relatively well presented). The creative surge in 1960s Czechoslovakia—especially the new wave of film§ but also theatre and literature—led to the appearance of Czech theatre companies in London's World Theatre Season. This stimulated the writing

* It was here that in 1983, after I had been vainly ordering copies of *Divadelní noviny* (*Theatre News*) for 1967, a courageous assistant in the reading room alerted me in a whisper to the existence of the (unsignposted) *zvláštní fondy*—special deposits of politically sensitive material—in the attic. An official letter from the Department of Theatre Studies at Charles University allowed me to access the attic and read *Divadelní noviny*. My temper tantrum when the *zvláštní fondy* refused to release the papers for photocopying led to an appointment with a higher authority, which rather strangely took place in a public corridor. The authority prevaricated by requiring another letter from my department, which felt, however, that it had pushed the barriers far enough, and arranged for me to borrow copies from a personal archive.

† Details of all the publications mentioned in the Introduction are in the Bibliography.

‡ I would also like to thank Martin Pšenička for drawing my attention to the fact that Jan Císař's book is part of an ongoing dialogue between different schools of Czech theatre historians, particularly with reference to the (untranslated) *Dějiny českého divadla* (*Divadelní revue*, 1/2011, pp. 161–164).

§ See Peter Hames, *The Czechoslovak New Wave* (1985).

of reviews and newspaper articles by British journalists and theatre critics, in particular the American professor, Henry Popkin, in *The Times*. These are now buried in archives, although Martin Esslin's brief chapter on the Czech Theatre of the Absurd appeared in the second edition of his seminal book on the subject. The Havel phenomenon was beginning to emerge at this time, and his first plays were published in English in the late 1960s; however, their potential was hampered by the well-meaning attempts of his translator to retain control. In the West, Václav Havel has tended to overshadow other Czech playwrights of this period, although one is grateful for his theatrical biography by Carol Rocamora (*Acts of Courage*) and literary biography by Kieran Williams (*Václav Havel*). A major project to translate Havel's theatre writing and publish it in English was recently refused funding.

Otherwise, information on theatre produced in the Czech lands is largely inaccessible to students and researchers who do not know Czech. Enormous frustration is caused by the fact that the nation that has probably done the most to document and analyse its theatre experience has done so little to make it systematically available in a world language. With some exceptions, publications available in English are lightweight and/or occasional, without an overall strategy. The publishing house *Pražská scéna* occasionally publishes in English, as does the Theatre Institute, mainly on aspects of contemporary theatre; this is also the case with the Theatre Institute's periodical *Czech Theatre*. One edition of the Cabinet's scholarly periodical, *Czech Theatre Review*, has been published in English; a second is due. English editions of the internationally oriented periodical *Svět a divadlo*, published as *World and Theatre*, also appear sporadically.

Returning to books published abroad: If one covers the field chronologically, the political story of how the National Theatre came to be built is told in Stanley Kimball's *Czech Nationalism: A Study of the National Theatre Movement 1845–83* (1964), while *National Theatre in Northern and Eastern Europe: 1746 to 1900* (edited by Laurence Senelick, 1999) uses contemporary documents to bring alive the stage of that period. John Tyrrell's *Czech Opera* (1988) and Brian S. Locke's *Opera and Ideology in Prague: Polemics and Practice at the National Theater, 1900–1938* (2006) shed some sidelights on theatre practice in the late nineteenth and early twentieth century. Given how little has been published in English on the Czech avant-garde between the wars, it is not surprising there is virtually nothing on the equally dynamic and innovative avant-garde theatre. An exhibition in 1990 in Oxford and London produced a catalogue on the Devětsil arts association; MIT published a monograph on its leader Karel Teige in 1999; and Derek Sayer's *Prague, Capital of the Twentieth Century: A Surrealist History* came out in 2013, but none of them has much to say about the Liberated Theatre or E. F. Burian. The only extended studies in English on the Liberated Theatre and Burian's D34 have again been Jarka Burian's articles, republished in *Leading Creators*. More is available on the work of the interwar Prague Linguistic Circle, which was ahead of the world in its development of the Structuralist analysis of theatre: *Semiotics of Art: Prague School Contributions* (1976), edited by Ladislav Matejka and Irwin R. Titunik, has papers on the semiotic analysis of theatre; Keir Elam analyses these in *The Semiotics of Theatre and Drama* (1980). The first book specifically on the Prague School and theatre semiotics, *The Semiotic Stage* by Michael L. Quinn, was published in 1996 after the author's death, and *An Approach to the Semiotics of Theatre* (2012) by one of the original Structuralists, Jiří Veltruský, in 2012, eighteen years after his death. Hot off the press is the *Theatre Theory Reader: Prague School Writings* (2017). Its anthology format is a model for publications in English that would disseminate Czech theatre analysis and criticism.

The case is similar with the Czech repertoire, only a part of which is available in English. It was 1999 before any of the classics of the late-nineteenth-century village drama became available in English; the first was Gabriela Preissová's *Her Stepdaughter*, otherwise known as *Jenufa*, followed in 2002 by *Maryša* by Alois and Vilém Mrštík (with an essay by Jan Grossman). The other plays of this genre, including the wry comedy *Our Proud Peasants*, are still not available. The interwar period is represented by Karel (and Josef) Čapek's plays, either in dated 1930s translations (*R.U.R.* and *The Insect Play*) or in more acceptable recent versions (*Čapek: Four Plays*, 1999). The plays by the more interesting František Langer do not seem to have been translated into English, except for a dificult-to-obtain version of *On the Periphery*; the only other I know from this period is Arnošt Dvořák and Ladislav Klíma's *Matthew Honest*. The 1960s fared better; all of Václav Havel's plays are available, sometimes in editions that include plays by his colleagues: He shares *Drama Contemporary: Czechoslovakia* with Klíma, Kohout, Kundera, and Uhde; *The Vaněk Plays* with Dienstbier, Kohout, and Landovský; and *Czech Plays* with Fischerová, Klíma, and Topol. Josef Topol's *The End of Shrovetide* is available in the Visegrad Drama series, but existing translations of plays by Milan Uhde and Arnošt Goldflam are not on general sale. It is unfortunate that one of the most notable playwrights of the 1960s, Alena Vostrá, is not among them; she helped to continue the Czech tradition (strongest in the nineteenth century, especially with Gabriela Preissová) of women writers with insight into the shifting zeitgeist.

An online search for material begins with the English pages of the Theatre Institute site. The papers of some candidates at Czech universities who have written their dissertation or diploma work in English are available on the internet, as are some papers on Czech theatre studies by English-speaking scholars. On the other hand, the number of books on theatre in Czech continues to grow, in spite of what one would expect to be a limited readership; not just commercial publications (those too), but also serious criticism and analysis. In 2016, the Janáček Academy listed around twelve Czech periodicals that dealt exclusively with aspects of theatre (I am counting dance, puppetry, and amateur theatre, but not opera, as this overlaps with music generally). Of current periodicals, the most useful for historians is the *Divadelní revue* (*Theatre Review*), published by the Cabinet for the Study of Czech Theatre. I have included in the Bibliography only those books and periodicals directly relevant to my work.

When I first had the idea for the dissertation that became this book, the Iron Curtain still divided Europe, and the Cold War seemingly stretched for decades ahead of us. I wanted to put on record achievements that could not then even be mentioned in the Czech lands. I wanted to celebrate the free spirits of the past and present who saw resistance to totalitarianism as a self-evident activity. I wanted to honour those who believed in theatre as the ethical heart of society. This still applies.

PROLOGUE

Freedom will never be obtained through crying and lamenting; it will only come through hard work... No nation has ever secured it overnight; a sensible man will not despair but work even harder.
–Karel Havlíček, 1848

Freedom is not something we wait for, some gift, but our task. We create our freedom by thinking and working freely, by wresting it out through our own specific actions.
–Václav Havel, 1968

In the revolutionary year of 1848, Karel Havlíček, politician and journalist, was a member of the Bohemian delegation that hoped to establish a provisional government for the Lands of the Bohemian Crown under a federal Austria. The previous half-century had seen the growth of a movement (retrospectively described as the National Awakening) to re-establish the Czech language and a sense of Czech identity, a movement in which the theatre was to the forefront. The delegation's aim was defeated by the absolutist government that returned to power in Vienna the following spring.

In 1968, during the emotional months that followed the Warsaw Pact invasion of Czechoslovakia, patriotic citizens flocked to revivals of operas and plays dating from the National Awakening. Bedřich Smetana's *Libuše* and Jaroslav Vrchlický's *Drahomíra* evoked legendary figures from Bohemia's heroic past; audiences identified with the sentiments expressed onstage and thereby renewed their optimistic belief in their own moral superiority. Three months after the invasion, the magazine *Divadlo* (*Theatre*) held a discussion to assess the phenomenon.* The playwright Václav Havel opened proceedings by observing that the sense of community was strongest when that community was threatened, but that the response needed to be practical, not emotional. The current phenomenon substituted emotion for action: It was a surrogate programme, pseudo-activity, even fraud. Like Havlíček, Havel rejected a national identity that consisted of slogans and flag-waving in favour of building a responsible society based on ethical principles.

In Havlíček's time, the frustration of 1848 was partially sublimated into a campaign to build a Czech National Theatre, which eventually opened in 1883. Until the late nineteenth century, intellectual life in Prague, an administrative centre of the Habsburg Empire, was for the most part conducted in German. The elegant, stone-built Estates Theatre was patronised by the German-speaking educated classes, since performances in Czech drew only a limited audience from the lower classes (although Czech-language theatre thrived in the countryside). A handful of enthusiasts saw it as their task to create an audience, and to stimulate a sense of national identity, Czech dramas were often based on heroic events from Bohemia's past. It was the proliferation of sentimental and indiscriminate nationalism that drove Havlíček, himself a patriot, to protest.

The *Divadlo* debate of November 1968 similarly concerned the morality of the way in which the theatre was feeding the emotions of the Czechs. The theatre director Jan Grossman responded to Havel by saying that at the time of the National Awakening, theatre had been based on a collective experience, and that he saw the continuation of this on the avant-garde stages, where people "did things for themselves," rather than in the established theatres. In the Bohemian lands, he argued, particular resonances, not necessarily artistic but also nationalist, linguistic, and cultural, contributed to the sense of theatre being a movement related to movement in society (noting that "in our papers, theatre performances are listed under 'culture,' not under 'entertainment' as for example in England"). However, every stick has two ends. Havel had spoken about the substitution of emotion for action, but Grossman pointed out that in the nineteenth century the theatre itself was used as a substitute for political action. Under abnormal circumstances substitution was bound to happen, Grossman argued—just as we drank ersatz coffee during the Nazi occupation.

The Brno playwright Milan Uhde agreed with Havel about the dangers of sentimental patriotism; an age like the present, he believed, was ripe for the formation of false myths, and even in their own time, these historical dramas

* November 1968; the transcript of the discussion was published in the January 1969 issue of *Divadlo*.

had perpetuated a distorted view of life because they simplified the complicated truth of history.

The frequently praised heroic nature of the Czech theatre arose out of times like the late nineteenth century, which were quite unheroic, continued Grossman. In his eyes, this distortion was repeated in the 1950s, a time of conformity when it was incumbent on the citizen and artist never to step out of line. The theatre became "a museum of heroism and revolution." The fact that the substitution of theatre for political action should be significant at all came about because of the theatre's engagement with developments in politics and society. Underlying all progressive trends was a sense that a theatre's programme—its dramaturgy—was not a mere season of productions, but related to movement in society. Therefore, although the writer might resent being cast in the role of a freedom fighter, the pursuit of artistic aims had in itself political results, as it was the pursuit of objective truth.

Counter to expectations, in the two decades that followed the *Divadlo* discussion—one of the direst periods of this totalitarian state, with all its sanctions and censorship—there was an intensely political dialogue being conducted between stage and audience, before the very eyes (or over the heads) of those charged to prevent it. Although it involved mainly the small stages, it was not necessarily absent from the "stone" theatres. The risks could involve demotion, dismissal, loss of profession, damage to family life—standard treatment under Normalisation. The qualities that made this possible were ethical as well as artistic, and followed a trail that led onwards from the struggling, quarrelsome, impoverished "national revivalists" of the turn of the eighteenth and nineteenth centuries.

"Every true art fights for freedom," claimed Grossman, "for freedom of knowledge, of a way forward, of further new projects. As Havel says, for the authenticity of man."[1]

I BOHEMIA RESURGENT

NATIONAL AWAKENING

Under Rudolf II Habsburg at the turn of the sixteenth and seventeenth centuries, Prague, capital of the Bohemian Crown Lands,* was a place of experiment and adventure. Under Rudolf's brother Matthias, however, Vienna became the seat of power and Prague a provincial city. The revolt of the Bohemian Estates against Matthias's withdrawal of their rights and privileges inaugurated the Thirty Years, War; by the end, the overwhelming majority of the Czech nobility had been killed or driven into exile and their estates distributed among nobility from German-speaking lands. Habsburg absolutism was imposed, the Estates retained only nominal powers, and the country was re-catholicised. It was the reforms of Empress Maria Theresa and her son Josef II more than a century later that provoked the movement known as the Czech *Národní obrození*—the National Awakening, Renewal, Revival, or Rebirth.

Influenced by Enlightenment philosophers, the Habsburgs sought to improve the lot of their subjects by rationalising the state and civic life. Government was centralised in Vienna—ensuring that the language of bureaucracy would be German throughout the Empire. The Bohemian Estates lost even their nominal powers, and local officials were appointed from Vienna as imperial civil servants. Josef's reforms in education put the schools under state control, made elementary schooling compulsory for boys and girls, and admitted Protestants and Jews to universities, where the teaching language was changed from Latin to German.

* Bohemia, Moravia, Silesia, and, in the fifteenth century, Upper Lusatia.

Native German speakers had a natural advantage in their working life. Aspiring members of other language groups aimed to acquire a fluent command of German and to conform to Austrian codes of behaviour. They could thus anticipate a career that would raise them above their provincial roots to the higher levels of German-speaking society. In Prague and other centres, Czech was spoken mainly by the lower orders: tradesmen and domestic servants. Ambitious parents, whatever their native language, sent their children to German-language schools and were conversant with German learning and literature.* Books, magazines, and newspapers were published in German. In the late eighteenth century, essentially nothing of literary value, including drama, was written in Czech. As in Vienna, the Prague repertoire was dominated by Italian opera and German-language comedy, pantomime, and burlesque.

However, this did not mean that Czech-language theatre did not exist before the National Awakening. The population in the countryside and the smaller towns of Bohemia and Moravia (except for the German settlements in the border regions) had continued to speak Czech. Folk customs, songs, and music were still part of traditional life. The rituals of the church, the visits of strolling players and puppeteers, were highlights of rural life. There was a healthy tradition of vernacular Czech drama stretching back over several centuries. This native tradition included the liturgical drama of the Middle Ages which, although interrupted by the Hussite Wars, served as one of the diverse sources of material for the popular or folk theatre. In the mid-sixteenth century, the school drama, performed in Latin, became an important area of cultural development. The plays served an educational function, mainly in the form of dramatisations of Biblical stories. Some of the school dramas were translated into Czech, and incorporated elements of the older folk plays. One author who belonged to the humanist tradition was the "Father of Modern Education," Comenius (Jan Amos Komenský), born in Moravia but exiled for his Protestant faith. Comenius took refuge in Leszno in Poland, where in 1630, the year that Sweden's intervention in the Thirty Years' War offered hope of a return home, he published his *Škola hrou* (*Schola Ludus*). It was a textbook containing eight dialogues for his students to perform—not for an audience, but so they might enjoy their studies and learn through doing.

The first permanent private theatre in Prague was opened by Franz Anton Reichsgraf von Sporck, in his palace on Hybernská Street in 1701; it was followed in 1739 by the first public theatre, the Kotzen Theatre, a converted market hall on the street now known as *V kotcích* near Old Town Square.

* These ambitions ended disastrously in the mid-twentieth century when, after the Nazi occupation, most inhabitants with German as their first language were expelled from Bohemia and Moravia.

From the 1770s Emperor Josef II, inspired by Gotthold Ephraim Lessing's analyses in the *Hamburgische Dramaturgie*, began to reform the Viennese theatre. Lessing, a philosopher and playwright, envisaged a *Nationaltheater* which would be a public institution, determined neither by the taste of an aristocratic owner nor by reliance on the box office. Contemporary theatre was to be clear and resonant, taking classical principles as a standard, but relating them to the direct experience of the audience. Modern drama was to be based on reason, requiring the audience to feel the passions of the actors and to transform them into "virtuous actions." The audience was to be directly involved in the complex art of theatre, one that would make them conscious of their identity as part of a wider society.

In 1769, the new director of the Kotzen Theatre, Johann Joseph von Brunian, influenced by the German reforms, designated his theatre a *Nationaltheater* and began to stage a repertoire of serious drama (in German). In 1771, the theatre ran into financial difficulties and as an experiment Brunian staged a Czech-language production of the popular German farce *Herzog Michel*, calling it (in Czech) *Kníže Honzík* (*Count Johnnie*). It was performed by the regular actors of the company, whose first language was German and whose Czech pronunciation was problematic. It seems to have been well attended, but did not lead to regular performances in Czech.

The Kotzen Theatre changed hands, and in 1781 the company was taken over by Franz Anton Josef Graf von Nostitz-Rieneck. Born into an old Lusatian family, he was a German-speaking patriot who defended the interests of the Bohemian Lands against Austrian centralisation. He decided to construct at his own expense a purpose-built theatre—the *Graflich Nostitzsches Nationaltheater*—next to Charles University and in the middle of the fruit market (*Ovocný trh*). Opened in 1783 as an assertion of Bohemian patriotism and intended to show that Prague could vie with Vienna, it is famous above all for the triumph in 1786 of Mozart's *The Marriage of Figaro* after its lukewarm reception in Vienna, and for the première of *Don Giovanni* in 1787.* The fact that the first production, Lessing's *Emilia Galotti*, and subsequent productions were performed in German did not imply a lack of patriotism. Not only were there no plays in Czech nor actors to perform them; there did not seem to be any audiences eager to watch them either. In 1785, as a commercial experiment, the management tested whether there might be an audience for plays performed in Czech. On Sunday afternoons, when the lower classes had their free time, bilingual actors from the company appeared in plays translat-

* When the theatre was restored in 1984 (after it had been used as a location for Miloš Forman's *Amadeus*), it was found that Count Nostitz had in his haste built the theatre almost without foundations. Excavation, reinforcement, and reconstruction lasted for eight years—far longer than it had taken to build the theatre.

ed from German. In 1798, after the Count's death, the theatre was purchased by the Bohemian Estates and its name changed to the Theatre of the Estates (*Das Ständetheater*, in Czech *Stavovské divadlo*).

The Enlightenment appeal to the intellect coincided with a concern among Bohemian patriots that the Josephine reforms were contributing to a decline in the use of the Czech language, and and as the language disappeared, so too would customs and traditions, even Czech history. They feared a future in which the educated classes would consider themselves Austrian first and Czech secondarily. With this in mind, the historian and philologist Josef Dobrovský—whose first language was German—started work on his *Lehrgebäude der böhmischen Sprache* (*Grammar of the Czech Language*, 1809), a landmark of the National Awakening. More scholars and writers emerged, publishing books and articles—written in Czech or translated from German—and embarking on projects to promote the Czech language. Among these were the forged manuscripts of Zelená Hora and Dvůr Králové (*c.* 1818), a carefully prepared hoax intended to prove that Czech had been a literary language as early as the tenth century. Dobrovský, who recognised their inauthenticity, was villified by more gullible revivalists.

One of the most effective ways of promoting the Czech language was through theatre, which in time became an arena for disputes over two tendencies: one that wanted to popularise the Czech language and attract a wide audience through entertainment; another that saw this approach as demeaning the Czech language. The second faction set high standards in composition and linguistics, with the aim of demonstrating that Czech held a worthy place among European languages. Controversies ensued over whether it was better to cultivate original writing in Czech, however clumsy the first attempts, or to concentrate on translating established works and on finding appropriate Czech equivalents.

Czech-language theatre was inextricably involved with the National Awakening. It became both a tool and a symbol. It was practiced largely by amateurs like the Thám brothers: Karel, who made the first translations into Czech of Schiller and of Shakespeare (through German), and Václav, who in 1784 published the first anthology of Czech verse. The same year the brothers delivered a petition to the Town Council asking for "a Czech-German theatre in the New Town of Prague," since:

> Every sensible person who is also acquainted with history is aware that the art of acting has always had a great influence on a country's morals and that, in many cases, it has assisted in sharpening public awareness and education. However, a large proportion of people are deprived of the enjoyment and beneficial influence of performed plays because of their inadequate knowledge of the German language; the petitioner is therefore

convinced that the regular presentation of plays in Czech to such a public will ensure that good entertainment is provide quite cheaply in place of a vulgar kind of amusement.[2]

Nevertheless, it was 1786 before the Thám brothers were able to open the Patriotic Theatre (*Vlastenské divadlo*) on the Horse Market (now Wenceslas Square). Despite being designated "Imperial and Royal" by Emperor Joseph II, the theatre was popularly known as the "Hut" (*Bouda*). The opening production was *Gratitude and Love to the Homeland*, a morally improving play adapted from August Wilhelm Iffland's German original. The historian Jan Císař estimates that in the first two years 120–140 new plays in Czech were performed,[3] including what is believed to be the first original drama in Czech, Václav Thám's *Břetislav and Judith or, Abduction from the Cloister* (1786). The audience consisted of domestic servants, craftsmen, tradesmen, and students, but numbers were too thin to make an all-Czech repertoire viable, and performances had to be scheduled in German too. In spite of the prestige of a visit from the emperor, the Hut was abandoned in June 1789 amid complaints that it disrupted trade in the market, but chiefly because it was not financially viable.

One of Josef II's reforms had been to close down approximately half the houses of religious orders in the empire. This enabled the company from the Patriotic Theatre to move to a theatre space set up in the library of a former monastery of Irish Franciscans near the Powder Tower, known as *U Hybernů*. Certain distinctive elements of Czech theatre were emerging: theatre practitioners who saw the medium as educational as well as entertaining, an audience drawn from ordinary people, the use of everyday life as a dramatic subject, an awareness of the importance of language, an ability to disguise the intended message, and consciousness of the emotional power of history and of the subversive nature of justice. Historical plays were popular, especially those dealing with the problems of servitude, while new plays on contemporary life were set in a lower-middle-class environment. The Czech-speaking performers were young and enthusiastic, but although they saw themselves as reformers rather than revolutionaries, political repression and instability arising from the Napoleonic Wars caused many setbacks, and the end of professional performances in 1809.

Josef II's reforms stalled after his death in 1790 and in some respects went into reverse. The French Revolution and the Napoleonic Wars shook belief in rationality, and the ideas of its proponents were outlawed by the new regime in power in the Austrian Empire, in which Klemens Wenzel von Metternich played a major role. His conviction was that stability had to be maintained in Europe, and that any revolutionary movement had to be avoided at all costs.

This effectively suppressed political involvement by patriots seeking to restore power to the Bohemian Estates, and the national revivalists had to content themselves with cultural activities. Bohemian aristocrats focused rather on the Society of Patriotic Friends of the Arts (*Společnost vlasteneckých přátel umění v Čechách / Privat Gesellschaft patriotischer Kunst-Freunde*), predecessor of the National Museum and the National Gallery, and the Foundation for the Czech Motherland (*Matice česká*, 1831), which was to support the publication of books in Czech.

It was in this atmosphere in 1824 that Jan Nepomuk Štěpánek, leader of an amateur theatre company, was appointed director of what was now the Royal Theatre of the Estates. He had the opportunity to reintroduce professional Czech-language performances and was himself the author of popular comedies based on everyday life (*The Czech and the German*, 1816). He also adapted plays from the German repertoire (*The Bandits at Chlum*, 1815). The choice of the local setting of Chlum, a Czech-speaking village to the west of Prague, helped the audience to identify with the characters. Štěpánek was the first to introduce opera in the Czech language, even including original Czech operas. However, his revivalist critics condemned the idealised and romantic stories of his repertoire as mere escapism.

The National Awakening was still just the work of a handful of patriots, trying to engage the interest of Czechs in their own language, literature, and national identity, but unable to agree even among themselves. According to practitioners such as Štěpánek, the theatre was a public platform that could be used to popularise the Czech language. According to his critics, the theatre was a temple of the arts that should propagate only what was highest and noblest in Czech culture. It was often difficult for playwrights and performers to live up to the ideals formulated in patriotic circles.

One active critic was the enterprising young Josef Kajetán Tyl, a hotheaded talent who in 1833 took over a Czech-language journal he named *Květy* (*Blossoms*). It was an instrument through which he could promote his concept of Czech identity, and he used its pages to express his frustration with Štěpánek's choice of repertoire and inadequately rehearsed productions. Tyl was also working as a part-time actor at the Estates Theatre, but left to start his own amateur theatre company, housed in the refectory of another of Prague's redundant monasteries, the Theatre at the Theatines (*Divadlo u Kajetánů*) in the Lesser Quarter. In its three-year existence, it set new standards of production for Czech performances. Many of the performers were writers for *Květy* (they included the poet Karel Hynek Mácha, author of *Máj* (*May*,* 1836)

* *Máj*, according to some scholars a Romantic poem, according to others an ironic poem in Romantic guise, is one of the darkest and most complex works of Czech literature.

and the group was founded largely to promote work of Tyl's teacher, the Hradec Králové schoolmaster and playwright Václav Kliment Klicpera.

Klicpera's plays, witty and fast-moving with vivid characterisation, appealed to educated speakers of Czech more than the robust farces of Štěpánek. He drew on a wide range of genres from parody to poetic drama, and his knowledge of the classical and neoclassical drama influenced the structure of his plays. Among the most popular were the anti-heroic *Hadrian of Rheum* (1817) and *Everyone for his Homeland!* (1829). Tyl also wrote for the ensemble, and in 1835 his verse drama about the shepherd Čestmír rebelling against the stultifying atmosphere of the countryside showed him as a Romantic playwright, the hero modelled in some ways on his own restless nature. Nevertheless, the play ends with the individual's reconciliation with society. This may have represented the policy of nationalist writers to advance through trust and cooperation; it certainly made it easier for the play to pass the censorship. Tyl wrote in other genres too: dramas of contemporary life, fairy tales, and histories. One of his comedies, *Fidlovačka* (1834), included the song *Kde domov můj?* ("Where is My Home?"with music by František Škroup), which later became the Czech national anthem. *Fidlovačka*, set in Tyl's home environment, portrayed everyday life among the Czech lower classes (there were no others): shoemakers, journeymen, woodcutters, seamstresses, singers, dancers, dudes, waiters, whores, a blind fiddle-player, and Mamsell Margarethe, the German housekeeper. In *Švanda the Bagpiper* (1847), Tyl again takes the theme of the "wanderer" but brings him thankfully back to his home in Bohemia. The emphasis was love of the homeland, and Tyl's voice was growing increasingly assured. In 1847, *The Miners of Kutná Hora*, in which Tyl reworked a historical theme to make a political point about workers' unrest, was at first banned. Audiences stormed the theatre for the première of *Jan Hus* (1849), based on the life of the fifteenth-century Bohemian martyr, critical of the Roman Catholic Church and thus implicitly of the Habsburg Monarchy.

By this time, Tyl had become a major figure in national life; in 1846 he was appointed director of the Czech section of the Theatre of the Estates, and in March 1848 he was one of those who met to demand from the Habsburg regime the rights recently confirmed for the "Lands of St. Stephen" (Hungary)—the unity and independence of the "Lands of St. Wenceslas." In July he was elected to the Constituent Assembly, which in September passed the Act of Emancipation. The ending of the *robota*, or statutory labour, initiated a major development in urban society, as the emancipated peasants made their way to the towns, swelling the labour force and increasing the Czech-speaking population. It meant the beginning of the industrialisation of Bohemia, with iron and steel works, engineering, and textile production. However, as far as political life was concerned, all attempts at autonomy collapsed after the failure of the October Revolution in Vienna. In May 1849 the new absolutist regime imposed a new constitution which treated the whole Empire as a unitary centralised state.

The writer Karel Havlíček Borovský had also been a Czech delegate of the Constituent Assembly; with the historian, philosopher, and politician František Palacký, author of the *Dějiny národu českého v Čechách a v Moravě* (*History of the Czech Nation in Bohemia and Moravia*; 1848–1876), he led the Czech liberals who sought a federal solution for the Empire. Havlíček was a fierce critic of all he saw as sentimental and lacking in thought. Having planned to work for the nationalist cause as a priest, he was expelled from the seminary for insubordination. Originally a supporter of Pan-Slavism, he was disillusioned by his experience as a tutor in a family of the Russian aristocracy. As editor of *Pražské noviny* (*Prague News*, later renamed *Národní noviny*, or *National News*), he made sure its coverage and editorial comment equalled that of the German-language press. He saw Czech literature of the period as being too influenced by the German Romantic style, whose fancifulness and vague phraseology did not suit the Czech idiom. Havlíček challenged ideas that were indiscriminately accepted as patriotically correct; he saw no value in encouraging original Czech writing when it was of poor quality and thought it better for writers to learn their craft by working on translations. He was also highly critical of Tyl's theatre practices—he would have preferred no cooperation with the authorities rather than a compromise, and regarded the policy of Sunday matinées at the Estates Theatre as accepting the second-rate status of the Czechs. Havlíček's emphasis was on the need for hard work rather than emotional talk for the achievement of nationalist aims; he did not blame external factors for the subservience of the Czech people, but the passivity of the Czech character itself.

In 1849, thanks to the efforts of the Prague lawyer and active politician Alois Pravoslav Trojan, who had been an amateur actor with Tyl in the 1830s, an open-air arena for summer entertainment opened, with Tyl as director. It was built in the settlement of Pštroska in Vinohrady, a pleasant area known for its gardens and vineyards, and was the first of several arenas to be built outside the boundary of the New Town. The plays chosen were not of literary merit, but delighted audiences with their comedy, spectacle, and topical jokes. The arenas became a popular feature of Prague summer life for the next half-century. Karel Havlíček, however, considered the semi-permanent structures to be yet another compromise of the Czech theatre enthusiasts with the Austrian authorities, writing in *Národní noviny*:

> For a long time we have worked so that our nation would have what every cultured nation has—its own theatre. […] On Sunday afternoons for a short time, when no one else

wants the building anyway, miserable plays are produced for us. And even these are presented thanks only to a few enthusiastic souls. Czech actors receive nothing, while their German counterparts are well paid. Now the present Provincial Board is embarrassed by such an example of "equality." So Hoffmann, director of the German theatre, requests that the board vote all of 9,000 fl. to build us a summer arena. This they think is equality!

We protest in advance against such equality. If this plan were to be carried out we would end up with a wooden hut where we could only present simple plays in a poor style to a vulgar audience. I believe that if the Provincial Board can offer us nothing better, we must request that they do not concern themselves and that the matter be postponed until the sitting of the first Bohemian Diet...[4]

The outspoken and ailing Havlíček was exiled to Brixen in the Tyrol and died in 1856, shortly after his return. His ideas had influenced some of Tyl's theatre colleagues who, while agreeing with the concept of theatre as an educational tool, reacted against Tyl's repertoire of plays that glorified the past and offered happy endings achieved by superhuman means. Tyl had lost his post as director of the Czech-language theatre company in 1851, returning to the roads of Bohemia as an itinerant actor. Shunned and unpopular with the authorities, he died on tour in 1856. His place had been taken by Josef Jiří Kolár, in the 1830s an actor in Tyl's Theatre at the Theatines. There had been tension between them in the past: In 1841, Kolár's refusal to play as cast had provoked Tyl to punch him in the face. Kolár had taken Tyl to court for insulting him "in the presence of... colleagues, in the most outrageous and illicit manner, grossly impugning his honour and person, attacking him with the most disgraceful names and striking him violently with his fist in the area of his temples and eyes."[5]

NATIONAL THEATRE

Monarchist control under the nineteen-year-old Emperor Franz Josef had been restored in the Austrian Empire with the Constitution of 1849. Policy was dictated by the minister of the interior, Alexander von Bach, who revoked the semi-independence won by Hungary, outlawed political activity, tightened censorship, and placed education again under the Roman Catholic Church. Seeing that all hope of political gain was lost, a group of Czech political and cultural patriots led by Alois Pravoslav Trojan obtained permission to form a Committee to Build a Czech National Theatre (*Sbor pro zřízení českého Národního divadla*). František Palacký (later to be known as the Father of the Nation) was appointed president, and the committee members (including Tyl) were people active in national and political life whose hidden agenda was to inspire the Czechs to a collective effort. Collections took place throughout Bohemia and Moravia and even among Czechs living abroad—"for example, Dr. A. H. Wratislaw, whose grandfather emigrated from Moravia to England, sent us 5 gulden from Cambridge."[6] But in spite of popular enthusiasm, the Austrian government's insistence that it should control public collections and subscriptions made the committee's task difficult. The original concept, which was to include a concert hall and café, was vetoed by the authorities and permission granted for a theatre building only.

In 1856, a site was purchased on the banks of the Vltava and in 1862 the Provisional Theatre (*Prozatimní Divadlo*) was built at one end of the site. It was a controversial decision, as many patriots were afraid that the Provisional Theatre would take the impetus out of the campaign for a National Theatre. However, the tight hold of Bach absolutism was relaxing by the beginning of the 1860s, and there had been an expansion in Czech cultural life. This included the foundation of an arts club (*Umělecká beseda*), a writers' association (*Svatobor*) and a choral society (*Hlahol*, where Bedřich Smetana became chorus master).* There had also been an increase in the number of periodicals published in Czech, while another aspect of nationalism consisted of *okrašlovaní* (beautification). The first of numerous local *okrašlovací spolky* (beautification associations) was founded in 1860 with the aim of improving the environment; initially the physical environment but by the end of the century the intellectual environment as well. Societies abounded, providing care for the countryside, the maintenance of traditional customs and a spirit of voluntary cooperation; their activities included puppetry, and helped to consolidate the association of puppetry with pratical patriotism.

It was in the end the Provisional Theatre that enabled the Czech actors to become accomplished professionals, as it provided the company with a permanent stage on which to rehearse and perform and, from 1864, the opportunity to perform every day. It also inspired Bedřich Smetana to think in terms of a new kind of opera that would draw on aspects of national life and character. The son of a brewer, Smetana had made friends with Karel Havlíček while at school in Německý Brod.† Inspired by Havlíček's nationalism, in 1843 Smetana followed him to Prague, where, as well as studying music and trying to earn a living, he was one of an assertive bunch of patriots that manned the barricades in the Prague Uprising of 1848. Fighting alongside Smetana was his future librettist, the ardent nationalist Karel Sabina. In 1862, Smetana had hopes of being appointed head of opera at the Provisional Theatre, but it

* *Svatobor* and *Hlahol* still exist; the latter resident since 1905 in the art nouveau building on the Masaryk Embankment designed by Josef Fanta.

† *Německý* means "German"; after World War II (and the deportation of the German-speaking population) the name of the town (in East Bohemia) was changed to Havlíčkův Brod.

did not happen until 1866. Smetana shifted the theatre's operatic repertoire from its Italian focus to Czech works—the repertoire included not only his own compositions but operas by new young Czech composers—and raised standards, not least by establishing a school attached to the theatre.

Josef Kajetán Tyl's former rival, Josef Jiří Kolár, now head of the Czech company at the Estates Theatre, had originally opposed the concept of the Provisional Theatre, but in the end led the drama company there from 1866 until 1876. Whereas Tyl had wanted to use theatre as an educative medium for the Czech-speaking population, Kolár was more interested in extending the theatre's resources to make a wider appeal to the public. A university graduate, he had travelled Europe as a tutor and become familiar with a range of literature before turning actor. In his time at the Provisional Theatre, translations from Gogol and Turgenev were performed, as well as French plays touching on social and political questions. Nevertheless, historical plays retained their popularity, since they were able to bypass the censorship by disguising current preoccupations as events from other times and other lands. Kolár was also known as one of the finest nineteenth-century interpreters of Shakespeare, as well as a translator of his plays. The translation of Shakespeare has been, from the time of Karel Thám to the present day, a rallying point for the Czech nation; the taunt that an earthy language such as Czech was unable to interpret the bard's high ideals and noble sentiments was a challenge that no literary translator could ignore, and consequently new translations are produced for every generation. In 1864, the Czechs celebrated the tercentenary of Shakespeare's birth as an expression of their independence of Austria and its German culture. They staged a magnificently dressed assembly of 230 characters from Shakespeare, processing to a triumphant march specially composed by Bedřich Smetana. The event culminated with a speech by an actress dressed as Perdita from *The Winter's Tale*:

> Do you apprehend the truth concealed in the legend? A babe banished to a foreign shore, yea, *perdita ars bohemica*, her father's land denied her... *Perdita ars bohemica* is this very child who... has returned to her home to find love and good will. Let us not, therefore, spoil this sacred moment by reviving bitter memories. Perdita, once lost, is home again.[7]

However, this major event took place, not in the cramped Provisional Theatre, but in the New Town Theatre (*Novoměstské divadlo*)*—a wooden structure seating over a thousand, built in 1859 to satisfy public demand. The desire to press ahead with the National Theatre was stimulated and the time seemed to be propitious. Bach had fallen from power in 1859; a movement to-

* In 1886 replaced by the elegant *Neues Deutsche Theater*, now called the State Opera (*Státní opera*).

wards federalism had been made with the October Diploma of 1860, and the provincial assemblies revived (though hope in them was to prove illusory). In 1865, Richard Belcredi, born in Moravia and a law graduate of Prague University, became minister for state affairs and head of Franz Josef's government. The emperor announced his intention to come to Prague and be crowned king of Bohemia.

In 1866, the Committee for the National Theatre announced a competition for the design of the theatre. Of the plans submitted, the choice fell on the most ambitious (by the thirty-three-year-old Josef Zítek—"probably the most gifted architect in Central Europe between 1860 and 1880").[8] Construction began in 1867, the year that "Old Austria" came to an end and the new era of the Dual Empire inaugurated. The Magyars had won their autonomy, setting their conditions. The hopes of Czech patriots rose—if the Lands of the Crown of St. Stephen could be autonomous, why not the Lands of the Crown of St. Wenceslas? But there were political reasons why not; and by this time Belcredi was out of office and Franz Josef no longer interested in being crowned king of Bohemia.

For a while, enthusiasm remained high. In May 1868, the foundation stone was laid by Palacký. Celebrations resembling coronation festivities lasted for three days, with processions, street decorations, speeches, fireworks, a regatta, choral singing, banquets, and performances of Tyl's *Švanda the Bagpiper* and Smetana's *Dalibor*. Everyone had to be represented, and invitations sent "to all the outstanding men of learning, artists, dignitaries, and others whose names are famous in Bohemia, Moravia, Slovakia, Galicia, Styria, Carniola, in the Kingdom of Croatia-Slavonia-Dalmatia, in Serbia, Montenegro, Slavonic Turkey, Prussian Poland, and Russia."[9] They came from even farther away—representatives from Czech communities in France, England, and America. Board and accommodation had to be found for 60,000 visitors (and their horses); schools were turned into dormitories, and the military supplied 3,500 new blankets. The foundation stone of the theatre was brought from the mountain Říp from which, so says the legend, Forefather Čech* claimed the surrounding territory for his people. Nineteen more foundation stones from historical places in Bohemia and Moravia were ceremonially transported to Prague to be laid alongside.

At the end of the festivities, Jan Neruda, writer, theatre critic, and diligent Committee member, wrote:

* Čech (i.e., Czech) was one of two (or possibly three) brothers who, in the mists of time, set out from Eastern Europe to find new and more peaceful lands. From the sixteenth century, Čech was denoted the father of the Czech nation.

Like the happy folk in the poem, we walk with excitement and a radiant gaze, our chests are as transparent as crystal, we can gaze into the depths of each other's hearts to see the same joy flickering with a calm, holy fire... Another great moment in Czech history; everyone was happy!

We don't want to go back to everyday life, we don't want to leave the beautiful rosy nest of our memories, all we want to do is rock ourselves in the golden rays of recent days....

The celebrations are over. Our guests have said farewell and left for their distant homelands; we hope they will not forget little mother Prague and their Slavonic brothers. The folk from the countryside have returned to their domestic employment, the students have put themselves to their studies again, the craftsman and labourer laid aside their formal clothes and we too, in our journalistic and literary trade always prepared for the struggle, we continue from where we were before the days of celebration. We all have the same work and the same purpose: to furnish our country with a national and universally human consciousness, a firm moral basis, and a deep, comprehensive culture... The future of the nation lies in its spiritual culture, that is what gives it strength, and it is the awareness of that strength that leads it to the summit of glory![10]

Neruda's exalted mood reminds us of the atmosphere of the Velvet Revolution of 1989. Yet eight years later the theatre remained unfinished, funds exhausted, and its importance almost forgotten. There had been an increase in official resistance to Czech nationalism, as well as political infighting among the Czechs. Like the Communists a century later, the Habsburgs had their informers (one of them was Smetana's patriotic librettist, Karel Sabina).* František Palacký was now in his seventies; no one of similar calibre had emerged to lead the Committee, and the cost of materials and labour had risen. Nevertheless, after further efforts and negotiations, the first performance of *Libuše*, Smetana's opera about the legendary princess who prophesied the founding of Prague, took place on 11 June 1881 in celebration of the wedding of the Habsburg heir, Crown Prince Rudolf. It was planned that *Libuše*, which Smetana had written in 1872 still in the hope of Franz Josef's coronation as king of Bohemia, should be reprised for the real, patriotic opening on St. Wenceslas Day (28 September). But on 12 August, a fire that started on the roof burned the theatre down to its foundations. No one was killed or even injured, but although the evidence pointed to a negligent workman, it remains a cause célèbre still today. The nation was distraught, provoking the mockery of the Vienna press:

Theatres have burned before in Germany, France, England, and Italy, and dramatic art has not died out, nor even suffered. The Czechs act as if the burning of a theatre left the

* See the 1985 Karel Sabina project, p. 250.

The National Theatre, a symbol of Czech identity, caught fire and was burnt to the ground shortly before its official opening in 1881. (Courtesy of Wikimedia Commons)

> Czech muses completely without shelter, actors without income, and as if Czech literature must cease for many years. The Czechs, however, generally overstress national and political events.[11] *

The nation's spirit had been moved; donations flowed in, improvements were made to the original design, and within two years, the National Theatre was rebuilt.† It reopened in November 1883, again with a performance of *Libuše*. The population of the Bohemian Lands took pride in the knowledge that each personal contribution, however small, had contributed towards the theatre. The decoration was magnificent—the foyers at every level covered with frescoes by leading artists of the patriotic movement such as Mikoláš Aleš. The subjects included legends from the Czech past, historic landscapes of Bohemia and Moravia, and allegories relating to Czech national identity.

* Poignantly, in December that year the Ringtheater in Vienna burned down with the estimated loss of 384 lives.

† The original architect Josef Zítek, embittered by political infighting, was not involved.

Above the proscenium arch, the audience could read the words *Národ sobě*: "From the Nation to Itself." The theatre is still known as the *zlatá kaplička*, the "golden chapel"—a reminder of the early patriots' ideal of what a Czech-language theatre should be: a temple where Czechs may come to experience all that is finest in the Czech culture and character.

The National Theatre provided a stage for what had been prepared in the Provisional Theatre: a professional company performing both the regular European repertoire, and new plays by Czech authors. Shakespeare and the classics were still produced in the Romantic style, as were the verse dramas by Julius Zeyer and Jaroslav Vrchlický. At the same time, production was influenced by a visit in 1878 from the German Meiningen Company, with its emphasis on the ensemble rather than on the individual actor. Productions of Ibsen's works had taken place in the Provisional Theatre as early as the 1870s, and Kolár produced Chekhov's short play *The Proposal* in 1890; *The Seagull* however was considered too innovative for the National Theatre, and was a failure when produced at Pavel Švanda's Theatre in Smíchov in 1898.

František Adolf Šubert, director of the National Theatre from 1883 to 1900, encouraged a new wave of Czech playwrights in what became known as the "village drama" movement, which had its roots in the popular tradition of the countryside and the scenes from Prague life by Klicpera and Tyl. This "new wave" directly addressed the question of Czech identity connected with the mid-nineteenth century movement of population from the countryside to the towns, especially Prague. The dramas were set in specific parts of the country, using the local dialect, customs, dress, and folk music. They reminded people of their origins and close ties to the land, and at the same time opened up issues relating to a changing society. Age-old traditions came into conflict with contemporary values. *Our Proud Peasants* (1887) by Ladislav Stroupežnický, a comedy of village intrigues and comeuppances, met with hostility from the critics because of the banality of its subject: rivalry for the position of village nightwatchman. Nevertheless, it grew to be extremely popular and is still part of the repertoire.

Another "village drama" still frequently performed is *Maryša* (1894) by Alois and Vilém Mrštík. Maryša, the lively daughter of the farmer Lízal, is not allowed to marry the impetuous youth Francek, with whom she is in love. Her father, for reasons of property and power, promises her to Vávra the miller, a widower who beat his first wife. In a highly charged second act, Maryša pleads in turn with her neighbour, mother, grandmother, father, and finally Vávra himself, to save her from this marriage. In her eventual submission, she tells Vávra: "It will be a life to make you want to drown yourself."[12] Having subjected herself to social conventions, Maryša in the fourth act rejects the chance of freedom offered by Francek's return. In the end she poisons Vávra and waits coldly to be taken to justice.

Two of the most powerful of the village dramas are by a woman, Gabriela Preissová. In *The Farmer's Woman* (1889)* Eva, a humble dressmaker, regrets having spurned the son of a wealthy landowner and years later spends the summer with him while they work as seasonal harvesters. Misled by the example of the doctor's wife, divorced and remarried but accepted in society, Eva reasons that her lover will divorce his present wife. The doctor's wife, however, is a "foreigner" (from another part of the country) and a Lutheran to boot. She is allowed to be unconventional; the landowner's son is not. Finally realising the power of social convention, Eva drowns herself in the Danube. Preissová's second play, *Her Stepdaughter* (1890), also takes the role of women in society as its theme. Leoš Janáček's opera *Jenufa* focuses mainly on the younger woman; Preissová was more interested in her stepmother, the Kostelnička (sacristan). This proud and morally scrupulous woman is driven by the pressures of society to drown the illegitimate child of her cherished stepdaughter; one of Preissová's most eloquent scenes shows Kostelnička on her knees before Jenůfa's indifferent seducer. However, in her condemnation of society she went too far for the Czech critics, who wrote of the "unsympathetic and embarrassing atmosphere that one might expect from the pen of a young literary hothead rather than that of a woman."[13] The play was dismissed as vulgar, foolish, and contemptible. Distressed by the scandal, Preissová returned to writing for children.

Meanwhile, a theatre entrepreneur and leader of a successful travelling company, Pavel Švanda ze Semčic, took advantage of the fire at the National Theatre to establish his own private theatre across the river in Smíchov. In the 1880s, he competed with the National Theatre in staging the new European and Russian repertoire, including Ibsen's *Enemy of the People* and *Rosmersholm*. In 1886, Švanda took over the management of the first professional Czech-language theatre in Brno, the two-year-old Provisional National Theatre (*Prozatimní národní divadlo*). Here too he presented contemporary Czech and foreign drama: Gabriela Preissová and Henrik Ibsen. Even after Švanda's death in 1891, his Prague theatre presented Chekhov, Tolstoy, and dramatisations of Zola. With the expansion of the Czech-speaking cultural elite, there was an audience for more theatres, and in 1898 a gap was filled by the Theatre at the Exhibition (*Divadlo na Výstavě*), part of the Urania pavilion at the 1898 Exhibition of Architecture and Engineering; the wooden structure was later rebuilt as the Urania Theatre in the garden of the First Prague Municipal Brewery in the Holešovice district of Prague.

* The basis of the opera *Eva* (1899) by Josef Bohuslav Foerster.

From 1900, the drama company at the National Theatre was effectively led by Jaroslav Kvapil, who brought it into the mainstream of established European theatre. In these closing years of the Austro-Hungarian Empire, Czech culture was, so to speak, catching up with European thought of the last fifty years. The liberalising of the Vienna government and the maturing of Czech political attitudes provided an atmosphere in which new ideas were lived through very quickly. Prague's population was still expanding, with country people seeking openings in the construction industry and new factories. Districts outside the city boundaries such as Vinohrady were rapidly covered by housing for the new population. The flow of the Vltava was regulated and terraces of grand apartment blocks along its banks gave their owners a grandstand view of the castle against the changing skies. Josefov's insanitary old ghetto was swept away and a new street plan stamped on it, culminating in the Neo-Renaissance House of Artists (or Rudolfinum)* across the road from the Old Jewish Cemetery. The Czechs deliberately asserted their nationalist sentiments by building their extravagant Municipal House (*Obecní dům*) in the heart of the German-speaking quarter of the Old Town.

Jaroslav Kvapil was a politician, journalist, critic, poet, and dramatist as well as a theatre director and the librettist of Antonín Dvořák's opera *Rusalka*. He regarded theatre production not just as the solving of technical problems, but as the work of an artist who controlled the different elements of theatre to create an emotional atmosphere answering the play of ideas. He was skilled in creating a harmonious whole, an impressionistic stage picture answering the mood of the play. František Langer, after watching rehearsals for the première of his play *On the Periphery*, left a description of Kvapil as a conscientious and confident director, comparing his direction of the lighting to the instructions of a sea captain who knew the map by heart: "Flood downstage right with red and blue, add a little white light, bring up some yellow from stage left, angle a white spotlight from the box stage right, bring up such and such lights from behind the borders."[14] A playwright himself, Kvapil respected the author's text and presented it as it was written, without intervention. Theatre was for him the play of ideas and he was more concerned with issues of the intellect and the emotions than with dramatic climax or documentary detail. Later critics described his work as lacking dramatic impact. Kvapil was described as "the Reinhardt of the Czech stage"; however, Jan Císař points out that Max Reinhardt did not have to focus on the complex social and political relationships that formed the context of Kvapil's artistic work.[15]

---

* Designed by Josef Zítek, architect of the National Theatre, and Josef Schulz.

Jaroslav Kvapil was fortunate to work with an exceptional generation of actors, on whose experience he relied, and whom he encouraged to study the psychological workings of their characters. The leading performers were his wife Hana Kvapilová (who died unexpectedly at the peak of her career) and Eduard Vojan. Vojan's *Hamlet* (1905) reflected Kvapil's philosophy and principles—an educated prince with a deep moral sense, and an ironic judge of the world. In 1906, Kvapil brought the Moscow Art Theatre to Prague as part of its first international tour. The actors impressed Czech audiences above all by their complete absorption in their work; still more influential was the Moscow company's repertoire, consisting of Ibsen and the first performances in Western Europe of Chekhov's major plays. Critics noted that in their attention to detail their performances approached those of the Meiningen Company nearly thirty years earlier.

The changes in politics and society provided a range of themes for the theatre. Kvapil and his company sought new techniques to portray a complex contemporary world. Writers such as Jaroslav Hilbert emerged, whose *Guilt* (1896) examined the hypocrisy of middle class society exemplified in a family drama. In a reaction against the objectivity of naturalism, Kvapil directed his own play, *Princess Dandelion* (1897, music by Josef Bohuslav Foerster), in which a fairy-tale princess falls in love with the peasant folk hero Honza, but cannot tolerate the reality of everyday life in a country cottage. She fades into a state of melancholy and in the end floats off into the snow-filled clouds. In the methods used to remind the Czech public of their national inheritance such allegories were close to Symbolism, as was *The Lantern* (1905) by Alois Jirásek, in which the threatened linden tree represents the Slavonic spirit.

Now that Czech-speaking theatre had been legitimised, a new generation emerged to assert its own ideas about what the theatre should be. Dissatisfied with the repertoire of the National Theatre, young people created their own experimental stages. These groups were largely peripatetic; many of the Prague halls they performed in are still venues for amateur performers today. Influenced by Antoine's *Théâtre-Libre*, by the Moscow Art Theatre, and by the Paris Symbolists, and led by conflicting personalities, the ventures lasted only a few years or even months. One of the earliest, the Intimate Free Stage (*Intimní volné jeviště*, 1896–1899) was founded by a group of artists from the *Moderní revue*, a monthly journal of writings condemned by its opponents as "decadent." (Edited by Arnošt Procházka and Jiří Karásek, the *Moderní revue* reflected a society in transition. It rejected the Czech obsession with historicism and looked to Nietzsche's nihilism for interpretations of the new age; it was influenced less by Viennese culture than by the writings of Baudelaire and the French Decadent poets.)[16] Influenced by Zola's theories about literature as an accurate reflection of contemporary life, the Intimate Free

Stage saw itself as part of the contemporary movement towards Naturalism in the European theatre, and productions included Strindberg's *Creditors* and *Wedding Night*, as well as Karásek's own claustrophobic and agonised *Burning Soul* (1899). Karásek's inaugural speech emphasised the relationship between the actor and the audience, unimpeded by scenery and technology. In the critics' eyes, however, the deliberately naturalistic performances merely indicated the actors' lack of professional technique, and audiences were confined to a few enthusiasts. The most significant of later experimental theatres were the Vinohrady Academicians (*Akademikové vinohradští*) in 1910, the Lyric Theatre (*Lyrické divadlo*) in 1911 and the Arts Theatre (*Divadlo Umění*) from 1912–1914—all essentially the same group.

Though they had their own public and their significance in the development of the avant-garde, the experimental stages were not closely related to the interests of the general public or to national and political concerns. More relevant to the former were the arenas and *cafés chantants*, to the latter the literary cabarets.

ARENAS AND TINGLE TANGLE, CAFÉS CHANTANTS, AND CABARET

While the Provisional and the National Theatres sought to raise the cultural standards of the Czech public, popular entertainments were still being presented in the summer arenas. Built in gardens outside the city boundaries, they were vulnerable to the weather, and the national red and white flag was flown if a performance was scheduled to take place. The first to have a moveable roof was the New Czech Theatre (*Nové české divadlo*, 1876). In the 1880s this became a subsidiary stage of the National Theatre; other summer theatres, such as Pavel Švanda's Pštroska Arena (*Aréna ve Pštrosce*, 1869), were run independently. The repertoire and acting style of the arenas differed from the established theatres. The plays were mainly vehicles for performers and effects men, consisting of comedies, farces, sentimental stories, fairy-tale plays, and even operettas. Music was an important element (as it was in the established theatre); the action was interspersed with songs, often not entirely relevant to the subject. Some performances bordered on circus and variety, with acrobats and clowns. There were performers who played only in the arenas, but for Provisional Theatre actors it was a duty—a burden for some, a pleasure and a relaxation for others. Although essentially Romantic in style, the acting drew on folk traditions that had survived in the itinerant companies of Bohemia. Some straight actors found their real home in the arenas, and developed broad types that resembled *commedia dell'arte* but were drawn from the contemporary environment. Communication was largely through movement, mime, gesture, song, dance, costume, and mask. The popular Jindřich Mošna (a famous Shylock at the Provisional Theatre, and an actor for whom Jirásek and Stroupežnický created roles) studied the arena types he played (tailor or cobbler) directly from life. Although a feature of the arena acting style was grotesque exaggeration of certain features—nose, chin, belly, feet—Mošna managed without these aids. The actors' freedom was not only physical; through satire, songs, and jokes they could express opinions that were unutterable in the Provisional and National Theatres. Audiences appreciated the physical feats of the actors, the colloquial language, and the topicality of the content.

The arenas also exploited their technical resources, achieving stage effects that amazed and delighted the audience: folding scenery for sudden scene changes; revolving backcloths for travel scenes, live animals, fireworks, projections, and wind, rain, and thunder machines. For country audiences, "theatre" meant the Prague arenas. The performances were the highlights of working people's lives; they repeated the jokes and sang the songs. In the late 1870s, when it seemed that the National Theatre would never be built, the summer performances were still full of delight. The audience felt a rapport with the arena performers, whom they regarded as friends and allies.

The popularity of puppets continued; the traditional "Kašpárek" (Punch) character helped to satirise and subvert the Austrian administration. Another form of entertainment with its roots in the early nineteenth century grew in popularity at this time. Groups of friends gathered in local inns, mainly outside Prague, and entertained each other with songs, sketches, and musical interludes. There were verse recitations and short stories, naïve humour, sometimes dance, card tricks, or a cartoonist. The evenings were known as *besedy*, from the verb *besedovat*, meaning "to get together and have a good time."* The intellectuals of the National Awakening recognised the educational value of such evenings and in the 1870s and 1880s encouraged their development into the *deklamační akademie*, amateur groups performing recitations and short scenes. They also influenced the Czech version of the imported Viennese *tingl tangl* and the Parisian *cafés chantants*, absorbed into Czech culture as *šantány*.

The *šantán* entertainments began in the corner of a room in an inn, performed by travelling groups moving to a new venue each night. Gradually a programme was built up; a group would perform at certain inns on set nights

* *Beseda* could also mean the group of people so gathered, the place where they gathered, and even a journal. The term survives, e.g., in the *Malostranská beseda* on the corner of Malostranské náměstí (Lesser Quarter Square).

of the week. A special room or part of the garden was set aside, a raised stage improvised, and by the 1880s groups were attached to their own inn. At first, *šantány* were frequented mainly by men and their content was broad and suggestive. As their respectability improved, they became suitable places for a family outing. The programme ranged from folk songs to opera and operetta, including parodies, travesties, musical jokes, comic songs, and even musical clowning, juggling, and conjuring. An important element in the programme was the *kuplet*, a form of song derived from ballad and folk song, often using a waltz or polka melody. Its predictable format and repeated refrain enabled it to carry a range of subjects and ideas. *Kuplety* had originally appeared in the programme of the arenas, but tended to interrupt the continuity of the performance. In the *šantány*, the *kuplety* pleased audiences by their use of local jargon and topical events; they commented on stories of local life or of international or national importance. Their heroes were the common Czech people and those mocked were the rich and pretentious. *Kuplety* were typically chauvinistic, often insulting German and Jewish Bohemians. The double meaning or illicitly introduced verse often escaped the censors, who were more tolerant of the *šantány* than they were of the legitimate theatres. Often it was necessary to put together all the elements of the performance—words, music, costume, gesture—to discern the politically or socially subversive intention of the *kuplet*. Costume and gesture might work in opposition to the words, as in the 1868 *kuplet*: "Everyone likes a bit on the side" (*Každý si rád odskočí*), ostensibly about an unfaithful husband, but with a shift in meaning when sung by an actor dressed in the uniform of an Austrian general. Much depended on the personality of the performers; only some of them intended to criticise the regime or draw attention to social conditions. Many were uneducated, aiming to entertain with innuendos about runaway lovers and unfaithful husbands. Costume roles (including female impersonations) were popular, an essential item being a specific hat, beard, or apron. Scenery was often no more than a curtain, but stage properties were important, often grotesquely large: an enormous parasol or spectacles, or a toy hobby horse for a pompous officer. In the intimate space, where the performers often moved among the audience, accuracy of gesture and expression was important, and it was essential to gain the audience's attention in the first moments. Characters were drawn from life; a particular walk or an expressive gesture could delineate a character.

Some performers became household names: for example, František Leopold Šmíd as the "Prague Pepik," a kind of cheeky cockney in checkered trousers, cap, and coloured scarf. Šmíd also wrote a number of scenes that were played in the *šantány* such as *Battalion Inn* (1893), based on the true story of the degradation of a Prague lawyer. Such short plays tended to reflect the everyday environment of their audiences: the Czech working and lower middle classes, journeymen, soldiers, cabmen, servants, and students. The atmosphere was similar to the English music hall, with the added tension of two languages and two communities. One of the most popular performers was Josef Šváb-Malostranský, who even appeared in the first short films made in the Bohemian Lands. Šváb-Malostranský's gift was for parody, mocking not only the more naïve forms of the *šantán*, but also the sentimentality of the newly fashionable cabaret stages. His quick wit and musical timing raised the standard of the *šantán*; but at the turn of the century a new and more sophisticated "small stage" emerged, in the form of the literary cabaret.

Cabaret was slow to arrive in Prague. The first professional Prague cabaret opened in 1910, shortly after the visit of the Polish cabaret Momus. It was based in Lucerna, the elegant complex of art nouveau passages built by Václav Havel's grandfather Vácslav Havel and entered from Wenceslas Square and Vodičkova Street. Under the direction of Jaroslav Kvapil (still head of the drama company at the National Theatre), Lucerna performed in both German and Czech. It was stylish and elegant rather than provocative, the softly lit settings (designed by Josef Wenig) creating a nostalgia for old Prague. Audiences were attracted by the songwriter, singer, and compère Karel Hašler, whose ballad "Our Dear Old Czech Song" (*Ta naše písnička česká*) was especially popular under Communism. Hašler, a commanding figure, was known for his cultured wit and sophisticated humour. A popular actor at the National Theatre (and later in film), he was sacked for insubordination in 1916; at the same time, the outspoken patriotic spirit of his songs brought him into conflict with the Austrian authorities. In 1919, he opened a music shop on the corner of Wenceslas Square and Vodičkova Street.* The writer Jaroslav Hašek performed in a very different style, in rough working-class pubs. By the end of the nineteenth century he was already a notorious mischief-maker, and in 1907 he joined the Anarchist movement. Hašek had two audiences: his own friends, who appreciated the deadpan humour of his performances; and the uninitiated general public, duped at first by his outrageous inventions. He was a perpetrator of the "mystification"; one such was the foundation of his "Party for Moderate Progress within the Bounds of the Law."

Hašek also performed at the cabaret Montmartre in the Old Town, opened in 1913 by the cabaret performer Josef Waltner. The old house in Řetězova Street provided a more relaxed setting for performers such as Hašek and Ferenc Futurista than the gilt and plush of Lucerna. Exhibitions of paintings

* In the 1990s, the dancer Lída Myšáková used to reminisce about the time when, as the pâtissier's daughter from the Rondo-Cubist house in Vodičkova Street, she would eagerly run on errands in the hope of glimpsing handsome Mr. Hašler in his shiny top hat.

by the Cubists and other modern artists were also held here, and the first shimmies and tangos in Prague were danced on the four-by-four parquet.[17] The semi-professional cabarets that sprang up in the early twentieth century had no commitment to any party political line, and their satire mocked every political party; this independence increased their appeal to the intelligentsia. The most famous, led by the law student Jiří Červený, was called the *Červená sedma*—the "Red Seven" or "Seven of Hearts."* It was founded in 1903 in Hradec Králové by a group of students who had created their own library (the *Mansarda*, or Garret). This, influenced by the *Moderní revue*, included everything opposed to their parents' values: mysticism, anarchism, paradox, Realism, Romanticism. In 1909, the Seven of Hearts began to perform "academic entertainments" in a Prague restaurant. They mixed parodies of Shakespeare, Ibsen, Tolstoy, Maeterlinck, and Wilde with ironic and sentimental chansons and lyrics. In 1910, they gave their first official performance in Prague, a parody of *Carmen*.

Jiří Červený graduated the following month, but his German was not good enough for him to find an appropriate legal position. His father was prepared to finance a six-month stay in Germany; Červený chose Munich, where at night he visited the cabaret, making friends with the performers. Back in Prague, his group spent their days rehearsing and their nights in an artist's studio, talking about politics, literature, ancient history, religion, and art; playing guitar; drinking spirits; and putting their programme together. Often their sketches were written immediately before the performance or even improvised. They used dance and mime, caricaturing contemporary types with the help of *commedia dell'arte* characters. One of the group—a graceful performer, more serious than the others—later studied with Émile Jaques-Dalcroze in Germany; known as Carratera (and sometimes Ore Tarraco), his real name was František Kulhánek. Music was an important element; they adopted the costumed *kuplet* from the *šantány*, and "musical jokes"—such as national songs with a political gloss that escaped the censor because the point lay in the combination of words and music. The design did not involve scenery so much as puppets, shadow play, projections, line drawing, and "mock puppets" (actors from the waist up). Parody was consistently popular, satirising well-known artistic or political events, humorously or scathingly exposing narrow-mindedness, stupidity, and megalomania. Grand opera was often parodied, frequently individual performers. Other subjects for parody were Parisian *Grand Guignol* and American detective stories, such as *Harry's Case*. For this, the central item was a large black coffin, which became a useful trunk

* There were actually six in the company; Červený explained the seven with reference to *The Three Musketeers*.

for transporting stage properties—to the consternation of fellow travellers. The group's sense of the absurd also pervaded the games they played among themselves: language games, or games of chance applied to everyday life.

The group became professional in 1913, with some reluctance, as they wanted to reject both the polished respectability of Lucerna and the vulgarity of the *šantány* (they declared themselves disgusted by the hypocrisy of a public that accepted the sexual suggestiveness of the *šantány* yet professed itself shocked by the social satire of the Seven of Hearts). They were joined the same year by Eduard Bass, whose father had sent him to France to set up business contacts but spent his time in Parisian cabarets. His poetry and humour added a French artistry until then lacking in the Czech cabaret. He wrote or translated his own material—for example, the songs of Yvette Guilbert. Bass disliked the nostalgic, evocative staging of Hašler's appearances, believing that whereas in straight theatre the actor works indirectly through character, in cabaret the artist must work through his own personality, setting up a direct relationship with the audience. He performed with the lighting at full intensity, introducing himself as he stood by the piano, the words of his songs in his hands. His aim was to be natural and to celebrate the ordinary things of life, the shared pleasures of Prague rather than its romantic mysteries. Bass saw the genre of cabaret as the product of a culturally sophisticated society:

> Cabaret... originates only where social life has developed to a certain level of cultural and material prosperity. Only where the life of the nation has grown to such a degree is it possible to allow a certain measure of luxury, only then is the ground prepared for a healthy basis of the art of the cabaret.[18]

In his pamphlet *How cabaret is done* (*Jak se dělá kabaret*, 1917) Bass drew attention to the specific elements which formed the basis of cabaret; the many-sidedness of its different parts; the need for a simple and continuous contact between stage and auditorium; the ability to improvise; and most of all the personality of each of the performers. These issues would be of central importance to the small theatres of the 1960s.

TURN OF THE CENTURY

In the closing years of the Habsburg Empire, Prague society was imbued with tense and often conflicting dynamics. The Bohemian Lands were still part of Austria; civil servants, business travellers, the aristocracy, and the intelligentsia moved frequently and easily between Prague and Vienna. Artists, architects, and craftsmen trained in Vienna, returning to teach in the schools and work in the industries of Bohemia and Moravia. German-language culture was in many respects flourishing. Praguers spoke and wrote in a pure form of the language alien to more mobile Germans and Austrians, a singularity that in some ways made their work more universal. Johannes Urzidil, a younger contemporary of Kafka, noted that in Prague German, the written and spoken language were one: "This absolute integration between the languages of life and art is probably the strongest source of the peculiar form and impact of the Prague writers."[19] He described how "thanks to the wealth of her national, social, and confessional facets, Prague could offer her authors writing in German, the intellectual potential of a city, a capital, and one more glittering than many a European metropolis far richer in population."[20]

German-language theatre still had a presence in Prague, although opera performances at the dazzling National Theatre attracted even German audiences. The *Deutscher Theaterverein*—whose founding members included German-speaking aristocrats, industrialists, politicians, and bankers—could not allow Richard Wagner's operas to be presented in the inadequate Estates Theatre, now the *Königlich Deutsches Landestheater*. An appeal was launched and funds raised to build the exquisite *Neues Deutsches Theater*, which opened with Wagner's *Meistersinger* in 1888. A significant contribution to the new building was made by Jews living in Prague, who formed a large part of the audience (and company; the first director, Angelo Neumann, was Jewish). The Czech *Divadelní listy* (*Theatre Pages*), however, wrote that "another German theatre in Czech Prague is utterly superfluous, since one theatre is perfectly sufficient for 20,000 Germans and a few thousand Jews."[21]

On another level, Franz Kafka's account of his fascination with a visiting Polish Yiddish theatre troupe performing on an improvised stage in the Café Savoy, written over several days in October 1911, turns into a reflection on the Czech theatre:

> Would like to see a large Yiddish theatre as the production may after all suffer because of the small cast and inadequate rehearsal. Also, would like to know Yiddish literature, which is obviously characterized by an uninterrupted tradition of national struggle that determines every work. A tradition, therefore, that pervades no other literature, not even that of the most oppressed people. It may be that other peoples in times of war make success out of a pugnacious national literature and that other works, standing at a greater remove, acquire from the enthusiasm of the audience a national character too, as is the case with *The Bartered Bride*, but here there appear to be only works of the first type, and indeed always.[22]

Almost twenty years after the opening of the *Neues Deutsches Theater*, the Czechs built themselves another imposing theatre, this time in Vinohrady, a district familiar to habitués of the summer arenas: the *Divadlo na Vinohradech*. The development of elaborately equipped theatres lit by electricity gave greater prominence to the stage picture, while at the same time Adolphe Appia and Edward Gordon Craig were developing ideas that would eventually rely on modern technology for their realisation. Influenced by the Wagnerian ideal of the *Gesamtkunstwerk*, the designs of Appia and Craig were nonrepresentational, the use of proportion and space determining—as well as being determined by—the stage action. Appia was concerned with the "hidden life" of a play, which should be expressed not only in the dialogue and acting but also through the complete integration of scenery, music, and lighting. Their influence reached Kvapil in the early years of the century. In his productions of Maeterlinck's *L'oiseau bleu* (1912) and Claudel's *L'Annonce faite à Marie* (1914) he replaced painted settings by non-illusionistic scenery. His partnership with the designer Josef Wenig, whose atmospheric stage pictures harmonised with Kvapil's integrated concept, began with Tyl's *Švanda the Bagpiper* in 1913 and lasted until Kvapil's revival of his own *Princess Dandelion* in 1938.

Among those who moved freely between the Czech and German worlds was František Zavřel, a talented young artist and friend of Max Brod, with whom he translated Czech plays into German. Zavřel began his career in Germany in 1905, working in both Munich and Berlin, where he came under Reinhardt's spell. In January 1914, Zavřel was invited to direct Arnošt Dvořák's *King Wenceslas IV* in the Prague National Theatre (with Eduard Vojan and Karel Hašler in two of the leading roles). At the Švanda Theatre later that year he reprised two of his Munich successes: Wedekind's *Lulu* (in his own translation) and Gilbert and Sullivan's *The Mikado*. Next came a production at the Vinohrady Theatre of *Don Quixote Achieves Wisdom* by Viktor Dyk, an ironic contrast of the dream with the reality and a play deemed impossible to stage by Kvapil. The following year Zavřel died of tuberculosis in a sanatorium in Davos. Visually, he had brought a new dynamic to the stage, choosing artists with no theatre experience as his designers. His work with light and shadow contrasted with Kvapil's harmoniously framed picture, creating a dramatic tension that could be seen as the first manifestation of Expressionism on the Czech stage. He also intervened in the structure of the text, when it was possible working with the author to create a taut, dramatically effective text. František Langer, after seeing Zavřel's *Lulu*, described him as a new kind of director on the Czech stage: "A director of this kind is responsible for everything, beginning with the choice of author and ending with thorough attention to the most varied details. Almost everything onstage, or even everything, is the work of the director... the actors are only puppets... he is his own dramaturge."[23] Such directors, he continued, were endowed with enormous, even feverish, industry and conscientiousness, and were full of practical and witty ideas that came together in a unified way.

Creative interchange was no longer bounded by the borders of the Austrian Empire. Czech artists drew their inspiration from further afield and were beginning to express themselves in the language, not of the Secession, but of Cubism and Functionalism. The key year was 1905, marked by an exhibition of Edvard Munch in Prague. It was the inspiration for the foundation of the Eight (*Osma*) in 1907, a group which included Emil Filla, Otakar Kubín (Coubine), Bohumil Kubišta, and the cabaret performer Emil Artur Pitterman. It was *Osma* that opened Czech art to French Cubism and, drawing on the inheritance of the Bohemian Baroque, led to the evolution of Czech Cubism. *Osma* was followed in 1911 by the Group of Fine Artists (*Skupina vytvarných umělců, SVU*). Leading members of the *SVU* included the artist, stage designer, and writer Josef Čapek, who had studied at the School of Applied Arts and, with his brother Karel, spent 1910 in Paris. Here they met the Czechophile Guillaume Apollinaire, with other members of the Parisian avant-garde. As the century turned and Czech ties to the German environment continued to weaken, French cultural influence was crucial to the rising generation; it was to be overtaken, however, by the conflicting aesthetics of America and revolutionary Russia.

II INDEPENDENCE: THE FOUNDING AND FALL OF THE FIRST REPUBLIC

IN THE NEW REPUBLIC

After the Great War, the Czechs found themselves not merely an autonomous land within a federal Austria, but (in a union with the Slovaks) an independent state in a newly configured Europe. The person who did the most to bring this about was a university professor of humble origins, Tomáš Garrigue Masaryk. Masaryk had spent the war in exile, mainly in America, negotiating with the Allies while keeping in touch with his *Maffie*—an organised underground network operating in Prague. One member of the *Maffie* was the National Theatre director Jaroslav Kvapil, who in 1916 directed the first of a series of Shakespeare plays, with Eduard Vojan in the leading roles. It was both a gesture of support for the Allies and a reminder to his countrymen that they could look beyond the borders of German-speaking Europe. In 1917, Kvapil initiated a Writers' Manifesto, and in 1918 a National Oath of Allegiance. With the establishment of independent Czechoslovakia, Masaryk became the new republic's president, and Kvapil head of the Ministry of Education and Culture.

On one level, this was a time of idealism, confidence, and euphoria. In economic affairs, however, the government faced grave problems, and the basis of a strong left-wing front was forming. Among artists there was a desire to make up for lost time, to catch up with the rest of Europe. No one drove himself harder than Karel Hugo Hilar, a dramaturge and versatile author appointed director of the Vinohrady Theatre in 1914 at the age of twenty-nine. Although temperamentally he and Kvapil were opposites, they resembled each other in their broad knowledge of literature, especially contemporary, and their ability to translate that knowledge into a theatrical experience. Absorbing the influence of both Kvapil and Zavřel, Hilar epitomised the dynamic and highly motivated, but precarious, years of the First Republic. His work was eclectic, reflecting the shifting patterns of contemporary European movements (a feature he shared with Kvapil). As Expressionism superseded Symbolism, Hilar learnt from Zavřel not only its visual principles, but also how to edit and adapt a text to his own stage methods, often reworking the lesser-known classics to suit his chosen theme.

At the Vinohrady Theatre, Hilar worked with a loyal and enthusiastic team. In 1919, he found a like-minded set designer in the architect Vlastislav Hofman. In an article for Zavřel's journal *Scéna* in 1913, Hofman advocated the need for theatre reform; he responded to the ideas of Edward Gordon Craig by arguing that Craig "obviously failed to penetrate inside the organism, but merely stylized the literary form by a simple conceit," continuing:

> One could say nowadays that there are three approaches that assume a common view of the necessity for reform. The first method, in principle the most correct, is the search for something typically new. This seeks to transpose literary intensities into artistic intensities *directly*—through a simultaneous combination of visual and sound effects on some abstract idea of artistic intention. ... It is about making literature into a visual art, the material portrayal of dramatic motive forces consisting of words and their resolution as space, movement, sound, and light, operating together.... The second method, the only one capable of acting as a transition to modern experiments, is that of Craig. Liberating the stage from Naturalism, Craig brought about an imposing calm in the play, a severe, grey, even melancholic atmosphere. The characters are lost to the eye among enormous vertical screens; through its lifelessness and regularity of rhythm his method achieves the appeareance of a fatefulness, an aura of Symbolism.... The third method by which the stage is often—erroneously—modernized, is to bring to it the sentiment and practices of contemporary decorative forms in architecture and painting.[24]

Although in his early theoretical writings Hofman invoked Craig (who in those years was better known in Europe than Appia), it is likely that his postwar collaboration with Kvapil work owed more to Adolphe Appia. Rather than looking for perfection in a single set, Hofman thought in terms of successive settings, adapting the Czech tradition of painted scenery to Appia's theory of rhythmical forces.[25]

Hofman's first design for the theatre, Hilar's production of Arnošt Dvořák's *Hussites* in 1919, was a sensation. Even Jindřich Honzl, a left-wing activist critical of Hilar and mainstream theatre, wrote that the production was "so outstandingly new and stimulating, more detailed reflection has to be devoted to it."[26] The stage was dominated by the Hussite symbol of the chalice as the head of Christ edged by flames, and the motifs of striking colours and strong diagonals echoed through the change of painted backcloths for a series of scenes. However, Hofman rejected the concept of Expressionism with its German connotations, and preferred the term Fauvism. While *The Hussites* relied on painted backdrops, with Hilar's move to the National Theatre in 1921 Hofman had the opportunity to create sets that were simultaneously monumental and subtle, geometrically precise and highly flexible. For Hilar's *Oedipus Rex* (1932), a double spiral staircase on a revolve rose to a massive lintel overhanging the great doors of the royal palace. An exponent of Cubist and Rondo-Cubist architecture, Hofman translated this style to the stage. His three-dimensional use of stage space and of lighting that defined the changing stage areas was to influence Czech theatre design for the rest of the twentieth century.

Hilar had moved to the National Theatre in January 1921 to fill Kvapil's vacant seat. However, he had to contend not only with actors accustomed to Kvapil's more relaxed regime, but also with playwrights such as Karel Čapek and František Langer, who were offended by Hilar's lack of respect for the text. Nevertheless, Hilar's productions of Čapek's plays at the National Theatre (including the Expressionist *Insect Play*,* which he directed in 1922, in 1925, and again in 1932) brought Čapek world fame and productions in America and throughout Europe. František Langer achieved similar international success with plays about moral problems faced by essentially ordinary people in real situations in modern life.† Among the most popular were *A Camel Through a Needle's Eye* (1923) and *On the Periphery* (1925). Max Reinhardt, at that time reaching the height of his European fame, directed the first in Vienna and the second in Berlin.

At the National Theatre, Hilar faced criticism on every side; even Václav Vydra, who had been one of the Vinohrady team, and played Zavřel's Don Quixote, began to mock Hilar's methods, writing later:

> We saw how after a while Hilar emulated Zavřel, when up to then Kvapil had been his model. We were witnesses when he moved on to Reinhardt and then Jessner, but never with any inventiveness of his own. Then it was the turn of Tairov; as though at his instigation, Hilar had his actors crawling up ladders. He also enthused over the slogan "silent theatre," but I remember that being used by Stanislavsky and Chekhov fourteen years

---

* Karel's brother Josef Čapek, who co-wrote *The Insect Play* and designed the sets for the first production, created more than thirty sets for the National Theatre.

† Langer, a medical doctor by profession, was captured in Russia during World War I, after which he joined the Czechoslovak Legionnaires, who fought on the side of the Allies and controlled the Trans-Siberian Railway.

ago! When Expressionism was no longer "the thing," out of the blue he adopted *die neue Sachlichkeit* but what was a novelty for Hilar was already passé in Germany...[27]

Hilar suffered a major stroke in 1924, after which he shifted to the more sober style of *die neue Sachlichkeit* (*New Objectivity*). He invented for it the term Civilism (still in use in Czech culture). Some critics believed that this less assertive approach brought its rewards in a more balanced approach to the text. Hilar died of a second stroke in 1935.

Jindřich Honzl, a disciple of early Soviet theatre, contrasted what he saw as Hilar's superficiality with Vsevolod Meyerhold's painstaking research. Honzl also criticised the fading world of cabaret and the conservatism of cabaret performers, as imitations of Karel Hašler patronised by the "insensitive nouveaux riches." Jiří Červený blamed the decline of cabaret on the economic situation that put ticket prices out of the reach of ordinary people, and on the public's search for novelty, as it turned to the cinema and dance hall. The Seven of Hearts lost its following and was wound up at the end of the 1921–1922 season. Červený, whose lack of proficiency in German was less of a handicap now that the Czechs were no longer Habsburg subjects, returned to the legal profession.

The politically and socially anarchic Emil Artur Longen was more uncompromising. Longen was known first as an artist; until expelled for insubordination, he had studied painting at the Academy of Fine Arts. In 1907, under his real surname of Pittermann, he was a founder member of the group of artists known as the *Osma* (Eight). However, as a writer he could turn his hand to journalism, biography, fiction, and playwriting, and he was equally versatile as an actor. His acting was physical rather than psychological; he drew on the *commedia dell'arte*, on circus, and on folk theatre. One of his cabaret roles was the *fin de siècle* decadent, nerves destroyed, sustained by drugs. Červený described his recital of Paul Leppin's hedonistic poetry as "sending shivers down the spines of the spectators." Franz Kafka was more caustic:

Cabaret Lucerna... A milksop face—Longen (the painter Piterman [*sic*]), mimic jokes. A production that is obviously without joy and yet cannot be considered so, for if it were, then it wouldn't be performed every evening, particularly since it was so unhappy a thing even at the moment it was created that no satisfactory pattern has resulted which would dispense with frequent appearances of the whole person.[28]

Longen's dream was to start a popular cabaret in Rieger Park at prices the proletariat could afford, but he was never able to obtain the financial backing. With his wife Xena he restlessly wandered Europe, poverty driving him to accept work he despised. After the war he earned a living in Paris from painting, journalism, and cabaret performances. He returned to the Czechoslovak Republic in 1920, and after an unsuccessful experiment with the Cabaret BOOM (*Kabaret BUM*), borrowed money to start his own theatre group, the Revolutionary Stage (*Revoluční scéna*), housed in the basement of the Hotel Adria. Longen belonged to the Anarchist circle of Jaroslav Hašek, and was the first to adapt *The Adventures of the Good Soldier Švejk* (1921) for the stage. Other productions included Vladimir Mayakovsky's *Mystery-Bouffe*, Georg Büchner's *Woyzeck*, Arthur Schnitzler's *La Ronde*, and F. L. Šmíd's *Battalion Inn*. In October 1920, the recently founded newspaper of the extreme left, *Rudé právo*,* wrote of the Revolutionary Stage's "clean and fearless Socialist nature." In spite (or because) of this, the theatre was closed down in January 1922 on the grounds that it contravened fire regulations. While the actors sued him for unpaid wages, Longen moved to Berlin, where he briefly ran the *Wilde Bühne*. In the intervals between drinking bouts, Longen acted in films, including adaptations of his own plays, wrote for the papers, and completed two biographies (of Jaroslav Hašek and Vlasta Burian). Xena, described by the dancer Nina Jirsíková as an "unforgettable" actress, was frustrated in her hopes of an engagement at the National or Vinohrady Theatres. Her greatest stage success was the leading role in *Tonka of the Gallows* by the Prague German "Raging Reporter" Egon Erwin Kisch (with songs by Karel Hašler). Kisch's play about a country girl turned prostitute was filmed as the first Czech talkie in 1930—but without Xena, who had thrown herself from the window of their Žižkov apartment two years earlier. Longen wrote the novel *Actress* (*Herečka*, 1929) as a memorial.

Some cabaret performers found a niche in other areas of popular theatre. Among them was Ferenc Futurista, who had occasionally worked with the Seven of Hearts and adopted his name out of admiration for Marinetti and the Italian Futurists. Futurista's stage appearance was large and shambling, with uncoordinated movements and a skull-like face distorted into a grimace. His grotesqueness was exaggerated by stylised makeup and incongruous costume—he might appear in a sculptor's smock or in faultless evening dress. His use of language was crude and colloquial, and his voice harsh and unpleasing. He developed the character of a coarse misogynist, widower, or elderly bachelor, which he portrayed with vulgar and emphatic gestures, reminding the audience of folk drama. His humour was more bitter and destructive than the ironic wit of Bass or the artistry of Longen; his monologues were convoluted and illogical, and he mocked not only traditional targets for satire—the

* *Rudé právo* (*Red Justice, Right*, or *Law*) was founded in 1920, when the extreme left-wing split from the Social Democrats to form the Czechoslovak Communist Party, formally established in 1921.

official bureaucracy, the self-interested clergy—but also attitudes prevalent among the general public.

Another cabaret artist and comic actor who remained popular until the end of World War II was Vlasta Burian. His gift was for identifying and drawing out the essential features that characterised a voice or type, and he was skilled at keeping a serious face in absurd situations. Longen portrayed Burian and Futurista in *Actress* under the names Dolan and Moderna:

> Dolan surpassed Moderna in the versatile power of his voice, capable of imitating all singing voices from bass to a woman's mezzo-soprano. He was as good as any artist in the world at whistling with his fingers and at imitating animals and musical instruments. He had such a presence onstage that he dared to venture on a new programme without any rehearsal or the usual preparation. All he needed was a few anecdotes and essential jokes, with which his wife Lola had to prompt him from the wings, and he had the whole performance in hand. In Moderna he smelt dangerous competition for the future; he detested him, although in order not to make an enemy of him he pretended to be friendly.[29]

Vlasta Burian formed his own company, where he played Chaplinesque roles of "the man in the street"—postman, office worker, or hospital attendant—who comes into conflict with officialdom and the stuffy middle class.

DEVĚTSIL AND THE AVANT-GARDE

> It is the serviceability of modern art that gives it its direction in life. It must get out of the atmosphere of museums and breathe the strong, fresh air of the earth. Let it be marked by splendid entertainment and genuine delight, just like the cinema, circus, or football match. Let it take for its own that technical perfection and flexibility that belongs to the athlete and the acrobat, the shameless functionality of its own machine. Let it be completely accessible and traditional; but by that we do not mean traditional in the sense of a specific ethnography. Mankind is the same from pole to pole: the modern proletariat.[30]

Karel Teige—architect, artist, and critic, as well as cofounder and secretary of the left-wing avant-garde group the Devětsil (an ambiguous title, the name of a flower, but also translatable as "nine strengths")—was writing for the Devětsil's collective publication of the same name in 1922. His words reflected not only the European artist's celebration of the twentieth century but also certain tensions inherent in the outlook of the Czechoslovak artist of Teige's generation.

One of the landmark publications of the interwar avant-garde, *Abeceda* (*The Alphabet*), a cycle of poems by Vítězslav Nezval, danced by Milča Mayerová, photographs by Karel Paspa, cover and photomontage by Karel Teige, originally published in 1926. (Reproduced by permission from Vítězslav Nezval, *Abeceda*. Prague: Torst, 1993, 19.)

The Devětsil was founded on 5 October 1920 by young people mostly from middle-class backgrounds; some of them were school friends from the secondary school in Křemencova Street, in Prague New Town. They were a generation for whom the Habsburg Empire was a childhood memory, who had been too young to fight in the Great War, and who were already impatient with the society and culture of the First Republic. Full of spontaneous but unfocused revolutionary feeling, they were on the one hand shocked by the divisions and injustices in their own society, by poverty and inequality; on the other, they were children of a new world, delighting in modern art and new discoveries, in colour, movement and light, in new technology and new structures. It was the tension between these two motivations which over the next decade provoked members of the Devětsil into activity and experiment. Many of its members later made their names as artists (Toyen, Jindřich Štyrský) or architects (Antonín Heythum, Jaromír Krejcar), poets (Vítězslav Nezval, Jaroslav Seifert) or performers (Jiří Voskovec, Milča Mayerová). In the dynamic atmosphere of the new capital city, ideas quickly flared and took hold. Decades later, under Communism, the musician and historian Václav Holzknecht mourned:

> There are no more cafés or other such forums as jolly, spontaneous, and informal as the pre-war cafés, where one could sit over a single coffee... for goodness knows how long... where you could meet up with just the person you wanted to see, or mix with someone come across by chance.[31]

The young dancer Milča Mayerová, returning to Prague after the sober discipline of a Laban training,* recalled the café meetings and conversations, their absurdities, arguments, contradictions, energy, enthusiasm, and sarcasm in discussing new poems, French books, foreign magazines, Dada manifestos, Surrealism, Constructivism, new theatre: "It was a whirligig, a dazzling fairground, a kaleidoscope of thoughts, a celebration of new understandings, manifestos, and struggles."[32]

Members of the Devětsil felt themselves to be part of a revolutionary international movement superior to Czech nationalism. They advocated active involvement in social change and supported the general strike called in December 1920 by the left wing of the Social Democrats. The strike, a protest against unemployment and exploitation, was accompanied by rioting, arrests, and some deaths, but was short lived. Karel Teige cancelled the Devětsil's first planned public evening of recitation (to be held in the Mozarteum on Jungmannova Street) with the words: "It is inadmissible to recite poetry at the same moment as the police are shooting down the workers in the streets of Prague."[33] The poet Jaroslav Seifert wrote:

> I found myself in front of the parliament building,† a few steps from where the worker Josef Kulda fell. It was the first time in my life I've been so near death. Excitement and fascination later drew me back to the same spot, while the blood still lingered between the cobblestones as under the fingernails of a murderer. With wide eyes and a thumping

---

* Rudolf von Laban, born in Pressburg (Bratislava) in 1879, was a pioneer of modern dance, and his training system was adopted in many countries around the world.

† Also (and currently) known as the Rudolfinum, in honour of Emperor Franz Josef's son and heir.

heart I relived for myself the terrible fatefulness of those moments.... The battle was of course lost, but the word "revolution," so many times repeated, did not fall from sight. As poets we returned to our verses, a word I pronounce with such professional pride as a soldier the word "sword" and a farmer the word "plough."[34]

At the start of the Devětsil, many of its poets belonged to the "proletarian" movement, which expressed sympathy with the working class's supposed needs. Its chief exponent, Jiří Wolker, believed that the role of the revolutionary artist was to identify himself with the experience of ordinary people:

[The critic] in today's *Lidové noviny** furiously lays into my article/lecture on proletariat art, castigating both me and the Devětsil. A front line has been formed and is being clarified.[35]

But by 1922 Wolker was already meeting opposition within the Devětsil, whose members were making a distinction between the involvement of artists in political activities and the involvement of their creative work. Its opinions shifted towards the freedom of art. A letter to Teige from the French playwright Charles Vildrac reflects the views he found in Prague:

Most of the people I met among your friends are teachers, intellectuals, and artists as impecunious as me. I'm an Anarchist rather than a Communist, in any case utterly independent, as a poet should be. But I'm too concerned with social injustice for my sympathies not to be with the Communists.[36]

Karel Teige's correspondence with the international avant-garde strongly influenced the development of the Devětsil. The Soviet theatre director Alexander Tairov wrote to him:

Your proposal for mutual cooperation seems very interesting.... I am organising for the future a literary bureau in Moscow whose aim will be to create close and regular contact between Russia and a whole range of authors, poets, painters, and other personalities active in European art. I would be very grateful if you could send me news and information about the Czechoslovak theatre.[37]

Correspondence was maintained with Marinetti and the Italian Futurists, with Tristan Tzara, André Breton, Louis Aragon, Philippe Soupault, Paul

* *Lidové noviny* (*People's News*), founded by Adolf Stránský in 1893, was closed by the Nazis and then by the Communists. It was revived as samizdat in 1988 and subsequently restablished itself as a national daily.

Eluard, and Henri Barbusse, with John Heartfield, George Grosz, and László Moholy-Nagy.

The Devětsil's 1922 collection contained not only material by its own members, but also translations from Ilya Ehrenburg, Ivan Goll, and Jean Cocteau. It was richly illustrated with reproductions of children's drawings and film posters, of Cubist works of art and postcards of Paris and New York. Ferdinand Leger's cartoons of Charlie Chaplin were there, along with Rousseau, Chagall, the modern automobile, and photographs of agricultural machinery in America. In his concluding essay "Art Today and Tomorrow," Teige mentioned that he chose the kind of illustrations that could be found pinned round a student's dressing room mirror. It was eclecticism, but a specific eclecticism, based on a belief in art as the product of a process of imagination that disregards previously existing forms. It was a process of renewal that rejected everything that had become familiar and accepted as convention.

The artists of the Devětsil rejected not only the conventions of Naturalism but even the manifestations of the Symbolist and Expressionist movements which had been adopted, especially in the theatre, as part of the official culture. They were trying to find a new imaginative relationship with the public, to provoke the audience by the use of allusion, juxtaposition, invention, and metaphor, in a method later described by Arthur Koestler as "the law of infolding."[38] In the mid-1920s, this movement acquired the name "Poetism," a term coined by Teige and defined by him in the May 1924 edition of the art and literary magazine *Host*, a poetry not of texts but of the five senses, deriving its character from the tension between the functional and the rational.

Poetism shared with Cubism a desire for simultaneity of expression, with Futurism a liking for the realities of modern civilisation. Like Constructivism, it was concerned with form and material. Like Surrealism, it trusted in the imagery of dreams and the logic of spontaneity. Poetism, in its meetings, publications, and recitations, expressed a lightness, a gaiety, a playfulness, a delight in life and living. It has been described as a Czech variant of Dada; but to those involved there was a commitment and a seriousness of purpose which did not correspond with the destructive elements of true Dada. Jaroslav Seifert, František Halas, Konstantin Biebl, and Vítězslav Nezval were among the Poetists, but their number also included novelists, musicians, linguists, and dancers. The type of theatre envisaged by the Poetists owed more to film than to traditional theatre, for whose audience, in Teige's words, "'To be or not to be' had ceased to be a question."[39] Film combined the new technology with the excitement of visual images, especially in the person of Charlie Chaplin, the embodiment of the Devětsil's delight in modern civilisation and protest against its dehumanising effect. The theatre was to abandon literary texts

Cover of the Czech edition of Alexander Tairov's *Notes of a Director*, translated by Jindřich Honzl as *Osvobozené divadlo* (*The Liberated Theatre*) and supplemented by Honzl's own essays, 1926.

and to draw its inspiration from what was internationally comprehensible: cinema, circuses, and the music hall; acrobats, fairs, and mirror mazes; fireworks, carnivals, and street demonstrations. In losing the dramatist it would gain "the poetry of the five senses," for its different parts would no longer be illustrating thoughts and actions plotted by the author but relating to the inner consciousness of a total work of art. Nor would it resemble Wagner's *Gesamtkunstwerk* with its multiple layers, but would rather be a synthetic work of art, precise and economical in the interweaving of its different elements. In autumn 1925, the theatre branch of the Devětsil came into being, jointly led by Devětsil members Jindřich Honzl and Jiří Frejka. On Honzl's suggestion, the title being taken from Alexander Tairov's *Notes of a Director*—translated by Honzl as *Osvobozené divadlo*, or the "Liberated Theatre."

"THE DARING THREESOME":* HONZL, FREJKA, E. F. BURIAN

JINDŘICH HONZL AND THE DĚDRASBOR

The scene is an open-air stadium, 26 June 1921. Fanfares celebrate the Victory of the Proletariat. Revolution makes a joyful entrance, greeted by a throng of children waving scarlet flags and scarves, working-class women with bunches of red flowers in their outstretched arms, and workers marching with hammers and rifles. Finally, the arrival of the Leader of the Revolution, carried above the heads of the crowd: a man of the working classes, born in the mean streets of the city and sworn to fight against the misery of his existence.

The Victory of the Revolution was performed in the first Spartakiad, celebrating the founding of the Czechoslovak Communist Party (May 1921) by a dissident branch of the Social Democrats. It was a riposte to the patriotic Sokol movement that had been a channel for Czech nationalist sensibilities in the nineteenth and early twentieth century, but which, according to the left wing of society, now had to be superseded. For the secondary-school science teacher Jindřich Honzl, it was his first theatrical production. Born into a working-class family in the Vysočina, the highlands between Bohemia and Moravia, he had become a founding member of the Czechoslovak Communist Party. The role of the Leader of the Revolution was played by a professional actor, Josef Zora, with whom Honzl ran the Dědrasbor (*Dě-lnický dra-matický sbor*, Workers Dramatic Chorus) from 1920 to 1922.

The Dědrasbor began with 120 members but grew to 4,000 for the Spartakiad performance. Karel Teige prepared the design while Zdeněk Nejedlý, a leading music critic and historian, wrote the score. All the performers were factory workers: "people until then untouched by the old theatre."[40] After their day's work they came to be coached by Honzl and Zora in breathing, posture, pronunciation, and rhythmical movement. Honzl simplified the material to suit the capabilities of the performers:

* This subtitle refers to Antonín Dvořák's book *Trojice nejodvážnějších* (1961), which for three decades was one of the few available studies about the interwar avant-garde. Dvořák, who first appears in our story in 1941 as a student with high hopes just released from concentration camp, developed over the decade into an embittered Communist.

I even had to restrain the workers, because I didn't want to see grotesque imitations of actors; for that is what the contemporary amateur theatre is, pathetic imitations of the professional theatre—and that is a humiliating role for the working man.[41]

Honzl saw the Dědrasbor as a revival of the values of Ancient Greece, with the chorus and audience as fellow creators in the poet's work. The Dědrasbor performed pieces by Wolker, the idealistic Communist poet S. K. Neumann, and Alexander Blok. They appeared on Longen's Revolutionary Stage and at Pavel Švanda's theatre in Smíchov, as well as in the workers' own factories. Eventually Honzl became dissatisfied, believing that they were still relying on the communicative methods of the existing theatre.

Honzl published his first collection of essays *The Spinning Stage* (*Roztočené jeviště*) in 1925. Teige's first book, *Film*, appeared the same year, as did Nezval's first collection of poetry, *Sham Poker* (*Falešný Mariáš*). Also in 1925, Honzl, Teige, and Jaroslav Seifert visited Soviet Russia as members of a cultural delegation. The political and artistic influence of the Russians had a lasting effect on Honzl's work and led to his book *Modern Russian Theatre* (*Moderní ruské divadlo*, 1928). He felt akin to Meyerhold in wanting to get rid of past aesthetics in order to discover a deeper reality. Abandoning the stylisation of his work with the Dědrasbor, he aimed to investigate the functional possibilities of the different elements of theatre. The Liberated Theatre was formed shortly after the delegation's return from the Soviet Union; administratively it was independent of the Devětsil (although the executive board included Teige). The first production was Jiří Frejka's adaptation of Molière's *Georges Dandin*.

JIŘÍ FREJKA AND CONSTRUCTIVISM

Jiří Frejka also came from the Bohemian-Moravian Highlands, where wild boar and mouflon are hunted in the ancient forests. Born into an old family of foresters, he came to Prague to study briefly at Charles University and the Conservatoire, but preferred to devote himself to experimental theatre. Early in 1925, the twenty-year-old's Molière adaptation, *Cirkus Dandin*, was presented by his amateur group Experimental Stage (*Zkušební scéna*) in the Masaryk Hall (now the Žižkov Theatre).* Frejka emphasised the non-literary nature of his kind of theatre: "Theatre is not only what is played, but also how it is played."[42] He acknowledged the influence of the Russian avant-garde, particularly as mediated through Vladimír Gamza, two years his senior.

* Žižkov, which came within Prague city boundaries only in 1922, is a traditionally working class district.

Cirkus Dandin, directed by Jiří Frejka and designed by Antonín Heythum for the Liberated Theatre, 1926. (Reproduced by permission from Antonín Dvořák, *Trojice nejodvážnějších*. Prague: Mladá fronta: 1988, app.)

The Poet and the Women by Aristophanes, directed by Jiří Frejka and designed by Antonín Heythum for the Theatre of Youth, 1926. (Courtesy of the Museum of Czech Literature)

Gamza, Czech born and brought up in St. Petersburg, lived his short life intensely. Influenced by Stanislavsky and Yevgeny Vakhtangov, on his return to his homeland he became an actor at the Vinohrady Theatre, but moved to Brno in 1924 and founded his own Czech Studio (*České studio*). He introduced Constructivism to the Czech theatre with his set for František Langer's *On the Periphery*. Among his collaborators were E. A. Longen and Xena Longenová. Gamza went on to found the Arts Studio (*Umělecké studio*) in Prague. The periodical *Host* described his company as "full of youthful zeal and enthusiasm… sacrificing every personal interest to the creation of a particular acting style."[43] The principles behind Constructivist stage design were to dispense with decorative features and to rely on the functionality of the set as a space in which the actor can play, an environment that will stimulate his imagination. To do this, the actor needs the perfect physical coordination and control of the body that Meyerhold aimed for in his "bio-mechanics." Meaning was conveyed, not by internally evoked emotion, but by the precision of each external movement.

Frejka's designer for *Cirkus Dandin* was the architect Antonín Heythum, who created a set made up of platforms, staircases, ropes, and brightly painted scaffolding for the young actors to fill with movement and activity. *Cirkus Dandin* became a *commedia dell'arte* romp, "disguising Dandin as a foolish Pierrot."[44] The actors were less concerned with the theory of Constructivism than with the excitement of their performances; Jarmila Horáková wrote:

> I could play well because the construction gave me lots of ideas, of movements, I could choose what to do at the last moment and it was always natural. The slightest changes in the constructions shifted the scale of movements. The actor was keyed up before every performance, even after a hundred reprises.[45]

The stage was not only a platform where the actors could perform (*hrát*) but also a playground where they could frolic (*hrát si*). Jindřich Honzl wrote in *Rudé právo*:

> It was apparent… what the bright young actor and the spirited and pretty actress mean to this new stage work, for their joints haven't yet stiffened into the dull and careful movements of the official actor. This… is mirrored in the enthusiasm of the audience.[46]

HONZL, FREJKA, AND THE LIBERATED THEATRE

The Liberated Theatre opened in the theatre known as *Na slupi* (after its address in a street below the old fortress of Vyšehrad) on 8 February 1926 with a revival of *Cirkus Dandin*, followed on 17 March by Honzl's production of Ribemont-Dessaignes's *Le Serin muet* (also designed by Heythum). Honzl and Frejka wanted to create a poetic theatre—not poetic drama, a text written in verse, but a theatre of metaphor where the inventiveness of the performers would awaken the imagination of the audience. Frejka wrote that it should appeal to those who were not concerned with "'Art' pickled in historical brine, but *art* as *concrete and immediate* as the machine we assemble, as the paint we mix."[47]

A double bill directed by Frejka opened on 17 April, the first half poetry, followed by Vítězslav Nezval's *Telegrams on Wheels*. Frejka and Nezval aimed to capture the spirit of Poetism with unexpected analogies, visual surprises, playful metaphors (the Fish-girl throws kisses to her lover the Sailor; they are fishes, which he catches in his mouth), and contemporary characters: the Radio-telegrapher, the Negro, and the Businessman. In the rapid sequence of scenes, verse followed prose, dance alternated with pantomime, and radio voices chased the cries of the street vendors. Frejka saw Nezval's composition as being musical in concept: "a sequence of lyrical poems, linked by ensemble scenes, which in themselves carry the action."[48]

Honzl's second production at the Liberated Theatre was Guillaume Apollinaire's "Surrealist drama" *Les Mamelles de Tiresias* (translated by Jaroslav Seifert) in October 1926. Apollinaire had been an inspiration and model for the poets of the Devětsil; they had been influenced by his games with the laws of time and ideas of viewing reality from different angles used in *Le Passant de Prague* (written after his visit to Prague in 1902). Other features of his work—the freeing of fantasy, the disregard of logic, the enjoyment of popular entertainment—also appealed to the Liberated Theatre.

The group worked feverishly on the new production. František Zelenka—a keen young architect engaged to design for Hilar at the National Theatre while still a student—laid aside his top hat and gloves to paint the scenery himself.* The young Miloš Nedbal (a fellow pupil of Voskovec and Werich), chosen to play the leading role ("maybe because I was a blank sheet of paper") later remembered:

> We began to rehearse in the theatre cellar. A small place was left next to the heaps of coal, and on that Honzl drilled us; every word, every gesture, every step. I sweated like a horse. I even cried a little. And all the time I was afraid in case Honzl would take me by the collar and throw me out.[49]

---

* Zelenka's final stage designs were created in 1944 in Terezín.

Honzl's direction enlarged and simplified the stage action, insisting on precise movement and gesture from the actors, and using exaggerated props such as a gigantic inkpot and glue bottle, balloons, and megaphones. The music was played onstage on an assortment of percussion instruments by the young composer E. F. Burian, in the role of the People of Zanzibar.

Teige thought Frejka and Honzl could outstrip Tairov and Meyerhold in:

> ...the new theatre poetry, stripped of ideology, literature, psychology, and sentimentality. From playing theatre they made real play, scientific play, play for society... as difficult as chess, as enjoyable as tennis, as destructive as poker.[50]

But in 1927 the coalition was dissolved. Frejka saw himself as a practical man of the theatre, able to take any play and turn it into spontaneous entertainment by the use of Constructivist or *commedia dell'arte* techniques. Honzl, on the other hand, considered that the choice of play was important; he wanted a studio-type theatre that would go beyond competitive "styles" towards a response to specific texts.

FREJKA AND THE THEATRE DADA

Frejka formed a new company called the Theatre Dada (*Divadlo Dada*). He was joined by several members of the Liberated Theatre and the Devětsil, including E. F. Burian and the twenty-year-old composer Jaroslav Ježek. Their first production in April 1927, directed by Frejka and Burian, was Jean Cocteau's *Les Mariés de la Tour Eiffel*. Thirteen titles were staged in just over a year; the most successful were the "merry evenings" (*veselé večery*), a kind of literary cabaret satirising state bureaucracy, false cultural values, and glorification of Czech history, punctuated by dance, *kuplety*, acrobatics, and jazz. The critic A. M. Píša wrote:

> The young authors and the actors... understood that their revue must be in a way a daily paper of its time, brief and colourful, amusing and aggressive, reacting with a sharp and immediate humour to the events and heroes of the day.[51]

When Dada closed, Frejka went off to the Bauhaus in Dessau, where he became involved in Oskar Schlemmer's production of the *Triadic Ballet*. On his return he published his first book *A Man Who Became an Actor* (*Člověk, který se stal hercem*), helped to found a new cultural revue, *Signál*, and planned an international exhibition of modern theatre. At the beginning of 1929, he and E. F. Burian founded the Modern Studio (*Moderní studio*, based in the

Umělecká beseda [Arts Club]).* Here, in a quiet corner of Prague's Lesser Quarter they played a programme of jazz farces, parodies, adaptations of classics, a pioneering attempt at a Japanese Noh play and performances by Burian's "Voiceband."

E. F. BURIAN AND THE VOICEBAND

In the dying days of Austria-Hungary in autumn 1918, Emil František Burian, the privileged scion of a family of internationally known opera singers, ran away from home. A fourteen-year-old volunteer guard, rifle in hand, he was intoxicated by the excitement of nationalism and wore his tricolour proudly in the streets of Prague. For several months he lived rough among the homeless. On his return he decided to study music at the Conservatoire; in 1923 he joined the Communist Party and the same year embarked on writing an opera based on Maeterlinck's puppet play, *Alladine et Palomides*. Two years later, his first completed one-act opera was staged at the National Theatre, and he had started a review *Tam-tam*, devoted to modern music. A member of Devětsil, he was excited by international avant-garde art. In 1926, he published his first two books: *Modern Russian Music* (*O moderní ruské hudbě*) and *Polydynamika*. With Vítězslav Nezval he read Freud, Einstein, Dostoyevsky, Marx, and André Breton; they discussed Dada, the unconscious, parapsychology.

As a musician, Burian was growing up in the last decade of Leoš Janáček's life. He regarded "our Janáček" as one of the true modern artists, marked by "unrestrained activity."[52] There was an affinity in their fascination with everyday sounds: "music… in a telephone receiver, in the dust of centuries-old registers, in the flag that flapped above the Castle in a mad whirl" (Janáček);[53] "The melody of speech… the clanging of dustcarts, the tramway, the barking of dogs, the murmur of water, laughter…" (Burian).[54] Burian was one of the first musicians in Prague to discover jazz, describing its rhythms and harmonies as "the music of the street, contained in every individual."[55] An affinity between Burian and Janáček appears too in their attitudes to the spoken word. Janáček took notes of the quiet resignation in the voice of Smetana's daughter and of a railway guard's announcements in German and in Czech; of a woman calling her hens: "[the Czech language] is not inherited song-like boasting…. It is the vigour of broad fields and the worthlessness of the dust…"[56] Burian too deplored declamatory speech in the theatre: "Few actors

* The Arts Club, formerly the home of the recently deceased Vladimír Gamza's Arts Studio; today known as the Theatre Na prádle, after the neighbouring twelfth-century Church of St. John the Baptist Na prádle (at the Laundry).

deliver their lines with a view to the form of their construction. Few directors cultivate the Czech accent to let shine the constellation of sounds..."[57]

Burian conceived the Voiceband with Honzl and Zora, as a successor to the Dědrasbor. He wanted to free the voice from dependence on melody and from mechanical recitation; to draw the listener's attention, dulled by familiarity with content, to the structure of the word and sentence and to a renewed understanding. He used vocal sounds such as whistling and hissing as well as words, claiming an analogy with jazz: "As the jazz band introduced new instruments, so the voiceband frees the human voice from the bondage of symbols..."[58] With the aid of Roman Jakobson's studies,* Burian distinguished between stress-based speech, traditional in Czech recitation, and that based on quantity. He considered the Voiceband to be closer to theatre than to recitation, and incorporated other theatrical elements such as stylised dance. Jarmila Kröschlová described her work on suiting dance to the rhythmic arrangement of the spoken word: "It had its own strict order, a finished form, unusual musicality, and a powerful expressive effect."[59]

The Voiceband gave its first public performance in April 1927 at the Theatre Dada. The programme included excerpts from works by the nineteenth-century writers Karel Hynek Mácha and Jan Neruda, and Devětsil member Adolf Hoffmeister, followed by Jaroslav Seifert's "Honeymoon" (*Svatební cesta*) in the rhythm of the Charleston, danced by Milča Mayerová and Saša Machov—the "russianised" stage name of the dancer and choreographer František Alexander Maťha: talented, extravagant, temperamental, and openly homosexual. The Voiceband was incorporated into Theatre Dada productions, and in the interval between Theatre Dada and the Modern Studio, twice toured Italy. The opening production of the Modern Studio in April 1929 was the Voiceband's version of Karel Havlíček's satirical epic, "The Baptism of Saint Vladimir" (*Křest svatého Vladimíra*). Seventy years after Havlíček's death, the censor still found it necessary to make some cuts.

When the Modern Studio closed, the paths of Burian and Frejka separated. But the Liberated Theatre survived—in unforeseen circumstances.

VOSKOVEC, WERICH, AND THE LIBERATED THEATRE

Early in 1927, an amateur revue had opened in the Arts Club. The actors and musicians were students, the scenery cheaply painted on large sheets of wrapping paper. One of the initiators, Jiří Voskovec, was among the first members

* See "The Prague Structuralists," p. 75.

of the Devětsil.* He had studied at the Lycée Carnot in Dijon, at the same time contributing to the Devětsil publication *Život* (*Life*) and producing some of the first collage poems seen in Prague. Back home he wrote reviews for a film magazine, wore a cap after the Soviet model, and attended the Law Faculty, where he resumed his friendship with Jan Werich. Here they made fun of the stuffiness of their teachers and enlivened their fellow students with games and practical jokes. They were bored by conventional theatre, preferring the summer arenas and the cinema, especially the American two-reelers. They relished the exotic settings and the *anglo-saský* (Anglo-Saxon, easily modified to *anglo-šašký*, from *šašek*, clown) humour with its grotesque situations and knockabout comedy. Their favourite music was Dixieland jazz, translating the lyrics with the help of a dictionary ("sugar baby" gained a new meaning).

Vest Pocket Revue (the title was in English, in accordance with the vogue for all things American) was written in response to a newspaper advertisement for a play competition. A parody of the sophisticated revues *à grand spectacle*, full of student jokes and wordplay, it made lighthearted fun of the clichés of both the conventional and the avant-garde theatre. Locations ranged from the Great Wall of China and the Eiffel Tower to Hradčany, using the illustration from a well-known brand of safety matches. Between scenes, the two students would entertain the audience with dialogue based on the student banter they had perfected over the years. These *předscény*, or forestage appearances, were soon the most popular part of what became known as "V+W." Devised only days before the première—or even on the same day—from notes made in a café or dressing room, they were always topical and, as the years passed, increasingly political. They were capable of variation not only in content, but also in rhythm, timing and emphasis, responding to the reactions of the audience. Wordplay was an important part: V+W played with homonyms, neologisms, hyperbole, anachronism, association, dialect, jargon, occupational slang, imported words and expressions, and literary and academic Czech. Voskovec saw it as a variation of Poetism rather than a parody of it. Teige described the language as "Surdada" or "Hyperdada," celebrating a delight in living and in the possibilities open to man; it provoked laughter at the absurdity of everything "sententious, profound, majestic, impassioned, bombastic, erudite, and patronising." Voskovec later postulated that they saw life through a prism whose three angles were "Fun, Poesy, and Satire."[60] From the start, Voskovec was the "intellectual," Werich the down-to-earth Czech. Their stylised clown makeup linked them with a range of antecedents: *commedia dell'arte*, circuses, American silent film, and Slavic folk art.

* He was temporarily expelled in 1926 for playing the romantic lead in the film *May Fairy Tale*.

In the early V+W revues, the games in the *předscény* were intended only to provoke laughter; but in the course of time their fields of reference became wider and their targets more specific. They mocked the contemporary middle classes with their season tickets for the National Theatre, easy praise for second-rate art, and cheap nationalism. As the economic crisis worsened, they commented on the "gilded youth" and the poverty in the streets. Their political satire arose out of their method of creative improvisation. In developing a theme through association, allusions to contemporary events would occur which would immediately be interpreted by the audience. Comparisons of the published text with recordings show how they would deviate from the basic script and then return to the original starting point.

Vest Pocket Revue caught on. Frejka quickly booked it for two showings at the Theatre Dada; then Honzl engaged V+W for the Liberated Theatre (performing in the Adria Theatre) and 208 performances were given there over the coming year. Voskovec and Werich still had time to prepare and rehearse the *Smoking Revue* ("smoking" in the Czech sense of dinner jackets), with the same intention of "laughter for laughter's sake."

Honzl's move made good commercial sense. The popularity of V+W helped to pay for his own more experimental productions at the Liberated Theatre, consisting of Marinetti, Cocteau, Ribemont-Dessaignes, Philippe Soupault, André Breton, and the Czechs Adolf Hoffmeister, Vladislav Vančura, and Vítězslav Nezval. One of Honzl's most successful productions was Alfred Jarry's *Ubu Roi* (1928), translated by Voskovec. It was played in a rapid succession of cartoon-like scenes, parodying the popular genre of historical drama (which was still reminding the Czechs of their historical greatness). The future Surrealist Jindřich Štyrský designed properties of grotesque size, while Werich brought a gross good humour to the title role. The bright young Communist journalist Julius Fučík wrote:

> The atmosphere in which the Liberated Theatre enfolds its audience from the first note of the original music; the excitement with which the public reacts, that gives one a new faith in the theatre, so mutilated, so ruined, on the official stage.[61]

Honzl, however, was frustrated by the small audiences attending his avant-garde productions and in 1929 accepted the post of head of drama at the State Theatre in Brno, while the Liberated Theatre moved into larger premises at the theatre *U Nováků* (At the Nováks) on Vodičkova Street, opposite the Myšák pâtisserie in the Rondo-Cubist house. However, Voskovec and Werich found it hard to repeat their early success. "Box office kitsch, patronised by upper class misses," sneered the left-wing critics. "A few witty ideas don't constitute a work of art!"[62]

Jaroslav Ježek, the handicapped son of a Žižkov tailor, became one of the most popular, even loved, members of the avant-garde movement. The world he saw through his pebble glasses was clouded and blue, and inspired his most famous blues number, "Dark Blue World" (*Tmavomodrý svět*). The melancholy world through which he blunders his way is, he tells us, not only his personal world but one shared by all of us. In spite of poor hearing he studied as a classical musician and composer, and was particularly receptive to new movements in modern music: Stravinsky, Schoenberg, Bartók, Debussy, and Les Six. In 1923, aged sixteen, he startled the Conservatoire by playing Ravel and Hindemith at his audition. J. B. Foerster, Josef Suk, and Václav Talich all led classes at the Conservatoire in Ježek's time. Just as the barriers were dissolving in the theatre and the visual arts, in music too the boundaries were widening. "The gates of music are opening," Leoš Janáček told his students at the opening of the Brno Conservatoire in 1919, "and its tones are not restricted to the field of instruments. The laws of music exist in all living beings, in rhythm and in melody, and by these rhythms we measure ourselves and the universe."[63]

While studying at the Conservatoire, Ježek also composed accompaniments for his friends' poetry; for example, Nezval's "Blues" from *Pantomima* (1924). He was drawn to American jazz, especially Duke Ellington and Louis Armstrong, and introduced his friends to Gershwin's "Rhapsody in Blue." While playing improvised jazz, he found the same rapport with the audience that the young stages were reaching for: an immediacy which demanded constant awareness from the audience, and from the performer a sensitivity to atmosphere, together with a mastery of technical skills. Ježek understood the creativity of improvising within a basic construction:

> For myself, I am deeply convinced of the necessity and validity of jazz as an art, for there are within me areas I could speak of and expose in no other way, and I am similarly convinced of the propriety of its use, since the outcome of several works of mine at the Liberated Theatre strengthened my opinion of the inherent qualities of song and dance in jazz.[64]

In the summer of 1929, Voskovec and Werich tried to persuade Ježek to sign a contract with the Liberated Theatre; at first he hesitated, not wanting to lose his reputation as a serious composer. He also had offers from other theatres, including the National, for which he had composed the music for G. K. Chesterton's *The Man Who Was Thursday*. The future of the Liberated Theatre hung on his decision; however, on 10 December 1929 *Fata Morgana*, with Ježek's "Fata-Morgana Fox," "Equatorial Rag," and "Bloody Moon

Rhapsody," inaugurated almost a decade of V+W+Ježek revues. Voskovec and Werich had been inspired in Paris that summer by the touring Broadway hit *Blackbirds of 1928*. Ferenc Futurista was engaged, and František Zelenka and Bedřich Feuerstein designed sets and costumes full of colour and invention. They were joined by the choreographer Joe Jenčík, defecting from the Lucerna cabaret despite financial enticements. One of the troupe of six "Girls" he brought with him was E. F. Burian's future choreographer, Nina Jirsíková. In her memoirs, she recalled that the teamwork with Jenčík and the company spirit were unique. The performers worked long hours but were decently paid, and above all there were none of the intrigues that prevailed in other theatres. Over the next eighteen months, Voskovec directed three more jazz revues, each one full of Ježek's marches and blues, foxtrots and American folk songs: "The Weary Blues," "Dynamit Fox," "Mercedes Tango," "Song of Buffalo Bill," "Bugatti Step," and "Isabel Waltz." But, as Voskovec put it, in the brief time that had passed since their carefree *Vest Pocket Revue*, the American financial skyscraper had collapsed. The world was topsy-turvey, and hastening to its ruin:

> Whereas the vigorous Liberated Theatre was once ruled mainly by eloquent student wit and intellectual Dada humour, full of literary parodies and social analogies, today it has become a major entertainment centre, eager to satisfy the many-sided tastes of the broad masses of the public.[65]

THE TURN OF THE DECADE

For all its political shortcomings, the young republic of Czechoslovakia had been well managed economically,* and had reached the height of its prosperity in 1929. It was in this mood that the young avant-garde directors had taken on new challenges. Jindřich Honzl spent two seasons (1929–1931) in Brno, which had a reputation for allowing the arts and learning more freedom than Prague. Before the founding of the Republic, Brno had been more closely linked with Vienna than with Prague, and until 1945 had a large German-speaking population. The citizens of Brno and Vienna used to employ the same architects to build their houses, the same musicians to play the same tunes *zum Kaffee und Sachertorte*, the same painters to paint the ceilings of their churches. Brno was no backwater; the *Deutsches Stadttheater*

---

* Czechoslovakia's economic soundness was established by the first postwar minister of finance, Alois Rašín, assasinated by an Anarchist in 1923. Václav Havel wrote a play about him in 1988 (see "The Theatre and the Velvet Revolution").

(now the Mahen Theatre), which opened in 1882, was the first theatre in mainland Europe to have electric light installed, designed by Thomas Edison himself. Brno also had a thriving Czech-language intellectual and cultural life; in 1884, it had been the first city after Prague to open its own professional Czech theatre, the Provisional National Theatre. In the 1920s the two most influential personalities in the Brno theatre were Leoš Janáček and the writer and dramaturge Jiří Mahen, who was to end his life when the Nazis occupied Czechoslovakia in 1939.

In Brno, Honzl found himself constrained by a director's administrative responsibilities in managing a large theatre and ensemble. He disappointed his colleagues in the Devětsil by failing to implement the radical programme they expected. He managed only one avant-garde play by a Czech author: Vladislav Vančura's *Teacher and Pupil* (1930). The programme comprised contemporary foreign authors (Jean Cocteau, Valentin Kataev), classic Czech and foreign authors (Klicpera, Ben Jonson)—and far too many drawing-room comedies.

E. F. Burian, who had similarly accepted an engagement in Brno, was equally disappointed. He arrived in 1929 as director of the newly founded Studio of the National Theatre, but his production of Machiavelli's *Mandragola* met with little success and the studio soon closed. After a season in Olomouc, Burian returned to Brno National Theatre, where, as his culminating production and on the heels of Jiří Frejka's première at the Theatre of the Estates, he directed Nezval's *Lovers from the Kiosk* (1932).* Frejka presented the comedy, superficially an ironic portrait of bright young things (Helena, bored by her chess-playing husband, flees to the arms of his brother Benjamin, a Parisian journalist), as a demonstration that the younger generation saw beyond the hypocritical Victorian morality of contemporary Prague society. Critics objected that the interpretations were in the spirit of psychological realism[66] and that the actors killed the poetry (the play was written in alexandrines). Frejka denied this, coining the term "magic realism" a quarter of a century before it came into common usage.[67] Feuerstein's designs[68] show a realistic functionalist set with neoclassical elements; Burian, on the other hand, kept the poetry and set the action in a lyrical abstract space, composing a score that in future productions became an integral part of the script. Both directors had problems with censorship; in Brno, a policeman was stationed in the wings at every performance to ensure that Vladimír Šmeral in the role of Benjamin did not deliver his closing poem in praise of the Soviet Union. At the end of the season, Burian—like Frejka, still only twenty-eight years old—returned to Prague as one of the thousands unemployed.

---

* A German-language stage until 1920, the Estates Theatre was now part of the National Theatre.

Honzl had returned to the Liberated Theatre in the autumn of 1931. He directed only one more experimental production: Nezval's *Fear* (January 1934), but took over from Voskovec as director of the jazz revues. At the same time, he continued his theoretical work on the aesthetics of the theatre. He became associated the Prague Linguistic Circle (1928–1939, also known as the Prague School), one of the phenomena that accompanied the rich ethnic and cultural mix that formed the First Republic.

The formation of the PLC in the mid-1920s brought together Russian and Ukrainian émigrés, Czechs and Germans. Its leaders included the Russian scholar and Brno professor Roman Jakobson and the Czech researcher into Russian Formalism Jan Mukařovský. Prague became a major centre for the study of semiotics; the Prague School started from the classic understanding of Saussurean semiotics, and developed new methods of literary analysis. Aesthetics, music, and theatre also came within its remit. Theatre offered the best-equipped laboratory for such study, and there were excellent conditions in Czechoslovakia in the 1930s; traditional theatres strongly influenced by the Realist, Symbolist, and Expressionist movements operated alongside experimental avant-garde stages; there was a practising tradition of abstract art and an awareness of Surrealism, as well as models of study from the fields of linguistics, literature, aesthetics, and philosophy, and openings for research in anthropology and sociology. The components of theatre performance, their qualities and relationships, were analysed by the scholars of the Prague School.

In some respects, Honzl followed the ideas of the musicologist Otakar Zich, a precursor and contemporary of the PLC who only became a member in the last year of his life. In 1931, the year of Honzl's return to Prague, Zich published *Aesthetics of the Art of Drama* (*Estetika dramatického umění*). In this he gave equal weight to elements of the theatre beyond the written text, emphasising the interrelationship between them and also indicating that, as the complete structure was greater than an analysis of its parts, there were two aspects to performance: the technical creation of performance onstage and the performance as experienced by the audience. He distinguished them by reference to the "stage figure" (*herecká postava*) created by the actor and the "dramatic character" (*dramatická osoba*) developed in the mind of the audience member—in Zich's concept, two sides of the same coin.[69]

Honzl investigated the concept of defamiliarisation, or foregrounding—a term that indicates the emphasis laid on one feature of performance in order to focus the audience's attention.[70] (Even in Naturalism, where it appears that real life is faithfully depicted, it is the detail and exactness of the setting that is foregrounded for the audience, in contrast with classical or Romantic staging, in which the actor is foregrounded.) Thus one of the conditions in a stage production is the shift in an audience's expectations; Honzl analysed how, once the signifying roles of the elements had been identified, information could be transferred between them and conveyed by settings or by speech, by gesture or by image. The stage director should compose his production so that the audience perceive his process of thought through the unexpected juxtaposition and contest of familiar elements.

FREJKA AT THE NATIONAL THEATRE

In the autumn of 1929, in the middle of activities at the Modern Studio, Jiří Frejka had accepted an invitation to direct a guest production at the National Theatre (Marcel Achard's updated *commedia dell'arte* pastiche, *Jean de la lune*, which Frejka retitled *Marceline*); from January 1930 he was engaged there permanently—as Hilar's assistant until 1933, and as a director in his own right until 1945. Frejka's main achievement at the National Theatre was to build up a company of actors with whom he worked on principles derived on the one hand from Naturalism and on the other from Meyerhold and Tairov (whose work he experienced firsthand as a delegate to the First Moscow Theatre Festival in 1933). He aimed at a style that would appeal to conventional National Theatre audiences and simultaneously convert them to the avant-garde ideas of the small theatre. Influenced by the French, he staged Jean Giraudoux and Jean Cocteau. He worked on new ways of using the stage space, with the help of technical advances in mobile scenery and stage lighting. From the start, he worked closely with František Tröster, whose complex sensitivity to angles of vision in the stage space gave an extraordinary dramatic quality to Frejka's productions: In *The Government Inspector* (1936) the drunken Khlestakov proceeded through the vertiginous doorways of an enfilade that lurched and swayed around him until he collapsed on a couch that tilted up from the front of the stage. In *Julius Caesar* (1936) the early scenes were played under a massive sculptured horse and rider "bestriding the narrow world," while the Capitol was overshadowed by the dictator's head, which split and crashed to the ground on Caesar's murder. Europe was already under the shadow of another dictator.

"The era of Devětsil Poetism is now quite at an end," Vratislav Effenberger later wrote. "Poetry no longer wants to come out to play."[71] Tensions were increasing in Europe. The Russian Civil War had sent thousands of refugees flooding to the West. In the early 1920s, President Masaryk and the Czechoslovak government instigated a generous programme of humanitarian aid

Julius Caesar by William Shakespeare, directed by Jiří Frejka and designed by František Tröster for the National Theatre, 1936. (Reproduced by permission from František Černý et al., *Dějiny českého divadla*, IV. Prague: Academia, 1983, 199.)

for exiled Russians,* with the hope that the Bolsheviks would be overthrown and order restored. Thousands settled in communities across the country, ranging from workers through students to intellectuals (including the poet Marina Tsvetaeva). Among them were members of the Moscow Art Theatre, which had found itself cut off by the fighting while on tour, and which in 1919 created the Prague Group of the Moscow Art Theatre.[72]

The Czechoslovak Communist movement, until now more in sympathy with the Mensheviks than the Bolsheviks, was itself in crisis; in 1925, one-third of its parliamentary deputies resigned from the Party in protest against Comintern interference. A power struggle ensued; Moscow backed "the Karlín† boys" led by Klement Gottwald, the belligerent son of a Moravian ser-

* *Ruské pomocné akce* (Russian Relief Action). According to Lesley Chamberlain in *The Philosophy Steamer*, "Czechoslovakia spent more than all other European nations put together on Russian refugees."

† Karlín, since the floods of 2002 rebuilt as the commercial centre of Prague, was at this time a working-class district where the Communist Party had its headquarters.

vant woman. In March, seven writers resigned in protest against the bolshevisation of the Party; some of them later returned, but not the poet Jaroslav Seifert. The Fifth Congress in February 1929 saw the defeat of the intellectuals and a massive purge of the Party. Gottwald, in his maiden speech as a member of parliament in December, openly acknowledged that the Communists took their orders from Moscow and that, when the time came, they would "wring your necks." The deputies laughed; yet when President Masaryk abdicated in 1935, the support of the Communist deputies in parliament was needed for Masaryk's protégé, Edvard Beneš, to be elected president. Earlier that year, Masaryk's government, threatened by growing Fascism in Germany and Italy, signed a Treaty of Alliance with Soviet Russia. The Czechoslovak right-wing parties were divided, while among the German-speaking minority, the *Sudetendeutsche Partei* led by the gymnastics teacher Konrad Henlein was increasing in numbers and influence.

What had happened to the international avant-garde? mourned Honzl in 1934. In Italy, what had become of Marinetti and Luigi Pirandello? In Germany, of the theatre at all? In France, had the struggle of Charles Dullin, Gaston Baty, and Jacques Copeau been in vain?* If the French could arrest Aragon for his poetry, then German-style Fascism was creeping over the borders. The avant-garde theatre could not exist in isolation; it needed a public stage: "The avant-garde is not only a question of technique... it is a question of an opinion, an interpretation of a world of impressions and feelings, a clear answer to a social reality."[73]

The Surrealist Group of Prague was formed in 1934, including Honzl, Teige, and Nezval among its members. It was a darker and weightier movement than the more luminous Poetism, recognising forces hostile to independent thought, and demanding greater commitment. Effenberger wrote:

> Honzl, like Teige, was led to Surrealism—this is no paradox—by its penetrating sense of reality, of the actual utility of poetry for which beauty, fictitious and divorced from society is insufficient, but which wants to share in the transformation of life.[74]

The left-wing artists of the Devětsil had progressed from Poetism to Surrealism; however, at the Moscow Congress of Writers in 1934 they heard Stalin's representative Andrei Zhdanov declare that the task of art was to depict reality in its revolutionary development, and promote Socialist Realism as the official style of the Soviet Union. To the Czechs, this was reactionary conservatism, denying the advances made in modern art. Vítězslav Nezval

* Dullin, Baty and Copeau had modernised the French stage by introducing new playwrights, reforming stage design, and rethinking stage conventions.

defended Surrealism, but the following year was forbidden to speak at the Paris Congress, from which André Breton was banned. Orthodox Communists in Czechoslovakia condemned experimental work and identified Surrealism with Fascism. In 1938, Nezval recanted and, to Teige's indignation, declared the Surrealist Group disbanded. Teige held the group together, but Nezval steadily inclined towards the Moscow faction, in the postwar years becoming an enthusiastic supporter of Stalin.

At the Liberated Theatre, Honzl retained the basic format of the jazz revue with its absurd but logical story, while the political satire intensified. They were living in an age when the irrationality of Dada and the cruelty of King Ubu ceased to be nightmares in the minds of poets and turned into reality. An early sign was the flood of beggars on the streets—not old professional beggars, but new young amateurs surprised to find themelves there. In *Golem*, (1931) Werich sang "A Prague Java" about the charm of living in snow-covered Prague—as long as you were not one of the freezing poor. The next production, *Caesar* (1932) parodied the rise of Mussolini and the arrogance of the Blackshirts. *World Behind Bars* (1933) disparaged narrow-minded nationalism. *The Ass and Its Shadow* (1933) was another classical allegory, alerting its audience to the causal connection of unemployment and need with the rise of demagogues like Hitler. Hostility towards the Liberated Theatre crystalised into a campaign. In *The Hangman and the Fool* (1934), Don Carriera, who assumes power in a South American state, was such an obvious caricature of Adolf Hitler that performances were violently disrupted by Nazi sympathisers. The theatre that had once vowed to stay out of politics was now so effective in its satire that the German Embassy in Prague made an official protest to the Czechoslovak Foreign Ministry. In the summer the company was disbanded.

> Once, to rule, a king must have a hangman and a fool;
> Now we have a fool who is both hangman and king.[75]

E. F. BURIAN AND DÉČKO

E. F. Burian returned from Brno to Prague in the summer of 1932, when the Czech economy, which had long withstood the Depression, was finally feeling its impact. He joined a new cabaret group, the Ace of Hearts (Červené eso), where he performed with Ferenc Futurista and a black American jazz singer known as Art La Nier. The cabaret's biggest success was *The Ship of the Living* (December 1932), directed by Burian. The theme resembled Mayakovsky's *Mystery-Bouffe*: We are all passengers in the same ship, bound on the same dangerous voyage, but some are travelling first-class and some steerage. The left-wing critics were enthusiastic: "We saw that these are artists who want to do more than tickle the bourgeoisie; they have opened their eyes and understand dialectically what is happening around them today." Burian appealed for funds to establish a new theatre company and gathered round him like-minded friends; the group formed a collective, each drawing a subsistence wage.* Opening in the Mozarteum in Jungmannova Street in the autumn of 1933, the company was known as D34; the number changed at the beginning of every autumn season, to indicate change and movement—particularly, with the number outstripping the year, "progressive" movement. "D" (referred to familiarly as Déčko) signified not only *Divadlo*, but also drama, history (*dějiny*), labour (*dělnictvo*), youth (*dorost*), and much more that Burian considered to be aggressive "today" (*dnes*). Their manifesto, which Burian gave to unemployed workers to hand out in the streets of Prague, declared: "We will draw together in our programme all the young talent which… disagrees with the existing theatrical regime and wants to sweep the theatre clean of its stinking corpses…"[76] Burian intended to make Déčko a central meeting place, a way of life. The actor Vladimír Šmeral later remembered:

> Déčko was not only avant-garde, it was a centre for the avant-garde. There you could find the avant-garde from music, poetry, and design as well as the theatre. If after one production the critics came to some conclusions… then along came Burian with another production and stood those conclusions on their head.[77]

The emphatic political content of some of the plays in the first two seasons and the exaggerated simplicity of their production made them targets for parody by Voskovec and Werich in *Keep Smiling* (1934). Burian congratulated them through clenched teeth:

> I enjoyed it very much… The parody of D35 has a very witty text. Unfortunately the direction didn't quite hit it off. Even the Voiceband is unsuccessful. I think Honzl has actually parodied the style that was current before we left for Brno… I'm sorry I couldn't have directed a parody of our theatre myself. I should have offered to do it. What else? You've made great ideological progress. The scene between the two unemployed is superb…[78]

Burian called for a repertoire of plays ignored by the official theatres and imposed a contemporary interpretation even on established texts. *The Merchant of Venice* (September 1934) became a play about bourgeois hypocrisy,

---

* When the Liberated Theatre was temporarily closed in 1935, choreographer Nina Jirsíková found another position for a salary of 1,800 crowns a month. But when Burian invited her to replace Saša Machov at Déčko, she accepted his offer of 600 crowns a month as both choreographer and costume designer without hesitation.

small-mindedness, prejudice, and betrayal. In the programme to Wedekind's *Spring Awakening* (1936) he wrote: "Those who see in our children the inheritors and continuers of our work... can no longer look with tolerance on today's crippling of everything that is healthy in our children."[79] He continued to experiment with techniques, making use of puppets in *The Mannequins' Ball* (September 1933) by the Polish Futurist Bruno Jasieński and in a new production of Nezval's *Lovers from the Kiosk* (November 1935). In other productions he asked his actors for stylised performances resembling waxworks or automata.

Burian responded to the increased militarisation of Europe in one of his most deeply felt productions: *War* (January 1935). This was a montage of voice-band and dance, based on traditional texts collected by the nineteenth-century poet Karel Jaromír Erben. The concrete incidents of common life were celebrated in their joy and pain, wealth, and loss: "The old women mutter on about the price of potatoes, the needy fellow grumbles over his broth, and they become lightning flashes illuminating fleeting twists of history."[80] Burian's aims were political, taking the view that the strength and hope of the nation resided in its common people, and it was they who suffered when their leaders declared war. To do this he took the familiar—not only plays, but also folk songs and stories—and presented it from a new angle. For this purpose, he consciously manipulated the different elements that make up a theatrical production. Unlike Bertolt Brecht, he did not try to maintain the autonomy of the different elements, but rather believed that they should lose their divisions in the formation of a new whole. In this whole, the different elements would work together in complex and changing relationships where any one of the parts could be dominant or substitute for another. He adapted his chosen texts to become part of a scenario on a theme of his choosing. "The dance in *War* was not only in the dancers' feet," wrote Jaroslav Kladiva, "the word danced too, the verse danced from syllable to syllable, from rhyme to rhyme, whirling in assonances and springing in metaphors."[81] Burian could, like a film director, select the most precise and effective medium of communication at a given moment. Jiřina Stránská, playing the title role in *Věra Lukášová* (1938, adapted by Burian from the novel by Božena Benešová, with his own music), remembered her tears when she first heard the overture to the play: "It was not that it was sad. It summed up in the most amazing way the whole of Věra's spirit."[82]

If any of the elements dominated it was that of music, for as well as composing much of it himself, Burian assembled his productions like musical compositions, on the basis of a scenario (or libretto), and saw the relationship of the director to the actors as analogous to the conductor and orchestra. The music, dialogue, and action flowed like a score, reciprocating but never

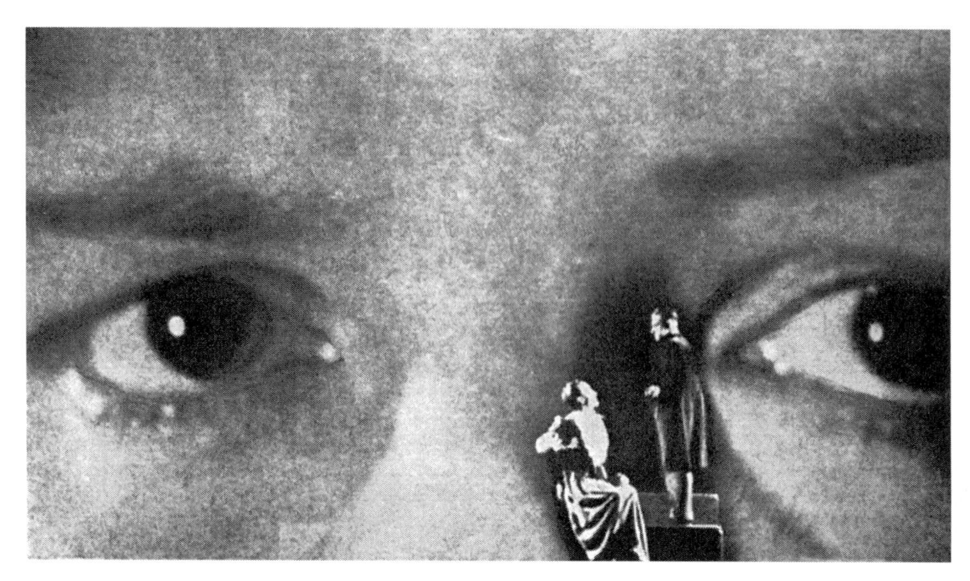

Spring Awakening by Frank Wedekind, directed by E. F. Burian and designed by Miroslav Kouřil for D 36, 1936. Burian used changing projections on a gauze that could be lit from behind or in front. (Reproduced by permission from Antonín Dvořák, *Trojice nejodvážnějších*. Prague: Mladá fronta: 1988, app.)

overlapping. In this "multi-voiced" drama, economy was both a principle and a necessity. The continuous flow of action had to be achieved with invention on a stage measuring approximately six by four metres. Burian worked closely with his designers, especially the architect and ardent Communist, Miroslav Kouřil. He joined D34 at the age of twenty-two and with Burian produced one set after another, inventively created for the small stage. Use was made of rapid changes of acting areas on a variety of stage levels, and the multiple capacity of the space realised through the dynamic use of lighting. In some productions, this experimental use of lighting was combined with the introduction of projection and film that led to the creation of the Theatregraph technique. The first theatre director to incorporate projection and film into his productions had been Erwin Piscator in the Berlin Volksbühne and the short-lived Piscator-Bühne (e.g., for Ernst Toller's *Hoppla* and *Wir leben!*, and for Jaroslav Hašek's *Good Soldier Schweik*, both 1928). However, although Burian sympathized politically with Piscator's revolutionary theatre, his motivation for using film was different. Whereas Piscator used mostly documentary film for an epic didactic, effect, Burian was more concerned the interplay of different voices and the role of film in the appeal to changing moods or emotions. By making his own film sequences for specific productions and to fit his libretto, Burian ensured that the filmed material corresponded not only with the content but also with the style and production. In *Spring Awakening*, the objects featured in the projections—Wendla's daisy field, Melchior's win-

May by Karel Hynek Mácha, dramatised and directed by E. F. Burian and designed by Miroslav Kouřil for D 35, 1935. (Courtesy of the photographer: Miroslav Hák)

dow—were enlarged to a gigantic size, which stressed the characters' vulnerability. *The Sorrows of Young Werther* (1938) was interpreted as a Surrealist dream of Werther on his deathbed: "Dream entered reality and reality into the dream, characters changed into symbols and prose alternated with verse and song."[83] The changing projections were of a distant countryside, the emphasis on the isolation and individuality of the characters. In *Eugene Onegin* (1937), film was used for certain key sequences such as Onegin's sleigh ride to the ball, where the screen showed details of his ride; a voice-over spoke his thoughts and memories; and Tatyana materialised onstage to respond to these thoughts.

The poetic theatre, with its free flow of images, its ability to juxtapose and contrast, its power to suggest a mood or allude to an idea, gave Burian the means to present his audience with what he believed were the serious topics of the age: conformism, capitalism, militarism. The Theatregraph was used not only for its aesthetic qualities but also because, with its use of foregrounding and detail, it could bring the performance closer to the public. But some of the left wing found his work insufficiently dogmatic; they disagreed with his principle of putting artistic truth before what they believed to be the political truth, and the opposition grew stronger after the 1934 advocacy of Socialist Realism. Burian chafed against this; he defended Meyerhold against official criticism, especially after Meyerhold's visit to Prague in the autumn of 1936. Meyerhold had watched Burian's production of *The Barber of Seville* (1936), a poetic commitment to the Spanish Revolution and protest at the murder of Federico García Lorca. Burian fiercely defended the right of an artist to pursue the truth and emphasised that there may be things in a work of art not immediately comprehensible to the average spectator. His version of *Hamlet*, which he called *Hamlet III* (March 1937, following a version of *Hamlet* by Jules Laforgue)* emphasised still more strongly the theme of the individual artist struggling for free expression in a dogmatic society, whether of the right or the left.

THE FETTERED THEATRE

> Dear Friends,
> We need... a Liberated Theatre first because we have been missing our favourite theatrical personalities and also the kind of theatrical culture which your theatre meant to us; and secondly because democracy too needs a touch of humour, laughter, and satire. A gloomy and starchy democracy ceases to be a democracy.
>
> Yours,
> Karel Čapek[84]

In November 1935, Voskovec, Werich, Honzl, Ježek, and the choreographer Saša Machov came back together to launch the Fettered Theatre (*Spoutané divadlo*) in the small Rokoko Theatre of the Lucerna building on Wenceslas Square. Their new production, *The Ballad of Rags* (November 1935), was a great success. Vsevolod Meyerhold, attending a performance the following year, embraced Voskovec and Werich onstage during the curtain calls, and wrote: "Not until today, in the shape of the unforgettable partnership V+W, did I behold again the 'zanni' and was once more enchanted by performers rooted in Italian improvised comedy."[85] *The Ballad of Rags* told the story of the fifteenth-century French poet François Villon, who, having stabbed a man in self-defence, hides from the gallows among the down-and-outs of Paris. In the prologue and epilogue of the play, a parallel was drawn with the poverty of the unemployed in contemporary Prague. The ending of the play, where the actors directly addressed the audience, came close to Brecht's didactic techniques.

The company soon returned to the theatre *U Nováků* on Vodičkova Street and resumed the name of the Liberated Theatre. In Germany the papers

* Jules Laforgue, *Hamlet, ou les suites de la piété filiale*, first published in *La Vogue* (November 1886).

Jiří Voskovec and Jan Werich in *Caesar*, directed by Jindřich Honzl for the Liberated Theatre, 1932. (Photograph from the Czech News Agency)

wrote: "The name 'Liberated Theatre' is indeed very appropriate; the artistic method really is liberated from any kind of constructive activity, any love towards their nation and country, any maintenance of healthy respect and discipline."[86] The four productions leading up to the summer of 1938 maintained opposition to German Naziism, and the subjects closely corresponded with current events (the Spanish Civil War, the annexation of Austria, Hitler's demands for the Sudetenland). In September 1938, the Munich Agreement was signed and in November, during rehearsals for a new production, the Ministry of the Interior withdrew the Liberated Theatre's performing licence.

It was known that the Gestapo carried a list of the Czech intellectuals to be interned as soon as the whole country was occupied and there was no doubt that the comedians would be on it. Voskovec and Werich arranged to leave for the USA, taking Jaroslav Ježek with them. However, whereas the two able-bodied men quickly asserted themselves in American society, Ježek was lost in the alien environment. He was befriended by members of the Czech émigré community, one of whom he married three days before his death in a New York hospital. Later in the war, Jan Werich was playing one of Ježek's recordings in a radio studio. Benny Goodman, impressed by the sound, came to ask whose work it was.

"He's dead," replied Werich. "He was a Czech and his name was Ježek."

"But that was done here, wasn't it?" asked Goodman.

"Here?" exclaimed Werich. "That was recorded long ago, back home."[87]

III UNDER THE PROTECTORATE

In 1937, after ten years absence, Karel Čapek returned to the theatre with *The White Plague* (also known as *Power and Glory*). Set in an unknown land, the nameless Marshal clearly represents Hitler, and the eponymous plague, creeping Fascism. The physician Galen confronts them both, but is trampled to death by the mob before he can deliver the cure. Possibly the most direct and dramatically effective of Čapek's plays, *The White Plague* was translated and staged in a diminished number of countries. In *The Mother* (1938), with its echoes of Maxim Gorky and Bertolt Brecht, Čapek confronted his lifelong position of pacificism. The decision of the eponymous heroine to sacrifice her one remaining son for the defence of the homeland was a reflection of his own response to the potential devastation of Czechoslovakia. In June that year, Čapek invited delegates from the International Congress of PEN Club to watch the Czechoslovak Army in military exercises, demonstrating that the republic was prepared to stand up to Hitler if her allies remained loyal. The target of vicious attacks by Germanophile Czechs, Čapek was urged by friends to go into exile. In September, France and Britain signed the Munich Agreement, granting Czechoslovakia's borderlands (where her defences were concentrated) to Nazi Germany. Czechoslovakia was not consulted. In December, in the ominous period before the final occupation of Bohemia and Moravia, Čapek died in his villa in Vinohrady. His passing went virtually unmarked; the management of the National Theatre lacked the courage to lower its flag to half-mast, and the National Museum claimed it had no coal to heat the Pantheon for a funeral ceremony.* Once the Protectorate of Bohemia and Moravia had

* According to Andrés Pérez-Simón in his doctoral thesis (p. 175), the Nobel Committee refrained from offering Čapek the literature prize for fear of offending Hitler.

been established, the Nazis had no reason to act magnanimously towards the Czech intellectuals. In Hitler's eyes they had been thoroughly obnoxious in the pre-war era, not least in their support for German refugees. According to him, the theatres had behaved particularly badly, in 1935 even encouraging Erika Mann's satirical *Pfeffermühle* to tour German-speaking parts of the country and then appear in Prague, first in the *Unitaria-saal* and then the *Kleine Bühne*, one of Prague's favourite intimate theatres.*

Although the theatres in Prague played regularly through most of Nazi occupation, they were closely followed by the censors, and increasingly tight limits were placed on the repertoire. The occupiers were determined that theatre should serve as propaganda. After the assassination in 1942 by parachutists of Reinhard Heydrich, Reich-Protector of Bohemia and Moravia, theatre workers had to set an example to the nation. Called to an extensively publicised ceremony in the National Theatre on 24 June, many of the cultural elite signed the *Slib věrnosti říši* (Pledge of Allegiance to the Reich). Shortly before the opening of the 1944–1945 season, all Czech theatres were closed (Brno theatres had been closed in 1941). Concert and dance halls were also shut down, cinemas showed only selected films, and no new books were published. In the same year, Czech collaborators published a list of twenty-one "degenerate artists,"including the designer František Tröster. Banned from the theatre and put to forced factory labour, he escaped and went into hiding. He joined the armed underground resistance, but was captured and imprisoned. Other actors, artists, musicians, and writers were also forced into the German war effort. By this time, unaware that the Third Reich was near its end, the Germans were making clear their intention to wipe out Czech culture.

As a leading director at the National Theatre, Jiří Frejka did not play an active part in the resistance. Nevertheless, his productions were remembered for maintaining the morale of the Czech audience and their sense of identity. Working almost exclusively with the classics, he used techniques of allusion and juxtaposition to convey meanings unrecognised by the German censors. His particular milieu was comedy—Josef Kajetán Tyl's *Švanda the Bagpipe*r and Richard Sheridan's *The School for Scandal*. His adaptation of Plautus, *Pseudolus the Fox* (1942), was enthusiastically remembered for its presentation of the disfranchised slave fearlessly seeking justice. With František Tröster in hiding and then prison, Frejka's designer for this and several other wartime productions was Jiří Trnka (later famous for his charmed manipulation of puppets in film). Another theme of the forester's son was the countryside of Bohemia and Moravia, particularly the "blue remembered hills" of Frejka's native Outěchovice.

---

* Regrettably demolished in 1999 for commercial reasons approved by the Prague City Council.

One of the boldest spirits in the Protectorate was the popular actress Anna Sedláčková, who in 1938 started her own company in Déčko's former home, the Mozarteum. She built up a following with a series of middle-of-the-road comedies—Oscar Wilde and Václav Štech—but the production of two plays by Karel Čapek provoked the ire of collaborators and after Sedláčková's refusal to sign the Pledge of Allegiance to the Reich, the theatre was closed. Although allowed to reopen in 1944, the company then followed a conventional repertoire.

E. F. BURIAN AND THE GESTAPO

From Munich onwards, Burian was under pressure to close Déčko and lie low; it was suicidal not to do so. Under the slogan "Modern theatre serves, but is not servile," he not only kept Déčko open but expanded it. The Mozarteum had always been inadequate for what he wanted his theatre to be, a centre for modern Czech culture. He moved into the basement of an extension to the Legiobanka* on the shopping street Na Poříčí, and held a retrospective exhibition of Déčko's work. Seminars for the "Friends of Déčko" (founded in 1939) continued, with speakers including the poet Nezval and the Structuralist Jan Mukařovský. Some of these were published among poems, illustrations, and musical extracts in the programmes edited by the poet Vladimír Holan; for D40, these measured a massive thirty by thirty centimetres and the covers made of brown parcel paper. The fourth number (8 February 1940) carried Jindřich Chalupecký's article "The World in Which We Live," which launched Group 42 (*Skupina 42*), a movement in art and literature celebrating the everyday drama of life, its mysteries and its miracles. Teachers who had attended Déčko as students came with their pupils from the working class districts of Žižkov and Libeň. A school for acting and theatre design was established, and a children's theatre called d41. The actors' working day involved study and training as well as rehearsals; Nina Jirsíková's dance classes at 8:00 a.m. were preceded by an hour of French language. Rehearsals lasted from 9:00 a.m. until 2:00 p.m. Jirsíková remembered the discipline as sometimes inhuman, but the company understood why. The new season's repertoire contained twenty-one original works by Czech authors; Burian knew that many would quickly be banned, and wanted to be able to replace them at a day's notice. Zuzana Kočová, a pupil at the school, described the atmosphere before performances:

* The Bank of the Czechoslovak Legions, designed by Josef Gočár with sculpture by Jan Štursa and Otto Gutfreund, was built in 1921–1923 in honour of the role of the Legions in the Great War.

People look round the exhibition, buy themselves books at the bookstand, hand over photographs of Burešová, Šmeral, Burian, to be stamped: "D40, Centre for Modern Czech Culture"; they read articles in the programme or just chat among themselves, smoke, drink black coffee at the buffet.

After a while the Déčko signature tune [for the start of the performance] sounds for the third time... Silently Burian crosses the foyer, greets the usherettes with a lifted finger or some comical gesture and goes down the corridor to the office. Everyone knows: he's going to write. He works from half past eight in the morning and is the last to leave the theatre, late at night. He hardly feels at home anywhere else...

Now they have banned *War*, Klicpera's *Everyone for his Homeland* and even *Věra Lukášová*.[88]

Some of Burian's most memorable work was produced in the first years of the occupation: the two *Folk Suites* (1938 and 1939); his adaptation of Viktor Dyk's story, *The Pied Piper* (1940); and Nezval's *Manon Lescaut* (1940).

The inspiration for the *Folk Suites* arose from Burian's belief that it was traditional folk theatre that was responsible for the survival of Czech language and identity in the countryside during centuries of German-speaking rule. He quoted the Russian folklorist Petr Bogatyrev, a member of the Prague Linguistic Circle, whom he said knew more about Czech theatre than all the native critics and dramaturges put together:

Over and again, we find that the most celebrated periods of the theatre are where the artists understood their time, where they reacted to it spontaneously, where they were absorbed by the fates of the audience, their joy and pain.[89]

Looking back to the eighteenth century, when the baroque left its mark on the architecture of almost every town and village in Bohemia and Moravia, he emphasised the difference between the art of the nobility—found in parks and churches—and that of the people, found in the language of village and cottage, which still reflected their Gothic origins. These country plays were performed at a fair or funeral, in a village square, or in a living room.

The first *Folk Suite* was made up of three plays from Moravia and southern Bohemia: *The Martyrdom of St Dorothy*, *Salička* (a Shrovetide entertainment), and *Bacchus the Beggar*. The costumes, unlike those of the nineteenth-century "village drama," were not representative of specific locations but designed to evoke the village atmosphere of any part of the country. In the *Second Folk Suite*, Burian emphasised the theatre context by putting his actors into the roles of villagers performing their own work on a small stage with a primitive proscenium and a set made from rough wood, straw, reeds, and old cloth.

The theme of both suites was resistance against an unjust tyrant. The poet František Halas wrote of Burian's work:

> He sees not only the germinating blossoms; he is familiar with the miraculous work of the sap, building the body of the song, and he knows the struggle of the roots, groping down into the dark for lifegiving nutrients.[90]

In dramatizing *The Pied Piper*, Burian switched Dyk's emphasis on the romantic, rebellious Pied Piper to the clumsy but good-hearted fisherman Sepp Jörgen. With the use of projections and colour filters, Hamelin became a labyrinth of lanes and alleyways disappearing into an infinite horizon. Burian composed the incidental music using unconventional instrumentation of clarinet, harp, and mixed choir. The dissonances emphasised the ambiguity of the Pied Piper's behaviour. The play was heavily censored, but the audience grasped the implications of the old legend.*

Early in 1941, Jirsíková was preparing a ballet, *A Fairy Tale of Dance*, about a country where a cruel queen forbids the population to laugh, sing, or dance. The collaborationist publication *Vlajka* (*The Flag*) wrote: "Mr. E. F. Burian apparently thinks he's living in 1937 and not in 1941!"[91] The first performance for the Friends of Déčko was well received; the second, on 11 March, was disrupted by a claque of collaborationists. Kočová remembered:

> When the Gestapo arrived the next morning the theatre was in perfect order. The latest première was being photographed onstage and the pupils were at their lessons in the small smoking room.
>
> In the large smoking room Burian sat alone at a table with the theatre accounts, trying to work out how to improve the wages of some dissatisfied members of the company.
>
> Without commotion they led him upstairs. After a short while Cajlajs [Jiří Süssland][92] and other Jews reached the steps of the bank by the service lift, as always. At least that worked out. [The other students] climbed the familiar circular staircase, one after the other leaving from backstage, past Burian surrounded by those strangers. The single file must have been never ending! Someone, perhaps from fear, caught back a sob; mostly the pupils greeted him with *au revoir*, more distinctly than ever before.
>
> In front of the theatre they split up as ordered and in less than half an hour all the more experienced of them were sitting in the café of the White Swan† opposite, like faithful dogs driven from the threshold, who creep as close as possible to their master's doorstep.[93]

---

* Jan Mukařovský of the Prague Linguistic Circle analysed Burian's achievement in turning Dyk's poetic prose into dialogue, in his essay "Dialog a monolog," *Listy filologické/Folia philologica*, Year 67, no. 3/4, 1940.

† *Bílá labuť*, the Functionalist department store built in the 1930s and still in use today.

Nina Jirsíková, the composer Zbyněk Přecechtěl and the (student) assistant director Alfréd Radok were arrested at the same time. Before this, they were taken to the Petschek Palace in the street now known as Politických vězňů (Political Prisoners'). Hundreds of Czechs were interrogated, tortured, and murdered in this state-of-the-art office building, seized by the Gestapo after its Jewish owner had fled the country.* One of Burian's obsessive memories was of being led down the corridor by the Gestapo and passing his student on his way out of the building. Alfréd Radok,† Burian claimed, "could not look him in the eyes."[94] Přecechtěl and Radok were soon released; Jirsíková spent the next four years in Ravensbrück. Burian was held first in the Small Fortress in Terezín, then in Dachau and other concentration camps. The reasons given for the closure of the theatre were, first, that the stylised gestures (soldiers' goose steps) in the new ballet were defamatory; secondly, that "Friends of Déčko" was an illegal organisation; and thirdly, that Déčko was a centre of Marxist resistance.

THE LITTLE THEATRE FOR 99 AND OCCUPIED PRAGUE

With Voskovec, Werich, and Ježek in America and the Liberated Theatre closed, Jindřich Honzl had returned to teaching and working in film. However, in 1940 the Borový publishing house (now owned by Jaroslav Stránský, son of the founder of the newspaper *Lidové noviny*) offered him a modest opportunity to stage performances in the basement gallery of their bookshop in the art nouveau building *U Topičů* on Národní třída.‡ On the Vltava embankment, Honzl interviewed the twenty-year-old architecture student Antonín Dvořák for the post of head of design:

> Honzl offered me a dry, almost transparent, sinewy hand, looked at me sharply with his bulging eyes, sort of laughed his dry and bitter laugh, and I was completely thrown from my carefully prepared speech...[95]

Honzl—"gaunt, with a pale, sharply featured face, wearing a little grey stew-pot hat; a sober citizen, scarcely resembling anyone from the theatre"—questioned Dvořák on his experience in the concentration camps: fourteen months in Dachau and Buchenwald. For Honzl, this information was more

---

* The building today houses part of the Czech Ministry for Trade and Industry.

† Radok, whose Jewish father died in Terezín, subsequently went into hiding from the Gestapo, but was eventually confined in Klettendorf Labour Camp.

‡ In 1949 it was taken over by the state and became the publishing house Československý spisovatel. Today it houses a branch of Raiffeisen Bank.

relevant than Dvořák's theatre experience. In any case, the duties of the head of design at this theatre were very basic; they involved finding and making props, setting out ninety-nine chairs for every performance, and removing them afterwards when the theatre reverted to its function as an art gallery.

The Little Theatre for 99 (*Divadélko pro 99*) originated with a group of artists who exhibited in the Borový art gallery. They began to present poetry evenings under a licence applying to audiences of under one hundred, while the Gestapo were more preoccupied with the repertoire of the National Theatre across the road. One of the literary programmes was *I See a Great City*, a collection of prophecies about Prague from the time of Princess Libuše onwards; the anonymous compiler was Jewish: Vincy Schwarz. Another production, which included elements of music and design, was based on the poetry of Jiří Orten (Ohrenstein) and directed by his friend Gustav Schorsch (both Jewish). It was the popularity of the literary evenings that had led Borový to invite Honzl to consolidate the group. Honzl realised that there would be little opportunity to implement his political ideas, but that he could work on his theories about what constituted "theatre." On a small podium with no wing space and only free-standing spotlights, Honzl created productions which moved Czech audiences with the conviction that they were a nation with its own culture and destiny.

The first truly theatrical piece to be staged here by Honzl was *A Story of Love and Honour* (1940): a montage of letters between the nineteenth-century writers Jan Neruda and Karolína Světlá. Honzl wrote in the introduction to the printed version:

> The dramatic montage, as I worked it out, was after all an experiment. But in fact I proved its right to exist and its effectiveness in front of an ordinary audience, while a few experts (only a few) did not consider it worthy of interest.[96]

Honzl tried to avoid sentimental emphasis on the love affair between two writers, being more interested in the problem of artists working in a narrow social environment.*

> The first aim was to gauge the living spirit of [Neruda's] work, to prove the inseparable bond between life and poetry, illuminate it from documents relating to his life—his let-

* In 1977, during the stifling period of Normalisation, Otakar Vávra based a film with the same name on the same story. Jiří Šotola wrote the script; Jiří Bartoška (Jan Grossman's *Don Juan*, May 1989) played Neruda.

ters to Karolína Světlá, his literary legacy—so that our audience could recognise Neruda again and afresh.[97]

As Honzl's work progressed he realised that in Neruda and Světlá he had characters who expressed themselves with emotions as powerful as in fictional drama, and that their conflict with the society of the 1860s was more intense than any expressed in the contemporary theatre. He did not need to write any new dialogue. The narrator and the four actors playing the roles of Neruda, Světlá, and Světlá's sister Sofie Podlipská, stood almost motionless:

> Gestures were replaced by the movement of facial muscles. Facial play became especially distinct in the small space because [the actors] were illuminated by the beam of a spotlight at the moment they spoke... The whisper of quiet speech in which an actor expressed himself in the small space mirrored every internal feeling far better than in the theatre, where acoustic considerations deprive the actors of the possibility of more subtle inflections.[98]

No attempt was made by the actors to resemble the characters whose words they read; instead, photographs of Neruda and Světlá were projected onto a screen. Simple properties were used: a flower, a letter, a bibelot. Audiences later recollected both the aesthetic and the moral qualities of the production.

The next two productions, *Songs of the Czech Pedlars* and *The Two Loves of Mikoláš Aleš*, were based on similar principles of montage but with more theatrical elements. In the first, Honzl recreated—with costume and mask, puppets and shadow play, and the juxtaposition of comic and tragic elements—the songs of the spring festivals, known to most of the audience only from cabaret parodies. The content was politically innocent, but educated Czechs recognised that Honzl drew his material from the eighteenth century, the period of suppression of the Czech language. The next production integrated projections of the paintings and drawings of Mikoláš Aleš, one of the young artists who had decorated the foyers of the National Theatre; the script was compiled from letters exchanged between Aleš and his love, Marina. The emphasis was again on the Czech artist struggling to reconcile his artistic calling and his human emotions.

The frequency of performances at the Little Theatre for 99 grew from one to several a week. However, the collaborationist press *Vlajka* (*The Flag*) and *Árijský Boj* (*The Aryan Struggle*) was out to track down the pre-war avant-garde, and the Borový publishing house was afraid to extend Honzl's contract. The company moved to a small hall in the Smetana Museum by the Charles

Bridge, but after the arrest of Julius Fučík and execution of Vladislav Vančura in 1942, Honzl decided to lie low. He held home seminars for young actors and technicians in his small damp apartment, and even arranged some performances there.

Antonín Dvořák took his opportunity to lead the company in the Smetana Museum; its nature, however, changed and it lost the artistic cohesion it had had under Honzl. Part of the group moved to a small theatre also close to the Charles Bridge, another part worked in the Arts Club across the river, calling themselves the Studio of Intimate Theatre (*Studio intimního divadla*) while a third group became the Independent Theatre (*Nezávislé divadlo*). Those remaining at the Smetana Museum renamed themselves the New Ensemble (*Nový soubor*) and were joined by some of E. F. Burian's former pupils. Directors experimented in the small hall with light and shadow; the actors' movement was replaced by dynamic effects achieved with mirrors and projections. Working with them was the adventurous young designer Josef Svoboda, son of a master-joiner in Čáslav. Svoboda had studied with Frejka's designer, František Tröster, and experimented with amateur theatre friends in his hometown. His most ambitious design for the company, for Jiří Karnet's *Roaming*, never reached the stage, as the Nazis closed all Prague theatres before the opening of the season. Svoboda wrote later:

> The scenography—for which I had a detailed scenario—evoked the impression of a stalactite cave (for us it was the environment of the Nazi protectorate). Necessary changes were made solely by lighting and by film and slide projects, with an awareness that the actors on the stage and on film had to be the same. Of course, I drew from everything that E. F. Burian had tried before me.[99]

Meanwhile, at *U Topičů*, Borový had engaged Honzl's former assistant Josef Šmída, barely twenty years old. The new company for the 1941–1942 season, composed largely of E. F. Burian's actors and students, was called Windmill (*Větrník*). Šmída's first production, *A Portrait of Antonín Dvořák*, was largely derived from Honzl. It was the third production that established the programme of the theatre: *Garlands of Wounds*, a staging of German baroque poetry. Compiled by the renowned Jewish translator of Shakespeare, E. A. Saudek, it was attributed to his fellow translator Aloys Skoumal (both could have been executed for such a crime). The suffering of the population during the Thirty Years' War, their longing for justice and defiance of tyranny as expressed in German poetry of that time corresponded to the feelings of the Czech population in 1942. The emotional subtext was not understood by the German censors, who allowed the text to be performed uncut as tribute to German culture. Šmída worked with five women's and six men's voices, concentrating on pitch, inflection, and intonation, sometimes using a chorus and sometimes a solo voice, so that the performance resembled one by Burian's Voiceband. He used a minimum of lighting, with the actors' faces picked out by spotlights.

Another side of Šmída's work was inspired by the Liberated Theatre, with its combination of gag-type comedy and Dada humour. He saw the internal world of the imagination as being contrasted with the external world of oppression and force, represented by the Realist style favoured by Nazi ideology (and by Stalinist Russia). He revived scripts by the Brno playwright Jiří Mahen, including *Castaways* under the title *Goose on a String* (1942). This was not a conventional comedy, but a piece full of clowning, acrobatics, juggling, circus gags, movement, and play. Šmída's work in the genre included *Lemonade Joe* (1944—best known in its 1964 film version), a parody of the Wild West adapted as a satire on the occupiers. The tradition of the recitation evening, built up from individual passages and dialogues, continued with *Likajdovic's Auntie* and its theatrical use of the Žižkov jargon; *Come to Stay!* (1943), based on an ethnographic study of fairy tales by J. S. Kubin; *The Doss-house Coin* (1943), based on short stories by Karel Schulz about young lives bounded by poverty and war, the four walls representing their prison; and *A Sentimental Romance* (1943), from the writings of the nineteenth-century writer Božena Němcová. The actors, in costume and makeup, took this into the Prague suburbs, acting out incidents and then discussing them. With Šmída's adaptation of *The Adventures of the Good Soldier Švejk* (1945, staged immediately after the Liberation), it was one of Windmill's most popular productions.

Audience members remember experiencing every performance at Windmill as resistance to the occupying powers. The future dramaturge Jan Kopecký, reviewing them for *Lidové noviny*, was careful to refer to "literary evenings" rather than theatrical performances.[100] Šmída gradually moved away from Honzl's stylised performances towards more realistic acting. Actors in his company—Radovan Lukavský, Vlastimil Brodský, Miloš Kopecký, Miroslav Horníček—became some of Czechoslovakia's most popular performers, almost like a brotherhood, with careers stretching to the end of the twentieth century. Their colleague Zdeněk Stránský was killed on the terraces of the National Theatre during the Prague Uprising of May 1945.

TEREZÍN AND THE CONCENTRATION CAMPS

After his arrest by the Gestapo, E. F. Burian was taken first to the ghetto town of Terezín (Theresienstadt), and later moved around different concentration camps. Internment did not bring his theatrical activity to an end, nor that of other Czechs held in camps and prisons. Behind bars and in surroundings that more easily bred selfishness and desperation, the difference between amateur and professional disappeared in a longing for national solidarity and culture. It was simplest for internees to put together performances on cabaret lines, or cultural evenings—mixtures of songs, recitations, and brief sketches. However, sometimes performances of classic works were mounted, plays by Klicpera, Stroupežnický, Kvapil, and Jirásek; occasionally original plays were staged. There were some theatre groups made up of different nationalities; more often the groups were based on nationality. The closed town of Terezín offered the most favourable conditions.* It was more difficult to work in Buchenwald, Sachsenhausen, and Ravensbrück, and almost impossible in the death camps of Mauthausen and Bergen-Belsen; although even in the death cells, stages were improvised and recitations performed.

Theatre in Terezín began in attics and cellars, with songs and verses. The first cabaret performances took place at Christmas 1941. After Terezín became a closed camp in 1942 activity increased, on rough stages in courtyards and temporary buildings, with groups led by such people as the twenty-four-year-old Gustav Schorsch, who in 1943 presented Peter Kien's *Marionettes* and Gogol's *The Wedding*; and Karel Švenk (Schwenk), who initiated and directed many satirical cabaret shows. Theatre performances in Terezín included cabaret, voiceband, puppetry, folk plays, classic dramas, children's theatre, and even opera. The architect and theatre designer František Zelenka, whose career had risen meteorically in the 1920s, was deported to Terezín in July 1943. He spent the last fifteen months of his life improvising sets and costumes for cabaret and drama productions. In October 1944, after the propaganda film *Der Führer schenkt den Juden eine Stadt* had reassured international opinion and given the Nazis a free hand with Terezín, Zelenka was one of thousands shipped out for extermination.

Meanwhile, among the horrors of Buchenwald, the cabaret group Bohéma performed satire and parody. Josef Čapek worked with a German-speaking group in Sachsenhausen before his death in Bergen-Belsen, while Czech students performed verse satires there on an international stage. In Dachau, E. F. Burian sang jazz with a satirical cabaret group. Nina Jirsíková crossed paths in Dresden with Karel Hašler, on his way to an icy death in Mauthausen. Later she remembered a Christmas performance she gave in a packed dormitory at Ravensbrück:

---

* German and Czech Jews were rounded up in wooden cabins in Prague 7 on the site now occupied by the Park Hotel. Trains from Bubny station transported them through Rudolf II's game reserve, down the Vltava and the Elbe Rivers to the ghetto town of Terezín, or directly to the concentration camps.

For the first time I stood face to face with a public which tore at my heart. That beloved, dirty, piteous public in their striped uniforms, whose eyes, full of understanding, shone on me in place of spotlights. It was a sad pantomime I improvised that day.[101]

IV LIBERATION, VICTORIOUS FEBRUARY, AND WHAT BECAME OF THE AVANT-GARDE

BRIEF WINDOW: 1945–1948

"Say what you will," wrote Milan Kundera of the period after 1945, "the Communists were more intelligent. They had a grandiose programme, a plan for a brand-new world in which everyone would find his place."[102] When in 1945, in a deal between Stalin and the Western powers, the Red Army liberated Czechoslovakia by advancing from the east,* the Communist politicians, led by Klement Gottwald, came back from Moscow with high aspirations and the knowledge that they had an obedient and lethal network on the ground. President Beneš and the government-in-exile, on the other hand, returned from London bruised and exhausted by their struggle to get Czechoslovakia's rights recognised by the allied powers. Beneš entered his country from the East, via Moscow, in the wake of the Red Army, and for several months the government sat in Košice in eastern Slovakia. Fearful still of the German presence in the Lands of the Bohemian Crown (and under pressure from Moscow), Beneš obtained Western approval for laws ordering the expulsion of the historic German-speaking population.†

Czechoslovakia had not suffered bombing raids like those in Germany, nor was her capital city razed to the ground as in Poland. Nevertheless, the war had been brutal. Armed (and unarmed) resistance had been crushed early on. Blood-red posters listing the names of those executed were regularly

* American troops could have liberated Prague from the west, but were under orders to stop at Pilsen.

† Over a hundred acts passed by the government-in-exile and in Košice became known as the "Beneš Decrees," although the term is often applied only to the acts on the German expulsions. The decrees were approved by parliament when it regathered on the significant anniversary of 28 October 1945.

pasted up around Prague. In retreat, the German soldiers took their revenge on Czech civilians, including children. In retaliation, stray Germans and collaborators were caught and lynched by the Czechs. The Soviet liberators, meanwhile, had their own lists and abducted members of Russian families who had settled in Prague in the 1920s and 1930s, as well as selected Czechs and thousands of Slovaks.* Most notorious of all were the "wild expulsions" of German-speaking inhabitants between May and August 1945, carried out by the local authorities, police, and zealous volunteers with the complicity of the higher authorities. After the Potsdam Conference the expulsions were carried out under the aegis of the Allies, but still in conditions of immense deprivation, violation, and suffering.[103] The brutality of war was carried over into peacetime.

Beneš was anxious to conciliate the meft, and through them the USSR. Right-wing parties were banned—not simply the far right, but centre right parties such as the Agrarians, an important force in the First Republic. The Beneš Decrees included a Nationalisation Act that came into effect in October 1945, confiscating without compensation all businesses with over five hundred employees. The theatres had been nationalised even earlier; whereas, after World War I, the cultured, intelligent, and wise Jaroslav Kvapil had been appointed head of the Ministry of Education and Culture, in April 1945 President Beneš appointed the no less cultured and intelligent, but unfortunately not very wise, Zdeněk Nejedlý (who had spent the war in the Soviet Union). One of his first actions (June 1945) was to cancel all the licences and permits granted to private entrepreneurs and impresarios and take the theatre as a whole under his own control.† The Communists were riding high, and in the 1946 elections won 38 per cent of the vote. It entitled them to some of the key ministries—fatefully, the Ministry of Information and the Ministry of the Interior.

The theatres were already in a critical condition; ordered to reopen two days after the liberation in May, they had to rethink their purpose and their repertoire, until now determined by wartime conditions. Morover, Nejedlý's abrupt withdrawal of concessions from private theatres left many actors and technical staff unemployed. One rich current of theatre life was gone forever: the German-language theatre. Dominant until the late nineteenth century, it had been pushed into second place by demographic and cultural changes. Back in November 1920, a band of Czech nationalists had forcibly taken over

* The Soviets had lost millions of young men and needed to replenish their labour force. Technically, Slovakia had been an enemy country, so they could justify exporting entire villages of able-bodied males to fill the gap. Many of them never returned from the Gulag.

† Jindřich Černý points out that although Nejedly's action had no legal basis, it was not challenged in the courts.

the Theatre of the Estates and thrown the legitimate German company into the street. (President Masaryk was so angered by this act of aggression, he refused to set foot in the Theatre of the Estates ever again.) Now, in September 1945 the *Neues Deutsches Theater* was renamed the Grand Opera of 5th May (*Velká opera 5. května*) with a production of Bedřich Smetana's *Brandenburgers in Bohemia*. Countrywide, the last traces of the old German traditions disappeared and their theatres were occupied by so-called progressive—and often ruthless—Czech youth.*

Theatre people, even more than those in other spheres of life, faced accusations of having collaborated with the Nazis. One was Zdeněk Štěpánek, grandson (or great-nephew; the sources are not clear) of the robust nineteenth-century theatre entrepreneur, Jan Nepomuk Štěpánek. Zdeněk Štěpánek, a greatly respected leading actor and former legionnaire, was accused of having too close a relationship with top Nazis; banned from the Czechoslovak stage, he was not allowed to return for several years. The "King of Comics," Vlasta Burian, who had been running his own theatre since 1930, was not so quickly exonerated. Some of his sketches and songs were allegedly anti-Semitic, but there were other motives—such as envy—behind the charge of collaboration.† He was cleared in a trial held in 1945 and in another in 1946, but at a third trial the secret police blackmailed Goebbels's mistress, the film star Lída Baarová, into testifying against Burian. He spent three months in prison, lost his theatre and property, and above all his reputation. His name was cleared in 1994 (after research by the theatre historian Vladimír Just), long after his death. Lída Baarová, then in her late seventies, retracted her earlier testimony.‡

The promotion of Czech identity and national values was no longer in the hands of the small stages that had been so courageous during the occupation, and many of them disappeared—including the Windmill (for a while Josef Šmída found refuge with Jiří Frejka in the Vinohrady Theatre). On the other hand, new small stages proliferated as young people who had been children at the start of the war found a release for their energy. These initiatives are largely unrecorded, as many of their participants emigrated after 1948 and the traces of their activity did not survive Communism.

* They could be as ruthless towards their fellow countrymen. In 1945, Honzl's former assistant Antonín Dvořák expelled Anna Sedláčková's company from the Mozarteum (see "Under the Protectorate," p. 89) to make way for his own (abortive) venture, the Theatre of the Revolutionary Guards (*Divadlo Revolučních gard*).

† Under the Protectorate, this son of a Liberec tailor wore a fur coat and was chauffeured in a white limousine.

‡ For a sympathetic treatment of Burian's fall, see the Czech Television serial *Bohéma* (2017), scripted by Teresa Brdečková.

Miroslav Kouřil, E. F. Burian's designer, had been feverishly diligent during the war, and at the turn of 1944 and 1945 had founded the underground Revolutionary Trade Union Theatre Council. With the end of the occupation, convinced of the need for radical reorganisation of the theatre on the Soviet model, he used his wartime network of contacts to influence the fluctuating situation, earning the nickname "Richelieu." He was not overjoyed when Burian arrived in Prague on 6 June 1945. Burian, who had swum ashore when the RAF sank the prison ship *Cap Arcona* with the loss of over four thousand lives, found his return to Prague an anticlimax. He had expected a hero's welcome and *carte blanche* under the new dispensation, but Kouřil had made other plans in his absence. One of Kouřil's initiatives had been to put together a group *Obratník*, "Turning point,"* indicating the turning point between war and peace.[104] Based on principles of Soviet theatre management, the group had started work covertly in the last months of the war. Kouřil was (he claimed) expecting Burian to be grateful for a company that was ready and waiting for him. Burian, however, was not interested in a group of inexperienced semi-amateurs (and was dismayed to see how the real spoils had been divided during his absence). He returned to Déčko on Na Poříčí, now shabby and ill equipped. One of his first productions was *Romeo and Juliet* (September 1945), subtitled *The Dream of One Prisoner*, and incorporating songs he had learnt in the concentration camps. It did not appeal to the public, which preferred to escape from wartime memories. Déčko was in any case too small for Burian's ambitions; for four months he took on the operetta theatre in Karlín, on top of three companies in Brno with plans for two in Olomouc and another in Zlín, as well as the management of the Zlín film studios. To this, he added editorship of the weekly, *Kulturní politika* (*Cultural Policy*), and a regular radio programme.

There was disappointment on all sides at Déčko. Audiences fell away, and Burian blamed the dissatisfaction in the company on the machinations of critics who (he claimed) would rather he had never returned from prison. The company that had remained loyal to the leader incarcerated by the Gestapo lost confidence in him, and the majority left in 1946. Burian engaged new actors, including the young Otomar Krejča from the steel-making town of Kladno: "Not only was [that Kladno actor] allowed to be there daily, sit there, watch, listen—he would be appearing on that very same stage on which *War* had been performed!"[105] Nevertheless, Krejča too left after one season. Jan Grossman, who worked with Burian several seasons later, recalled how he was full both of energy and misunderstandings:

---

* The term is usally applied to the Tropics of Cancer/Capricorn, but does not have a precise English equivalent.

Somebody who loved improvisation and changed from day to day, who loved people, hated people, had wonderful ideas, had no strength to realise them, had his team proclaimed the sort of theatre that is a collective... but actually... it was a dictatorship.[106]

Obratník, spurned by Burian, was entrusted by Kouřil to Burian's former student, the ambitious Zdeněk Míka.* In the summer of 1946 the group toured Bohemia, using the back of a lorry as a stage and performing a political piece by Burian's dramaturge Jaroslav Pokorný, *Behold the City!* At the end of the summer they settled in Prague as the Young Pioneers' Theatre (*Divadlo mladých pionyrů*); later, on Party instructions, they moved to Zlín† as the basis of a permanent ensemble. Here, as the Theatre of the Workers (*Divadlo pracujících*), they became part of the Communists' re-education process. Míka seized his opportunity, invited his comrades to Zlín, and implemented a Stalinist repertoire. In 1947 he directed *The Shoe Factory*, an "exposure" of the pre-war "brutality" of the capitalist Baťa family based on a novel by the overlooked (and vengeful) advertising artist Svatopluk Turek.‡

Another company that had been operating clandestinely before the war ended was the semi-amateur group Youth Drama Studio (*Dramatické studio mladých*) from Pelhřimov in southern Bohemia, led by the brothers Oldřich and Lubomír Lipský. Their satirical production *The Broken Trilogy* had been widely performed clandestinely; in June 1945, it opened at the Smetana Museum and was an immediate success. Oldřich Lipský wrote of how the production had been built out of the poverty and disillusion of six years of war: "*The Broken Trilogy*, a conglomeration of rags, waste paper, little ditties, old scabs, and whatever lacks sophistication."[107] The group found a permanent home in the Artists' Union and called themselves the Theatre of Satire (*Divadlo satiry*). They were joined by the poet Josef Kainar and the musician Harry Macourek who had been touring their own illegal wartime cabaret in the Ostrava region. Macourek was still a student at the Conservatoire, where his sister was part of a four-woman modern dance group; they too joined the Theatre of Satire. Their second production, *The Armoured Circus*, was compiled by the company out of sketches, songs, gags, and dance. Within a circus framework, jugglers and acrobats, clowns and bareback riders satirised the brutalities of war and its aftermath—the Nazi leaders' escape to Argentina, the dropping

* Míka did not noticeably feature in earlier versions of this book; when I revised the text he began to emerge as a shining example of Communist opportunism. I had forgotten I already interviewed him in April 1984; unearthing my notes on the interview, I found I had at that time recorded (on good authority) that he was indeed a "scoundrel."

† Zlín was the home of the Baťa family's model shoe manufacture enterprise; in an effort to eliminate Baťa from memory, the town was renamed Gottwaldov from 1949–1990.

‡ Turek published the novel under the pseudonym T. Svatopluk. In 1954 it was made into a film, but this was not as popular as the play. See Mariusz Szczygiel's *Gottland* (2006).

of the atom bomb on Hiroshima. More cabaret-style productions followed; sometimes with loosely connected items, sometimes with a more consistent theme. Those who worked there included the director Alfréd Radok; designer Josef Svoboda; and pre-war choreographers Nina Jirsíková and Laurette Hrdinová. The small theatre was always full, and Harry Macourek later recalled that there had been something of a Dada atmosphere; it was a centre for young artists who held exhibitions in the corridor and gathered at the tiny bar. Looking back from the dark Stalinism of 1953, the Slovak specialist in small-form theatre Ján Kalina wrote defiantly:

> The progressive, daring, innovative Theatre of Satire, in spite of all its mistakes and formalist tendencies, was a platform for aggressive satire against reactionaries at home and abroad. In its zest for youth, in its élan, this stage continued in the good traditions of the Liberated Theatre.[108]

Jiří Voskovec and Jan Werich came to performances, as did Jiří Červený and Eduard Bass, and Oldřich Lipský claimed they would gladly have joined the company if they had been invited. Bertolt Brecht, returning to his first place of exile, attended the première of *Circus of Hope*. He invited Lipský and the young actor Miroslav Horníček to Berlin; Lipský sent a postcard home, an aerial view of the Brandenburg Gate standing among the ruins of Berlin. "In the middle of all this—us," he wrote.*

Miroslav Horníček joined the Theatre of Satire in 1947 with his colleagues from the Windmill, Miloš Kopecký and Vlastimil Brodský. He felt, however, that the early élan had disappeared. Harry Macourek later remembered that their original sharp satire had been blunted in the changing political climate. In 1947, the company staged its first satirical drama: *The King Doesn't Like Beef* by Vratislav Blažek; it ran for 275 performances. Blažek's second play *Where Is Kuťák?* was banned after its preview in October 1948.† The authorities had decided that the allegory, in which self-appointed bureaucrats bungle the launch of Noah's Ark, was too pessimistic for the new society (in reality, too near the truth). In 1949, the theatre was closed down and Blažek wrote nothing more for the stage for ten years.

Voskovec and Werich, back from the USA, revived some of their old productions, but to Jindřich Honzl's disappointment, the Liberated Theatre did not reopen:

---

* Interview with Oldřich Lipský, 29 May 1984. The postcard was signed jointly by Lipský and Brecht.

† The same year the Theatre of Satire rehearsed the first postwar mime production, *Cirkus*, choreographed by Nina Jirsíková with Miroslav Horníček as Pierrot; it too was banned for ideological reasons.

> You say, dear Voskovec, that "the Liberated Theatre played out its role with Munich" and that "one shouldn't revive a spectre." Indeed, who would wish to resurrect the spectres of destruction and death? But isn't the assertion that "the Liberated Theatre played out its role" wishful thinking rather than fact? Isn't the intense desire that the Liberated Theatre should not return rather a desire that Munich should not return?[109]

Voskovec sensed what lay ahead under the Communists, but failed to convince Werich (and certainly not Honzl, who had rejoined the Party in 1945). In 1948, Voskovec left for France, and in 1950 to America (where he was held for a year on Ellis Island, on suspicion of being a Communist sympathiser). He built a successful career in film, playing foreigners conversing in imperfect English. The witty juggler with the Czech language was silenced. Werich, meanwhile, regarded as *persona non grata* by the regime, was sent to work as a dramaturge in the Barrandov Film Studio. In 1949, he played Goering in the Soviet film *The Fall of Berlin*, shot at Barrandov; and (more congenially) Rudolf II and his baker in *The Emperor's Baker—The Baker's Emperor* (1951), directed by Martin Frič and released in an international version as *The Emperor and the Golem*. After 1955, he was allowed to revive his former roles on the stage of the ABC (formerly the *Theatre U Nováků*, the old home of the Liberated Theatre) with Miroslav Horníček as his partner. Through this, and occasional film and TV appearances, he remained close to the Czech public. Meetings between Voskovec and Werich were rare, but in the mid-1950s a correspondence began, which, when published in 2007/2008, helped to ease the loss still felt by the public.

Jindřich Honzl continued to work with the Little Theatre for 99, which re-formed in May 1945 as the Company of Youth (*Soubor mladých*). When in July Honzl was appointed to the triumvirate leading the drama company of the National Theatre (under the directorship of the politically powerful and well-connected actor Václav Vydra) he was allowed to incorporate the group into the strucure of the National Theatre. Minister Nejedlý provided them with a former operetta theatre in the Old Town. In October 1945, Honzl outlined in a brochure the programme of the Studio of the National Theatre (as it was renamed), describing it as a symbol of the constant renewal of theatre. There were around twenty young people in his studio; Honzl looked for those interested in the multi-sided aspects of the theatre. Interviewed in the 1980s, the designer Jiří Nesvadba (who often deputised for Honzl during his illnesses and commitments at the National Theatre) remembered the years from 1945 to 1948 as a golden age. They lived together as a family, sharing each other's homes, taking holidays in the mountains, and playing improvisations en route (to the confusion of their fellow passengers). Nesvadba recalled that as a director Honzl did not like to dictate but debate; he would spend hours with an actor searching for the clear precision of facial expression or gesture. Sometimes rehearsals brought the actors to tears, with Honzl dissatisfied—unable or unwilling to demonstrate what he wanted, but recognising it when it came. Forty years later, Nesvadba believed the company could still perform just as Honzl had rehearsed them.

Lída Myšáková was head of dance in the Studio, and Josef Pehr, manipulator of glove puppets and shadow theatre, was in charge of puppetry. Myšáková later remembered how Honzl was far more at ease with the young Studio performers than with the National Theatre actors, and recalled the contrast between Honzl's cold and often difficult personality in rehearsal and his sudden kindnesses. In the Studio's first year, Honzl created his own scenarios from texts such as Julius Fučík's *Report from the Gallows*.* The opening production, *Teacher and Pupil* (December 1945) was staged in memory of its author, Vladislav Vančura, who was also executed by the Nazis. The revival of the poetic, Surrealist piece was performed with stylised movement against projections of photographic montages by Toyen. Later that season, Honzl would stage another of Vančura's adaptations, *The Prague Jew* (from J. J. Kolar's work of 1871), which accentuated the Jew's courageous and patriotic characteristics.

Other members of the National Theatre thought that the Studio was a drain on resources, and in 1946 Jaroslav Stránský, then minister of education and culture,† ordered it to vacate the theatre in the Old Town. It then performed twice a week in the Theatre of the Estates, but made itself unpopular with demands for rehearsal space. After a fight for funding, Honzl gained the Mozarteum, where he directed Jan Bartoš's schizophrenic *Missing* (1947). Jindřich Černý later described it as being linked with his Surrealist experiments of the 1930s: "If any other director but Honzl had staged such decadent nonsense, the Communist critics would have launched an offensive."[110] Another production was Antonín Dvořák's dramatisation of the novel by the Socialist Realist author Jan Drda, *Little Town in Your Hand* (1947), an evocation of a small Czech town. In the programme, Jan Mukařovský compared the Studio of the National Theatre with that of the Moscow Arts Theatre—a place where young actors learned from the more experienced while feeding the results of their experimental work into the mainstream. The established company did not see things that way, and resented the studio as Honzl's personal fiefdom. He was marginalised in the leadership and in the 1947–1948 season directed only one play, *The Government Inspector*, with the main company. A chronic stomach complaint (aggravated by a wartime diet of dry bread) often drove

---

* Fučík, hanged in a Berlin prison two years earlier, had become a Communist martyr, and *Report from the Gallows* a sacred text.

† Stránský both followed and preceded Zdeněk Nejedlý as education and culture minister (July 1946–Feb 1948).

him to his bed, so that he directed through Dvořák or, in the case of the Studio, Nesvadba. At the end of the 1947–1948 season, Honzl disbanded the Studio.

SOCIALIST REALISM

"At last we were going to run our own affairs," wrote Ladislav Mňačko of the Communist *coup d'état* in Fenruary 1948. "At last the people were masters, nobody would be able to deceive us, sell us to our enemies, betray us."[111]

Gottwald had succeeded in deceiving the master of the diplomatic arts, President Beneš, and the squabbling democratic parties. After the 1946 elections, the Communists had taken control of the ministries allocated to them (Finance, Information, Interior, and Internal Trade) while at the same time infiltrating those ministries they did not yet control and the inner committees of the democratic parties. A paramilitary force (*Lidová milice*, People's Militia) was secretly recruited in factories countrywide. In February 1948, Beneš accepted the ill-judged resignations of twenty-four non-Communist ministers; the government fell, and Gottwald took over.

Czechoslovak society, coarsened by war and resigned to force, for the most part looked for ways of coming to terms with the status quo. By the end of 1948, membership of the Communist Party had risen to two and a half million, one in three of the adult population. The past was renounced and in Milan Kundera's "brand-new world": "Every man is a note in a magnificent Bach fugue, and anyone who refuses his note is a mere black dot, useless and meaningless."[112] Up to 250,000 citizens left the country "illegally"– the dispossessed, and those who could not live in a country where they could not breathe freely.

Among the priorities of the new regime was the passing of a Theatre Act that came into effect on 1 April 1948. With licences to run private theatres already cancelled, the new law decreed that theatres could only be "set up and run by the State, the provinces, the districts, or the communes."[113] Control of the theatres returned to Zdeněk Nejedlý, reinstated as minister of education and culture. Nejedlý had an obsessional belief in the cultural significance of art, and had been condemned as early as 1919 as a "false moralist."[114] During the First Republic he had propagated Smetana as the Czech composer *par excellence*, condemning Dvořák and Janáček as "cosmopolitans." Eva Soukupová, founder of the Theatre Institute, later described him as "a frog in the spring of our postwar culture."[115] As minister,* he was responsible for the

* Jiří Menzel included a fictional portrait of Zdeněk Nejedlý (played by Vladimír Šmeral) in his film *Larks on a String* (made in 1969, released in 1990).

dismissal of hundreds of university teachers, and for destroying the lives of musicologists with whom he differed. Some spent long years in prison for their musical transgressions. (One music critic was sentenced to thirty-nine years imprisonment.)

Nejedlý's Theatre Act increased the authority of Miroslav Kouřil's Central Theatre Commission (*Ústřední divadelní komise, ÚDK*) by incorporating it into the ministry. It was renamed the Theatre and Dramaturgy Council (*Divadelní a dramaturgická rada, DDR*).* The whole theatre network was centrally managed from this hub, chaired by Miroslav Kouřil and with Antonín Dvořák as one of the councillors. Local authorities that operated theatres were subjected to a second authority enshrined in the Theatre Act, the Theatre Promotion Commission (*Divadelně propagační komise, DPK*), which came under the Ministry of Information led by one of Gottwald's "Karlín boys," Václav Kopecký. Kopecký, who hid a treacherous nature under a mask of joviality, appointed as chairman his (unrelated) namesake, the dramaturge Jan Kopecký. Action Committees were set up overnight in every theatre (and other organisation) with the power to decide policy, manage finances, and hire and fire. The first of many purges began, and four hundred workers from theatre and film—directors, actors, dramaturges—instantly lost their jobs. In January 1949, the practice for heads of theatres to be screened politically by the Action Committees of their own theatres was introduced.

The intensification of the Cold War had increased fear of the enemy both within and without. The world of the arts and education could not be separated from the world of politics. Security lay in thinking along the same lines as those to whom one entrusted one's political future. It was now said that an avant-garde was no longer needed. "Progressive" ideas could be presented on the major stages and were no longer the property of the small theatres. Nor was satire required in the new society; it was part of the old world that had disappeared in 1945. All the "borderline" stages with permeable or flexible content—fringe, "small forms" of different types, variety, cabaret—were rounded up to be placed first under public administration, later eliminated. Some of their members joined the official theatres, while others emigrated.

In this context, the arts had to be seen as integrally involved in social development, in future planning as well as in retrospect:

> Dramatists understood that they had to support from the foundations the building of Socialism in the Czechoslovak Republic, and that drama must become a powerful weap-

* The following year, Miroslav Kouřil enhanced his power by becoming editor-in-chief of the newly founded theatre journal *Divadlo* (*Theatre*). This replaced three existing theatre magazines that were being liquidated; one of them was Jindřich Honzl's *Otázky divadla a filmu* (*Questions of Theatre and Film*). Twenty-one years later, *Divadlo* would meet the same fate as the journals it had supplanted.

on in this struggle, since drama can actively contribute to the rapid development of the social situation.[116]

The "negative features" of "Democratic Realism" (Naturalism), those that say "this is how the world is" were condemned as pessimistic and depressing. Popular dramatists of the "nihilist period" between the wars were attacked, in that "this drama fails to present a strongly emotive recognition of the contemporary world, but aims rather at sensuous and sentimental feelings, the cult of the moment and often even the cult of scandal."[117] Confidence was essential, both in a splendid future and in the workers of the present who were to bring it about. Socialism was an achievable utopia to be brought about through the planned enlightenment of human nature. The optimism of Socialist Realism lay in presenting models of future perfection for inspiration and emulation, while avoiding the risk of submitting them to the kind of questioning which could cause them to fall apart.

As in the Soviet Union, some writers responded by setting their plays in factories, quarries, and railways, in an effort to depict the contemporary conflicts of the workers, and indicate solutions. Writers were encouraged to dramatise the problems of the countryside during Collectivisation. Some playwrights (Vojtěch Cach, Milan Jariš, Miloslav Stehlík) wrote plays that held up dramatically; others were eventually criticised for their "hollow didacticism." One of the leading exponents of Socialist Realism was the energetic young Communist Pavel Kohout. His first play *The Good Song* (1952) had an immediate success at the Czechoslovak Army Theatre (formerly Vinohrady) with the close friends Jiřina Švorcová and Vlasta Chramostová in the leading female roles.* The same year, Kohout co-scripted the colour film *Tomorrow There Will Be Dancing Everywhere.*† The insistence that love for the "people's" music was inseparable from love of the Communist Party was typical of the propaganda that eventually drove young people to reject their folk customs and traditions. Favourite fairy-tale allegories and legends also became a part of Communist propaganda (for example, Jan Drda's *Romance of Oldřich and Božena*, 1953). In historical drama, playwrights searched for patterns of social change, and the nationalist tradition was approved as being ideologically correct: "The indelible part of the fight for Socialist Realism is organically linked with the Tyl-Jirásek tradition."[118] The nineteenth-century classics were regularly performed, but followed a pattern Jan Grossman described a decade later as leading to their simplification and generalisation.

---

* A quarter of a century later, the two actresses stood at diametrically opposed political poles.

† This was the source of the title for Aleš Březina's 2008 opera *Tomorrow There Will Be...*, in which Soňa Červená played the role of Milada Horáková.

The role of the director diminished so much during this period that in 1957 the critic Jiří Hájek could write that: "The production was suspected of Formalism if the performance showed any signs whatsoever of the director's intentions. The director was guilty simply by being the director!"[119] It was a situation that Ivan Vyskočil parodied in the early 1960s in his story "The Incredible Rise of Albert Uruk." Albert Uruk is employed as a theatre director precisely because he has "absolutely none of these artistic notions, fancies, urges, or desires."[120] At the same time, stage designers were developing their technical skills in the reproduction of illustrative effects such as the workings of factory machinery. Socialist Realism dictated a return to the theatre of illusion, to conventional scenery. Designers found some freedom in designing for opera and ballet. As Vyskočil commented in "Albert Uruk": "The designer, after all, is the fellow who looks after the art side of the theatre, and [the performers] all wish to look artistic."

The emphasis was on the Stanislavsky-trained performer. Writing for *Divadlo*, Vladimír Šmeral, Burian's former leading actor, ridiculed followers of Meyerhold* and those described as practitioners of Formalism. He cited such "tricks" as having the hero perform with his back to the audience until the climax of the play, and condemned the intensity of "Expressionist" action. Šmeral continued:

> The Formalist stage can captivate the audience through the fantasies of colour, tones, movement, lights, and all possible stage means. However, Realist art must captivate the audience through the thought and life of man.[121]

Relevance to "the thought and life of contemporary man" was considered the most important aspect of Socialist Realism. Form, although in practice indivisible from content, does not have a political commitment and therefore to be concerned with form is to be apolitical. However, as every work of art has to have some kind of form, the only way not to be concerned is to adopt the most conventional, and therefore invisible, form. It is the opposite principle to the Structuralists' defamiliarisation. Pre-war Structuralist research was now rejected, its practitioners (such as Jan Mukařovský) adapting their thinking to Marxist literary criticism; others (Jiří Veltruský, Karel Brušák) preferred to live permanently abroad.

Modern dance was condemned as Formalist, while the highly artificial classical ballet was sufficiently traditional to be accepted as Socialist Real-

* E. F. Burian, on his return from the concentration camps, asked in vain after Meyerhold. He had been tortured and executed by firing squad on Stalin's orders in 1940, although no information emerged until the 1950s.

ism. In 1951, the head of the National Theatre ballet company, Saša Machov, faced charges of sabotage. As a homosexual, he was already, as Jindřich Černý put it, "predetermined for liquidation."[122] Machov, a veteran of Déčko and the Liberated Theatre, had escaped from Nazi-occupied Bohemia to become the leading choreographer for the Royal Theatre in Athens. When Greece was invaded in April 1941, Machov joined the British Army and fought in the North Africa campaign, including the Siege of Tobruk. He was stationed in Palestine, where his duties included secondment to the Jerusalem Opera, and the choreography of scenes from *The Bartered Bride* (sung in Hebrew). When the Czechoslovak battalion was transferred to Britain, Machov was greeted with delight by the Czech theatre director Ota Ornest, who had reached London in 1939. Ornest had been asked by the British theatre director Eric Crozier to find a Czech choreographer for *The Bartered Bride*, his first production for Sadler's Wells Opera. Released from the army for the task, Machov was a gift from heaven:

> The new production by Mr. Eric Crozier, with decor by Mr. Reece Pemberton, has the advantage of Czech supervision. The dances have been arranged by Mr. Sasha [sic] Machov, who himself leads them with that grace at once virile and leisurely which makes Slavonic dancing so attractive to watch. The performance has, therefore, an unusual authenticity...[123]

The production and its success must have heartened President Beneš, who attended the première, and the exiled Czechs. Machov went on to direct *Cosi fan tutte* (1944) and *Madame Butterfly* (1945) at Sadler's Wells. Despite these successes, however, despite the theatre and film contracts on offer (and against the advice of his compatriots), Machov returned to Czechoslovakia. Full of ideas, he planned to stage Benjamin Britten's new opera *Peter Grimes*.* But in a cultural environment dominated by Nejedlý and the Communists, neither Machov's service in the British Army nor his experience with Sadler's Wells Opera counted to his credit. As international relations polarised, it became clear that it would be inappropriate to stage a contemporary British opera at the Prague National Theatre.† After 1948, Machov was increasingly terrorised, with regard both to the artistic integrity of his work and to his private life; his lover, the Slovak poet Theo Herkeľ Florin, was caught up in the show trial of Foreign Minister Clementis, who in 1952 would be executed alongside

---

* Crozier had introduced Machov to Britten, and he had been involved in the preparations for the world première of *Peter Grimes*. He should have created the role of Dr. Crabbe in London, but film commitments prevented it.

† The Czechoslovak première of *Peter Grimes* did take place in Brno in 1947, but it was 1979 before a production was staged by the Prague National Theatre.

General Secretary Slánský. The secret police attempted to blackmail Machov into collaboration. In 1951, he was responsible for a Prague Spring matinée at the National Theatre at which the audience showed greater enthusiasm for the Czech dancer Miroslav Kůra than for the Soviet State Prize winner Askold Makarov. Zdeněk Nejedlý, watching from the ministry box, condemned the applause as political provocation. Kůra was exiled to Košice in the east of Slovakia. Saša Machov took poison and died. For years, it was forbidden to write or even speak of his suicide.*

The death occurred the same year of Karel Teige, described as "one of the few whose stature in Surrealism is comparable to that of Breton."[124] It was André Breton who circulated the information that Teige took poison after a police interrogation. Teige's friend, the poet Jaroslav Seifert,† claimed that this was mere invention; that after being viciously attacked in the press as a "Trotskyite degenerate," Teige had been working day and night to finish writing his books. One October day he was missing; his mistress found him collapsed in a Smíchov tram shelter. He died the same day of a heart attack.[125,‡]

The "brand-new world" promised in 1948 was not materialising, and fear drove the regime to find scapegoats for the delay. The time had come for show trials and executions—first, the democratic politician Milada Horáková and her "collaborators," then even the general secretary of the Communist Party, Rudolf Slánský. Gottwald's men learnt from their Soviet "teachers" how to torture and brainwash defendants into confessing their guilt. The trials were broadcast live on the radio and piped into classrooms. The judiciary consisted of volunteers fast-tracked at Workers' Law School to administer "Socialist justice." The state procurator at Horáková's trial was the aspiring actress Ludmila Brožová; having failed to get into drama school, Brožová had spent a year at the Workers' Law School. In 2009 she was sentenced to six years' imprisonment for her share in the judicial murder of Milada Horáková.

At every level, people were urged to watch out for the enemy. Thousands of Czechs and Slovaks disappeared—lawyers, priests, shopkeepers, businessmen—executed, imprisoned, or thrown out of their work and home. Without warning, someone could be intercepted on the way home or taken from their

* The following year, the head of the ballet company of Brno National Theatre, Ivo Váňa Psota (artistic director of the Metropolitan Opera ballet in New York during the war) suffered a stroke and died, after similar criticism.

† When Teige died, Seifert was still in favour with the regime. This definitively ended when he signed Charter 77.

‡ Barely a handful of people attended Teige's funeral; of his own generation, only Seifert and the artist František Muzika. When Vítězslav Nezval died in 1958 he was given a state funeral, and hundreds followed his coffin to Slavín on Vyšehrad. Seifert—winner of the Nobel Prize for Literature—was also entitled to a state funeral when he died in 1986, but it was held under the auspices of the secret police.

bed in the early hours. A net of informers began to establish itself—you could be arrested for having the wrong friends, reading the wrong books, telling the wrong jokes—or for nothing at all. Having the right opinion on artistic matters could be a matter of life or death. The lighthearted games and experiments of the pre-war left-wing avant-garde had led its practitioners into a labyrinth of terror and fear.

THE DARING THREESOME AND THE THIEF OF HAPPINESS

From the 1930s through to the Nazis' closure of the National Theatre in 1944, Jiří Frejka had been responsible for a series of productions intended to foster the Czechs' sense of identity and patriotism. In Miroslav Kouřil's postwar reorganisation, however, it was inappropriate for a non-Communist to hold a major post at the National Theatre; nevertheless, Frejka was appointed to the important directorship of the Vinohrady Theatre. Even before 1948, he began to develop an influential political circle, entertaining important Communist functionaries—including General Secretary Rudolf Slánský—at Vinohrady premières. In February 1948, he belatedly joined the Party and submitted to screenings and self-criticism, for a while enjoying Kouřil's protection.* The company at Vinohrady was bitterly divided between Frejka's supporters and his enemies. As far as his artistic programme was concerned, Frejka tried to keep it untainted by political allegiances, and the quality of his productions and variety of his repertoire attracted audiences of a size bitterly envied by more politically minded theatre directors. One of his successes was George Bernard Shaw's *St Joan* (1948) in which he cast his former colleague from the National Theatre, Jiřina Štěpničková, in the leading role. Shaw's frequent invocations to the "west wind" and the final line of the play: "O God that madest this beautiful earth, when will it be ready to receive Thy saints? How long, O Lord, how long?" evoked an emotional response in the audience. It was to be one cause of Frejka's downfall, but still he resisted intimidation by the actors' union, and in 1949 he cast as Hamlet, not the powerful Vladimír Šmeral, but the young actor from the provinces, Otomar Krejča. Accusations mounted: discrimination against union members, poor financial management, overpayments to some favoured employees, inability to run the theatre in harmony with Party tasks, lacking the qualities of a Socialist director...[126]

* Within a few years Kouřil had lost his power and influence. In 1972, however, after being marginalised for two decades (as head first of the National Theatre Scenographic Laboratory [*Scénografické laboratoře ND*], then of the Scenographic Institute [*Scénografický ústav*]), he was made a professor at Charles University, replacing reform-minded colleagues purged under Normalisation (in particular the former dramaturge Jan Kopecký, who spent the next decade as a manual worker for the Water Board).

The decisive blow came in June 1950 when the Ministry of Defence took over the Vinohrady Theatre, renamed it the Czechoslovak Army Theatre (*Divadlo Československé armády*) and dismissed Frejka without even the favour of a farewell performance.

In February 1951, Frejka was offered a position at the Karlín Operetta Theatre. It was intended as a humiliation, but he created a team which included Alfréd Radok; the dramaturge Karel Kraus (whom he had met during the occupation at the Arts Club when Kraus was a young new playgoer); designer Jiří Trnka; comedian Vlasta Burian; and singer Soňa Červená (daughter of Jiří Červený of the Seven of Hearts). He devised a form of music theatre he believed would be closer to the "people" than the ubiquitous operetta. It seemed, however, that the people could not do without their operetta; moreover, Frejka's personal life was in shreds, and his closeness to the Slánský circle had put him under the surveillance of the secret police. On 16 October 1952, after Radok's dress rehearsal of Johann Nestroy's *Lumpazivagabundus*, Frejka shot himself with his hunting rifle. He died eleven days later.* Twelve years later, Karel Kraus wrote in *Divadelní noviny*:

> For a number of years the work of Jiří Frejka has not been discussed in detail or aloud. Therefore, the recent passing of the sixtieth anniversary of Frejka's birth also afflicted us with the knowledge of how little we know of him.[127]

Less than six weeks later, Frejka's St. Joan, Jiřina Štěpničková, was put on trial. The previous year she had embarked on what she thought was a chance to escape over the Czechoslovak border with her small son. The border was not yet fortified, and during this period hundreds fled the country by following a guide over rough terrain on foot at night. This time, however, the secret police had framed the actress. After a nerve-wracking rail journey, she and three-year-old Jiří followed the "guide" through the woods. Offering to carry the child if Štěpničková took his briefcase, the guide quickly disappeared with him, leaving Štěpničková with the briefcase (according to Vlasta Chramostová's memoirs, full of compromising materials) to be arrested within yards of the brook that marked the frontier. For weeks she was "missing," and some feared she was dead. Some colleagues at the Czechoslovak Army Theatre petitioned for the death penalty, on the grounds of attempted sabotage (citing the postponement of *Jan Hus* because of her illness, and her "anti-state" portrayal of St. Joan). The document has disappeared from the

---

* Frejka wrote a farewell letter to the Central Committee of the Communist Party, attacking Miroslav Kouřil and Vladimír Šmeral for "draining" Czechoslovak theatre, and suggesting they should be replaced by E. F. Burian.

archive, but quotations in the judge's summing-up confirm its existence. The act was to haunt those signatories still alive in the 1990s.* Štěpničková was sentenced to fifteen years hard labour, of which she served ten. Her little boy grew up to be an actor and to play the role of President Gottwald in a 1980s television serial.

Jindřich Honzl, who had lived virtually in hiding during the war, was not happy with his rewards. Moreover, he suffered from a chronic illness of the digestive tract, and his medication intensified his state of depression. He had surely not forgotten how in 1935 a promised engagement at the National Theatre had been blocked by a committee on which Jiří Frejka and Václav Vydra sat. Now he struggled to reconcile his idea of a Socialist theatre, developed over the last three decades, with the Zhdanov doctrine of "truthfulness of artistic description... combined with the ideological remodelling and education of the toiling people in the spirit of Socialism."[128] In August 1948, Honzl was reinstated as head of the drama company at the National Theatre, under the protection of Minister Nejedlý. He denounced the theatre's repertoire between 1945 and 1948, accusing it of having fallen into the decadence of the French and American bourgeoisie. He chose to direct the Russians—Gogol, Gorky, Sofronov—and the Czech classics, including his own adaptation of Tyl's *Jan Hus*. In 1949, he used his power to take the production of Gorky's *Philistines* out of the hands of another director, accusing him of attempting an "incorrect" interpretation. Rumours circulated, and anonymous letters. In another episode, Alfréd Radok collapsed when, at an official meeting shortly before the première of *The Chodsko Bride*,† Honzl accused him of financial, professional, and ideological incompetence. Specifically criticised were Radok's "empty Expressionist effects."[129] But Honzl himself was officially accused of being authoritative, unpopular, unwilling to accept criticism, and financially and technically incompetent.[130] Some of the National Theatre's leading actors, who saw themselves as the bearers of the theatre's historic mission, complained about Honzl's unremittingly painstaking method of direction. Preeminent was Václav Vydra, now in his seventies, and overall director of the National Theatre. He had seen off K. H. Hilar before the war and regarded the rest as mere arrivistes. In 1949, following a power play with Vydra, Honzl was sent on permanent sick leave. Although on the surface he was still honoured as a theatre historian, a leading expert on Soviet theatre,‡ and the

* Jiřina Švorcová offered a confused account of the incident, somehow managing to lay the blame on Vlasta Chramostová, in Graclík & Nekvapil, *Jiřina Švorcová osobně*, pp. 262–263. A more lucid account appears in Jindřich Černý, *Jiřina Štěpničková*, pp. 188–193.

† A new Socialist Realist play based on folklore (music by Dalibor C. Faltys, choreography by Lída Myšáková). After fourteen sold-out performances, Honzl abruptly removed the production from the repertoire.

‡ No one openly mentioned the fact that Honzl had not visited the USSR since 1935.

acceptable face of the interwar avant-garde, he could no longer do what he cared about most: create theatre for a living audience. In 1952, he entered a sanatorium, where he died the following year. One critic wrote about the enthusiast for the international avant-garde: "It was inevitable that Honzl's road eventually led to Realist theatre, to Stanislavsky, to the Realist tradition of our stage and dramatic art, to admiration for such actors as [Eduard] Vojan... to Socialist Realism."[131]

E. F. Burian had, in his early postwar productions, continued to work in the genre of poetic theatre—for example, his own play, *Love, Defiance and Death* (1946). At the same time he had tried to adapt to Socialist Realism, writing plays himself on contemporary problems. After 1948, attacks on his programme of poetic theatre increased. Jan Grossman remembered:

> He had these qualities which were condemned as Formalism... at that time didn't correspond with the Socialist Realism... he was quite schizophrenic, because as a very true member of the Party he tried to fulfil his duties and that was the Socialist Realism which was inwardly very alien to him, he couldn't do it, but he *did* it...[132]

Burian realised that a gap had opened between him and his contemporaries during his long absence in the prison camps. Called before the Action Committee, in the depths of self-criticism, he returned to this theme:

> I'm dissatisfied with my work. I don't mean I'm in a quandary about what to serve... but I'm in a quandary because I don't understand well enough what the new man wants, not the new man in the factories, but the new man in our auditorium.... I read Lenin, Stalin... who help me, and yet this isn't clear to me.... Many times I wanted to intervene in what you're doing, take it apart and make from it what I called art. Then I bethought myself. I reflected and said to myself that those who knock me back are maybe right. I thus managed to retreat *ad maximum* in my art. But suddenly I see that others go ahead—and I stand bereft of everything... The problem of Socialist Realism does trouble me. I was always a Realist. Then it came to me that during my absence they had begun to interpret my Realism differently. I'm not ashamed of reconsidering. I made many mistakes...[133]

One episode subsequently regarded as an ethical "mistake" was *Hotbed* (1950), generally believed to be a fictionalised treatment of Milada Horáková's life. J. A. Pitínský, who revived the play for *HaDivadlo* (HaTheatre) in 2008, argued that it was intended as an anti-Communist text. Burian's son Jan refuted this, expressing the family's view that the leading female character, a pre-war "salon Communist" who had drifted from the Party line to become a Trotskyite, was in fact a portrait of Burian's second wife, Marie Šubrtová.

After Stalin's death in 1953 and the subsequent condemnation of the "personality cult," it was suggested at Party meetings in the theatre that Burian had encouraged a personality cult around himself. For the first time, he delegated some of his directorial responsibilities:

> The attacks on the theatre were fewer when I stepped down. Some people now blame me for giving way. But I didn't go fishing as I was advised, nor did I commit suicide, I went on working behind the scenes.[134]

Some of Burian's problems were financial; after the war he resented having to beg for a monthly subsidy. From 1951 to 1954, Déčko was under the management of the army and was renamed the Art Theatre of the Army (*Armádní umělecké divadlo*), Burian having been advised that it was the only way to survive financially. Theatregoers noted the curtains slung from the balcony to screen empty rows of seats below, and Burian standing in the foyer, pompous and unapproachable in his colonel's uniform. For his part, he remembered the humiliating scorn of acquaintances who addressed him as "General" and accused him of having betrayed his art.

The former student Zuzana Kočová, now Burian's third wife, remembered the years up to 1953 as being those of his deepest crisis. In 1955 he embarked on a programme of revivals of his pre-war productions, but without some of his old collaborators, such as Miroslav Kouřil. His revival of *War*, described as "a polemic against the poverty-stricken, simplified, and puritanical displays of Socialist Realism,"[135] was followed by *The Beggar's Opera*, *White Nights*, *Věra Lukášová*, and *The Pied Piper*. In 1956, *War* should have represented Czechoslovak theatre at the *Théâtre des Nations: III Festival de Paris*, but the invitation was appropriated by the National Theatre. Two years later Burian celebrated Déčko's quarter-century with a festival of poetic theatre in Karlovy Vary, and then took seven of the productions to the USSR and Poland; on his return he was told that the new theatre building he had been promised was no longer available.

Burian was simultaneously under attack from the younger generation; in the spring of 1959, in the middle of an unsuccessful season of new work by young playwrights, he was accused by Pavel Kohout of being ignorant of most new writing, of never having seen anything by himself (Kohout), Jariš, or Peter Karvaš, and little by Stehlík.[136] Kočová nevertheless remembered the summer of 1959 as a time when Burian was full of excitement and plans for the future, before he died on 9 August. In an article published in 1969, the theatre historian František Černý recalled Burian's feelings of betrayal ten years earlier. Talking late into one May night in his apartment with its view of Prague Castle, Burian was still making plans for the future of Déčko. Černý saw again "the revolutionary poet and man of politics who once showed our youth the path to tomorrow... the fighter... who was not afraid of mistakes, for he knew that without them there would be no victory through which the Czech theatre would move ahead." As they stood in the doorway in the dawn light, Burian suddenly said: "I want to write a play. Černý, I have a great theme! It would be called *The Thief of Happiness*. You know, the thief of happiness, about a man who only gets pleasure out of destroying another's happiness. *The Thief of Happiness*. There are many such people among us, many! It would be a very useful play."[137]

AFTER STALIN

Three years after Stalin's death, in a closed session of the 20th Congress of the Communist Party of the Soviet Union in February 1956, First Secretary Nikita Khrushchev addressed delegates "On the Cult of Personality and Its Consequences." The speech, with its condemnation of Stalin, was soon leaked, and perplexed the leaders of the satellite countries. Many anticipated change—some fearfully, some optimistically. Some "forbidden" persons returned to their professions; some young people from "unsuitable" families were granted places at university or—for example—Prague's Academy of Performing Arts. In Czechoslovakia this tentative relaxation lasted until October. When the Hungarian Revolution was crushed by Soviet tanks, the process went into reverse.

In this situation, the Central Committee of the Communist Party was circumspect about the appointment of a new head of the drama company at the National Theatre. Zdeněk Štěpánek, who had been head since 1954, was worn out by attacks on him and on the company; and everyone knew that something had to be done about the weak state of the dramaturgy. Moreover, the company had been invited to the *Théâtre des Nations*[138]—the first tour abroad for a Czechoslovak theatre company under the Communist regime.* There were many contenders from the generation now in their thirties; among them Antonín Dvořák, who had lost his patron when Honzl died in 1953, and whom Štěpánek had replaced with Radok.† None, however, could match the authen-

* This was the invitation intended for E. F. Burian's production of *War*; but it was unacceptable for the Communist hierarchy that Déčko should take precedence over the National Theatre. The productions chosen were Karel Čapek's *The Robber* and Nezval's propagandist *Today the Sun Still Sets over Atlantis*, described by its director Radok as a "bombastic fraud." However, some small roles were played by young performers who later founded the mime group at the Theatre on the Balustrade. They took the opportunity of being in Paris to meet Marcel Marceau, so the tour was not entirely a waste of time.

† Štěpánek showed courage twice over, in re-employing Radok and in asking him to direct Čapek's *The Robber*, since Čapek had been long condemned as "bourgeois".

tic origins of Otomar Krejča—"that Kladno actor"—who had once joined Burian's company with such youthful enthusiasm. Krejča already had his enemies, including Dvořák and the actors Vítězslav Vejražka, Stanislav Neumann, and Eva Vrchlická (daughter of the poet Jaroslav Vrchlický). At the same time, he had some strong women on his side: the popular actresses Olga Scheinpflugová (widow of Karel Čapek) and Zdenka Baldová (widow of K. H. Hilar), as well as Eva Soukupová, who held a key position in the Ministry of Culture.

Krejča was rare among Prague intellectuals in being a genuine proletariat. He grew up in the Bohemian-Moravian Highlands as the son of smallholders "poor as church mice." His political education was gained in industrial Kladno and he took the Communist destiny of his nation for granted. He began as an amateur actor* and did not direct until relatively late in his career; however, within the decade he had become one of Europe's leading theatre directors. Since the late nineteenth century, directors had usually been drawn from the ranks of dramaturges, writers, and critics rather than actors, but, as Jindřich Černý wrote in his 1964 biography, with Krejča the aims of the actor, the theoretician, and the director were one.[139] Krejča followed the Structuralists' theories of theatre as a synthesis of different elements. He regarded the different contributions as equal, but as subordinate to the interpretation as a whole. In one of his earliest articles,† he identified two types of director: one who is faithful to the intended meaning of the play and the other who uses the text for his personal vision even if this is opposed to the original meaning. This had led to Krejča's break with E. F. Burian in 1946, and later that year he wrote: "The director must not only unite the ensemble but be united with them."[140] He chose instead to work under Jiří Frejka at the Vinohrady Theatre, where he played a range of roles in Shakespeare, Chekhov, Gorky, Frisch, and Langer. Here he came to know the dramaturge Karel Kraus, who had been working with Frejka since the end of the war.

In autumn 1949, Krejča directed his first production, Gorky's *Counterfeit Coin*, a controversial production which, according to the theatre critic of the Communist daily *Rudé právo*, failed "to school the general public concerning pre-revolutionary Russian society."[141] It was taken off after seven performances. In 1951 he was, like Frejka the previous year, required to move from the Vinohrady Theatre (now the Czechoslovak Army Theatre)—but in his case to the National Theatre. The Ministry of Culture had noted his proletarian background and had plans for him (although Krejča was only interested in his theatre work, not in Party activity). At first he was engaged as an actor,

---

* By the end of the 1950s, Krejča had played more than 150 roles, including his amateur work, film, and TV.

† "*Co je režisérismus?*" (When does directing become an -ism?) in *Divadelní zápisník*, February 1946. *Divadelní zapisník* was one of three new theatre magazines that started up postwar, all to be replaced in 1948 by *Divadlo*.

directing only one (unsuccessful) production, Oscar Wilde's *An Ideal Husband*. He continued to analyse scripts and in June 1955 published an article in *Divadlo* about a new play at Déčko: *Midnight Wind* by the young poet Josef Topol. Krejča had not yet seen Burian's production; his analysis was based entirely on the script. In this he emphasised that all the elements, not only the descriptive word, should be capable of communicating the idea of a play: "The dramatic character is a picture of the whole person, not only their speech. The word is only a part of a person's behaviour… It is wrong to try to capture in dialogue alone everything the characters live by…"[142]

Krejča was looking for new playwrights, even—or especially—those who had never (or rarely) written for the theatre. At the 2nd Congress of Czechoslovak Writers in April 1956 he was repelled by speeches in support of Socialist Realism by the popular playwrights Miroslav Stehlík and Pavel Kohout, and publicly refused to work with them. At the same congress, however, he noted a bold claim made by the poet František Hrubín, comparing Czechoslovak literature to a swan frozen in ice.

V THE GOLDEN SIXTIES

SPRING AWAKENING

AKORD CLUB, REDUTA, AND THE TEXT-APPEAL

"Cool cats in Prague would like to hep to the voice of George Suchy," reported Michael Alexander in May 1957, discovering Prague for the *Picture Post*:

> The Presley of Prague is 25-year-old Georg [sic] Suchy, a commercial artist by profession, an ardent Johnnie Ray fan. He makes up his own words… But at the Bystrica night club rock 'n' roll evenings, held twice a week, the guests may only listen not jive.[143]

This Presley of Prague, this Dada poet and graphic artist, compère and composer, may have been a fan of Western pop music, but it was in the avant-garde tradition of experiment and discovery. Jiří Suchý, described by one of his colleagues as "a free spirit," belonged to the tradition of artists who found the practice of their art to be a political act. Miroslav Horníček remembered the atmosphere of Prague in the mid-1950s: "I came to hear that somewhere in Prague rock 'n' roll could be heard. It was a daring word, and at that time was pronounced in the same breath as the word Imperialism."[144] Rock 'n' roll could be heard at Reduta, a makeshift club a couple of blocks up from the National Theatre. The war had been over for ten years, the Liberation and Victorious February belonged to the past and young people wanted their own entertainment. Curiosity about Western music and fashions did not mean disloyalty towards Gottwald's successor, the avuncular President Zápotocký, but excitement over what was novel and different. Brought up to believe in the moral rectitude of the leaders who had struggled in the fight for the Communist system, they were still unaware of the manipulation that promoted one man and destroyed another. Some young people found outlets for their creative energies in the organised activities of the Pioneers (*Pionýři*) and the Czechoslovak Youth Union (*Československý svaz mládeže, ČSM*). Others joined amateur choirs, to sing classical music, traditional folk songs, or even voiceband material. No less than in previous centuries, submerged longings were expressed in music. Organ concerts of music from Bohemia's past drew crowds of young people to St. James's in the Old Town, where they stood or crouched on the cold stone floors. All over the country, teenagers gathered in each other's homes, sharing scarce Western magazines and precious records, copying out the lyrics from the distorted sound of foreign radio programmes, imitating the rhythms on homemade musical instruments.

Jiří Suchý was born in 1931, the year Jindřich Honzl returned to the Liberated Theatre to direct Voskovec and Werich in *Golem*, Otakar Zich published *Aesthetics of the Art of Drama*, and the unemployed went on hunger marches. He grew up during the German occupation, as a member of the (underground) Karlín scout troupe performing in sketches by the campfire. For a brief period after the war there was an influx of British and American films; Suchý became a fan especially of the music hall stars—Jack Hulbert, Tommy Handley, George Formby—whom he felt to be close to the Czech sense of humour. He heard about Voskovec and Werich and, reluctantly (traditional theatre had always bored him), went to see *Caesar*. He was amazed by the informal relationship the performers shared with their audience and—just when the theatre closed and Voskovec left for the West—he began to collect their records, photographs, and scripts. Excited to discover a native tradition resembling the music hall, he read about the history of the *tingl tangl*, *šantán*, and cabaret. Jaroslav Ježek and the development of jazz excited him—the influence of Paul Whiteman, Jack Hylton, and their contemporaries. He was not interested in Brecht's theoretical writings, by now part of the "official culture," but found G. W. Pabst's film of *The Threepenny Opera* and especially the music by Kurt Weill an unforgettable experience.

Viktor Sodoma, Suchý's colleague in the (state) design studio of Promotional Productions (*Propagační tvorba*), sang and played the guitar with his wife Vlasta. Fans of Frankie Laine, Les Paul, and Mary Ford, they learnt their songs from Western broadcasts and set up an internal radio network to which Suchý began to contribute. At the same time he was writing a verse play for his father, a puppeteer, while reading Nezval and the Czech Poetists, together with Apollinaire, Morgenstern, Wilde, Baudelaire, and the Czech Decadents; and, even though they were blacklisted under the Stalinist regime, the works of Franz Kafka. In 1952 (the year that former General Secretary of the Communist Party Rudolf Slánský was executed as a traitor), Jiří Suchý started his compulsory military service: "I always thought that the idea of me as a soldier was absurd."[145] The experience shook him out of his private world; but his head was still full of Dada poetry and songs, stories and dialogues, rather than the military threat from the West.

Back in civilian life he mastered the double bass and formed a "group" with Viktor, Vlasta, and two friends. They called themselves "Akord Club," learned the latest American hits, and performed in Reduta, *Propagační tvorba*'s employees' club on Národní třída, below the Casino Bar (of ill repute), and the Bystrica night club. The manager saw that Akord Club was popular with young people, and proposed they should open to the public under his aegis. First they had to pass the tests set by the organisation which monitored performing artists, the Central Office for Musical and Artistic Activities (*Hudební a artistická ústředna, HAÚ*). Established in 1948 on the Soviet model, *HAÚ* was the regulating authority that made the decision about the entertainment activities of any enterprise. Performing artists had to undergo examinations not only in their field of expertise but also in Marxist-Leninist teaching on culture. (The sources are unclear on whether the Akord Club artists passed these tests or whether the Bystrica manager arranged for them to be waved through.) Akord Club also had to submit the texts of its songs to the state enterprise that managed restaurants and canteens (*Restaurace a jídelny*; the acronym *RaJ* translates as "paradise"). The group gave its first public performance on a Thursday evening in 1956. The entrance fee was two crowns, later raised to five. Friends had been telephoned, and fourteen arrived; the following week there were forty-four, and the week after, eighty-eight. Soon they were performing twice weekly: blues, rock 'n' roll, American folk songs, and the songs of V+W. In 1961, the magazine of Charles University recalled Reduta in its early days:

> They didn't play theatre here, but good jazz. Syncopated jazz and blues without gloss, reminiscent of the long-ago tamtam. In this modest room, where the lighting struggled through the cigarette smoke, where the dance floor was always empty (for we went to Reduta to listen), where the silence of the audience witnessed to the quality of the music, in this hall began not only the Theatre on the Balustrade but also Semafor and the later Reduta.[146]

Ivan Vyskočil ("Albert Uruk" was still ahead of him) remembered Reduta's special atmosphere with nostalgia: "There were these plush boxes, it still had the flavour of the First Republic."[147] Akord Club was allowed to take over the basement of the Bystrica because it seemed trivial and non-threatening, and as Vyskočil later observed: "The censors usually followed the theatres that

SVĚT IVANA VYSKOČILA

Na první pohled je svět autora četných povídek a několika divadelních kusů (Kdyby tisíc klarinetů spolu s Jiřím Suchým; Faust, Markéta, služka a já — rovněž s Jiřím Suchým; Smutné vánoce — spolu s M. Macourkem a P. Koptou; Autostop s V. Havlem) řízen, vlastně režírován pouze rozmarem svého původce. Svět, kde v Hlavní správě snů a zdání se dostanou za mírnou cenu létací sny, kde silou vůle se trčí ve vzduchu, kde andělé chodí na strážnou hlídku do putyk a barů, nepřipouští jen tradičně humoristické přeskoky z doby do doby, ze skutečnosti do sna, z opilosti do střízlivosti a naopak, nýbrž také extrémně moderní skoky z reality do kalambúru a říše pouhých slov, Alenčiny říše divů, dále třeba z ovzduší odborníka do prostředí uličníka s vyjádřením výrostkova světa ve specialistické terminologii, a jiná podobná kouzla. Princip vtipu — zklamané očekávání, které je nicméně splněno, ale jinak, zklamání vyplněním nebo vyplnění zklamáním, je zde vyhnán na vrchol: těmito přechody z extrému do extrému, které jsou si navzájem úplně cizí, je dán vtipu nebývalý rozsah, a bujná a skvělá kombinace této nejbohatší škály prostředků nás zprvu svádí, abychom v rozpoutání všech vazeb a všeho pevného spatřovali autorův účel sám o sobě.
Kdyby tomu tak bylo, připomnělo by nám to slova Bertranda Russella, že metoda postulátu liší se od zkoumání reality podobně

The opening page of philosopher Jan Patočka's essay on Ivan Vyskočil in the December 1963 issue of the journal *Divadlo*.

needed financial support. It's based on the opinion that the thing that costs a lot of money can influence the whole nation."[148] Before long, two hundred people were crowding into a room intended for ninety: "Young, thoughtful, exactly what Reduta needed. Players and listeners in close contact… played without breathing space, to constant applause."[149]

Towards the end of 1956, Reduta brought out the first of four issues of a magazine compiled by Jiří Suchý, full of cartoons, articles, information about Akord Club, texts of songs, and statements which echoed the feelings of the young audience: "We enjoy playing swing, we get our fun out of improvising hot jazz, sometimes during the evening we want to rest with a little cool jazz, and then we throw in a 'comedy song.' That's how we like it."[150] In the second issue, Suchý published an article by Werich's former partner at the ABC Theatre, Miroslav Horníček. Reduta was attracting some of the older generation, including Alfréd Radok. Among the visitors was the bubbly blonde singer Ljuba Hermanová, who had begun her career in the arenas and sung in Vienna and Paris. Once a star of the Liberated Theatre, she was regarded by the Communists as an unsuitable role model. "Wouldn't you like to sing with us?" suggested Suchý one night, and she did.

By 1957, the novelty of Akord Club was fading and it was soon to disband. The "Presley of Prague" was twenty-six and tired of carrying his double bass home to Nusle late at night. Ivan Vyskočil, a childhood friend, was among the regular audience. Vyskočil had studied at DAMU and later in the Department of Psychology at Charles University, specialising in the psychology of acting. Suchý, with eighteen months of semi-professional performances behind him, approached him with the idea to devise a more theatrical performance. The plan was to compose dialogue on the V+W model, but the attempt failed. Instead, they developed entertainments in which Vyskočil's monologues alternated with Suchý's songs, backed at first by Akord Club. Only a few friends attended the first evenings, and Vyskočil experienced the insecurity of being alone onstage: "The first three evenings at Reduta I had nothing at all written down, and that I started to write at all was the direct consequence of my failure, or to be more accurate, my bad feelings about those beginnings."[151] "But a negative beginning can be very helpful. People who were at first dissatisfied came again and again, and it was these with their reservations who gave us that extra flavour."[152]

As the evenings grew in popularity, more programmes were planned. Suchý and Vyskočil realised this was literary cabaret, but were unwilling to call it by that name. They invented the term "text-appeal" (*text-apel*), which they liked for its American hint of "sex appeal." Chiefly, however, they felt that the "appeal" to the audience expressed a relationship in which the response was an essential element of the performance. (There was no pressure to participate. Vyskočil did not like performance events in which the audience was manipulated, believing that physical participation is not necessarily active involvement; there is no real partnership.) The principle of the "text-appeal" was a significant step in the movement away from the didacticism of Socialist Realism.

The first advertised performance took place on 15 January 1958: *Of Human Troubles or, Moody Blues*. Jiří Suchý recalled:

> Ivan Vyskočil came on the podium in a black suit past its best and a black pullover, with what was still at that time a black beard, and, introduced by me, he began to speak. He spoke allusively, fluently, like a book. You had to concentrate on what he was saying—and that was what happened that evening in Reduta. One could feel little by little a shiver go down one's back, even if of course every now and then one unexpectedly had to burst out laughing, because those sentences spoken in such a serious voice contained so much hidden and even apparent humour, always original, unusual, and new.[153]

Four more text-appeals followed in the next six months, each with a specific theme:

Of Dreams and Follies
A Man and His Pint
Bring Them Back Alive, or Hunting
*Hi, Sorrow!**

Performances increased to three a week; some people came to every performance, for no two were alike. New stories and songs were inserted, others deleted, and sometimes characters or solutions might be changed. Although the performers had a working plan, its flexibility allowed them to vary the programme according to audience response. Vyskočil's stories were laconic and colloquial, with a dry black humour, but their popularity lay mainly in the choice of subject. In three stories from *A Man and His Pint*, a beer drinker muses on the significance of a pint in the hand; a young delinquent from a broken home casually answers a cross examination about his night out; and a drunk tries to interest other travellers at a tram stop in his philosophy of life. They were brief, open-ended tales, but told in such a way that the audience felt as though it were involved in a conversation. In a sense, it was the banality of the stories that the audience enjoyed. Jan Císař wrote:

> They were not themes you would usually find in Czech literature. Facts that until then had been shut up found their freedom. The destruction of convention begins through this freedom. For convention always originates where something cannot be seen—or is not allowed to be seen.[154]

No literature like this, arising directly from real situations, was published in the 1950s. Vyskočil's theoretical work on the psychology of acting interested him in the immediacy of performance. He remained distanced from the characters in his stories; even when speaking in the first person and in the voice of, for example, the delinquent boy, he never identified with the character, and was always prepared to modify characters and actions on suggestions from members of the audience:

> The situations in the earlier stories gave the audience the opportunity to stage their own play. We did not intend to perform, and in any case a play could not be performed on a stage of these dimensions, so people had to use their imagination to visualise what was happening.[155]

* An allusion to Pavel Kohout's 1957 success, *Farewell, Sorrow*.

Audiences crowded into Reduta to hear him; Vyskočil recalled that around ten o'clock they might be joined by some of the "loose women" on their way up to the nightclub. He also remembered:

> When the visitors' attention could be lured from their schnitzel, wine, and chat with their neighbour, then that was good. And when it was as though everyone in Reduta were sitting round one table, known to each other even perhaps we've met for the first time and maybe for the last, it was even better. This experience of relaxed togetherness was perhaps the best thing that the text-appeals provided.[156]

But as word about Reduta got about, its character began to change; many of the original fans sensed that the atmosphere was not the same, that Reduta was now frequented by those who liked to appear fashionable. A new group (including the future pop star Waldemar Matuška) replaced Akord Club and new entertainment was contrived by Suchý, Vyskočil, Horníček, and Jiří Šlitr (another musician and graphic artist who had been introduced to the group by Horníček). They called their show *Plentuch*, a neologism around which they created musical and verbal improvisations. Suchý and Horníček were performing at other venues as well—for example, *Mondays with Auntie* at the Café Vltava, based on Suchý's song "Blues for Auntie's Broken Arm." The audience was invited to ask questions: "Where does the dark go when you turn the light on?" The answer: "The dark is still there, but you can't see it."[157]

OTOMAR KREJČA AT THE NATIONAL THEATRE

Krejča became head of the drama company at the National Theatre at the same time as Vyskočil and Suchý were experimenting with the "text-appeal" at Reduta. They were completely dissimilar genres of theatre, and yet both set out to re-examine the nature of the relationships between the stage and the audience. Just as a new young audience attended Reduta, so a new young audience was attracted to Krejča's productions at the National Theatre. They were theatres in which the artists did not follow a pattern of what had gone before, but shared their own ideas with their audience.

Taking advantage of the deceptive thaw of spring 1956, Krejča began to build a team that included designer Josef Svoboda, director Jaromír Pleskot, and dramaturges Otakar Fencl and Karel Kraus (Kraus exceptionally, as he was not a member of the Communist Party). In 1959, they were joined by the actor and director Miroslav Macháček. Fiery in temper and under constant surveillance by the Communist authorities, Macháček had attempted suicide eight years earlier after having been dismissed from the Realist Theatre* as an "imperialist agent." Alfréd Radok was also part of the circle; his influence had helped to shift the dramaturgy of the theatre towards contemporary European drama and Czechoslovak playwrights who did not conform with the limitations of Socialist Realism. The inclusion of new writers was an essential part of the strategy; all the work with the authors involved long discussions and rewrites, in which Karel Kraus played an important role. In an interview in 1969, Krejča said of Kraus:

> Collaborators are necessary... The literary advisor† in our theatre department doesn't see his work only in the area of literary criticism—but in a theatrical, analytical, critical attitude. The literary advisor must consider the ensemble when choosing a play.... I don't think this work can be done by the director. If he's really strict with himself he's always too involved in his work. He does not have a broad view... The literary advisor is colder, more analytical, and doesn't have so much opportunity to grow into the work.[158]

The American interviewer noted how Krejča liked to work with other strong personalities prepared to contest his opinions. Actors have recalled how he demanded full commitment during the rehearsal period, challenging them to think through new solutions, forcing them to concentrate on every detail. The process demanded full engagement of mind and body and not all the National Theatre actors were capable of such involvement. Nevertheless, an ensemble formed within the company of actors who liked working with Krejča and he with them. Krejča did not choose his players on the basis of how well they could dissemble or on their ability to understand and interpret a wide range of different roles, but on whether they could bring something individual to a role, whether they carried within their own personality a quality they could communicate to the audience. One who could do this, and who became closely identified with Krejča's work, was Jan Tříska—a striking actor who had played a range of roles on stage and screen while still a student at DAMU. In 1959, he became the youngest member of the National Theatre. The critic Jan Císař later wrote of Tříska's roles with Krejča:

> In Tříska's physical actions—in the agitation and scornfulness expressed in his body and his voice—the dissatisfaction with himself and others was materially embodied; the rebellion against the surroundings in which his characters lived...[159]

---

* Formerly Pavel Švanda's theatre in Smíchov, renamed in 1945 and dedicated to Zdeněk Nejedlý in 1953.

† i.e. dramaturge. The interview, by an American, was published in English.

The legendary actor Miloš Nedbal similarly contributed his individual qualities:

> His military, erect bearing, exact articulation, juxtaposing with clarity, one sermonising syllable after another, as though the fate of the world hung on each, the expressively peremptory gesture, which irrevocably sums up what has been pronounced…[160]

Císař was not writing about the actors' performances in a single production but about the qualities they brought to a series of productions. When Krejča cast Tříska as Romeo and as Rafael in Topol's *The End of Shrovetide*, it was not to exploit a romantic lead but to emphasise the dissatisfaction and rebellion inherent in the actor's personality and expressed in the two roles. By this means, common or contrasting features in the two plays could be highlighted. With the minimum emphasis, Krejča was thus able to suggest recurrent issues through a series of contemporary and historical plays.

Between 1957 and 1961, Krejča directed seven major productions for the National Theatre.* Svoboda was the designer for all except Nâzim Hikmet's *The Eccentric* (1957), designed by František Tröster. He directed two classics by Josef Kajetán Tyl; *Švanda the Bagpiper* (1958), chosen to celebrate the National Theatre's seventy-fifth anniversary, is a domestic fairy-tale that tells the story of the thoughtless but lovable Švanda who leaves home to seek his fortune. Krejča dispensed with the usual folk environment for the play and staged it in a mysterious, colourless, neutral space, designed by Josef Svoboda. In editing the play, Kraus stripped it of its sentimentality. Jindřich Černý noted that, without adding to the text, Krejča shifted the emphasis from Tyl's message that home is the only certainty to Havlíček's more considered opinion that this depends on the values and attitudes preserved at home. In Krejča's production of Tyl's *Drahomíra and Her Sons* (1960), Jan Grossman noted that:

> Right from the start, the urgent concern is not what is going to happen, but what it means. The story's truthfulness and its implications are important, but far more important is the interpretation of the story.[161]

František Hrubín's *August Sunday* was premièred in the spring of 1958, a few months after the first text-appeal. Chekhovian in atmosphere, sophisticated in presentation, it would seem to have little in common with the shocking directness of the text-appeal. It is a story of the parting of the lovers Morák, once a poet, and Mixová, once a beautiful woman, and of their relationship

---

* Some of these were on the stage of the Theatre of the Estates, home of the drama company of the National Theatre, and at this time known as the Tyl Theatre.

with other visitors at a lakeside hotel, especially Mixová's young niece and her boyfriend. The roles of Morák and Mixová were played by National Theatre stars Karel Höger and Vlasta Fabianová, and Svoboda used all his technical inventiveness to create onstage the impression of a timeless summer's day, when sunlight filters through the leaves and distant music echoes across a luminous lake:

> A double projection was cast on two large projection screens joined at an angle of forty-five degrees at the back of the stage. The diffused light, through its oscillations, wiped out the join between the two projection screens and at the same time gave the set, which was actually shallow, the optical impression of unusual depth. Under the lower screen was mirror foil, which reflected the actors as though in water. The set changed according to the light and the projections, changed rapidly and fluently: morning was the time to bathe in a silver mist, at noon the sun scorched the skin, night was deep and dark.[162]

August Sunday was not narrative theatre in which interest depends on the story, but, like the text-appeal, a juxtaposition of scenes on an underlying theme concerning the conflicts and compromises made in the passage of life. Jan Císař noted that the dialogue between Morák and Vach, the former proprietor of a pâtisserie, is really a montage of two monologues on the theme of hatred towards youth. Like the text-appeals, the short scenes and monologues expressed facts specific to the individual characters, and it was for the playgoer to interpret them. Krejča and Kraus had collaborated closely with Hrubín on the writing of the play, which was very different from Hrubín's original concept of a historical fantasy. Jindřich Černý later wrote: "Krejča and Hrubín did not reveal a new kind of hero. They did something far more: They offered up on the stage material for the transformation of man—i.e. man himself."[163] The atmosphere of *August Sunday*—a moment in time poised on the edge of a lake—is in its way a distillation of the expectant emotion that marked the end of the 1950s.

Krejča and Kraus went on to work with Josef Topol as with Hrubín, although Topol's play, *Their Day* (1959), was performed more or less as written. Here again the theme was more important than the story, and as with *August Sunday*, the action took place within the space of one day in the lives of interrelated characters. The first play of this period to deal directly with "the issue of youth," it focuses on the conflict between youthful idealism and the conservative middle generation, led by the bureaucratic Dohnal (Miloš Nedbal). The frustration of Dohnal's son Vladimír and his friend Pavel is expressed in their rebellious relationships with their families and the small-town community. For the composition of alternating scenes, Svoboda made use of a moving track, three trucks, and ten projection screens that moved silently into different positions.* Onto these screens were projected the naturalistic images of the provincial town: house façades, streetlamps, advertisement hoardings, staircases, windows, etc. They were also used for passages of film, including, with integrated lighting effects, the death of Vladimír's uncle, a failed musician, in a road accident:

> One image slowly travelled down the side of the road, the other sped in the opposite direction at the speed of the car. Over the sound system you could hear the whirr of tyres and the scraping of brakes. The pedestrian—an actor—fell onstage; a second of darkness followed, the image stopped still and the noise of the engine disappeared into the distance. Then, on all the screens, an idyllic scene of an empty, grass-lined road. A man lay dead on the forestage.[164]

Hrubín's second and last collaboration with Krejča, *Crystal Night* (1961), a family drama uncovering deep-rooted conflicts, made less of an impact than *August Sunday*. Krejča was already deeply engrossed with Kundera on his first play, *The Owners of the Keys*, which was to open in April 1962. At the same time, his career was in a political crisis. He had led the drama ensemble of the National Theatre for five creative years (1956–1961), but was in constant conflict with the old guard. There was strong resistance, artistic and political, to Krejča's leadership, and official complaints about the (ideological) pessimism of his productions. He was criticised for paying too much attention to his own productions at the expense of other directors, and it was said that his preference for certain actors caused division within the ensemble. The conflict began to undermine Krejča at the National Theatre, and in August 1961 a report by the Central Committee of the Communist Party led to the dismissal of Krejča's two dramaturges, Otakar Fencl as well as the non-Party member Karel Kraus—and, as had been intended, Krejča resigned too.

In the tense atmosphere of the time, approval had been slow to be granted for Milan Kundera's first play, *The Owners of the Keys*, and productions (in cooperation with Krejča) had already been seen in Ostrava and Olomouc. Six months after Krejča's resignation, in April 1962, Kundera's play finally opened at the National Theatre. On one level, *The Owners of the Keys* belongs to the genre of World War II resistance drama. The action takes place in an apartment belonging to the middle-aged Krůtas (Miloš Nedbal and Blanka Waleská). In Krejča's production, the two rooms of the apartment—one of them inhabited by the Krůtas, the other by their daughter Alena (Marie Tomášová) and her husband Jiří (Luděk Munzar)—were represented by independently moving stage trucks. Thus two conversations could take place simultaneous-

* The first use of the Polyecran technique in a "proper" theatre (see Laterna magika later in this chapater).

ly, while a third viewpoint appeared in Jiří's "off-truck" visions, triggered by the arrival of the Resistance worker Věra. The moral sphere in which the visions appeared was intensified by a mesmeric "black hole" suspended above the acting area: a vanishing point created from rays of light focused on a mirror almost a metre square—Josef Svoboda's invention.

All the action takes place within the real time of an hour and a half, a fact emphasised by the collection of clocks belonging to Krůta. In his post-script to the published play, Kundera drew attention to the fact that *The Owners of the Keys* is really a one-act play and should be played without an interval. But within this space there are two storylines:

> The first storyline, the one the critics have described, is reminiscent of the regular run of occupation dramas, the second storyline... is perhaps more like the unfamiliar dramaturgy of the Ionesco type of anti- or pseudo-drama.[165]

Kundera described the two storylines as:

> Two voices... individual strands of thought are gradually examined and reworked by both voices, i.e. by both storylines; meaning that all the strands of thought... are in the play illuminated from both sides, from the point of view both of greatness and of pettiness.[166]

Although the action of *The Owners of the Keys* is essentially conventional, the use of montage sets up new relationships. Jiří's "heroic decision," which begins with his murder of the caretaker, condemns the Krůtas and their daughter to death. The story could have developed as a simplified generation conflict, but through the use of montage the focus shifted to the confrontation between the vitality of the Resistance and the oppressive materialism of the bourgeois. The Krůtas and Alena are innocent of the crime in which Jiří implicates them, but Kundera presents this as a deadly innocence; they are innocent because they cling to their own world of pettiness and materialism, symbolised by the ownership of the keys.

Kundera and Krejča were not interested in psychoanalysing the characters. Krejča wrote:

> The author is interested most of all in what the character says, not so much in how he came to that opinion. He is interested in what he does, less in the reason for it, the psychology of the action.[167]

Nevertheless, Kundera was correct in referring to the "regular run of occupation dramas," for the content of *The Owners of the Keys* is standard

Romeo and Juliet by William Shakespeare, directed by Otomar Krejča and designed by Josef Svoboda for the National Theatre, 1965. (Courtesy of the photographer: Jaromír Svoboda)

Socialist Realism. The hero is initially immersed in a bourgeois environment of convention, complacency, and romantic love, from which he is roused by a call to arms from the Communist brotherhood (in 1961 it would have been heresy to suggest there could have been a non-Communist Resistance). This may be why Kundera has not allowed the play to be published or performed since the late 1960s.

Krejča was to direct two more productions with the National Theatre. *Romeo and Juliet*, translated by Josef Topol, opened in December 1963. Jan Tříska and Marie Tomášová played the lovers. Krejča's first Shakespeare interpretation, fast-moving and physical, was unlike anything National Theatre audiences had seen before. On Svoboda's luminous set the action could move instantly from one playing area to another. Juliet's balcony hovers and seems to dematerialise. By casting the actors who had played the Krůta family in *The*

The End of Shrovetide by Josef Topol, directed by Otomar Krejča and designed by Josef Svoboda for the National Theatre, 1964. (Courtesy of the photographer: Jaromír Svoboda)

Owners of the Keys—Nedbal, Waleská, and Tomášová—as the Capulet family, Krejča emphasised Kundera's theme of a "young world" locked within the old one of their elders, who refuse to hand over the keys. Any other attempt to underline its contemporary relevance—such as modern dress—would have been superfluous. Jindřich Černý wrote that with *Romeo and Juliet*, Krejča had the audacity to take the timeworn slogan "young world of Socialism" seriously, and give it new meaning.[168]

Josef Topol's *The End of Shrovetide* is one of the most revealing yet multilayered pieces of writing to have come out of Czechoslovakia under totalitarianism. It took nearly two years for the Central Committee of the Communist Party and the Ministry of Culture to sanction *The End of Shrovetide* for the National Theatre. It was, however, premièred as early as April 1963 in Olomouc, with the director Jiří Svoboda working in cooperation with Krejča; interest was intense and by the end of the year, productions had opened in eight more provincial theatres (including Brno, Ostrava, and Hradec Králové), and in the new year, another three. Eventually, in November 1964, Krejča staged his own production in the National Theatre in Prague.

Like the authors of the village drama in the late nineteenth century, Topol set *The End of Shrovetide* in the Czech countryside in a time of change.

Topol himself grew up in a village and would have experienced in the course of Collectivisation the disappearance of ancient lanes and hedges, groves and ponds, together with the names that held them in the village memory, under the slogan "Fewer Boundaries, More Bread!"* As in the nineteenth century, values that have long been relied on become vulnerable when outside influences encroach. Does an old mare destined for the slaughterhouse have value, or a chandelier when it no longer hangs in its familiar place? A trumpet fanfare opens the play, but it echoes in an empty council office, merely a rehearsal for the empty ritual of Shrovetide, when once the community asked forgiveness for their sins. In an age of tractors and Collectivisation, time-honoured traditions are a parody of what they were—and yet the villagers remain aware of their symbolic power. The bureaucrats with their briefcases and utopian plans are left in discomfort.

Josef Svoboda's panoramas of puddled earth rutted by tractor wheels formed the backdrop for the shabbily clothed farm workers (Marie's bright new party dress is thoughtlessly trampled in the mud by the mummers) and for their disguises, enormous heads designed by the sculptor Jan Koblasa. There are sixteen traditional mummers—including the Bear and its Keeper, the Dandy and the Scarecrow, the Clown, the Chimney Sweep, and the Horse.† They are simply themselves, neither good nor bad, just as Topol's Party representatives are neither heroes nor villains, but local people who at times themselves merge with the natural elements. The ambiguity of the setting forms a counterpoint to the essential theme: the individual's responsibility for his or her own moral identity.

A web of connections is interwoven into the structure, and the threads begin to tangle as the characters hide behind masks and disguises; the crucial twist occurs when one character borrows a disguise from another and is challenged in that persona. The central character, Král (King), does not wear any disguise; and as the last farmer to resist Collectivisation, he tries to keep his children untainted by the carnival: "They're what I hear with, what I see with... I will turn into them, and my soul will nourish them..."[169] Nevertheless, they belong to the village, which includes a failing collective farm, an inefficient Party apparatus, and a manipulative barber, Smrťák (or Reaper—as in "the Grim Reaper"). Král's young counterpart, the rebel Raphael, son of a bourgeois architect and an émigré, is in love with Král's daughter Marie. He has plans for them to run away together; meanwhile, Král's simple-minded son Jindřich is mocked by the carnival players and dies in a pointless argument

* Topol's portrayal of disillusion with Collectivisation preceded Ludvík Vaculík's landmark novel, *The Axe* (*Sekyra*, 1966), by two years.

† Rather disappointingly, in the published English version, only the Hussar and the Corpse are specified and the rest are left anonymous.

with Raphael, whom he mistakes for the Hussar—killed by a sabre of which the Hussar had earlier said: "It won't draw blood. It's only poetry."[170] At the end of the play Marie, like Jenůfa, provides hope of redemption through her love for an outcast and murderer—in Jenůfa's case, her stepmother; in Marie's case, Raphael. The casting of Tomášová and Tříska as the lovers connected the production thematically with Krejča's *Romeo and Juliet*. It was Krejča's last production at the National before an absence that lasted thirty-three years.

LATERNA MAGIKA

When Karel Kraus was sacked from the National Theatre in 1961, he was given sanctuary by Eva Soukupová, from 1959 head of the Theatre Institute. Otakar Fencl moved to television. Another member of Krejča's team, the stage designer Josef Svoboda, emerged unscathed. In 2011, a documentary by his grandson Jakub Hejna voiced a suspicion that had simmered through the years—that Svoboda had paid for his successful career at home and abroad with reports to the Communists on the opinions and activities of his colleagues. Other colleagues angrily rejected Hejna's thesis with the defence that Svoboda was an apolitical figure totally devoted to his profession. Svoboda was unsurpassed on an international level in his confident ability to achieve a desired artistic effect through technical means.* In this field he was a genius, but he remained a technician rather than a truly creative artist. His role in Alfréd Radok's *Laterna magika*—which built on the earlier work of Burian, Kouřil, and Tröster—relied on the input of directors such as Radok himself, Miloš Forman, or Jan Švankmajer. With them, it had the potential to be the "theatre of infinite space" envisaged by Radok; without them, it turned into a clever attraction for tourists.

The *Laterna magika* was premièred at Expo 58 in Brussels, an iconic moment for the Czechoslovak public. Exceptionally, the Communist Party allowed the best of Czechoslovak talent to be involved in the creation of the Czechoslovak pavilion, and turned a blind eye to the political profile of artists and technicians involved.† As a result, Czechoslovakia won the award for the best pavilion in Expo 58, attracting six million visitors. This unprecedented artistic and social success ignited a new sense of national confidence, not to mention the *Brussels Style* that remained in vogue for the next three decades. The originality of Radok's *Laterna magika* and the ingenuity involved in its

* Comprehensively recorded in Helena Albertová's account of his career, *Josef Svoboda: Scenographer*, Prague, 2008.

† This can be largely credited to the eccentric and innovative František Kahuda, who succeeded the hardline Ladislav Štoll as minister of education.

combination of live and filmed action (the polyecran technique, derived from Burian's pre-war Theatregraph) had a major share in this success.

The Communists were eager to exploit their new popularity, but not at any cost. Radok was preparing the *Laterna magika*'s second programme, to open in spring 1960. Folklore had been a key element of the first, but now he wanted to take it a stage further by building the production around Bohuslav Martinů's cantata, *The Opening of the Wells* (1955). Written after nearly two decades of exile caused first by the war and then by Communism, Martinů's short work recalls the village traditions of welcoming springtime. Radok's staging reinforced the poignancy of the exile's longing for continuity with the past and the return to a purer way of life. After a few performances under closed conditions, the authorities ordered the elimination of *The Opening of the Wells*; the remaining fragments of the programme were to be pieced together and presented as the finished work. Ladislav Štoll, currently minister of culture, stormed at Radok, saying that he had failed to use the opportunity to glorify the achievements of the Soviet Union. Václav Kopecký condemned Martinů's work as the "morbid nostalgia of an émigré" and Radok's interpretation as a "wrong, ideologically malignant manifestation of Jewish Expressionism,"[171] ordering the filmed episodes to be destroyed.* Radok waited in vain for Svoboda to stand by him and resist the ban.† On 5 May 1960 Radok was sacked as director of the *Laterna magika*, and in September forced out of the National Theatre, of which it was administratively a part. For a time unemployed and devastated, he was rescued by Ota Ornest, at that time director of the Prague Municipal Theatres—then consisting of one company working in three central theatres (the Comedy [*Divadlo komedie*], Chamber [*Komorni divadlo*], and ABC Theatres). Ornest, with six years in London behind him, introduced crowd-pullers (mainly comedies) from the British, American, and French repertoire. Anchored there for the next five years, in 1964 Radok directed one of his finest productions, Romain Rolland's *Le Jeu de l'amour et de la mort*.

THE THEATRE ON THE BALUSTRADE

FOUNDING OF THE THEATRE ON THE BALUSTRADE

The narrow streets and courtyards of the Old Town of Prague shelter many halls and galleries. In 1958, the radio producer and Reduta regular Helena

---

* The pieces of film were rescued and hidden at Barrandov Film Studio.

† Svoboda later said that it was not a question only of Radok; it would have meant the end of *Laterna magika*, and the whole team that had worked on it.

The entrance to the Theatre on the Balustrade in 1966. (Author's personal archive)

Philippová, full of energy and optimism, discovered one such hall not far from the Charles Bridge. The building dated from the Middle Ages but had been rebuilt in the nineteenth century by the Association of Catholic Journeymen (*Jednota katolických tovaryšů*). It was now used by the Union for the Disabled (*Svaz invalidů*), whose deaf and mute members staged an annual mime show. Vyskočil was reluctant to regularise the informal text-appeals, but was persuaded by the enthusiasm of Suchý and the Reduta fans. One was a lawyer and Party member, working at the Ministry of Culture and influential in high places: Vladimír Vodička. He was also a songwriter and composer of some of the most evocative tunes of the 1960s.

Philippová's troupe of musicians, singers, and dance students swept and scrubbed, replaced rotten woodwork, and replastered the interior. Suchý, the graphic artist, painted the blue-grey stripes that are still a feature of the auditorium today. Only the electrical work was contracted out, although the converted paraffin lamps in the auditorium were chosen as the cheapest fittings available. Until 1966, the auditorium was heated by a wood stove to one side of the proscenium arch; there was no heating backstage. There was no wing space stage right, and only a few feet stage left; backstage facilities consisted of one room, and families still lived on the upper floors, looking down on the courtyard from the internal balconies.

While the renovation was going on, Vodička and Philippová were negotiating with the local council (*národní výbor*) to establish the basis for the theatre's legal existence. In a totalitarian system, it was not possible simply to start a theatre company—everything had to have its approved place in a hierarchy that culminated in the Central Committee of the Communist Party. However, a new Theatre Act had come into effect in November 1957 that allowed theatres to be administered by institutions, and not necessarily directly by the state. Without this, the small stage movement of the 1960s could never have happened. Vodička and Philippová agreed with the council for Prague 1 that the theatre would come under the cultural department (*osvětová beseda*) permitted to carry out small-scale cultural activity. Vodička's position as manager was confirmed when the Theatre on the Balustrade (*Divadlo Na zábradlí*) was granted independent status in 1959, and he remained there until 1991. Some suspected him of having too close a relationship with the authorities; others noted the periods of sick leave that coincided with the worst crises. His heart attacks, legend says, were exceptionally well staged.

Rehearsals began for a production with the working title *The Great Transformation*. The theme was the ideologically correct one of pacifism. Jiří Suchý's script was about an army whose weapons have changed into musical instruments and their barracks into a conservatoire. Suchý later wrote in a programme note:

> The word PEACE usually turns up cut out of shiny paper or cardboard and pinned with other fine words on the office wall. Whenever I see it like that, I have the feeling it ought to turn up in places where people are laughing and singing and having a good time. Because happiness, good cheer, and peace somehow go together.[172]

Vyskočil insisted that the story be no more than a thread on which to hang other episodes; he saw no need for a well-structured plot or dramatic conclusion. Philippová directed, but her ideas were in conflict with those of other members of the ensemble and she dissociated herself from the project. Antonín Moskalyk, a pupil of Alfréd Radok and his assistant at the National Theatre, was invited to take over. He remembered long rehearsals and improvisations, trying out new ideas, always searching, not knowing what they were looking for, never deciding on anything until it had been tried out on stage. Eventually the ensemble arrived at "something which fell between a cabaret and a loose theatre form."[173] The title was changed to *A Thousand Clarinets* and it was described as a *leporelo*—a children's picture book. Some of the "pictures" were mimed, some had dialogue, others were stagings of songs by Suchý, Vodička, Jaroslav Jakoubek, and Jaromír Vomáčka, the Reduta pianist who became the theatre's composer. Jiří Šlitr coauthored one song with Suchý, "Song about Love" (*Píseň o lásce*), sung by Ljuba Hermanová in the role of Zuzana, who sets the miraculous metamorphosis in motion. The scenes changed rapidly; one gag was piled upon another, often musical gags. There were two pianos onstage, one played by Vomáčka. There was no money for scenery; to brighten the sombre backdrop, Suchý designed a set of placards in the manner of the Russian Constructivists.

A Thousand Clarinets was premièred on 9 December 1958. By professional standards the production was uneven; Milan Lukeš warned of the danger "when everyone does everything."[174] Most highly praised were Hermanová's singing and a mime sequence by Ladislav Fialka, who was already working with his own group. Suchý had written himself a comedy role but was unused to working without a microphone, and his lines were redistributed. Despite the musical's shortcomings, the first-night audience cheered the company's zest and élan, and praised the novelty of form and content. Jan Kopecký wrote in *Divadelní noviny*:

> The playgoer... takes away not just a pleasant feeling that he's seen something worthwhile, where the ideas weren't laid on with a trowel, but also something inwardly a bit unsettling because serious topical questions can be heard beneath that understated entertainment. The word "peace" isn't a slogan here, but a living human desire.[175]

In spite of the première's success, the company—inexperienced in marketing techniques—played for six weeks to half-empty houses. But as word of mouth went round, audiences began to fill the theatre and stay behind after performances for discussions and debates in the auditorium or foyer, discussions which sometimes lasted into the early hours. Ivan Vyskočil encouraged the informal meetings, which for him were more interesting than the performance on stage. But even that was informal; three years later, a reporter on the newspaper of Charles University remembered nostalgically how they would sit "as they pleased," not "at the theatre," while Hermanová "stopped by to sing for them," or Vomáčka "picked out a tune on the piano."[176] The audience included established theatre directors and professors as well as students: Otomar Krejča and Miroslav Macháček, Ladislav Smoček and Jan Kačer, Evžen Sokolovský and Miloš Forman. Through the evenings of 1959, the foyer of the Theatre on the Balustrade became a forum for new ideas about theatre and presentation: "Theatre ought to be a proper actor in a proper costume, not amateurs helping themselves to whatever they want!"[177] "Why always play three-act plays when you know already what's going to happen and how it's going to turn out? Why not try something new?"[178]

The company put its next production into rehearsal. *Faust, Gretchen, the Maid, and I,* written by Suchý but adapted by Vyskočil and directed by František Čech opened on 27 May 1959. It was a version of the Faust legend set in the twentieth century and subtitled "A Morality"; Vyskočil describes it as a *fabulační kompozice*—a story put together from different elements. The revue-style structure of songs and short scenes was similar to that of *A Thousand Clarinets* but angled towards a specific aim. The intention was not simply to retell Faust and Gretchen's story but to relate it to contemporary life with the use of anecdote and allegory. The role of "History" was written for Ljuba Hermanová, who stepped in and out of the action and commented on it in song and narration.

Faust was portrayed by Jaromír Vomáčka as a modern aesthete: "a mean, cowardly creature, parasite and careerist, an immoral hoodlum, hiding his own corruption behind accusations of immorality in others."[179] Such a personality was familiar to anyone who had experienced the blackmailing tactics of the Communist authorities and/or the secret police. František Černý noted that Vomáčka's innocent face "made a thirteen-month-old babe look like an arrant existentialist."[180] Ivan Vyskočil and Karel Laštovka played the fifteenth-century devils Méfisto and Tvéfisto, whose message was that man brings his own evil on himself. At the heart of the play was Gretchen, "one of the girls of our time of whom one could say 'her reputation has been knocked around a bit'":

> The modern Gretchen talks like a hooligan, screws up her face, behaves appallingly, twists herself up in outlandish dances. But that is just on the outside. The authors—and the excellent performer herself, Emma Černá—know how to see beneath the skin; sometimes to a chilling extent. Such as when Faust asks her what her parents would say about her lifestyle and she roars in cynical laughter. Or when she runs from her problems to rock 'n' roll with the devil Tvéfisto. Or when, in the middle of all the merrymaking there are sudden moments of emptiness and sorrow.[181]

The production possessed a sharper and more immediate criticism of society than its predecessor. One critic noted of Faust: "It is enough to discover in him part of something we have all been carrying in ourselves, and I hope—as do the authors—that at least it makes us think."[182] Jiří Suchý did not appear in *Faust, Gretchen, the Maid, and I.* In the course of rehearsals, his role had again been cut to a minimum. To remind his colleagues of his centrality to the whole project, he threatened to leave. "When would you like to go?" they asked him politely: "Immediately, or at the end of the season?"

In between these two productions (in March 1959), Ladislav Fialka's mime group had premièred its first independent production, *Pantomime on the Balustrade*. Of the small theatre groups that proliferated in the late 1950s and 1960s, this was the first to establish an international name. Czechoslovakia had no tradition of mime, but in the nineteenth century, Josef Kajetán Tyl had written a novel claiming that Jean-Gaspard Deburau, the Pierrot of the Parisian Funambules, was born in Bohemia as Jan Kašpar Dvořák.* Deburau's fictional life was one foundation for Fialka; others were the teaching of Étienne Decroux and the work of Marcel Marceau. These were mediated through his teacher, Laurette Hrdinová, half-French, and a leading modern dancer before the war, when the avant-garde artists were inspired especially by the French model. Dismissed from the academy teaching staff by the Communists, who followed Stalin's preference for classical ballet, Hrdinová was smuggled onto the Prague Conservatoire staff in the mid-1950s as a specialist in traditional *commedia dell'arte* pantomime. There were native sources of inspiration too: In the late 1940s Saša Machov used his experience from Sadler's Wells Opera to stage a series of dance-theatre productions; these were followed by E. F. Burian's revivals of *War* and the *Folk Suites*.† A group of conservatoire students formed around Fialka's strong personality, and under Hrdinová's supervision, gave their first performances, *Cassander and Pierrot - Castaways*, *The Flower Girl*, and *At the Crossroads*, at a youth event in the courtyard of the Clementinum Library (June 1956), followed by *Pierrot the Baker* (August 1956).‡ The group included Zdenka Kratochvílová—one of the most expressive mime artists of modern times—Lída (Ludmila) Kovářová, and Jiří Kaftan; they were to be joined at the Theatre on the Balustrade by Jana Pešková (married to the rising young musician Libor Pešek), Josef Fajta, Ivan Lukeš, Božena Věchetová, and Richard Weber. The dimension that made Ladislav Fialka's ensemble exceptional was the ability of the members to develop their own characters (Weber as Harlequin, Kaftan as Clown) while still working together as elements of a single entity (briefly captured for posterity in a film clip of the "Metamorphoses" sequence from *Fools*). Most mime performers perform solo or with one or two subordinate performers; a performance by

* Josef Kajetán Tyl, *Pouť českých umělců* (*Pilgrimage of the Bohemian Artists*, 1836).

† E. F. Burian died five months after the première of *Pantomime on the Balustrade*, but there is no evidence that he saw Fialka's production; he had at that time engaged the Slovak mime, Milan Sládek, to work at Déčko.

‡ The men had to do their military service, which was the reason for the gap of almost three years before *Pantomime on the Balustrade*.

Fialka's ensemble filled the whole stage, and enthralled large audiences. The original group remained together for over a decade and travelled the world.

Pantomime on the Balustrade, still under Laurette Hrdinová's supervision, was described by Fialka as "an introduction to the art of pantomime, an historical and stylistic survey from its classical form of the mid-nineteenth century up to its appearance today." It was followed in January 1960 by *Nine Hats on Prague* in which the group collaborated with Ljuba Hermanová on a nostalgic programme of episodes from Prague's history. It had relatively few performances and is remembered as an example of the imperfect but appealing early work of a young theatre. *Etudes*, December 1960, consisted of miniature sketches, technically exact, with every superfluity eliminated. They enabled the company to consolidate its skills, and Fialka to make discoveries about the genre: "The language of pantomime cannot use symbols; it can interpret absolutely any sensation, but must express it through a concrete situation. The mime cannot play false, just as he cannot be both sitting and standing at the same time."[183]

With *The Journey* (also known as *Clowns*, 1962) the company for the first time based a full evening on one theme. This history of the clown was told in four episodes, beginning with the *commedia dell'Arte* and travelling through Deburau's Funambules and the touring circus until it reached the "great circus" of contemporary life. Nearly two years of work went into the production; whereas in *Etudes* the performers had developed the episodes by working outwards from a meaningful gesture, in *The Journey* they had to find the meaningful gesture while working within the given scenario. The insistence on precise technical work set the mime ensemble apart from other groups working in the small theatres, for whom enthusiasm was often a substitute for technical mastery. It was this that led Fialka to write a short book, *The Art of Pantomime* (*Umění pantomimy*, 1964), where he described in detail the cooperative effort which created a production out of "a thought or feeling" that was for him "the beginning and chief aim of pantomime."

The thoroughness of their work was rewarded. A nonverbal repertoire consisting of the flexible *Etudes* and the more substantial *Journey* attracted international impresarios; the mime company's first experience of the West was Berlin, where they felt as though a curtain had risen for them on an extravagant stage set. Invitations to Western Europe, the USA, Mexico, and South America followed, a dazzling opportunity for the inhabitants of a closed country. The impact of their experience was evident in their next production, *Fools* (1965), strongly influenced by the emotion of what they had seen and passed through, and its contrast with the prison that was their home. *Fools* represents the high point of the company's creativity, and was deeply suffused with the amazement, joy, freedom, longing, and pain of their experience abroad.

During the three years of preparation for *Fools*, "all the Adams, Eves, Clowns, Cains, Eurydices, Hamlets, and Ophelias patiently performed their somersaults and played Orpheus's song on their flutes. They beat their drums and repeated a hundred times the same motion, often merely for one purpose: not to do it at all."[184] Fialka allowed the production to grow organically out of the company's daily exercises and improvisation, their experiences and relationships, and their awareness of "the wealth of fantasy of the old tragedy and the new clownery."[185] The sources ranged from literature and music, through childhood and philosophy to folk rituals. Through reference to a shared cultural inheritance–the Bible, Ovid, Shakespeare, and Kafka–it aimed to express the unity behind all living things:

> I tried to grasp the secret hidden in the difference of similar things and in the similarity of different things. There is a certain unity and some all-embracing and connecting rhythm hidden inside them.[186]

This unifying element was suggested in different ways, one of which was the fleeting but recurring use of the mirror image, as when Ophelia momentarily comes face to face with her double, or in the climax and reversal of the Metamorphoses sequence: From a circular formation, the group passed from plant life through the bird kingdom and the animal world to the triumphant but cruelly destructive coming of man.

Fools was subtitled *The Strange Dream of a Clown* and the motif of the Clown and his gesture of incomprehension before an unknown power ran through the production. It was present not only in Fialka's roles–Adam, Abel, Hamlet, K–but in Eve, suffering in labour; in Hamlet's Fool, softly weeping; in the piping whistle of Offenbach's Barcarolle. It was there too in Cain's hand, raised to kill; the dictator's drumbeat; and the pain of Othello's eyes rolling behind a black mask. The whole company was sensitive to the rhythm of the production, an essential part of the months of preparation. Both Fialka and the composer Zdeněk Šikola preferred to rely on recorded music, but each actor played at least one instrument and Fialka saw training in intonation and harmony as essential to their work. Drums, recorders, a whistle, lute, trumpet, clarinet, and tuba were used not only in the interludes but also in the Hamlet sequences. Constant training sessions, sometimes improvising or changing roles, ensured the freshness and precision of the performance.

Some critics accused *Fools* of being illustrative. Fialka, however, intended the audience to grasp allusions and parallels from the simplicity of the presentation, not from a detailed interpretation. Others complained that it was difficult to understand; but most audiences delighted in the purples and golds, the swanlike figures against a midnight blue cyclorama, the trumpets, flowers, ladders, and bells. At the same time, they shared the emotions of birth and death, loss and searching, laughter and loneliness. Permanently sold out at home, *Fools* was a triumph at festivals and foreign tours; in London, declared "a sudden glory."[187]

The mime company was initially just one element of the Theatre on the Balustrade, which in autumn 1959 had advanced from its semi-amateur status to become a professional theatre under the jurisdiction of the City of Prague, with Vladimír Vodička as general manager. In November, a Sunday children's matinée was premièred: *The Parrot's Got All the As* by the Miloš Macourek, with lyrics by Pavel Kopta and music by Vodička. The performers were DAMU students; the production was directed by František Čech and later restaged by the students' teacher, Miloš Nedbal. The play—set in a schoolroom with a cast of parrots, monkeys, giraffes, rhinoceroses, a blackboard, and a cupboard—was well received; the daily *Lidová demokracie* (*Popular Democracy*) praised the spontaneity, naturalness, charm, and humour of the young performers.[188]

In December 1959, a student group calling itself the Black Theatre (*Černé divadlo*, later known in English as the Black Light Theatre) was invited to perform. Jiří Srnec, studying puppetry, had rediscovered the classic principle that in certain lighting conditions, actors dressed in black cannot be seen against a black velvet backdrop. His fellow students eagerly joined in experiments that were invited to European student theatre festivals. At that time, membership of a sporting, music, or theatre group represented a rare opportunity to travel, albeit under strict political supervision. The Black Theatre's first full-scale production, *What Next...* was premièred in a subterranean theatre in the Alfa arcade off Wenceslas Square (later the home of Semafor). In 1962 they were invited to appear at the Edinburgh International Festival and that, as Jiří Srnec later wrote, "opened the world to us."[189] The lighthearted invention of the programmes chimed with the mood of discovery at the time, but the Black Theatre never developed into anything more—paradoxically, maybe because it took itself too seriously.

In December 1959, twenty-six-year-old Libor Pešek, best known at the time as a jazz trombonist, had conducted his newly founded *Komorní harmonie* (Prague Chamber Harmony) at the Theatre on the Balustrade in a programme that included a new work by his fellow student Jan Klusák. It was the first Sunday concert of many at which Pešek's *Komorní harmonie* regularly premièred new music. Other concerts ranged from harpsichord and madrigals to folk songs, jazz, and recitations of Apollinaire and Nezval. December saw the beginning of a series of art exhibitions. František Černý suggested in

Divadelní noviny that the Theatre on the Balustrade and the Rokoko Theatre were growing into "the kind of young Prague cultural centres we need... their sympathetic attempts reminiscent of E. F. Burian and his pioneering concept of theatre in the broad cultural sense."[190]

Like the avant-garde between the wars, the artistic movements of the 1960s crossed the boundaries of the disciplines—contrasting with orthodox Communist cultural policy that compartmentalised the arts and tried to maintain the purity of the genres. Theatre, by its nature, draws on the other arts, and in the 1960s was closely associated with the new writers: Hrabal, Kundera, Škvorecký, Klíma, and others who were published, cautiously at first and then in larger editions of twenty, forty, sixty thousand copies, in slim volumes. Young people gathered spontaneously in each other's homes to read aloud and discuss the new works, many of which found their way onto the stage and the screen. The rediscovery of the inter-war avant-garde was a rich source of inspiration—works that had been out of print for two generations appeared in new editions. Experiments in visual art spilled over not only onto the stage but into theatre programmes and posters—the applied arts often had more freedom than the more politically sensitive fine arts. Nevertheless, here too Socialist Realism was disregarded, and abstract and experimental work could be exhibited. Among those who began to re-emerge were the Surrealists, including Vratislav Effenberger, Jan Švankmajer, and theatre designers Libor Fára and Josef Vyleťal. The group had survived in spite of persecution (which nevertheless continued to the end of the 1980s) and in the 1950s experimented with mime performances to libretti by Effenberger; titles included *Wedding Feast* (1950) and *The Last Will Die of Hunger* (1953). These were rehearsed at the *Na slupi* theatre but never performed in public. In December 1960 the eighteen-year-old Prokop Voskovec, whose family background* rendered him politically unacceptable as a drama student, decided to stage his own version of *Ubu Roi* on the small Radar stage in Prague's Holešovice. Already a Surrealist, Voskovec himself played Ubu with a cast of DAMU students, including the impeccably working-class Zdena Holubová as Mère Ubu. The local authority (*Obvodní národní výbor pro Prahu 7*) had initially been persuaded that the production was "anti-militaristic"; however, *Ubu* was banned after two performances—but not before it had been seen by Jan Werich and Alfréd Radok,[191] and briefly reviewed by Václav Havel.[192]

Many of these artistic and theatrical worlds interpenetrated with film, as in the case of Jan Švankmajer, who made his first short film, *The Last Trick*, in 1964. The Balustrade's opening production, *A Thousand Clarinets* (1958) was

* This included his uncle, by this time better known as the star of American stage and screen, George Voskovec.

adapted as a film in 1965. Cinema and the small theatres used the same actors (and pop stars) and were followed by the same audiences. The Czechoslovak New Wave was about to break, with, among others, Miloš Forman, Věra Chytilová, Jan Kačer, Jiří Menzel, Jan Němec, Ivan Passer, and Evald Schorm. It could be said to have begun with *Audition* (1963), Forman's cold-hearted survey of the starstruck amateur talent at Semafor's doors. By 1964, the premières were coming one after the other: *Everyday Courage*, *Diamonds of the Night*, *Loves of a Blonde*, *The Party and the Guests*, *The Shop on the Main Street*, *Pearls from the Depths*, *Closely Watched Trains*, *The Return of the Prodigal Son*, *Daisies*, *The Firemen's Ball*, *The Joke*, *All My Good Countrymen*. The wave could be said to have finally broken with Jiří Menzel's politically outspoken *Larks on a String*, made in 1969 but premièred in 1990.

IVAN VYSKOČIL AT THE THEATRE ON THE BALUSTRADE

Following the success of *Faust, Gretchen, the Maid, and I*, audiences had to wait nearly eighteen months for the Balustrade's next drama production, *Sad Christmas* by Vyskočil, Kopta, and Macourek in October 1960. The critics were expecting great things; *Sad Christmas* was a disaster. Influenced by Friedrich Dürrenmatt, it was a black comedy based on the idea of anti-mortality pills manufactured from corpses. One review read: "The (theatre's) search for its own profile here shows where the path does *not* lead."[193] There was praise for the greater professionalism of the ensemble; the joint direction by Ivan Vyskočil and Miroslav Macháček, and the team work of the actors, including Ljuba Hermanová, Václav Sloup (one of Miloš Nedbal's pupils) and Jan Preučil as the crematorium director who "with elegantly greying temples, palely powdered face, nervously shifting fingers, and decorative little yawns drew a deft caricature of the intellectual with a sensitive soul."[194] But in the same review Milan Lukeš described the play as a badly mixed cocktail of exotic ingredients which lacked punch and left a muddy sediment at the bottom. Jan Werich, who had taken to sitting in the theatre's busy office, was not amused by the play either.

For the theatre's next production Vyskočil chose a format closely related to the text-appeal. *Hitchhike* (1961) was a collage of separate pieces linked by the character of the Demonstrator. Vyskočil invited a young stagehand recommended to him by Jan Werich to coauthor the piece, Václav Havel. In the end, only three pieces (mainly by Vyskočil) were used: "Future Prospects," "Motomorphosis," and "Whither the Wind, Thither Pejča or, Which Way Gregor Blows." "Motomorphosis" took the form of a lecture on the recent phenomenon of humans changing into motor cars; "Future Prospects" depicted a family thrown into a new social situation by winning a car in a lottery; and the concluding playlet assessed human nature through different attitudes towards hitchhikers.

The direct approach of the Demonstrator, who linked the pieces, contrasted with the absurdist language and distorted values of the "acted" characters. In the playlets, the car was seen as a barrier to communication, the high road as neutral ground for an encounter, while hitchhiking itself represented freedom of choice, both for the hiker and the driver. *Hitchhike* also introduced what was to become one of Havel's recurring themes: the mechanisation of man as he invests his values in material objects. Vyskočil extended the principle of the text-appeal in a line at the bottom of the programme; the visitor was asked to fill in his own name: "For as audience you have played with us one of the main roles in this performance." As the Demonstrator, Vyskočil aimed to establish a personal relationship with the audience:

> For the performance to have its full ideological and psychological meaning, the Demonstrator and the audience must be in real, not "pretended" contact, he must talk to them as though he is the author of words and ideas that just occurred to him.[195]

The effect of this contact was to distance the three "acted" pieces, thus enabling the audience to analyse and evaluate the action in those pieces. The undisguised approach of the Demonstrator and the audience's response also contrasted with examples of deformed communication between the acted characters. They expressed themselves not only through a distorted sense of values, but also in the language with its use of cliché and wordplay. It was a theatrical device that Havel was to use in his own work, very soon.

Vyskočil invited Václav Hudeček, who had worked with Alfréd Radok at the National Theatre, to direct *Hitchhike*. Hudeček brought a firmer discipline into Vyskočil's liberal regime. He handled the technical elements with expertise, paying attention to lighting, costumes (embellished with road signs), and music by Jaroslav Jakoubek. However, analysing the production in *Divadelní noviny*, Jan Grossman noted that none of this was altogether to the advantage of the piece as originally conceived. Hudeček focused on the set pieces of wordplay and situation comedy and drilled the actors to perform them with stylised exaggeration and external precision of speech and gesture. Grossman felt that this emphasis on stage business and detailed perfectionism detracted from the intention of the script and overshadowed its analytic qualities:

> The required professionalization of staging implies a decreasing sensitivity for the individual characteristics of the Theatre on the Balustrade and thus its certain conventionalisation; this problem must be solved on both sides. The leadership must above all

achieve its own company feeling and... convince the actor that his primary task is not to play a role but to create modern theatre.

The Theatre on the Balustrade, led by Ivan Vyskočil, certainly has this strength, especially in thought and content, and in this is rare, if not unique.[196]

Ivan Vyskočil was also aware of this conflict between the pressures of professional theatre and his personal inclination towards "a theatre of encounters." *Hitchhike* played in repertoire with the mime ensemble for the next eighteen months, with no new premières by the drama ensemble (one was announced, but came to nothing). In October 1961, the newspaper of Charles University mourned the decline of the theatre, no longer experimenting, no longer a crossroads for talent.[197]

The theatre's early success had culminated with an internal crisis. Except for the mime ensemble, many of the founders had left (songwriter Jaromír Vomáčka had joined the *Laterna magika*), and functions had become more precise, with sharper distinctions between management, actors, musicians, designers, and technicians. All this was against the wishes of the polymorphic Ivan Vyskočil. Some years later he explained what he felt to be the misunderstanding of his work:

The critics' attitude arose from the idea that what we were doing was a semi-prepared form, a compromise... Today I can see it was natural for them at that time to assume that we still had not learnt how to do the conventional finished product. They wrote about the necessity of professionalism. For a critic the criterion is a certain form that he knows from experience. We cannot blame him for not being able to imagine any other form.[198]

Early in 1962 Jan Grossman was invited to become artistic director of the drama ensemble at the Theatre on the Balustrade. Vyskočil returned to Reduta.

JAN GROSSMAN AT THE THEATRE ON THE BALUSTRADE

On the question of whether theatre had grown away from the playgoer* or the playgoer from the theatre, the most pertinent answer could no longer be concealed; the playgoer was by his very nature a man of his time, a real individual sorting out the meaning of his own life—or if you prefer, his relationship to social reality—by means of his own experiences. While the theatre, taking the dogmatic approach of ideological and political plan-

* In Czech, the word is *divák*—"spectator" or "viewer." This word is commonly used where English would refer to "the audience."

ning, was oriented towards the abstract playgoer. This abstraction certainly seemed a lot more elevated and historically worthy than the mere concrete playgoers. There was only one thing wrong with the abstract playgoer; he didn't fill the theatre.[199]

So wrote Jan Grossman, shortly after his appointment as director of the drama ensemble at the Theatre on the Balustrade. Grossman, whose career as a literary scholar and critic had been blocked by the Communists, had turned instead to the theatre. He had attended the Prague English Grammar School before the war, and was at home, too, in German literature. He wrote analytically, with reference to the writers of the past—an approach that was not in accordance with Socialist Realism. In the late 1950s it became increasingly difficult for him to publish; he lost his position as editor on *Mladá fronta* (*Young Front*), the newspaper of the Czechoslovak Youth Union, and moved to the dramaturgy department of the National Theatre. Here he came under the influence of Alfréd Radok, whom he regarded as having been his most important teacher. When Radok was forced to leave the National Theatre in 1949, Grossman left with him, hoping to work with Jiří Frejka at the Vinohrady Theatre. Instead, he found a position as dramaturge at the State Theatre in Brno, where he directed his first productions. At this time the Brno theatre was under the directorship of the traditionalist Aleš Podhorský; the following year it passed to Zdeněk Míka, pursuing his upwardly mobile post-Zlín career.

In 1953 Grossman returned to Prague to spend the next three years with E. F. Burian. He took over from Burian direction of the third part of Zuzana Kočová's adaptation of Balzac's *Père Goriot*. Grossman regarded this production as routine; a continuation of the run of productions he had directed in Brno. In the autumn of 1954 he rehearsed a production which he felt set him on a direction of his own choosing. The play was the anti-militarist *Hagenbeck* (1920) by Fraňa Šrámek, best known as a lyrical poet. *Hagenbeck* belongs to an earlier period when Šrámek was full of revolutionary fervour. It is a political play, capturing the turbulent atmosphere of the last days of the Habsburg Monarchy. Grossman admired the aggressiveness of the play, the roughness of its writing, and the sharpness of its satire. It was for him a work in progress, a drama that can only be completed when confronted by an audience.

In 1956, during the illusory thaw, Grossman was allowed to return to his literary career, and left Burian to become an editor with *Československý spisovatel* (Czechoslovak Writer: before nationalisation, the Borový publishing house). His first article for *Divadlo* appeared in February 1957: "The Czech classics in the context of the contemporary Czech theatre," in which he analysed current productions of Tyl, Jirásek, Stroupežnický, and the Mrštík brothers at the National Theatre. Later that year he contributed articles about Ber-

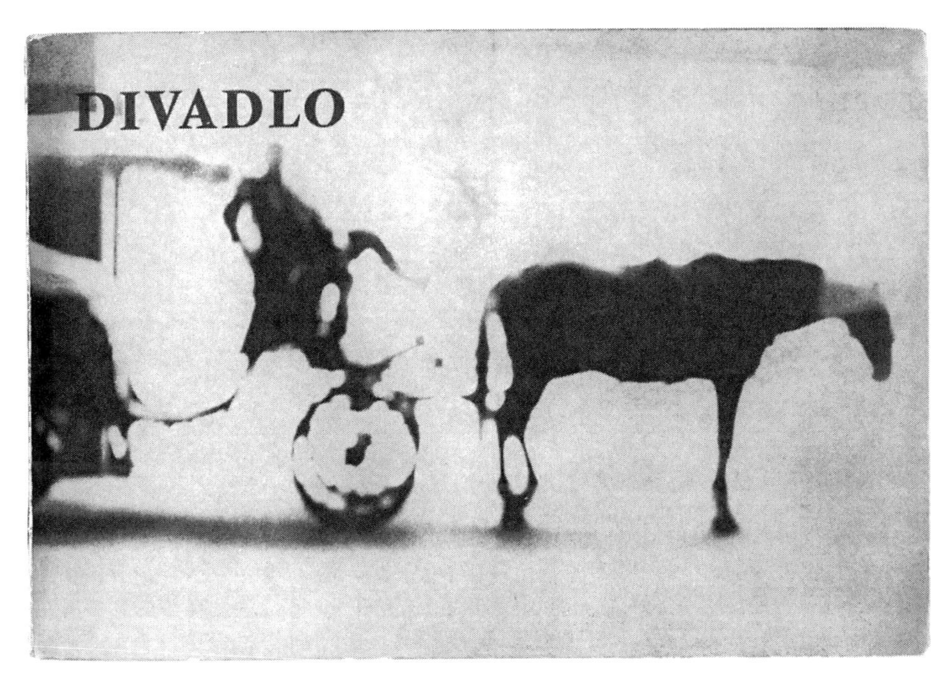

Cover of the journal *Divadlo* (*Theatre*), January 1964. Photograph by Josef Koudelka.

tolt Brecht, Eugene O'Neill, and the contemporary "crisis" in Czechoslovak literature. He became a regular contributor to *Divadlo*, joining the editorial board in March 1966.

In 1963, a seminar on the small theatre phenomenon was held in Karlovy Vary. The September issue of *Divadlo* was devoted to papers given at the conference, including those by Milan Lukeš, Jaroslav Vostrý, Karel Kraus, and Jan Grossman. Grossman introduced "The world of the small theatre"[200] with an analysis of the term "small theatre" and whether it was defined by physical space, company size, choice of material, or the actual performance. He believed that the audience sensed more intuitively than the critics what it meant; that the quality of "small theatre" was inherent not so much in its form as in its function. The concept "small theatre" was the expression of certain tendencies in a given artistic and historical situation, capable of performing a task in which conventional theatre had failed. Looking back at the development of the Czech theatre over the past fifteen years and analysing what had happened during the period of Socialist Realism, Grossman concluded that in practice the theatre broke with what it simultaneously extolled: its close relationship with contemporary life. In modelling its work on a previously conceived ideological framework, the theatre had simplified and even vulgarised the experience of a limited group of people; whereas each individual's relationship towards society is based on a continuous process of confrontation between his private world and the "whole world." The more single-minded the ideological approach, the more abstract was the effect of the presentation on the spectator, however realistic the theatrical presentation. Grossman believed that conventional theatre, more concerned with portraying static results than the processes that led to those results, had ignored the specific problems of its audience and failed to tap the personal involvement which leads to understanding. Theatre had lost the adventure of discovering the unknown reality, for its task was to show only what was already known.

At the end of the 1950s, he continued, with the relaxation of official insistence on Socialist Realism the range of theatrical possibilities had expanded, but still lacked that relationship with contemporary concerns. The long period of isolation had provoked uncritical adoption of Western forms and repertoire, which invoked the stigma of "cosmopolitanism." A superficial enthusiasm for Dürrenmatt and Brecht was combined with a "rediscovery" of the pre-war avant-garde—which for the most part meant using the means rather than turning to the principles. So that although the second period appeared to be the antithesis of the first, they shared a common feature: an inability to break with convention and to relate to the time.

Grossman continued by analysing those features that enabled the small theatre movement to change tradition radically. First, the small theatres were not part of institutions that had to look for performance material to keep themselves in existence; they had emerged in response to an urgent need to communicate. Consequently, and because they were small, they could have a flexible structure and avoid the usual administrative machinery. Thirdly, the nature of the small form meant that it was not expected to be politically committed in the same way as a full-scale play; it was able to slip through uncensored, expressing only the personal view of its author. Fourthly, it was theatre in a state of growth. The large theatres also used unconventional techniques (flexible time, metaphoric foreshortening, symbolism, alternation of narrative with drama, the actor stepping into the audience, and other tricks of breaking illusion), but they did so for the sake of experiment, rather than as an organic part of the content. The small theatres used a variety of material, not to prove that it *could* be used, but as a source of energy. Finally, Grossman considered the founders of the small theatres, few if any of them originating in the professional theatre. Entering the theatre without inherited traditional knowledge and techniques but anxious to communicate, they had to work their way towards a new professionalism, based on practice and experience.

The question of professionalism in the small theatres had been hotly debated since the previous autumn, wrote Grossman.* The combination of youth-

* See p. 181–182.

fulness, aesthetic naivety, improvisation, and bohemian negligence and liberality gave the impression of a workshop where the spectators' participation was welcome and necessary. What took place in the small theatres was not a definitive performance but work in progress. "Mistakes" were unimportant in this atmosphere of "incompleteness," which almost gave the impression that the participants were "playing at theatre." Grossman believed that this could not be a permanent stage, and that this "amateurism" should be the starting point for a new kind of theatre. He compared the development of a young theatre to that of a young writer who, after an early success, must work on his talent, set himself tasks, solve problems, and understand his limitations. But for a theatre this was a more complex process; this was where companies came into crisis, either disintegrating or finding an inner creative strength.

At the Theatre on the Balustrade, the process of professionalisation had begun at an early stage and the drama ensemble had oscillated between different tendencies: "One aim got in the way of another. Elaborately developed details obscured rather than supported the whole. The intended idea did not always find the most suitable and communicative means of realisation." These conflicts highlighted problems Grossman believed were common to the whole development of small theatre. He tried to distinguish between the Theatre on the Balustrade's overall purpose and the means used to fulfil it. He did not think the theatre would lose its special character if it stopped devising its own plays and drew on the "normal" repertoire. He was more interested in essential dramaturgical principles, which he defined as the effort to analyse the problems leading to contemporary conflicts, and then to choose the material and method to express them in the theatre.

To explain this, Grossman coined the word *apelativnost*, derived from the same root as the English "appeal" (and not unrelated to the text-appeal). *Apelativnost* is the quality inherent in a theatre production that does not reach a conclusion by answering the questions it has raised, but rather, by demonstrating them to the audience, invites its response. He had recognised the quality in *Hitchhike* and wanted the Theatre on the Balustrade to continue this analytical form of theatre: "Theatre, like all the arts, should not only describe life but help to change it. An old and simple truth; tireless and new must be the method of doing it."[201] He reiterated his belief in man, not in the abstract but as a specific individual, involved in a practical way in the increasingly complex pressures of the contemporary world. It is a world not of bare facts but of interpretations of those facts, a world of conventions, illusions, ideas, hopes, and fears. Art helps man to disentangle these impressions. It cannot solve problems, but it can expose them.

From this central point of his paper, Grossman returned to the question of the small forms—"songs, sketches, monologues"—with which the work of the small theatres originated. He saw them as being peripheral by their nature, but also material from which an artist like Chekhov, Hašek, Kafka, or Chaplin can create an integrated work of art. This integration was beginning to happen in the small theatres, but it could only be worked out through practice, not to a predetermined plan. This did not invalidate theoretical analysis; Grossman pointed out the close connection between the intellect and the imagination. Analysis was essential in identifying those moments in small form theatre capable of development.

Grossman quoted Milan Lukeš's paper at the Karlovy Vary conference, in which Lukeš put the small theatre movement into the context of a worldwide trend in theatre towards dialogue between stage and auditorium. Grossman described it as a trend that roots the theatre in the contemporary social situation. In a world that superficially offers greater opportunities, we are increasingly limited by bureaucracy—not simply paperwork, but fixed systems and structures that determine our actions, define our roles, and above all are self-propagating. It is a world where man is no longer the subject but the object; a completed world, which excludes the unexpected and individual. Human nature, especially in youth, looks for space for its own experiences and creativity, for adventure. Jazz and the small theatres were criticised for their escapism: "But escapism is not always the fault of the one who is escaping." Jazz, with its natural rhythms, its irregularities, improvisation, and incompleteness, was the human response to the twentieth-century world of bureaucratic uniformity. The popular forms of the small theatres were capable of unleashing a creative energy vital for the development of contemporary society.

Jan Grossman delivered this talk to the 1963 Karlovy Vary conference after a difficult year running the drama ensemble at the Theatre on the Balustrade. His first task had been to revive a theatre that had lost its reputation. Few of the actors in the *Hitchhike* ensemble were interested in remaining at the theatre. (Unemployment was not a threat under Communism, even in the acting profession. The correct number of actors was trained annually and actors could remain at the same theatre for life.) After many rejections, Grossman put together an ensemble led by Ljuba Hermanová, then appearing in Fialka's *Nine Hats on Prague*. With an assorted group of largely inexperienced actors, Grossman set out to demonstrate what he meant by a theatre which could "professionalise within its own means" and achieve productions which were more relevant, interesting, and provocative than those put on by the National Theatre, with its infinitely superior resources. He started by asking Miloš Macourek (best known as a children's writer) and Václav Havel to write a play in which Hermanová could star. Installed in an apartment with a typist, "for ages we tried and rejected all kinds of themes, until it proved that the best theme was how we tried and rejected all kinds of themes."[202] It was a play about the writing of a play, about the frustrations and miseries of writing about a fictional Hermanová and her husband, director, and dramaturge. Premièred in November 1962, it was called *Mrs. Hermanová's Best Rocks* (a pun in Czech, as *rok* means "year"). The designer was Vladimír Nývlt, with whom Grossman had worked in Burian's theatre; music was by Vladimír Vodička, lyrics by Pavel Kopta). Sergej Machonin noted that it was a production made up of "chanson, abbreviation, sketch, idea, joke, gag, music, a small stage, and a few actors."[203] Milan Lukeš commented that the theatre was "back to its old form."[204] It had returned to the simplicity of its beginnings; to making the best of its performers' strengths while ideas were articulated that could not yet be integrated into a unified dramatic structure. The critics praised Hermanová while recognising the satirical intention of the production. Macourek and Havel mocked not only the vulgarisation of such theatre forms as the *Laterna magika* but also, in the character of the dramaturge (Václav Sloup), the kind of people who live in a world of slogans, formulae, memoranda, and resolutions. It was a world more absurd than the Surrealists' creations, made specific by the meaningless procedures of its originators, who were not necessarily living a double life, but were totally convinced of the rightness of their actions and unaware of life's ambiguities and contradictions.

NO HEROES LIVE IN THEBES WITH OTOMAR KREJČA

Mrs. Hermanová's Best Rocks guaranteed Grossman the popular success he needed to bring the theatre back to public attention. While the production was taking shape, he was contemplating a major change of gear that, although in the spirit of *apelativnost*, would disrupt the public's expectations. The play he chose was Claus Hubalek's *Die Stunde der Antigone*, a verse play originally written for German television. This contemporary retelling of the Antigone story was adapted for the Balustrade under the title *No Heroes Live in Thebes* (November 1962). Grossman invited Otomar Krejča to direct, considering him "one of the few directors for whom directing means more than an expert, technically perfect staging arbitrarily based on his own taste."[205] (It was significant that the man who until recently had held the top job in Czechoslovak theatre should accept the invitation from a struggling fringe theatre.) Libor Fára designed costumes in stark symbolic colours against a set of simple sliding white cubes by Josef Svoboda. Sergej Machonin described the production as a play about truth—Antigone's truth and Creon's "truth"—and about lies, the lies on which the prosperity of Thebes is based.[206]

Grossman was criticised for staging a play apparently so distant from the Balustrade genre of comedy, text-appeal, and popular music. He was prepared for this reaction; in the programme for *Mrs. Hermanová's Best Rocks*, he had written:

> In many places the boom in these small forms became mechanised, limited to an effect that was forceful but transient… for the Theatre on the Balustrade the small form is not a dogma but just another starting point.[207]

In the programme to *No Heroes Live in Thebes*, he went further:

> The most interesting feature of small theatre was not these small forms but rather, as it were, its "appellative" ability, the ability to turn from the stage direct to the audience, to confront the play-event-problem with the audience's experience, to renounce elaborate illusionistic staging and concentrate everything on the substance, on the actual playing; on the idea, on the essence of communication and appeal.
>
> The moment comes—at least, that's how it seems to us—when the ability that has been cultivated by the small form and its forceful but transient means (allusion, gag, stage anecdote) has to be invested in a stronger and more organised form. New genres must be sought where the theatre can reflect contemporary life more consistently and in a wider measure.[208]

THE INVENTION OF THE GRENOBLE

To circumvent preconceptions, Grossman invented a genre of his own for the next production at the Balustrade: *The Demented Dove* (February 1963) was described as a "grenoble."

The Demented Dove began as the work of a Brno student, Radim Vašinka. In 1959, influenced by E. F. Burian, Vašinka and a group of Brno students (mainly of medicine and science) had founded a poetry theatre in Brno, *Divadlo X* (known as *X-ka*). On the strength of its guest appearance in Prague, Grossman invited Vašinka to work with him. Vašinka assembled poems by contemporary Czech writers (including František Halas, Josef Kainar, and Miroslav Holub) about the relationship of freedom of thought and action to freedom of expression. The everyday vocabulary, simple constructions, and concrete images appealed directly to the audience's intellect and imagination. Grossman asked Václav Havel for three contrasting speeches, demonstrating the deformation of language in official life. Inserted into the script and declaimed from one of the windows opening into the auditorium at gallery level, these speeches used the prevaricating phraseology of drama theory adapted to new ideological viewpoints:

The stage grenoble—and who would deny it, comrades?—is a theatrical genre that has stagnated here in recent years. Last year's conference on the state of our grenobles warned us of this.[209]

The history of the theatre has taught us that the appearance of the grenoble on the theatrical map is always a symptom of crisis; we call to mind for example the exceptional development of the grenoble in the age of darkness.[210]

The stage grenoble is, however, an unusually complicated manifestation, and today we know that it contains many positive features as well as many negative features.[211]

The fluidity of the sequences demanded a simple setting, which Josef Vyleťal provided in the form of three portable sets of wall bars. The actors could sit on these at different levels, or turn them sideways to represent the bars of a cage. Certain sections of *The Demented Dove* were linked by the staging; for example, in one sequence an actress was identified with the image of a caged goldfinch. She remained centre stage as through trapped by the surrounding dogmas and banalities, dominated by the "master"—a character whose features changed, but who remained essentially the same. Other passages were built on metaphoric contrasts or the juxtaposition of different levels of time. The actors did not identify with the voices, but demonstrated certain types in certain situations, sometimes through contrast:

Advice to follow a wise and cautious life is given by a lout, a fable about egotism is spoken in the wise and prudent tones usually reserved for the loveliest fairy tales, the story of a sordid love affair made to sound warm and tender.[212]

Jindřich Černý, in *Lidová demokracie*, commented on the variety of techniques employed by the actors and the wide range of tones: lyrical and parodic, playful and crude.[213] He defined the aim as a direct appeal to the audience to make a critical assessment of the information presented to them; Grossman believed that life (human relationships, speech, actions) is more bounded by convention than people realise, and he aimed to identify hidden reactions.

Karel Kraus wrote about the precise intellectual stress of the dramaturgy.[214] In emphasising the nature of each item through suggestion rather than realism, Grossman treated the poetry as material for theatrical performance. He further "theatricalised" the production by inserting the lectures and projecting drawings by Jiří Jirásek that "did not illustrate the theme of the evening but reworked it in their own perceptive way."[215] There was music on drums and double bass. The performance closed with an excerpt from a 1947 lecture by the avant-garde poet and disillusioned Communist politician František Halas. Grossman considered it a poetic and intellectual synthesis without parallel in postwar literature—a creed.[216] In part:

Be courageous and fear not. What use is knowledge without the courage to express it, even though painful. The silent will stand terribly accused.

The completion of the revolution is freedom; not an empty freedom, but a freedom that is law and conscious submission. It is a way of attaining the ideal. Be the epicentre of its radiance.

Live with it through its fevers and its chills; do not be a traitor to what you know, and do not listen without asking questions. Man again becomes the measure of things; his dignity must be restored.

Be humble, for humility is the greatness of proud souls.

Detest the idyll, assault it in its hiding places and in all its forms.

Your teeth are young and healthy, so refuse pre-digested pap and bite out your sustenance for yourselves.

Always take a stand against what is slick and tawdry.

Be stubborn rather than yes-men....[217]

VÁCLAV HAVEL'S *THE GARDEN PARTY*

Grossman's programme was built on three groups of plays. One was Western drama (particularly the Theatre of the Absurd) not yet seen in Czechoslovakia; another was classic works of literature in adaptation; and the third was the work of new Czech writers. The groups had themes in common, enabling the attentive playgoer to follow certain ideas from play to play, from Jarry's *Ubu Roi* through to Kundera's *Cock-up*. Grossman did not have the resources to audition for his ideal interpreters, but had to make the best of those he had. Nevertheless, wherever *Memorandum* is played in the world, the names of the three female characters evoke Marie Málková, Hana Smrčková, and Helena Lehká, who created those roles.* In the original production, their physical presence helped to link the themes to the rest of the Balustrade's repertoire.

Of the Czech writers who were premièred at the Balustrade, Václav Havel was to be most closely identified with the theatre. Born into a wealthy and cultured family, Havel had the misfortune to reach adolescence at the turn of the 1940s and 1950s, when privileges were reversed. Entrance to university required political vetting of the whole family, and instead of studying at the Film Academy, he found himself attending evening classes on the economics of motor transport. Denied the opportunity to study dramaturgy, he had to rely on his own resources. Curious about everything, he enjoyed the company

* In the case of the male characters, Havel uses the actors' surnames—although he sometimes plays with them: Sloup (column) becomes Pilíř (pillar).

of the intellectuals in his family's circle of friends and later, in spite of his shyness, sought out writers and artists for himself. Many (if not all of them) were out of favour with the authorities. Among those of interest were the members of the suppressed Group 42.* Aged barely twenty, Havel made his first public appearance in November 1956 at a conference of the newly founded literary magazine for young people, *Květen* (*May*), in defence of Group 42. It was an indication that this reserved reader had a practical mind and was able to deploy strategies, techniques, and operating details. In this respect, theatre practice, which began to interest him during his compulsory military service, brought together his intellectual and his practical abilities. The speech—delivered at the chateau of Dobříš in front of leading members of the Writers' Union—alerted the literary world to an unconventional young thinker. In 1959 Jan Werich, a family friend, offered Havel a job as stagehand at the ABC, where he not only learnt the techniques of the Liberated Theatre firsthand but also worked as assistant to Alfréd Radok on Chekhov's *The Swedish Match*. It was the start of a lifelong friendship, in which Havel's greatest wish was for Radok to direct one of his plays.† In 1960, Ivan Vyskočil, intending to use Havel's skills as a writer, offered him a post as lighting technician at the Theatre on the Balustrade. (It was still the time when everyone did everything.) Havel started work on *The Garden Party*, which, however, was still unfinished in 1963. Grossman despatched him to a mountain hotel to finish the play away from distractions.

The Garden Party follows the fortunes of the characterless Hugo Pludek (Václav Sloup), born into a parody of the conventional middle-class family. His parents talk in clichés that sound like solid traditional virtues but are meaningless distortions: "Dear son! Life is a struggle! And you are a dog! Stone walls do not an iron bar!"[218] Family connections win him an invitation to the garden party of the Liquidation Office, where he encounters two secretaries versed in everyday bureaucratic jargon. They are interrupted by Ferda Plzák (Zdeněk Procházka), a liberal-minded member of the new generation of officials: "You see, I'm quite an ordinary man made of flesh and bones, milk and blood; in short—as they say—I'm one of you!"[219] Plzák's views disorient the secretaries to the extent that they begin to talk about love in a parody of the Fraňa Šrámek lyric school of poetry, an experience from which one of them (Marie Málková) never recovers. Hugo listens and waits for an opportunity to experiment with language as a means to advancement:

---

* See p. 89.

† It seemed likely this would be *The Memorandum* in 1965, but circumstances intervened. Eleven years later, when Havel was in internal exile and Radok in external, Radok was engaged to direct Havel's Vaněk plays in Vienna. He suffered a fatal heart attack shortly after his arrival.

In fact, they were both sort of right and sort of wrong—or rather, on the contrary—both were wrong and both were right, weren't they? I mean, they were, were they not? [*Pause*] Yes, I agree, they were not, although I don't think they were.[220]

In a war of words, Hugo eventually defeats the director of the Inauguration Office (Jan Libíček). The play closes with a long monologue from the previously monosyllabic youth:

In man there is nothing fixed, eternal, absolute; man is continuous change—a change with a proud ring to it, of course! [...] Truth is just as complicated and many-sided as everything else in the world—the magnet, the telephone, the poems of Branislav, the magnet—and we are all a little bit what we were yesterday and a little bit what we are today; and also a little bit we are not.[221]

The subject of *The Garden Party* is language—or rather, the political abuse of language. Havel, who had suffered compulsory re-education in Marxism-Leninism, was alert to cliché, phraseology, and the verbal conventions most people take for granted. He recognised the difference between language forged out of personal experience and the platitudes adopted to increase a person's self-esteem: "For truth is not only what is said, it depends on who says it, and why."[222] The characters in the play control and manipulate each other by a mechanical use of language which is both grotesque and terrifying; terrifying, because to the Prague audiences in the autumn of 1963 it was instantly familiar. They realised that the robotic characters onstage mirrored behaviour in the outside world and that, as part of the same mechanism, they themselves were being similarly controlled and manipulated.

Some critics judged that Havel lacked theatrical qualities: "He is not in fact a dramatic author. He is an author able to see very clearly the philosophical problems in life... He dissects such problems like a physician."[223] Jan Grossman saw it differently. He recognised that although Havel's material was not traditionally theatrical, its relevance evoked a response from the audience. The Czech word *zkouška* means not only "rehearsal" but also "test" or "examination." The small theatres were testing the truth and relevance of their work in an appeal to the audience. Grossman wrote in 1967:

Havel functions as a dramatist not when he is invited or when there are plays to be written, but at the moment when he senses the latent dramatic quality of his theme, when he realises that dramatic expression is the *only* and *necessary* expression of his material... However much he has learned from other people's models, Havel derives his dramatic method from his own view of reality and from his own subject, one he has discovered in it the principle characteristics of the dialogue; these remain the most valuable feature of both [*The Garden Party* and *The Memorandum*] and the essence of their universal resonances.[224]

Havel was not an author who saw human beings as pitiful insects, destroyed by forces they could neither see nor understand. The characters in *The Garden Party* are abstract mechanisms, perfectly (Hugo) or imperfectly (the secretary played by Málková) adapted to a mechanical society. The human beings who interested Havel were the ones in the audience; they were capable of response and had the ability to change things. Although he was often classified as a playwright of the Theatre of the Absurd, Havel's philosophy was never nihilistic. It was rather that his ideas of structure and technique were influenced by his early reading of writers difficult to obtain in Czechoslovakia, such as Arthur Adamov and Samuel Beckett. Of Eugene Ionesco he wrote:

Ionesco's plays showed me much that was valuable, for example, that one can talk complete nonsense onstage and yet the play will give an impression of being "true to life" or, on the contrary, one can talk as though "true to life" yet the play can be complete nonsense. But I don't want to set myself up as Ionesco's pupil. Suppose he were to come and give me a lesson.[225]

Grossman doubted whether Havel's plays belonged to "the so-called art of the absurd." A point regularly made but worth reiteration is that situations which appear illogical and absurd to citizens of a Western democracy were familiar occurrences within Czechoslovakia and the other Soviet bloc countries. There was nothing more absurd than everyday life. Havel's treatment of such situations was a natural progression from the satire of the small form theatres. Karel Kraus observed that although *The Garden Party* is a four-act play, in content it more closely resembles the one-act play which "leads primarily to an analysis of the situation, ascertains, mirrors (maybe distorts) a social of psychological action or a character. It does not draw the spectator into the play but provokes him, does not suggest a solution but counts rather on his intellectual revolt."[226]

He pointed out that drama with an opinion to express tends naturally towards the choice of a specific image, rather than drawing the audience in to identify with the complex conflicts of the characters onstage.

The characters in *The Garden Party* had no existence outside the function they performed on stage; they fulfilled their specific role and then dematerialised as efficiently as Hugo at the end of his final speech. He extended the limits of the genre by moving from variously formulated attacks on a multitude of targets to focusing on a single object (the abuse of language). The process of pruning away superfluities had taken place not only in the writing but in the rehearsing.

The use of musical techniques, frequent on the small stages, is not immediately apparent. Paul Trensky, however, has pointed out how Havel uses changes in tempo, repetition, retardation, and gradation to promote the action of the play.[227] A further link with the small stages is in the device of the "gag" as Havel describes it in his essay "The Anatomy of the Gag" (*Anatomie gagu*). In this he analyses three gags from silent film and notes that a gag is created where conventionally acceptable activities are juxtaposed in a way that disrupts our expectations. The gag also possesses its own internal logic; it defies our presuppositions with a perfectly explicable chain of events. Vladimír Mráček, in his thesis "Václav Havel & Co." (*Václav Havel a ti druzi*), described Havel's language structure as a series of gags created from two basic elements, neither of which in itself is absurd, only in relation to the other. For example, Pludek's juxtaposition of cliché and proverb: "The middle classes are the backbone of the nation. And why? Not even a hag carries hemp-seed to the attic alone."[228]

Grossman had invited Otomar Krejča to direct *The Garden Party*, as his second production for the Balustrade. Krejča again brought Jan Klusák with him as composer and Josef Svoboda as designer; a remarkably "Olympian" team to concern itself with a young author's first play. However, the rehearsal period coincided with that of *Romeo and Juliet* at the National Theatre, where Krejča's star was rising again, and direction of *The Garden Party* can be credited in part to Grossman. Krejča turned a blind eye when Grossman and Havel feared that Josef Svoboda's design, a technically complex mirror structure, undermined the directness of the play. The overnight vandalisation of the set before the play opened remained a mystery for nearly half a century, and *The Garden Party* was performed within a simple molecular frame.

UBU ROI, BECKETT, AND IONESCO

With *The Garden Party*, Jan Grossman was launched on a programme that over the next five years would bring the Theatre on the Balustrade to the forefront of European theatre. Havel's controversial success was followed in less than six months by Grossman's production of Alfred Jarry's *Ubu Roi* (May 1964); a programme insert connected the production with Jindřich Honzl's Czechoslovak première of 1927. The adaptation by Grossman and Miloš Macourek of the translation by Prokop Voskovec* incorporated Jarry's sequel,

* Elder brother of Jiří Voskovec, and father of the actor and theatre director bearing the same name (Prokop Jr. is remembered chiefly for his daring production of *Ubu Roi* in 1960).

Ubu enchainé, which fascinated them "by its merciless unmasking of the bureaucratisation of freedom–freedom which becomes a strictly controlled order"[229] and parts of *Faustroll* and *Ubu sur la butte*. It was presented as a travesty of a Shakespeare history play where the wheel of fortune rises and falls, not in an empire of majesty, but on a dunghill. In a world created out of the rubbish of contemporary society, the clumsy, brutish Ubu becomes the personification of totalitarian government. *Ubu Roi* confronted the audience with a world not far removed from *The Garden Party*, peopled by characters living out a petty existence protecting their valueless status and possessions. Peter Brook wrote about the production in 1968:

> This version ignored every one of Jarry's images and indications. It invented an up-to-the-minute pop-art style of its own, made out of dustbins, garbage, and ancient iron bedsteads. M. Ubu was no masked Humpty Dumpty, but a recognisable and shifty slob; Mme. Ubu was a sleazy, attractive whore; the social context was clear. From the first shot of M. Ubu stumbling in his underpants out of bed while a nagging voice from the pillows asked why he wasn't king of Poland, the audience's belief was caught and it could follow the Surrealist developments of the story because it accepted the primitive situation and characters on their own terms.[230]

Jan Grossman had been preparing the production since 1962, when there had been a possibility that Jan Werich (who had played Ubu at the Liberated Theatre in 1928) might take the leading role. In 1964 it was played by Jan Libíček, "a tun of a man with the face of a dissatisfied Gouda cheese."[231] He delivers the famous "Merdre!" (in Czech, *Hovnajs!*) as a throwaway line in response to Mère Ubu's sensuously outstretched arms. The characters were identifiable types, with costumes emphasising or discretely underlining the roles: Mère Ubu (Marie Málková) in a short tight skirt and high heels, the King (Zdeněk Procházka) taking a military salute wearing a shabby but neatly pressed civilian suit. Sometimes the images might be more complex. Jan Přeučil played the composite character Čuřislav as a parody of Austro-Hungarian correctness in a liftboy's uniform. Stage furniture and properties were similarly employed for economy of meaning. Like children playing on a wasteland, the actors made use of the discarded utensils of everyday life provided by the designer Libor Fára. The objects took their meaning from how they were handled: The bedstead could turn into a saluting dais or prison bars. In the chapel scene, two sceneshifters entered and as they shifted the props, perfunctorily bowed before the "altar" (the bedstead) and crossed themselves with holy water from the "stoup" (a dustbin).

The soundtrack by Zdeněk Šikola was a combination of dodecaphonic music, traditional Czech wind music, and *musique concrète*, recorded by a seven-piece orchestra (bass clarinet, tenor saxophone, trumpet, trombone, drums, accordion, and violin). For the leading motif he chose the melody of a running brook, incongruously fresh and clean in the context of such foul, sweating visual images. Some passages were accompanied by romantic interludes of programme music: banal images of birdsong, brooks, mills, and meadows contrasting with the ugliness onstage.

Grossman intended the playgoer to ask questions about what he saw onstage. To this end he brought Alfred Jarry's pataphysical theories and machines into the printed programme, the foyer, and the auditorium. Jarry, who invented the concept of pataphysics in the course of writing *Ubu Roi*, defined it as the science of imaginary solutions. Grossman presented the machines as images of materialism, of those processes in life which society tends so carefully that they work to perfection, but only to their own advantage. In his published analysis of the production,[232] Grossman drew a parallel between these innocuous machines and the most absurd machine of all: the Nazi machine for genocide. It did not take a great stretch of the imagination to see an analogy with the mechanics of the existing regime. The production, for all its robust comedy, carried a dark contemporary relevance, whose roots Grossman acknowledged to be as much in Kafka as in Jarry.

In the spring of 1964, Jan Grossman invited Václav Hudeček, director of *Hitchhike*, to rehearse a double bill of Ionesco's *The Bald Prima Donna* and *The Lesson* and, concurrently, Beckett's *Waiting for Godot* – the first Beckett to be staged in Czechoslovakia. Hudeček was one of the most knowledgeable Czech directors on the new drama and had even met Beckett when in Paris with Alfréd Radok and the *Laterna magika*. Hudeček had recently run a series of Sunday afternoon readings at the ABC Theatre to introduce authors of the Absurd, such as Edward Albee, and was later to stage the first Czech productions of such works as Friedrich Dürrenmatt's *Romulus der Grosse* and Jean Genet's *Le Balcon*.

Grossman chose the plays by Beckett and Ionesco not only because they were important works performed for over a decade in the West and not yet seen in Prague, but also because they fitted the dramaturgical programme of the theatre. In *The Bald Prima Donna* (December 1964) Hudeček directed the actors to move in a mechanical, stylised manner, delivering the dialogue with puppet-like monotony. The critics preferred this to *The Lesson*, which Marie Málková and Josef Chvalina performed in a lower key with greater naturalism. Between the two pieces, Kaftan and Weber from Fialka's ensemble performed a mime interlude, *Tenant*; between the two parts of *Waiting for Godot*, which premièred the following night, Fialka himself performed an interlude, Beckett's own *Act Without Words I*. The link between the two productions was further underlined by Libor Fára's design of both programmes: the small, square format carried text interspersed with uncaptioned photographs and marked up with a proofreader's red pen, suggesting it was still in preparation. The robust Jan Libíček played Estragon as an artless child, naïve and open-hearted. A rising inflection in his voice suggested he was speaking in questions. Václav Sloup gave Vladimir an apathetic stoicism, his eyes the only mobile feature in a melancholy face. One clown was observing, the other questioning; both of them components of an anonymous machine.

The first reaction of the public was one of curiosity; once the initial excitement was over, critics began to assess the relevance of the productions. Zdeněk Hořínek wrote in *Divadlo*:

> Don't we ourselves have our own little Godots, onto which we project our illusions that something will turn up which will save us from "all this," which will give meaning to our life? Isn't the meaning of Hudeček's production above all a challenge to us to think about ourselves?[233]

In giving tentative voice to the possibility of *Waiting for Godot* being a parable of Socialist society, Hořínek was recognising that Grossman's choice had not been mere opportunism. Grossman was aware that there was a cultural necessity for the plays to be performed in Prague and believed he had actors in the ensemble who would fit the roles; but these reasons were secondary to the relevance of the plays in the theatre's repertoire. The influence of Ionesco on Havel's writing has already been mentioned, so it was natural for plays by Ionesco to follow Havel's first play and precede his second. However, the links were not only with Havel but with the world of Jarry and that of Kafka as well. The use of language as a manipulative weapon, the waste of man's life in futile activity, the reduction of personality to the point where one individual is interchangeable with another—these were themes directly relevant to contemporary society. The implications of *The Lesson* were even more sensitive, both in the play's presentation of cultural dominance and in its depiction of authority.

The Ionesco plays were more immediately accessible to the audience, but greater critical interest was shown in *Waiting for Godot*, with Hořínek writing that "the ascetic Beckett is an author of a higher order than the more productive and more dazzling Ionesco."[234] The issues in Beckett are more ambiguous than Ionesco's specific targets, and for most people their significance can only be appreciated in performance. *Waiting for Godot* provoked more spontaneous but less certain reactions. Grossman felt it to be, of all the plays at the Theatre on the Balustrade, the most open-ended and the most demanding in its appeal to the audience.

HAVEL'S *THE MEMORANDUM*

The theatre's next première followed in July 1965: Václav Havel's *The Memorandum*. Grossman's Theatre on the Balustrade was by now an important centre of cultural and intellectual life in a society which had changed radically in the previous decade, and whose rate of change seemed to be speeding up. An easing of the political situation had been indicated in May 1960, on the fifteenth anniversary of the Liberation, when an amnesty released more than five thousand political prisoners sentenced for "subversion of the republic" and similar crimes.* From the beginning of the 1960s, foreign travel became possible in selected cases: carefully supervised groups of sports competitors, singers, and dancers; and reliable members of the Czechoslovak Youth Union (potential Party members). Writers who had been banned since the late 1940s, or never allowed at all, gradually began to be published. Interesting articles appeared in magazines and newspapers. Even consumer goods became more accessible; and in 1965–1966 oranges were for the first time available *all through the winter*.

The Memorandum is set in such a changing society. As with *The Garden Party*, the main theme is exploitation through mechanised language, but it received a completely different treatment. Comparing the two plays, Jan Grossman wrote:

> The characters in *The Memorandum* are no longer treated with the same deliberate and provocative "purposefulness." They do not serve just as an exaggerated illustration of the author's concept, but mature in a more organic and consistent way; they are themselves that concept, and the concept itself in them—the author has disappeared behind the story and his actors.[235]

The action arises out of the discovery by Gross, the managing director of a firm whose business we never discover, that a new bureaucratic language, Ptydepe, has been introduced into the firm without his knowledge. The purpose of Ptydepe is to clarify communication by using a different expression for every shade of meaning. (It was created for the purpose by Havel's brother, the mathematician and philosopher Ivan.) In four spiralling perambulations from his office through the Ptydepe classroom to the translation department, Gross passes from ignorance through bewilderment and humiliation to a self-justifying involvement in what he knows very well to be an unjust society. Certain passages are allusions to the political brainwashing of the 1950s. Sergej Machonin wrote in *Literarní noviny* how these passages reminded him

* They still had to live in impoverished and humiliating circumstances.

The Memorandum by Václav Havel, directed by Jan Grossman for the Theatre on the Balustrade, 1965. (Courtesy of the photographer: Jaroslav Krejčí)

of the way people had conformed both as a whole and in their personal lives, and of the still fresh history of the loss of feeling, reason, and character.[236] Václav Havel was not only making a historical reference, but also exposing the dangers of all those systems which attempt to control man and his destiny.

The emphasis on inflexible structures is reflected in the construction of the play, whose precise divisions contain constant and mechanical repetitions of routine actions. The regular drip of water into a tin can was the idea of Grossman's assistant director, Lída Engelová. The first scene of each of the four triplets focuses on Gross's struggle for power with his deputy Baláš; the second treats the audience to a grammatical analysis of Ptydepe; and the third shows Gross out of his depth in the Translation Centre. The repetitions of the first set involve inventories, audits, rubber stamps, the tribulations of the accounts department, and the trips by his secretary Hana for milk and rolls; in the second set, they focus on subtleties of meaning in Ptydepe; and in the third, they assume Ubu-like proportions. In contrast with the ascetic academism of the Ptydepe classroom, the privileged staff of the Translation Centre pamper themselves hedonistically. Gross is overlooked as they hurry to the canteen, attend a party in the next office, or disappear with an urgent need to relieve themselves. There are constant references to roast goose, glasses of beer, gingerbread, and the need for a snack bar. The secretary is occupied with shopping for their lemons and melons, making coffee, and ironing Helena's underwear. Gross pleads with Mašát and Kunc for at least a cigarette, as they draw on rich cigars.

The relationship with *Ubu Roi* is even closer when we realise that we are in the presence of a pataphysical machine. The life of the office is independent of the outer world. Procedures are self-perpetuating (Baláš is able to compromise Gross after Gross transgresses a minor rule) and major changes take place (the removal of the Accounts Department to an unlit cellar) without the managing director's knowledge. To what end? The operation of this machine is irrelevant to anything outside itself. Ptydepe, manufactured to simplify office procedure, is exposed as being beyond human competence when the last remaining student creeps defeated from the classroom. The frenzied activity of office routine was emphasised in Jan Grossman's production by the lowering of a shadow curtain between scenes, against which the activity of the stagehands was silhouetted in red lighting. Zdeněk Šikola's grand operatic persiflage accompanied the scene changes.

The characters in *The Memorandum* seem literally more "flesh and blood" than those in *The Garden Party*. Jan Libíček, playing the role of Baláš, said: "I find I like *The Memorandum* much more than *The Garden Party*. It is a more mature piece of work with better dramatic construction and gives the actors more possibilities."[237] The journal *Plamen* (*Flame*) commented that in the first play the language governs the actors, whereas in *The Memorandum* the characters have the opportunity to "decide" and "do" as well as to "say."[238] But the flesh is only the coating of a collection of animated attitudes. It is the human feelings of the imperfectly adapted secretary (Marie Málková again) which lead her to sacrifice herself to the expediency of others: "No one ever spoke to me so beautifully before," she whispers after Gross has justified his reasons for endorsing her dismissal. Gross himself, though fully understood by Czech audiences, caused confusion among Western critics. His range of language is more complex than that of the other characters, encompassing pre-war humanism and contemporary liberalism as well as the clichés of Socialism. Both his humanism and liberalism are superficial. Gross's values are banal and he fights only for his own position. Apparently a victim, he is actually a more dangerous conformist than the others. With Gross in charge, the process of depersonalisation can continue unchallenged. He resembles Josef K in Grossman's version of Kafka's *The Trial*, who also acquiesces in a system he recognises as deformed and inhuman.

The Memorandum was followed in January 1966 by another "grenoble," *Thrift*, directed by Grossman's protégé Jaroslav Gillar. This ninety-minute montage was composed from a prologue and six stories by the Polish writer Sławomir Mrożek, who had emigrated to France and Mexico less than three years earlier. Jan Přeučil, who a few months previously had presented a programme of stories by Mrożek and Vyskočil at Reduta, starred in what was virtually a solo performance. *Thrift* was received warmly, though with some disappointment that the theatre had not chosen one of Mrożek's plays instead of this montage. Přeučil was praised by *Divadlo* as an interpreter of Mrożek, "above all in his understanding of the meaning of abbreviation, implication, and hyperbole."[239] Others suggested that Přeučil's tour de force was too emphatic and overly tragic for these understated, naturalistic, and often wryly humorous stories.

GROSSMAN'S *THE TRIAL*, AND THE END OF AN ERA

For several years, Jan Grossman had been meditating on Franz Kafka, a banned writer in the first years of the Communist regime. The journalist Milena Jesenská—an independent spirit who died in Ravensbrück—had been the first to translate Kafka into Czech. Jesenská had been closely associated with Kafka and with the Devětsil; Kafka, who was virtually bilingual, had more friends among the Czech avant-garde. His writings were banned under the Protectorate and again unavailable after the Communists took power. Neverthe-

The Trial by Franz Kafka, dramatised and directed by Jan Grossman for the Theatre on the Balustrade, 1966. (Courtesy of the photographer: Jaroslav Krejčí)

less, intellectual circles were fascinated by Kafka, and in 1958 *The Trial* was published in a new translation by the great German-speaking scholar of the Czech language, Pavel Eisner. In 1962, a debate opened about the differences between Jaroslav Hašek and Franz Kafka, both born in 1883;[240] the following year, the eightieth anniversary of their births, a conference on Kafka's work was held in the Czechoslovak Academy of Sciences' Chateau Liblice. International participants included Roger Garaudy from France and Anna Seghers from East Germany. The official aim of the conference was:

> ...to attempt a multisided evaluation of Kafka's work from the positions of Marxism-Leninism and, with a view to the close connection of Kafka's work with the Prague environment and development of Czechoslovak culture, to create the conditions for Czech literary science to utter a significant opinion on the Kafka issue.[241]

As well as reinstating Kafka—and acknowledging that a German-language culture had once coexisted in the Bohemian Lands—the conference had an underlying significance in that it allowed subjects that until then had been discussed only in private to be debated in public, sometimes heatedly. The issue at stake was whether a work of art could be interpreted in its own terms or whether it must be approached from a predetermined standpoint based on the cultural analysis made by the secretary of the Soviet Central Committee (known as the Zhdanov Doctrine, and published in Czech in 1947). This polarised world culture into "imperialist" and "democratic" and led to the condemnation of movements identified with the bourgeois past (including the avant-garde and formalism). After 1968, the authorities claimed that the Liblice conference was used to mask counter-revolutionary preparations for the Prague Spring. Kafka's writings, in theory permitted, became in practice unavailable. To mark his centenary in 1983, a volume of his short stories was published in a small edition; it sold out in a couple of hours. The novels were out of print throughout Normalisation.

The year after the Liblice conference, 1964, the proceedings were published as an attractively designed book (3,400 copies, a relatively small print run for the 1960s). In November, *Divadlo* focused on Kafka, publishing three of his short stories with articles by Jean-Louis Barrault, Jan Kott, and Czechoslovak contributors including Jan Grossman. Grossman opened his article "Kafka's Theatricality?" by explaining that it was not intended as a study of Kafka but preparatory notes for a staging of *The Trial*. Grossman wanted to be faithful not only to Kafka's novel but also to his method of working (i.e., his way of telling the story): "Interpretation cannot be the beginning or the pivot of such work. It only comes in at its end; it is the result which arises out of a complete realisation of the text, probably not apparent until its performance."[242] Grossman rejected the concept of the "Kafkaesque," of bizarre adventures taking place in a fantastic world. The quality of theatre he sensed in Kafka's work was not the Expressionist interpretation of André Gide and Jean-Louis Barrault, nor was it Orson Welles's more contemporary Romanticism. It was closer to the quality Grossman had recognised in the playwrights of the Absurd, and could trace in the very dissimilar work of Brecht and of Beckett. It lay in the factual reporting of simple events. Grossman drew attention to Kafka's precise and matter-of-fact style of writing, noting that Kafka's language is rarely complex or difficult to follow. He pointed out that *The Trial* is full of anecdotes, one of the simplest forms of literary expression (*The Castle* has even more). Each of K's encounters is essentially simple, like the units that make up *Waiting for Godot* or *Happy Days*; it is their juxtaposition that creates a cumulative effect, making *The Trial* the perfect scenario for an epic drama. The characters are not analysed in a psychological way; as we follow K's footsteps we see what he does, but not why he does it. Similarly, when we meet his colleagues, fellow lodgers, and other acquaintances we observe how they behave but are given no explanation for their frequently contradictory actions. On the other hand, Grossman wanted to avoid giving any scene or character a symbolic interpretation; each character has its own significance, but it is not a symbolic significance. The characters do not represent something; they *are* something: "The meaning is not outside the gestic process, but inherent in it," Grossman said later in an interview, and continued:

> Kafka's dramatic qualities are in harmony with the kind of theatre that does not aspire to illustrate the world, does not intend to thrill or preach to the spectator, but challenges him to a dialogue. It puts questions to its audience and awaits their answers... Without speaking about specific trials, our production sets out to attack all trials in which the spectator has in some way participated and to return to him a responsible attitude to the world in which he lives.[243]

The role of K, when Grossman came to cast the play, was allotted twice over, to two very different actors: Jan Přeučil, whose innate aristocratic quality emphasised K's sense of shock that a man of unsmirched reputation should be mistaken for some housepainter; and Ivan Palec, who showed K dismayed more by the essential absurdity of the proceedings. The practice of rehearsing two actors in one role is not unusual in theatres with a repertoire system; however, on this occasion Grossman used it to extend the meaning of his production. The two interpretations emphasised the possibility of any of us finding ourselves in K's position. The "everyman" nature of K could be brought out not by making him an anonymous representative of humanity, but by contrasting the characteristics of different actors in the same role.

The remainder of the characters in *The Trial* are glimpsed only as seen by K: inconsistent, vengeful, briefly sympathetic. Grossman saw K's tragedy as one brought about neither by force of circumstances nor by weakness of character, but by failure of will. He believed that Kafka's K was not a pathetic figure immobilised by an internal state or by an external situation that prevented him from making choices, but a free individual who simultaneously conforms to what he is denouncing. In his preparatory work, Grossman was challenging the attitude that man is a helpless cog in the machine of society. While the horrors of the modern world—bureaucracy, opportunism, sycophancy, hypocrisy, betrayal, egoism—are revealed in *The Trial*, responsibility cannot be taken away from the individual.

It had been on Grossman's mind to dramatise *The Trial* even before the impetus given by the Liblice conference, and his intention had been to ask Radok to direct the production. No record has been found as to why this did not happen. Rehearsals eventually began in 1965, but the text was not finalised until the early months of 1966. Anticipation had been stimulated by the reawakened interest in Kafka and by the reputation of the Theatre on the Balustrade. The première took place on 26 May 1966.

In the smothering darkness of the tiny theatre, a massive organ blast shatters the silence. Bright shafts of light briefly illuminate the black-clad figures as they glide, spring, duck, stride, swing through the scaffolding maze. They slip from corridor to bedroom, from antechamber to judge's podium, from cathedral to alley, disappearing into the shadows. Only the pubescent girls invading Titorelli's studio wear light-coloured dresses as they somersault from bar to bar. "Black, it must be black!" exclaims one of the warders as K dresses for his first interrogation. Shadowy figures, some played by theatre technicians, briefly identify themselves as clerks and petitioners. Long-legged Václav Mareš strides through K's office like a character from *The Memorandum*. K's bed becomes public property as the action revolves from the lodging house to the bank to the court; the three actresses we know from *The Memorandum* clasp him in urgent passion, then as swiftly slip from under him and are gone. Flexible as a contortionist, Málková glides through the Advocate's room, momentarily glimpsed in a white shift and carrying a branched candlestick "like a pagan ministrant, fulfilling her ritual role in an absurd mass."[244] Václav Sloup doubles as the student and as Block, his peasant face expressing both the egoism and the vulnerability of earthy humanity. Bowler-hatted Libíček as the First Warder plays Hardy to Jiří Krampol's Laurel as they bide their time before pulling the ultimate gag on Josef K.

Dodecaphonic variations on Bach motifs accompany transitions from one episode to another. Most of the sound effects are vocal, distorted telephone calls to K's office, murmurings in the court, and Smrčková's voice accompanying her own speech as the laundress, schizophrenically losing coordination; but the famous organ of St. James's in the Old Town dominates the soundtrack.

The organ seemed to composer Zdeněk Šikola to be the ideal instrument because of its impersonal quality; he felt that, unlike other instruments, it did not express any emotional quality of its own and therefore would not transfer or superimpose any emotion onto the text. Its "monumentality" was also appropriate in combination with the setting. Boris Soukup painted the span of a baroque vault on the cyclorama, dominant in dark crimsons, where shadowy figures suggested the existence of a higher reality. Jan Grossman had conceived the idea on a visit to St. Nicholas Church in the Lesser Quarter, at that time under reconstruction. Grossman gradually assembled on the acting area a construction of scaffolding poles, ladders, and platforms ("acquired" by stagehands from various sites in Prague; from the 1960s to the 1990s scaffolding obscured many of Prague's magnificent but crumbling churches and palaces. Much of this was semi-permanent, to stop the façades collapsing on pedestrians, and remained there for decades.) At a late stage of rehearsals (March) the construction was placed on a revolve which, because of the theatre's limited facilities, was built on top of the stage and turned by hand.

The images in *The Trial*—the cage, the labyrinth, the rituals of life and death—made a vivid impression on theatre observers from the West, who in the summer of 1966 were beginning to arrive in Prague; among them, Kenneth Tynan, Peter Daubeny, and Michael Kustow. They admired the physical virtuosity of the performers, the precision of their timing, and the remarkable effects achieved on the tiny stage of the Theatre on the Balustrade. Its international reputation coincided with a yearlong reconstruction of the old building; the drama and mime companies embarked on a complicated touring schedule that took them to Slovakia, Denmark, Israel, Russia, France, Italy, Germany, Austria, and the World Theatre Season in London, with *The Trial* and *Fools*. Jan Přeučil described the problems the actors had in establishing the essential contact with an audience with whom they shared neither a common language nor a common experience. He noted that moments of intense concentration could be achieved, and that in *The Trial* these were especially in the penultimate scene in the cathedral between the priest and Josef K. "I had the impression that even these foreign audiences found... questions which interested them and which were very real for them."[245] The London critics had been dazzled the previous year by Svoboda's kaleidoscopic play with tilted mirrors for Miroslav Macháček's production of the Čapek brothers' *The Insect Play*,* but the darkness of *The Trial* was another experience. "I've

* Macháček's production of the Čapek brothers' *The Insect Play* was premièred at the National Theatre in 1965, and was the first of a series of Czech productions to appear in the World Theatre Season in 1966.

never been made so conscious," wrote the *Observer* critic, "that what Kafka attempted was a twentieth-century Doom."[246]

After *The Trial*, Miloš Macourek's *Playing at Susie* (1967), which compressed the passage of one person's life into two hours, disappointed audiences, who felt it lacked contemporary relevance. (It had been two years in the making, with Václav Havel contributing to the script.) Jan Císař wrote in May 1968 that three or four years earlier it would have excited people by its expression of their own unspoken thoughts about the mechanisms to which they submitted.[247] Now, however, people were asking themselves more direct questions about their own responsibilities in the developing political situation, how to liberate themselves from unnecessary conventions, and where the limits of personal freedom lay.

Václav Havel approached some of these questions in *The Increased Difficulty of Concentration* (April 1968), directed by Václav Hudeček. The central character, Dr. Eduard Huml, is an "expert" in the science of human relationships who has himself lost his human identity. He is able to maintain an effortless flow of observations on the subject, apparently profound but essentially banal:

> By a value we mean that which satisfies some human need—semicolon—the structure of values thus always reflects the structure of human needs—full stop. We distinguish material values—for example, food, clothes, houses, etc.—from spiritual values—for instance, particular ideas or pieces of knowledge, relationships to other people, artistic experiences, etc.—full stop. Various people have at various times and in various circumstances various needs.[248]

At the same time Huml does not understand the significance of human relationships in real life. His liaison with his mistress is a mirror image of his relationship with his wife, while he seeks sexual excitement with his secretary, disregarding her identity as a person with her own life and relationships. He wears a mask of polite indifference and adopts the gestures and phraseology of conventional communication. The play is set in Huml's home, the place where one should be most free to "be oneself." It has been chosen as the venue for an experiment to identify the individuality of a human being; but the machine Puzuk, set to perform the task, proves more sensitive than the human beings in the play. The action consists of the encounters Huml makes during the day—with his wife, mistress, secretary, and the researchers—juxtaposed in a non-chronological order. It forms an image of Huml's life, which lacks any continuity or purpose. The Brno philosopher Josef Šafařík wrote in his afterword to the printed edition of the play:

> Unlike the traditional stage, which tries to persuade the "real" authentic man in the audience that the stage illusion is reality, Havel's intention is quite the opposite; he presents onstage the world of the machine era with technological "being without being" as its only reality, and leaves the man in the audience–from the point of view of science an inauthentic, abstract creature–to look into this mirror and decide for himself how distorted it is. "The problem of humanity" is being sorted out within the playgoer, not on stage.[249]

Havel's third play for the Balustrade was a development of the movement which began with the text-appeals at the end of the 1950s–an exposure of the consequences arising from the mechanical adoption of approved forms of language and ideas, intended to provoke audiences into thinking about the truth of their own experience. It was written at a time when political prisoners condemned in the early 1950s were being rehabilitated, and the evidence given in their trials reassessed. Two novels widely read at this time were Ludvík Vaculík's *The Axe* (*Sekyra*, 1966) and Milan Kundera's *The Joke* (*Žert*, 1967), in which the authors examined their personal experience in the context of historical events. Freedom of speech was infectious, and spreading rapidly in the hot summer of 1967, when opinions also raged over the Arab–Israeli Six-Day War. At the 4th Congress of the Writers' Union, held after a long delay in June 1967, the Ideology Department of the Central Committee held out against the attacks on censorship. It had resulted in Vaculík, Škvorecký, and others being expelled from the Communist Party, Kundera receiving a strong warning, and Havel (never a Party member) being sacked from the Theatre on the Balustrade on orders from above.

Although the onset of the Prague Spring made this sacking only temporary, the April 1968 première of *The Increased Difficulty of Concentration* was the last to take place in the Grossman era. When Grossman followed Vyskočil as director of the drama company of Theatre on the Balustrade, he achieved several things simultaneously. Among them, he maintained the traditions and myths of the past; identified colleagues able to interpret shared experience into theatrical language; and created productions with appeal to both the emotions and the intellect of audiences. In the 1960s, world fairs and international festivals had helped to bring Czechoslovak theatre to the public's attention; Grossman's position in international networks enabled cross-fertilisation to take place at an intellectual level, where, again to Western surprise, the seemingly isolated country had as much to offer as receive.

THE STATE THEATRE STUDIO (*STÁTNÍ DIVADELNÍ STUDIO*) AND OTHER SMALL STAGES

ORIGIN OF THE STATE THEATRE STUDIO

Soon after the Liberation, and Minister Nejedlý's abolition of the century-old network of private touring companies, the Ministry of Agriculture set up a programme called *Vesnické divadlo* (Village Theatre). It had to provide culture for remote and thinly populated areas (including those that had lost their German-speaking community). It was divided into units that travelled to the schoolrooms and pubs of small communities in its own buses, with costumes, stage sets, and equipment in trailers. The first unit was launched in December 1945; the following season there were three on the road, performing for children in the afternoon and adults in the evening; mainly plays by Czech authors such as Josef Kajetán Tyl (the casting requirements of the adult play dictated what show could be offered to children). At its most active, Village Theatre ran eleven units, including one that was German-speaking. In 1955, Miroslav Kouřil produced a illustrated textbook demonstrating different types of small stage, their technology, set design, and theory.* It was dedicated to "all the actors and theatre workers, most of their names forgotten, who sacrificed their art, life style, and individual fame to the travelling theatre in Bohemia, Moravia, and Slovakia, and whose memorial lives in the heart of our people." For the young actors, who collected financial allowances for being on the road, it was not too sacrificial a prospect. But by 1959, the pioneering enthusiasm had declined and the project, renamed the *Státní Zájezdové* divadlo (State Touring Theatre) had become the last resort of third-rate performers.

In 1961, an employee of the Ministry of Culture, Miloš Hercík, a fan of Jiří Suchý's Semafor Theatre who was aware of its precarious existence, used his influence to have the Village Theatre disbanded. He proposed that the funds be put towards a new organisation to be called the State Theatre Studio, which would provide a administrative roof for newly emerging small stages. The studio was to come directly under the Ministry of Culture, and not be answerable to local councils. The groups would have artistic freedom while standards would be maintained by offering short (one-year) contracts. (Vladimír Just, however, saw the purpose of the State Theatre Studio as less benign, as a check imposed on the small stages that had proliferated as a result of the Theatre Act of 1957.)†[250] Semafor was one of the first companies to be adopted.

---

* Miroslav Kouřil, *O malém jevišti* (*The Small Stage*), Orbis, Prague 1955.

† See p. 139.

Some of the State Theatre Studio groups are discussed under their own headings; others survived only briefly. Some had premises of their own while others toured. In 1970, however, the studio acquired a small theatre that it administered as a venue for several groups. Formerly known as the theatre club Olympik, under its new name Atelier, it had its own director and production team. Jazz groups played here, but it was also a home for cabaret and text-appeals. Vyskočil appeared with Pavel Bošek and the jazz singer Eva Olmerová; the satirical partnership of Jan Vodňanský and Petr Skoumal performed both there and at the Drama Club. The Brothers Just (Vladimír and Jiří) made their first appearances there, as did Jiří Dědeček with Jan Burian, the son of E. F. Burian and Zuzana Kočová. Actors from other theatres, such as Miloš Kopecký from Vinohrady, could present their own shows. Atelier also hosted companies visiting from the provinces, such as Kladivadlo* from Ústí nad Labem and Studio Ypsilon from Liberec. It survived for longer than the State Theatre Studio itself—until 1983, when it was closed for renovation. It provided an organisational basis for groups which otherwise would not have had an opportunity to get started, or a stage on which to perform. It reopened as the home of Studio Ypsilon, when it finalised its long drawn out move from Liberec to Prague.

SUCHÝ, ŠLITR, AND SEMAFOR

Rejected by the Balustrade Theatre in spring 1959, Jiří Suchý had returned to Reduta and started another theatre group in collaboration with the jazz musicians Jiří Šlitr and Ferdinand Havlík. They called it "Semafor"—literally "traffic lights" but also standing for "seven small forms"—*se-dm ma-lých for-em.* The number seven had other references, from legends and marvels to Jiří Červený's Seven of Hearts cabaret. They intended to develop seven of the small forms: black [light] theatre, children's cabaret, experimental film, puppetry, musical comedy, poetry, and the "theatre of masks," led by the Surrealist Jan Švankmajer. Premises were found in the *Ženský klub*—the Women's Club on Ve Smečkách (Smečky) street near the top of Wenceslas Square; the formalities of administration were again taken on by the cultural organisation *osvětová beseda*. The theatre, with its tiny strip of a stage, held an audience of 220. Young people crowded the theatre from the start, and the performers soon became national celebrities.

---

* Kladivadlo began as an amateur drama group of industrial workers—hence the wordplay on *kladivo*, hammer, and *divadlo*, theatre. (It also echoed the title of one of E. F. Burian's essays, "Come, Folk, to the Theatre with the Iron Hammers").

The first production, premièred in October 1959, was *The Man from the Attic* with music by Šlitr, and Suchý as the *malý lord* (the fictional Little Lord Fauntleroy). The central character, Antonín Sommer, exemplified the writer-intellectual who thinks himself an artist. The role alternated between Miroslav Horníček, Miloš Kopecký, and František Filipovský, chosen because of their links with small theatres in the past. The theme was the contrast between the artificiality of literature and the art of living, a criticism of worn-out conventions. However, the criticism was not in the dialogue, but in the dramatic shape. In "paper literature," a story is fixed, but when the *malý lord* reproaches Sommer for the fate inflicted on him and persuades him to re-write the story, Suchý was demonstrating that we can change our context and influence the course of events. The setting was merely suggested: a curtain on a line across the back of the stage and a stepladder to climb up and over it, suggesting the ascent to the attic. Four dudes (including the dashing Waldemar Matuška) interrupted the action with songs that became the hits of the day.

The Man from the Attic played to full houses for a year. The next musical, *What a Waste of Blood* (October 1960), told the story of the missing Vlastimil Drábek: a model schoolboy, he is sought by his anxious teacher and, independently, by the hooligan Harry Bedrna (Matuška) assisted by the town bookseller. Drábek has hidden himself away because he has discovered that sawdust, not blood, runs in his veins. At the end, the teacher stands accused of having created a stuffed dummy in place of a man. Radko Pytlík described it as a revue "directed against hypocrisy, pedantry, and dogmatism, standing for the interests of youth."[251]

Between the two musicals Semafor staged *Zuzana is Alone at Home* (1960), a programme of songs linked by Zuzana Stivínová.* The first part included mainly American music (Fats Domino, Elvis Presley); the second half, compositions by Suchý and Šlitr. A series of "Zuzana" productions followed: *Zuzana is Alone at Home Again* (1961); *Zuzana is at Home for No-one* (1964, directed by Antonín Moskalyk) and *Zuzana is Everywhere at Home* (1965). Just as popular was *Paper Blues* (February 1961), a literary cabaret "under the patronage of Mr. Christian Morgenstern."† Suchý wrote of Morgenstern:

> I don't find his poems fifty years old, as the calendar tries to tell me. I feel as though they were written yesterday, meant for Semafor... I used to like the Dadaists and their mag-

* Zuzana Stivínová had earlier taken over the role of Gretchen in *Faust, Gretchen, the Maid, and I* at the Theatre on the Balustrade. In 1964, she was cast in Jan Grossman's production of *Ubu Roi*, but emigrated, being replaced at Semafor by Zuzana Burianová.

† Christian Morgenstern (1871–1914), a German author of humorous verse and nonsense poetry who used subtle wordplay to mock sententiousness.

ical piling up of nonsenses, but I always had the feeling there was something contrived about them, lacking in warmth. Christian Morgenstern also piles up nonsenses, you might say, but with such love and understanding of mundane little things that one suddenly becomes aware of their meaning in life, not only as useful and practical objects, but as wondrous and inspiring things. A chicken, underpants, a funnel, a dray horse, a jacket...[252]

Paper Blues married poetry and music with the help of pop singers like Eva Pilarová. It set the path for Semafor's future programme, which abandoned the storyline treatment of the earlier musicals.

The Prague City Council soon regretted having allowed Semafor to come into existence, but its popularity made it difficult to close. At the end of the 1960–1961 season, a committee inspected the premises, pronounced them inadequate, and offered to restore the theatre over the summer break. When the company returned after their holiday, the theatre had been virtually demolished. Rehearsals began amid the rubble, but Suchý was told that for safety reasons the club could not be used as a theatre again. Working from the office (two by two metres), the company devised a programme whereby Semafor performed at other theatres when the home companies had their "night off." Over the next year Semafor appeared at thirty different venues, many outside Prague, travelling by public transport or sharing cars. Props, costumes, and musical instrument were stored in members' homes. Singers who had made their name with Semafor—Matuška, Pilarová—transferred their loyalty to more secure ensembles.

By spring 1962, the company was close to collapse, but was rescued by Miloš Hercík's State Theatre Studio. Their next home was the old wooden building *Na slupi* that had once housed the Theatre Dada and the Liberated Theatre. The auditorium was arranged like an amphitheatre with the stage at ground level, creating such good rapport between actor and audience that Suchý would gladly have stayed if the building had not been scheduled for demolition. In the autumn of 1962, the company moved to the basement theatre in the Alfa passage near Wenceslas Square, built for the popular actor Oldřich Nový in 1934.*

Two landmark productions had been premièred while the company was "on the road": *Six Wives* in Pilsen and *Jonah and the Tingle Tangle* in Gottwaldov (both in June 1962). (The Pilsen opening represented tactical support for the singer Eva Olmerová, who had been targeted by the secret police and

* In the 1990s the building was restituted to its former owners, who gave Semafor notice. For a while they performed on the small stage (Karlínek) of the *Hudební divadlo Karlín* (Karlín Music Theatre) before moving to Dejvice. Semafor's old foyer was converted into shops and no one who passes through the Alfa passage today would guess that a legend lies under their feet.

banned from performing in Prague.) Miroslav Horníček made his second appearance with Semafor in *Six Wives*, describing the production as "a kind of parodistic look at a fictitious diary of Henry VIII."[253] (An early version of *Six Wives*, involving Viktor Sodoma and Ivan Vyskočil, had been performed by Akord Club.) *Jonah and the Tingle Tangle* marked the first time the composer Jiří Šlitr appeared onstage at Semafor. Although inseparable from the Semafor legend, Šlitr was not officially a member of the company, and always kept his independence. Several years older than Suchý, he wrote music for television and performed in cabaret with Horníček, Filipovský, and Lubomír Lipský. His first collaboration with Suchý was at Reduta in 1957 with "Song for Hamlet" (*Píseň pro Hamleta*). However, while Suchý was engaged in founding the Theatre on the Balustrade, Šlitr associated himself with Alfréd Radok and his *Laterna magika* programme at Expo 58.

Suchý's attempts to form a partnership on the model of Voskovec and Werich–first with Vyskočil, then with Horníček, then Matuška–had not worked out. In persuading Šlitr to join him onstage, he found his partner: impassive and apparently slow on the uptake, speaking colloquially with a monotonous, clipped delivery. Suchý, in contrast, was the whole time on the move: impulsive, spontaneous, impatient. Suchý pursued an argument with the enthusiastic logic of a child; Šlitr, bowler-hatted and ponderous, would suddenly illuminate the stage with moments of Dada miscomprehension. Unlike V+W, S+Š never improvised on stage; their popularity lay in their apparent but carefully rehearsed spontaneity and the topical jokes they shared with the audience.

For many, *Jonah and the Tingle Tangle* embodied the legend of "old Semafor." Suchý abandoned the rock 'n' roll and echoes of Western hits which had brought him popularity, and connected with the tradition of the šantán and Music Hall. He brought out his archives and in fourteen days, with Šlitr's help, put together a programme of sketches, *kuplety*, comedy songs, and parodies. Their only props were two chairs, two microphones, a piano, and a girl in fishnet tights. As they recounted anecdotes about the mythical Jonah, the scene moved between Vienna, London, Milan, New York, Moscow, and the bar Honolulu in Paris. Suchý later wrote of the production:

> It was a kind of cabaret performance, but for us at Semafor it was something more. Something like our calling. The mythical cabaret performer Jonah [...] was in fact a symbol of our efforts. His humour and his songs were in a way the essence of Semaforism... Two companions [...] remember Jonah, about whom they know lots of ridiculous details and whose repertoire they have in miniature, while there is only one thing they are unsure of: whether he really existed or not.[254]

Jiří Šlitr and Jiří Suchý, and an unnamed member of the company in *Jonáš a tingtangl* at the Semafor Theatre, 1962. (Photographer: Vilém Sochůrek; courtesy of the Arts and Theatre Institute)

In 1963 Jaroslav Vostrý (soon to be head of the Drama Club) wrote of *Jonah* and *Zuzana*:

> It is difficult to imagine anything less like a play or indeed theatre in the usual sense of the word than these programmes—that is, in every element including the acting deliberately appearing to be nonprofessional.[255]

In the autumn of 1962, a debate arose over Suchý's attitude towards professionalism, a dispute which helped to clarify the criteria of the small theatres.* In a front-page interview with Leoš Suchařípa, editor of *Divadelní noviny*,[256] Suchý's remarks were taken as an attack on the established stages. The reaction he provoked, especially from the acting profession, led to a statement from the editor saying that although he did not agree with Suchý's views, he defended his right to print them.[257] Suchý, who had not anticipated such controversy, tried to explain that in his kind of theatre he could not use actors trained in the old school; he was in search of performers who came to the theatre without preconceived ideas. He was not interested in actors trained so perfectly in movement and diction that they could play any role, but in those whose relationship with the audience came from their own indi-

* See Jan Grossman's response to this debate the following year in this chapter: p. 151–153

viduality. He preferred to engage people from other professions rather than from the theatre; it was easier to train newcomers in technical skills than to rid them of unwanted mannerisms. He gave the example of Jiří Šlitr as the type of performer who at drama school would have been trained to relax, and coached out of "faults" in diction and delivery. In fact, it was these that appealed to the audience: Šlitr's apparent shyness and naivety, the tensions aroused by his awkward presence onstage.

Suchý's arguments led his critics to accuse him of amateurism, of trying to evade evaluation of his work by appealing to different standards. The dispute was still echoing in the 1980s, although actors on the main stages had by then learned to be more flexible and those in the small theatres were more competent technically. Suchý insisted that he abhorred lack of professionalism where it concerned the performer's "approach to work," whether in a straight acting role, a cabaret anecdote, or a pop song; and that this kind of professional attitude was less common among actors than among people in other professions. For Suchý, the role of Henry VIII in *Six Wives* was an example of the difference between "pretence" in acting and direct communication with the audience. Some people argued that the part should be played in Tudor costume with the actor simulating sixteenth-century manners, whereas Miroslav Horníček read Henry's diary dressed in an ordinary suit, sharing the jokes with the audience as one of their contemporaries. Suchý explained that he was not interested in the "character" of Henry VIII, but in the relationship of someone today to what was being said:

> As far as my work goes, I'm not concerned about experiencing a thing, identifying with it, but rather a way of distancing; the kind of theatre where the actor comments on what is happening onstage, whether by word, gesture, or attitude.[258]

Suchý cited Horníček as the kind of trained actor who could adapt to the needs of Semafor, one who had proven himself at the National Theatre before becoming Jan Werich's partner.

Suchý's theatre had bewildered many critics from the start. They confessed themselves at a loss with regard to the themes of the first two musicals—in the case of *What a Waste of Blood*, expressed with such black humour: "I do not know [...] what it is about, against whom it is written, what the moral is, what it is trying to convince the audience about. Take your pick. But most of all have fun."[259] The young audiences paid little attention to the plot of the musicals; they enjoyed the Western flavour of the songs, the humour of the wordplay, and the charismatic performers like Matuška. When Suchý abandoned the storyline, he disappointed audience members who had appreciated the satire and were hoping that Semafor would become a Liberated

Theatre as they remembered it. But satire was not Suchý's forte; he did not intend Semafor to be satirical. His theatre set out to celebrate the fun of life, love, music, and good company. Any satirical element arose out of the themes that interested their audience and the situations they had to deal in daily life.

Influenced by Morgenstern, Dada, Poetism, Voskovec & Werich, and the modern poets, Suchý's texts had a wider range than the contemporary pop repertoire with its generalised references to the emotions. Suchý had much in common with the "*Květen* Generation"—poets such as Jiří Šotola and Miroslav Holub, most of them older than Suchý, who wrote for the magazine *Květen* in the late 1950s (before it was closed down in 1959). Like them, he tried to release poetry from pomposity and cliché, and to evoke the simplicity of everyday experience: a lonely street or a neighbour's garden. Love and the beauty of women were recurring themes, but so too was comedy, often expressed in absurd anecdotes with a dark twist to the story. He learnt a lot from translating song texts, finding, as did Voskovec and Werich, that the sound and feel of the Czech language is fundamentally anti-jazz and awkward in interpreting the rhythms of the American lyrics. From Voskovec and Werich he learnt to play with words, compelling the Czech language to fit jazz, getting round its rules of accent and length, discovering the surreal effect of a right choice of word:

> This can only be done if you treat it in a jokey way, for fun, with word plays and rhymes, but also with ideas. Then anything goes. A lot depends on the interpreter, whether he understands the jokes.[260]

Many of Suchý's songs originate from a delight in the sound of certain words: *koupil jsem si knot* (I bought myself a wick), *tento tón mám rád* (I like that note) with their mini-explosions on "K" and "T." In "The Tulip" (*Tulipán*) the search for a rhyme led a reference to the Hussite defeat at the Battle of Lipany (Český Brod) and a pacifist theme emerged. When Suchý turned from the musical with its logical plot to the composition of "song-theatre," he found himself developing a programme of songs with their own internal connections, so that the production became a montage, each part contributing to the whole. Jan Císař wrote of *Jonah*:

> They talk about marrying and sing of the problems of Adam—and beauty and woman in general. They talk about the meaning of objects. They sing of a candle wick and the use of useless little things. The songs add to and extend the prose... the joining of two different phenomena on a level with a common meaning is a classic principle of unfolding montage.[261]

During the brief freedom of the mid-1960s, with an enthusiastic following, with Šlitr's partnership, and with organisational support from the State Theatre Studio, Jiří Suchý created a "theatre of songs"; not only his own, but those of visiting artists. Semafor was a place to share a love of life and living. There was nothing political or satirical in its programme; nevertheless, when the pendulum of freedom swung again, Suchý was to be one of those most fiercely harassed.

PARAVAN

In 1945, the actor Jiří R. Pick joined Jindřich Honzl's Company of Youth (later the Studio of the National Theatre), where he wrote plays about his experiences in Terezín. Much of his early writing tended towards Socialist Realism, but in the mid-1950s he began to write satirical short scenes and sketches, collaborating with the writer Milan Schulz on a literary cabaret. In 1959, he formed the group Paravan, performing in Reduta. Václav Havel was an early visitor, writing in *Divadlo*:

> [Paravan's] text basis is a montage of satirical verse and prose by Jiří R. Pick and Milan Schulz. Pick's items are witty; in places very witty. He knows how to make use of abbreviation in his humour, which takes many forms and always contains a crystallised idea. Pick's special characteristic is a kind of drastic quality, manifesting itself particularly in themes of emotional life. Schulz's parodies are, I think, fairly weak.[262]

Havel also criticised the lack of structure; one item followed another, mutually cancelling each other out. Features he liked were the use of improvisation, the way the performers mixed with the audience, and the "workshop atmosphere."

Several more productions were premièred in Reduta, of which the best remembered was *All My Granddads* (1962), a montage of songs from early twentieth-century cabaret, in particular the repertoire of the Seven of Hearts. The ensemble was put together ad hoc for each production, including both semi-amateurs and guest stars such as Jiří Suchý and Ljuba Hermanová. Guest writers also appeared, reading their own text-appeals as part of a programme; they included Ivan Vyskočil, Ludvík Aškenazy, the philosopher Ivan Sviták, and Josef Škvorecký, author of *The Cowards*.* Škvorecký became in-

* *The Cowards* (*Zbabělci*), a novel about youth and jazz reflecting Škvorecký's wartime experience in a small town, was published in 1958 and immediately banned.

volved in Paravan through his girlfriend (later his wife), the actress Zdena Salivarová, and later remembered:

> I liked the friendly atmosphere of the Textappeals [sic]—they had that atmosphere of conspiracy between the audience and the performers. The stories that we read, although they had to be shown to the censors, were often read in versions that had not been shown to the censors. The audience responded beautifully to every political allusion and allegory.[263]

Paravan was incorporated into the State Theatre Studio in 1962, as part of Reduta. In December it premièred its first fully professional production, a montage of songs and text-appeals, *Two Briefcases and a Dispatch Case.** The following October, Paravan staged Pick's *About My Murder*, an attempt at Absurd drama. A critic suggested in *Divadlo* that Pick, one of the first contemporary satirists, had been overtaken by more talented intellects.

In 1964, Paravan moved into the Women's Club on Ve Smečkách street—Semafor's former home, closed in 1961 as "unfit for use as a theatre." But Paravan was already behind the fast-moving times; small theatre groups were mushrooming, and the work of contemporary Western authors could be seen in the professional theatres. In the spring of 1964, *Divadelní noviny* noted that one performance attracted an audience of only thirty. Hercík made a decision, and on 30 October Paravan premièred its last production, *Kunst-appeal* (after Miroslav "Sláva" Kunst, the orchestra leader). *Divadlo* wrote, "The evening doesn't need to be a dazzling success; it can safely assume its all too familiar mood."[264]

In 1968, J. R. Pick inaugurated the *Kabaret Au* at the *Radiopalác* in Vinohrady. The company combined satire with striptease; for example, a semi-naked girl sang "Why do these old men stare at me so?" against a projection of three of the Soviet leaders. Early in 1970, the authorities closed down *Kabaret Au*.

THE DRAMA CLUB (*ČINOHERNÍ KLUB*)

> In other theatres emphasis is laid on how the social system affects people. We would rather show the opposite: how the way people behave creates the system.[265]

Hercík's decision had a purpose; Paravan was sharing the theatre in Smečky with a theatre company in the process of formation. A new play, *Picnic*, written

---

* Another case of wordplay in the Czech—the word for briefcase (*aktovka*) also means a one-act play, and the word for a dispatch case (*diplomatka*), a female diplomat.

and directed by Ladislav Smoček, was premièred in February 1965—although the Drama Club did not officially exist until 1 August 1965. Smoček had spent three unsatisfactory years with the *Laterna magika*, where he felt excluded from the creative team. He used his free time to write *Picnic*, a psychological study of four American soldiers trapped in a tropical jungle, for himself and his friends. Clearly derived from American literature, it was an unusual work for a Czech writer. Miloš Hercík liked the play and Smoček's ideas, and gave him carte blanche.

Smoček preferred not to lead the company himself, inviting his former fellow student Jaroslav Vostrý, professor at DAMU and editor of *Divadlo*. Vostrý had written a theoretical study about multiple approaches to a theme[266] and followed the dramaturgy of Krejča and Kraus at the National Theatre. He believed that the prerequisite for theatre was a mixture of creative talents; in this way, a necessary handicap (the number of people involved in a theatrical performance) could turn into a creative internal balance. Vostrý's ideal of a voluntary collective concurred with Smoček's more intuitive approach. The third member of the team was the actor and director Jan Kačer. Kačer had spent six years (1959–1964) running the Petr Bezruč Theatre for Children and Youth in Ostrava, where the repertoire had included works by Mayakovsky and Dürrenmatt, Viktor Dyk, Josef Topol, as well as Vítězslav Nezval's *Lovers from the Kiosk*. To quote an essay from 1969: "Kačer's work as a director in Ostrava was rooted in a combination of the lyrical musicality of Burian and the unsentimentality of Brecht."[267] Kačer's ideas were close to those of Smoček and Vostrý: a commitment to themes arising from human relationships; the importance of a contributing group of actors; and a belief that the group must pursue what it felt to be important whether or not it had "mass appeal."

It was from this that the name "Drama Club" originated: "drama" because the ensemble intended to produce straight plays rather than cabaret or text-appeals; and "club" to emphasise the idea of audience involvement ("club" did not imply exclusivity). Although it did not call itself an experimental theatre, the group's intention was to use the stage as a space for research. They rejected didactic theatre, believing that not only were there no known answers, but there were no known questions either. In 1969, Jaroslav Vostrý wrote:

> Just as in the choice of plays at our theatre, we refuse to illustrate previously formulated themes, so the individual productions are not mere illustrations of one dramatist's or one director's design; our theatre arises out of the conviction that a play is not a play only in the sense of a dramatic text, nor even in the sense of a piece performed on the stage, but a play/game (*hra*) in the original—and broad—sense of the word. Every play/

game is only a play/game insofar as it contains a space for fortuity, in spite of having been determined by inescapable conditions. It is this space for fortuity where accidental as well as intentional factors can make themselves felt, unforeseen as well as foreseen, particular, or individual as well as general. In short, a space not for one but for many possibilities. And so the theatre must always allow for change.[268]

Rehearsals at the Drama Club were more like workshops, guided by one of the directors but with the emphasis on improvisation. Long rehearsal periods were allowed, and when the play was by Smoček, the actor Pavel Landovský (*Rooms by the Hour*, 1969), or Vostrý's wife Alena Vostrá, the acting ensemble was involved in the scripting. The nucleus of the ensemble, which included designer Luboš Hrůza,* as well as actors Josef Somr, Petr Čepek, and Kačer's wife Nina Divíšková, came largely from Kačer's ensemble in Ostrava. Kačer said in 1968:

The idea you can build up a creative group within a year or two is an illusion. It's a life's work or, if I break it down a little, it takes at least six or seven years. People who take to each other find it terribly difficult to let in new people, because the organism is so fragile.[269]

The freedom of the rehearsal sessions, combined with the actors' awareness of each other's reactions and their trust in each other, created a range of possibilities of which the actor could ultimately select only one; the task was to show the audience that moment of choice, to convince them that in the given situation the character could not act otherwise, while at the same time making them aware of all the other possibilities. The theme that linked the Drama Club productions was the potentiality of chance becoming real: Machiavelli's *Mandragola* (1965), Dostoyevsky's *Crime and Punishment* (1966), Pinter's *The Birthday Party* (1967), and Kačer's most famous production, *The Government Inspector* (1967). This theme was clear in Alena Vostrá's first play, *Whose Turn Next?* (1966), seen in London's World Theatre Season (with *Mandragola* and *The Government Inspector*) in 1970. Much of Vostrá's play was a compilation of the actors' dialogue developed in improvisation. In the first scene, a group of students pass their time in a café playing word games and inventing absurd stories. They think up practical jokes to play on their elders, games that transgress the bounds of social convention. The games escalate, taking on a life of their own. Offsajd, one of the instigators, becomes caught

* Other artists who worked at the Drama Club included the Surrealists Libor Fára and Jan Švankmajer, as well as the graphic artist Joska Skalník, who was responsible for programmes, posters, and the organisation of art exhibitions.

up in a game of another's making, and is ridiculously and painfully humiliated. In December 1968, Vostrá followed *Whose Turn Next?* with the black comedy, *On a Knife's Edge*, in which the behaviour and activities of the residents of an apartment house (six rooms simultaneously on stage) are juxtaposed and overlap.

The Drama Club actors found that when the potentialities of chance are exploited to their ultimate, the result almost always ends in violence. If the boundaries to social convention are removed, man's latent aggressions come into conflict in situations that reflect the dangerous potentialities of our own everyday lives. This could be seen too in Ladislav Smoček's double bill, *The Maze* and *The Strange Afternoon of Dr. Zvonek Burke* (1966). In the first, an onlooker idly watches visitors disappear into a maze as he chats to the gatekeeper. Cries and strange noises begin to be heard from within and the onlooker realises there is no exit from the maze. As evening approaches, the gatekeeper forces him in and locks the gate. In the second play, now usually performed on its own, Smoček created a classic character of Czech comedy. Burke (in the original production played by twenty-three-year-old Vladimír Pucholt) is an amateur philanthropist, a gangling elderly gentleman whose mission in life is to spread sweetness and light, to counteract his suppressed feelings of hostility—represented by the detested *buchty* (jam-filled buns) he has courteously accepted over the years from his landlady (Jiří Hálek) and secreted in hidden corners of his room. Burke's landlady has, however, decided that the room is needed for her daughter (Nina Divíšková) and her daughter's fiancé, and gives Burke notice. The escalating consequences involve a locked door, a swallowed key, the embarrassment of Burke's visitor Mr. Tichý (Václav Kotva) caught short in the locked room, revelations of past *buchty* and multiple murder by Burke.*

In spite of the Drama Club's apparently more traditional repertoire, it was connected with other small theatres of the time by the techniques used to keep the audience in active mode, always aware of the choices being made and the possibility of influencing events. The actors never completely identified with their roles. Houselights were often left up for part of the action, emphasising the unity of stage and auditorium. In the small space, eye contact was frequent between actor and spectator. *Whose Turn Next?* opened with two characters identifying a girl—any girl—in the audience and addressing her. In notes to the play, Vostrý and Vostrá wrote:

* In 1983, the play was revived at the Kobylisy Theatre by Boleslav Polívka, who cast Hálek, Divíšková, and Kotva in their original roles and played Burke himself.

> We could say that the characters are merely displayed by means of the game; in this sense the principle of comedy is an artistic principle, i.e., an appearance is always involved, a "number," a showing-off, at times similar to a clown's act, pure comedy. But if we talk about principles we are talking about themes again; the fun we have from the play/game [*hra*] is one of them.[270]

Following the criticism directed at the amateur acting of the small theatres, the Drama Club emphasised the development of professional communication skills. Focus on detail was an important part of the performance. In London, the theatre critic of *The Times* noted that in *The Government Inspector*:

> The grotesque... emerges as a form of super-realism; microscopically observed human character blown up to gargantuan exaggeration, but never to the extent of severing its attachment to nature.[271]

Effective use was made of contrast; the *Times* again observed that in Jiří Menzel's production of *Mandragola*:

> Siro the servant (Jiří Hrzán) lolls in the sun unable to stir.... But once the trio (of conspirators) get moving they break into a brilliant gymnastic routine of tumbling, footstamping, triple back somersaults, spinning, calf-biting, and passing slaps at fleas around.[272]

Kenneth Tynan described how, in Evald Schorm's production of *Crime and Punishment*, Jan Kačer as Raskolnikov erupted from moments of quietism into "prodigies of physical abandon and emotional commitment."[273] Reviewers often mentioned the use of film techniques in Drama Club productions: the foregrounding of a particular piece of business, the contrast of the visual image with the spoken word, indirect means of expression. Vostrý had written a study on Eisenstein, and Evald Schorm, Jiří Menzel, and Antonín Máša, who directed at the Drama Club, were leading film directors of the New Wave. Some actors became famous through their film appearances: Vladimír Pucholt as the young seducer in Forman's *Loves of a Blonde*; Josef Somr as the philandering railway guard in Menzel's *Closely Watched Trains*. Actors from other theatres regularly visited the Drama Club, admiring the rapport between the stage and the audience and the spontaneity of the performances.

MARINGOTKA

Maringotka (Caravan) was added to the State Theatre Studio in autumn 1964. The name recalled the old days of the strolling players at the same time as suggesting a direct, practical approach to theatre. The founder was E. F. Burian's widow, Zuzana Kočová, appointed director of his theatre after his death but dismissed within the year. In 1962, she began to work with students at JAMU* in Brno on primitive rituals and ethnography. Her production of Burian's *War* was so successful that the group was accepted as a permanent company within the State Theatre Studio.† Kočová intended to create a contemporary poetic theatre, building on Burian's use of Czech folk traditions and supplementing them with the results of her own research. She was interested in the variable use of space to set up new relationships between performers and audiences. Adolf Scherl noted that in comparison with Burian, Kočová relied more on the spoken word and that her productions were less effective as synthetic theatre. This was partly because Kočová lacked Burian's musical ability and partly because, in spite of her vision of a dedicated ensemble full of initiative and zeal, Maringotka had problems in creating a permanent ensemble, still less the vibrant "club" atmosphere with exhibitions, discussions, and publications that had been Burian's ideal.

Maringotka's first production, Vítězslav Nezval's *Loretka*, a sentimental story of Prague bohemian life in the 1920s, was criticised as an unsuitable choice for inexperienced actors. Burian's *Folk Suite* the following year aroused greater interest, as did Kocová's own play *The Witch*. A collage of folk texts, it tells in ballad form the story of two brothers in love with the daughter of a woman believed to be a witch. Adolf Scherl described its theme as one of human feeling in conflict with the forces of fanatical dogmatism.

At the end of 1965, Maringotka was moved from the State Theatre Studio to the Czechoslovak State Song and Dance Ensemble. Under Communism, traditional art was treated as a commodity to be exploited for hard currency, and the highly trained professional ensembles (there were more than one) circulated in a hectic schedule of world tours. Intellectuals, reacting to this commercialisation, dismissed folk art as tourist kitsch. The conveyor-belt efficiency of the ensemble was a world away from Kočová's search for the roots of the old myths. She believed that the contemporary Czech theatre, in its wholehearted capitulation to the novelty of Western theatre, was losing an important stimulus that only the traditions of primitive theatre could offer. Another believer in the power of ritual theatre was Jan Kopecký, who had been distancing himself from hardline Socialist Realism. Kopecký's research had led to a series of revivals, starting in 1965, of folk plays from Bohemia and Moravia. These had been warmly received at the Realist Theatre in Prague.

* The Janáček Academy of Performing Arts in Brno, established in 1947.

† The production was invited to Verona, a rare opportunity in those years for Czechs to travel.

In 1969, Maringotka staged Kopecký's adaptation of the Biblical *Song of Solomon*. *Divadelní noviny* wrote:

> On a small podium, which it would be an exaggeration to call a stage, with the minimum of props and a piece of sheepskin as just about the only setting, director Zuzana Kočová puts into play the eternal wheel of allurement and longing, dream, and fulfilment.[274]

Acquiring premises on the slopes of Vyšehrad, Kočová began to develop Maringotka as a "theatre-club" where budding musicians, writers, and artists were encouraged to share their work with the rest of the audience. Each visitor was welcomed at the door; there was no set starting time, and the performance was followed by a discussion in which people shared their experiences. Kočová experimented with open staging: the action of one production took place entirely on a marriage bed; in another, the audience had to imagine they were entering a "real" apartment. Expelled from Vyšehrad in 1971, the company renovated a building in Husova Street in the Old Town. However, the local authority condemned the premises as unsuitable for public performances and they returned to a peripatetic existence. Maringotka was closed down in 1973 on the grounds that this was not an appropriate time for theatrical experiments.

THE THEATRE OF JÁRA DA CIMRMAN

In 1965, the radio producer Helena Philippová (instrumental in the foundation of the Theatre on the Balustrade) broadcast with colleagues a series of programmes which apparently came live from one of Prague's *vinárny* (wine bars)—the teetotal *Vinárna U Pavouka* (At the Sign of the Spider).* Habitués of Prague nightlife were at first surprised to hear of its existence; why had they never visited this lively nightspot, with its varied entertainments? One night a conjurer appeared, his amazing illusions breathlessly described by the radio commentator; another night an interview with a water acrobat took place. The clue was in the description of *U Pavouka* as a *teetotal* wine bar—like the entertainments, something possible only on the radio; it was a practical joke, maintained over weeks by Philippová and her radio colleagues, including the former schoolteacher Zdeněk Svěrák. Out of this "mystification" emerged the character of Jára (da) Cimrman, said to have been born in Vienna of Czech extraction at a date variously given between 1859 and 1873. Cimrman, it was

* The *vinárna* of the same name in the Old Town of Prague conversely took its name from the radio programme.

claimed, had been one of the most significant Czech dramatists, artists, poets, explorers, musicians, philosophers, inventors, and sportsmen of his day—if not of all time. The Theatre of Jára Cimrman (*Divadlo Járy [da] Cimrmana*) had been founded to rehabilitate his memory. After a short acquaintance, it becomes evident that Cimrman was untalented, ignorant, and given to sciolism. Cimrman is a satire on the Czech character, a self-mocking look at the trait that makes a genius out of every "little Czech person" (*malý český člověk*).

The group first performed as amateurs at the *Malostranská beseda* (Lesser Quarter Club) in October 1967 with *Act*, written by Svěrák and directed by Philippová. They turned professional in the context of the State Theatre Studio and their second production, written and directed by Ladislav Smoljak—a newcomer to the group—opened in November. However, the new partnership broke with Philippová, and Svěrák and Smoljak jointly took over directing as well as performing.

After 1970, the ensemble began performing in Reduta, and occasionally the Theatre on the Balustrade and the Žižkov Theatre, until in the mid-1970s they settled in their own theatre in the southern suburb of Braník.* The ensemble evolved an entertainment in two parts that became the model for most of their productions. The first half of the evening took the form of a seminar on some aspect of the life and work of Cimrman, illustrated by exhibits and musical examples; after the interval there would be a reconstruction of one of his works, such as an operetta (*The Inn on the Glade*); a detective story (*Murder in the Saloon Car*); or an opera (*Cimrman in the Realm of Music*). The theatre scholar Milan Obst wrote in *Divadlo*:

> The absurd comedy of these trifles comes nearest to the world of Smoček's Dr Burke, resting on a nonsensical situation put together with almost naïve carelessness and on parodistically exaggerated characteristics randomly gathered from Czech home life, school, and wherever possible.[275]

One feature of the Theatre of Jára Cimrman was that none of the performers had studied professionally as an actor; all of them came from other professions—translating, conducting, designing. As with Jiří Šlitr at Semafor, their appearances were marked by exaggerated unease and deliberate amateurism both in the delivery of their papers at the "seminar" and in the roles they play in the dramatic episodes. During the Normalisation of the 1970s and 1980s, their amateur, unorthodox ways made it possible for them to extend a helping hand to artists whom professional theatres were afraid to touch.

---

* In the 1990s the company relocated to the Žižkov Theatre.

For over fifty years, even after the death of Smoljak, the Theatre of Jára Cimrman retained its popularity with an audience that, Svěrák claims, is now bringing its children and grandchildren along to enjoy the performances. Among the younger generation there is a following attracted by the elements of Surrealist humour. Svěrák believes that the theatre's appeal lies in its emphasis on specific features of a common education and culture, much as Voskovec and Werich (whom Svěrák names as a major influences) used references from school humour and current fashion to evoke an atmosphere of shared humour. Many of the techniques are similar—wordplay, musical jokes, substitution, parody—although Jára Cimrman does not claim to have the range of the Liberated Theatre. Milan Obst believed that the significance of their humour went deeper than mere parody of popular forms; that it was satire on a common problem:

> Every age has its own Cimrman, its woe from wit, its monstrous forms of theory and practice. In every age there exists alongside the power of reason a meagre intellect, dancing in circles of sophistry, speculations, and conceptual swindling. And most of all, in every age, there are people who are willing or forced to take such pseudoscience seriously.[276]

KREJČA AT THE THEATRE BEYOND THE GATE

During the 1963 Karlovy Vary Conference on Small Theatres, Krejča's dramaturge, Karel Kraus, had realised that times were changing and that it was possible to work in more creative conditions than the bitter atmosphere of attrition in the National Theatre. By 1965 he and Otomar Krejča saw a way to recreate the kind of ensemble that had foundered a few years earlier. A relaxation in the political and cultural environment provided a window of opportunity, and Hercík's State Theatre Studio the necessary patronage. Krejča was not aiming to start something new, but to continue the work he had started at the National Theatre. This did not mean repeating what he had already done; his enthusiasm for multimedia productions, a reaction against the uniformity of the past, was waning, and his chief interest was in the practical work onstage with the actors: "Theatre is above all the ensemble, coming alive within the productions."[277] As the nucleus of the company, Krejča and Kraus engaged Jan Tříska and Marie Tomášová, Krejča's *Romeo and Juliet* of 1963, and other actors known to him personally. The writer and translator Josef Topol, author of *Their Day* and *The End of Shrovetide* was another member of the team. Like all members of the State Theatre Studio, they were on annual contracts that required full commitment. In terms of company numbers, the Theatre Beyond the Gate was one of the smallest in Prague, intending to avoid self-perpetuating administrative work, and to concentrate on the central work with the performers. "We defined its aims in a very simple manner," Krejča said later:

> To do only what we ourselves considered to be essential... only what, from beginning to end, would give us satisfaction and happiness in our work. Ultimately, after much effort and inevitable doubts we wanted to say, "Yes, this is what we wanted to express and this is how we wanted to express it, there is no other way to express it."[278]

The company had twelve months in which to prove that the work they wanted to do would interest others; Krejča was warned that if audiences fell below 60 per cent the theatre would be closed. He began with a one-act play by Josef Topol, *Cat on the Rails* (1965), virtually a two-hander for Tříska and Tomášová. Two lovers while away the time as they wait at a lonely railway halt; their relationship is laid bare in all its need and vulnerability. Krejča wrote of Topol, in an interview published a few days before the opening:

> He is convinced that the protagonist of contemporary drama is one who does not swim with the tide, who is full of doubt and uncertainty, who is always seeking. The protagonists of our theatre should be just such dissatisfied, searching personalities.[279]

Cat on the Rails shared the bill with Michel de Ghelderode's *Masques Ostendais*, full of colour, movement, masks, and music. The overwhelming success of the double bill enabled Krejča to spend a year working on the next production, Chekhov's *Three Sisters* (1966).

Karel Kraus later judged that of all writers, Chekhov held the most meaning for the Theatre Beyond the Gate. Krejča's first venture into Chekhov had been with *The Seagull* in 1960 at the National Theatre. Now he chose *Three Sisters* because he believed Chekhov would be the ideal author to help the actors develop, and he recognised that the ensemble had the right basic combinations for the roles at that time. The year spent in preparation, including several weeks of dress rehearsals, enabled him to work in detail with the actors in their responses and relationships. The British writer Hilary Spurling sensed this in 1969, at the World Theatre Season in London. Reviewing the production for *The Spectator*, she wrote:

> The whole production is criss-crossed by invisible lines, currents of attraction or revulsion, the passion flickering between Masha and Vershinin, between Soliony and Toozenbach, their eyes following Irena—all these seem to run like high voltage cables over the stage, while the bystanders barge and blunder in between.[280]

Nearly twenty years later, when Karel Kraus was showing photographs of the Theatre Beyond the Gate's productions to some young actors, one of them exclaimed: "Unbelievable–how one actor looks at another. That doesn't happen anymore."[281]

Three Sisters drew attention both nationally and internationally, visiting not only London but Paris, Zurich, Oslo, Rome, and fifteen more European cities.[282] Krejča continued to rehearse the production even after its première, constantly changing or creating new details. It remained in the repertoire for most of the theatre's lifetime, being followed by *Ivanov* in 1970 as part of Krejča's ongoing work with the actors on Chekhov; the process continued with a new production of *The Seagull* (1972). At the same time, the company worked on plays structured in a completely different way, but which Krejča saw as being complementary to Chekhov. One of these was Alfred de Musset's *Lorenzaccio* (1969), the story of a wild young idealist, himself corrupted within a corrupt court. Krejča told the story through the complex use of images summoned up by mirrors, masks, doubles, costume, and a constant shifting of the mass of actors onstage. Other directors also worked within the ensemble; Josef Topol directed his own short plays, *Nightingale for Supper* (1967) and *Two Nights with a Girl* (1967), and Helena Glancová directed Topol's translation of *Love's Labour's Lost* (1970).

Although technically a member of the State Theatre Studio, it could be argued that the Theatre Beyond the Gate did not belong to the small stage tradition at all, being the creation of a National Theatre director with an established reputation. The same could be said of Jindřich Honzl's Studio (1945–1948). There are parallels between Honzl and Krejča, both in their character and their life story. They were born within a few miles of each other on the windswept Bohemian-Moravian Highlands. They came from poor but hardworking parents; Krejča's family "scratched a living from the soil." Both joined the Communist Party out of conviction, but never followed a political career. Although chosen to lead the National Theatre drama company at different times in their careers, they were more interested in intensive work with a dedicated group, both of them driving their actors hard for long hours. Both were aware that when a theatre has to guarantee its "professional standard" there is little freedom to take creative, but crucial, risks. Both Honzl and Krejča were intensely involved in discovering the source of theatre, through rehearsal and through analysis (both published many theoretical articles). Both directors turned to the small stage because it is, in Peter Brook's words, an "empty space" where basic principles of theatrical relationships and communication can be investigated. Both were betrayed, personally and professionally, by the system in which they had invested their beliefs. What essentially divided them was the timing of the political betrayal that exposed the emptiness of that system. In 1967, a few months before the Soviet invasion, Krejča told an interviewer:

> It seems to me that the development of theatre worldwide is made up of a persistent centrifugal movement; it is an unceasing deviation, it is an obstinate repeating of efforts to circumvent its fundamental basis, i.e., the utter core of theatre: to cheat it, outsmart it, swindle and blind and deafen it.[283]

Krejča was granted a few years of relative creative freedom when, working with an experienced and cooperative team, he directed a series of productions which now feature in major histories of international theatre. When he created the Theatre Beyond the Gate, he could have returned to the National Theatre on his own terms, and many were disappointed he did not do so. He was more concerned with "theatre that is always at a beginning." His methods of getting back to the fundamental basis of theatre differed from those of the Theatre on the Balustrade or the Drama Club, but the very differences emphasised the fact that these theatres were engaged in a process of "searching" and the tensions between them were mutually reinforcing.

ROKOKO

Although young people were enjoying new freedoms, exemption from military service was not one of them. Even here, however, many "extracurricular" activities were available, including theatre. In the late 1950s, army policy was to replace large entertainment ensembles with smaller units whose development mirrored the civilian expansion of popular small theatres. One that made the transition to civilian life was led by Darek Vostřel, the ambitious son of the pre-war director of the Akropolis Theatre in Žižkov. In 1957, his group was offered the tenancy of the dilapidated Rokoko Theatre off Wenceslas Square (where Karel Hašler, Eduard Bass, Ferenc Futurista, Vlasta Burian, and V+W had once performed), provided they put it in working order. Their opening show in February 1958 seems to have passed unremarked; a second, *Ransacked*, quickly followed in March. The title *Ransacked* referred to items lifted from the repertoire of the turn-of-the-century cabarets, but the evening also included elements of contemporary satire; as did their next production the following October: *Up We Go the Rio Botičo*,* a montage of scenes by Ivan Vyskočil, J. R. Pick, Vratislav Blažek,† and others. Critics had reservations

* The Botič is a stream running through the Nusle Valley in Prague.

† After years in the wilderness, Blažek was back in town with *A Much Too Merry Christmas* at the Comedy Theatre (*Divadlo Komedie*), highly critical of Party opportunists and hypocrites.

about the quality of the performers, but young audiences did not care when they could hear topical ideas expressed in a way they had not heard in their lifetime. Productions included *Ba-po-po* directed by Antonín Moskalyk, *Was the Wolf Here?*, written and directed by Helena Philippová for children, and a revue, *Rokokokoktejl*. Early in 1963, Rokoko staged the first production in Czechoslovakia of a work by the Polish author Sławomir Mrożek, his one-act play *At Sea*, in a trilogy of Polish works (*3 x 3*). Later that year Rokoko staged *It's the Dragon* from the repertoire of Evening Brno.

In the early 1960s, Rokoko performances were praised for having higher technical standards than those of other small Prague theatres; later they were criticised for being showy and superficial (one critic daringly compared the lighting design for Waldemar Matuška singing "Jezebel" with the effect of taking marijuana).[284] The ensemble maintained its popularity with the younger generation by the discovery of popular new singers: the urchin-like Václav Neckář, blonde Helena Vondráčková and husky-voiced Marta Kubišová. Darek Vostřel was ambitious in wanting to expand Rokoko's activities, and in 1967 wrote in *Divadelní noviny* that they no longer wanted to do only cabaret, nor straight theatre, but rather music theatre; although the theatre lacked the necessary facilities, he believed they had the potential to achieve it. Rokoko closed for renovation in 1968 and reopened in October 1970 with Vostřel as Mr. Pickwick in a musical dramatisation of Charles Dickens. However, Normalisation policy no longer looked favourably on a theatre specialising in political satire, and Vostřel was forced to leave the theatre. In 1974, the ensemble was disbanded and Rokoko became a stage of the Prague Municipal Theatres.

VIOLA

A spotlight shone on the poetry *vinárna* Viola in the 1960s as the leading rendezvous for the international avant-garde. It could (and still can) be found at the back of the art nouveau "Prague Insurance Company" building on Národní třída, flanked on one side by the Academy of Sciences and on the other by the publishing house *Československý spisovatel*.* In its early days, Viola was a dingy space, the walls a greyish-yellow from cigarette smoke. The audience sat on bentwood chairs at rough tables, or stood listening at the window that opened onto the courtyard passage it shared with the only Italian *trattoria* in Prague. It was a meeting place for writers—Pavel Kohout and Václav Havel were regularly to be found here—and a landmark for foreign intellectuals:

* *U Topičů*, formerly the Borový publishing house that sheltered the wartime Little Theatre for 99.

Jean-Paul Sartre, Simone de Beauvoir, Allen Ginsberg, Paolo Pasolini, Kenneth Tynan. As Viola was a *vinárna*, jazz musicians could continue in jam sessions after the performance while the audience stayed to drink, listen, smoke, and talk until after 2:00 a.m.

The idea for the Viola poetry theatre had come from a group of actors: Jiří Ostermann, Jiří Martinek, and Drahomíra Fialková, who, with the help of an American long-playing record, persuaded the Reduta jazzman Luděk Hulan that there were other ways of performing poetry than the traditional recital. They called themselves the Poetic Cabaret and began to rehearse in a room where, for fear of interruption, they kept copies of Soviet poets on their desks. The group's first performance was given in the Kino Praha (now the Světozor) opposite Lucerna, between two short films directed by Věra Chytilová. They persuaded the head of *RaJ* (*Restaurace a jídelny*) to allow them to use a rundown *vinárna* a few yards up from the more famous Café Slavia, and advertised their first performance by leaving cards in other *vinárny* around Prague. *Whose is Jazz?* premièred on 22 July 1963. Hulan's compositions were combined with poetry by the Americans Lawrence Ferlinghetti, Gregory Corso, and Langston Hughes, and the Russians Yevgeny Yevtushenko and Andrei Voznesensky, as well as Czech authors including Ivan Diviš and Jiří Šotola. Instantly popular, it was the model for more programmes; the atmosphere was one of experiment, not always professionally accomplished, with performers who may not have been the best but who shared with their audience a desire to be where something new was happening. At Viola, new ideas were not only shared but also generated and some of them were, in the opinion of the Communist authorities, subversive. They knew that in the current climate it would be unwise to close down such a popular venue, so they looked for another solution. They found it in the person of the beatnik Jiří Ostermann, who had become involved with the homosexual underworld, drank heavily, and took drugs.

A well-timed and officially supported coup in April 1965 transferred the management of Viola to Vladimír Justl. Justl, expelled from Charles University in 1948 for political reasons, was a well-read scholar working as an editor in the Odeon publishing house. His specialism was the work of the poet Vladimír Holan, unpublished for fifteen years. In 1963 Justl had staged an arrangement of Holan's *A Night with Hamlet* at Viola. *A Night with Hamlet* is a complex poem which Justl made theatrically compelling with Radovan Lukavský and Marie Tomášová from the National Theatre. The appearance of such distinguished actors (especially Lukavský, who had been a notable Hamlet in the late 1950s) at a sleazy jazz dive shocked their contemporaries. But under Justl's management, Viola flourished as a professional theatre venue (in spite of the stage being only two metres deep). Leading performers and directors manoeuvred for an opportunity to work there, while openings appeared for those who were restricted from working elsewhere. Favourites performers such as Miroslav Horníček appeared regularly, but there were also opportunities for young directors such as Zdeněk Potužil from the Theatre on the Fringe and Lída Engelová, Jan Grossman's assistant on *The Memorandum*. Programmes compiled from the work of Jacques Prévert, Oscar Wilde, Jean Cocteau, Catullus, and Dostoyevsky entered the repertoire, alongside Czech poets Mácha, Hrubín, and Kainar. Some programmes included works as yet unpublished, such as Miroslav Holub's *Interferon, or On Theatre* (1984), directed by Jan Grossman. Grossman returned in 1987 with *Agathamania* by the HaTheatre playwright Arnošt Goldflam.

In the meantime, Viola went through a transformation. The smoke-stained walls and bare wooden tables of the jazz venue were replaced by a pink and white colour scheme, tablecloths, and muted lighting. In the view of Radim Vašinka, founder of X-ka, Viola had become Justl's *cukrárna* (patisserie), and the sense of risk shared by performers and audience had been lost.

ORFEUS

After leaving the Balustrade Theatre in 1963, Radim Vašinka had remained in Prague and formed the So-Called Theatre of Poetry (*Takzvané divadlo poezie*) (in defiance of his critics) on the model of the Brno X-ka and under the patronage of the University Art Ensemble (*Vysokoškolský umělecký soubor Praha*). In 1966, he found a mediaeval cellar on the Leser Quarter Square that the organisation had been using to store its archives. He obtained permission to renovate it and use it free of charge and called it Orfeus, after an inn that had once stood on the site.* Once the group had cleaned the two cellar rooms, several of them lived and slept as well as worked there.

Orfeus staged poetic works, some by foreign writers so little known that the literary agency DILIA had difficulty in tracing them to pay their royalties.† Its earliest efforts were montages of short pieces, but as it became more ambitious Vašinka began to stage one-act or even longer plays—plays that would not usually be seen in the theatres, and some of them for the first time in Czechoslovakia. For Vašinka the emphasis was on the staging; he thought the Viola productions were, while unconventional in form, as sterile as traditional poetry recitals. He believed the staging of a poem could bring to the

* The space was later (and is still) known as *Rubín* (Ruby).

† The *Divadelní a literární agentura* (Theatrical and Literary Agency) was the only such agency allowed to operate in the Czech Lands.

surface the poet's personal vision; could, through the use of movement, gesture, and costume, uncover hidden dimensions in the work. The cellar walls of Orfeus, scrubbed down, remained unpainted; the theatre's equipment, the most basic. Costumes, furniture, and props were acquired as cheaply but authentically as possible. Vašinka later recalled the audience attracted by Orfeus—from university lecturers to petty criminals, from secondary school pupils to flower sellers, from foreign intellectuals to workers at the ČKD heavy machinery factory in Vysočany. At the beginning of the 1970s, under Normalisation, the cellars became the property of the Socialist Youth Union.* Orfeus was expelled in 1972, after the start of Normalisation, and thereafter lived a peripatetic existence. The repertoire included an arrangement of the Čapek brothers' poetry, *The Ship of the Living*, and a version of W. S. Gilbert's *The Pirates of Penzance*, without Sullivan, and with the choruses treated as voiceband material. The amateur performers worked according to Vašinka's principle: "Poetry is something essential to life, by which man lives, and not something served up like dessert after dinner."

EVENING BRNO (*VEČERNÍ BRNO*)

One of the leading small theatres in Moravia was the satirical theatre, Evening Brno. Founded in 1959 by a group of actors and from 1962–1966, it was run by Evžen Sokolovský, at that time head of drama at the Brno State Theatre. In its early days it was a revue-type theatre—Eva Pilarová was a founder member, and Ljuba Hermanová joined the ensemble from 1963–1967—but progressed to more unified programmes without losing its communicative style. The first of these was *Hamlet IV, or The Elsinore Circus* (1962), a reworking by Vladimír Fux of the 1937 version of Jules Laforgue's *Hamlet* (*Hamlet II*) made by E. F. Burian (*Hamlet III*).† Further inspiration came from Voskovec and Werich, as models for the two intellectual clown-gravediggers who comment irreverently on the mores of their rulers. The duologues, touching on subjects such as the degeneration of power and the cult of personality, gave their interpreters scope for improvisation.

Hamlet IV was followed by *It's the Dragon* (1963) written by a collective authorship, including Fux. Written in the form of a folk legend, it is a satirical allegory in which the nonexistent dragon is a scapegoat for incompetence and abuse of power, and the dragonslayer an opportunist barber. In March 1964, Milan Uhde's *King Vávra*, based on Karel Havlíček Borovský's

---

* *Socialistický svaz mládeže* (*SSM*), the reincarnation of the *Československý svaz mládež (ČSM)*.

† See p. 84.

nineteenth-century satire *King Lávra*, opened at Evening Brno. This "nonstop nonsense" retells the Irish legend of the ruler with ass's ears (symbolising his stupidity) whom two idealists seek to expose, only to discover that the secret is well known and accepted by his subjects. Uhde put the script together from songs, sketches, gags, and duologues. It is not only about the corrupt nature of power but also about the attitudes and values of a public which subjects itself to what it knows to be a malfunctioning mechanism:

> Look here, young man, I don't know what you live on, maybe your fine words, but me, I've got a good appetite. Do you want me to kick the bucket? Us common folk want to get by. We got by, even when we were at war with England, and we'll go on getting by whether King Vávra's got ass's ears or not. And that's why I'm in service here.[285]

Uhde's satirical lines were to become the creed of the "common folk" of the 1970s and 1980s.

1968

In April 1968, the Theatre on the Balustrade returned to London to open the 5th World Theatre Season with Fialka's *Fools*, followed by Grossman's *Ubu Roi*. This year the company was reluctant to leave, even for a short time, a Prague that felt like the most dynamic city in the world.

The political intricacies of the Prague Spring are less important to this story than the cultural blossoming of the time. The gradually won freedom of thought and expression, manifested in literature, film, the theatre, and the media, accelerated with the political transformations. Ingrained caution in relationships between neighbours and colleagues dissolved, as "facts that until then had been shut up found their freedom." Censorship, overruled from above and ignored from below, was forgotten, and as spring turned to summer even its premises were handed over to the offices of *Literární listy*.* Discussions went on everywhere—in cafés and in trams, in queues and at swimming pools. Long, sometimes troubled debates were held between friends, spontaneous comments exchanged with strangers. As the summer got under way, newspapers sold out hot off the press, and were read avidly for the political and economic news. A nation normally indifferent to statistics educated itself through popular TV programmes that exposed the critical economic sit-

* The weekly *Literární noviny* (*Literary News*), at this time the house paper of the Union of Czechoslovak Writers, was at the centre of the political and intellectual battles of the second half of the 1960s. It was confiscated in autumn 1967 but returned in January 1968, when it was renamed *Literární listy* (*Literary Pages*). After the invasion and before it was closed down in 1969, it called itself *Listy*.

uation. The news was not all good; what was important was that it could be heard and read. The theatres, which had played a vital role in bringing about the new situation, now became secondary to the press, radio, and TV. People felt that the dramas onstage were lagging behind the drama of everyday life.

Not everyone was confident that "there would be no more fear." The National Theatre actress Marie Glázrová remembered Budapest in 1956, and prophesied blood flowing in the streets. The Balustrade stagehand and occasional actor Ladislav Klepal grumbled into his beard that everyone was blind to the obvious outcome. When, in mid-June, Warsaw Pact troops entered Czechoslovak territory for "manoeuvres," no one felt easy. At the end of June, Ludvík Vaculík's "Two Thousand Words that Belong to Workers, Farmers, Officials, Scientists, Artists, and Everybody" urged Czechoslovaks to become activists. Citizens lined up at makeshift tables in city centres to sign the manfesto. In mid-July, the Warsaw Pact leaders, without the Czechoslovaks, convened in Warsaw. The resulting letter to the Central Committee of the Czechoslovak Communist Party described "Two Thousand Words" as an attempt to foment anarchy and an organised political platform of counter-revolution. The broadcast of the Warsaw Letter was piped through the Balustrade Theatre sound system. Sitting at the director's table in the auditorium, Jan Grossman sunk his head into his hands and groaned out loud.

At the end of July, the Czech and Soviet leaders held talks at the border crossing of Čierna nad Tisou and after a Warsaw Pact meeting in Bratislava, the troops began to withdraw. Days of tension were followed by the deceptive peace of August. For the first time in decades, Czechoslovaks were free to travel abroad, and thousands did so. Others carried on working in the dusty towns, sending children and grandparents to enjoy the fragrance of the forests and mountains on the German and Polish frontiers; until one still summer night, when those borders were crossed by convoys of German and Polish tanks, while aircraft heavy with Soviet tanks flew low over Prague, thundering into our dreams. Telephones rang from house to house; in the darkness before dawn, people came onto the streets to see what horror had struck. More than a quarter of a million Warsaw Pact soldiers crossed the Czechoslovak frontiers that night.

VI "NORMALISATION"

In the irrational euphoria of the weeks following the Soviet invasion, the nation persisted in believing it had not been defeated. It seemed to be of one mind in its solidarity, its support of the leadership, and its opposition towards anyone regarded as sympathetic to the Soviet Union.* There were moments of heroism. But as the tide of hope receded, treachery began to emerge. The fact that Alexander Dubček and his reform Communists (all but one) had signed away the country's independence in the Moscow Protocol was still kept secret. Students obediently obeyed his instructions to scrub the statue of St. Wenceslas clean of protest slogans. In January 1969, dark columns of mourners still wound their way through Prague, following the coffin of Jan Palach, who burnt himself to death in protest at the national paralysis. It was the last public manifestation. When the second "torch," Jan Zajíc, immolated himself in February, the news was concealed and there were no crowds at his funeral. Czechoslovak society in the 1970s slid into the state of "Normalisation" described by Václav Havel as "Calm as a morgue or a grave."[286] In April 1969, Alexander Dubček resigned the leadership of the Communist Party to Gustáv Husák—a man who looked on his life sentence in the 1950s show trials as a "misunderstanding" which did not impair the rightness of Communist ideology. Husák had been one of the "reform Communists," yet under his regime those to whom the label had stuck were ruthlessly discarded, thrown

* One such was the theatre director Stanislav Vyskočil (a former member of Honzl's Studio), who, when I interviewed him in 1984, was still enraged over the inscription pinned to his office door by Pilsen's young theatre staff in September 1968: "Down with the collaborator" (*Pryč s kolaborantem*). Young people, he told me, always thought they knew better than their elders, and the moment a young person was dissatisfied, he or she was convinced that everything had to be changed.

almost literally on the streets. Those "reform Communists" who were only purged from the Party (*vyškrutnutí*) were fortunate; those who were expelled (*vyloučení*) would probably never work in their profession again. In the early 1970s, a document was circulated to key workers to sign, denouncing the Prague Spring as a counter-revolutionary act and welcoming the intervention of the "fraternal armies." All over the country, people were changing places—sometimes with a friendly agreement that the former head could stay on in a lesser capacity, in other places with opportunist greed and a taste for revenge. A secret list of "undesirable persons" began to be compiled: people who found it increasingly difficult to get work of any kind.

The "Normalisation" of publishing, education, and the arts was one of Husák's priorities. Out of more than 400 writers publishing in Czechoslovakia prior to 1968, around 170 were allowed to continue. Journals disappeared from the newsagents and books from the libraries (as they had in the 1950s); prisoners were tasked with cutting prefaces and epilogues by "forbidden" scholars out of editions of Marx and other Communist classics. The Union of Czech Writers (*Svaz českých spisovatelů*), established in 1969 after federalisation on principles laid down by the Union of Czechoslovak Writers in 1967) and led by the poet Jaroslav Seifert, was abolished as early as 1970; its members included many playwrights now unable to make a living in their profession: Topol, Landovský, Blažek, Uhde, Rejnuš, Karvaš, Pavlíček. Not only could their plays not be staged or broadcast; their names could not be mentioned in print or on air. Many established scholars and journalists, including theatre critics, were no longer able to publish their work: Sergej Machonin, Jindřich Černý, Karel Kraus. Researchers in academic institutes found that certain names had to be omitted from reference works. Nor could the names be mentioned of people who had been active in the theatre in the 1930s and 1940s but rejected Communism and in some cases remained in exile after World War II.* Work prepared for publication during the 1960s with references to now unacceptable personalities was shelved or destroyed. Some new books went straight off the press into the pulping mechanism; a few copies might be salvaged for the archives. One example of a book prepared for printing was Vratislav Effenberger's detailed analysis of the work of the Liberated Theatre. It was suppressed on the one hand because the name of the Surrealist Effenberger was again unacceptable to the Communist regime and on the other hand because of his serious and objective approach. Nothing has been published on the Liberated Theatre, during Normalisation or since,

* Bořivoj Srba, one of the founders of Theatre Goose on a String, after being banned from teaching (and travelling), worked for years on a study of Czech cultural activity in London that was finally published in 2003.

with the depth of Effenberger's analysis. An encyclopedia of Czech theatre artists, prepared during the 1970s by the Cabinet for the Study of Czech Theatre of the Czechoslovak Academy of Sciences was scheduled to appear in 1983, the Year of Czech Theatre. It was at the final proofing stage when its editor-in-chief Vladimír Just was told that it contained names that could not appear; nor, because this would be too obvious, could they be excised. The volume had to be reedited on different lines and was eventually published in 1988.*

The Arts Faculty of Charles University lost more than one-tenth of its teaching staff through emigration, early retirement, or dismissal; some departments were abolished, others were merged, such as Theatre and Film Studies with Music. Jan Kopecký, who had been appointed head of the department in 1968, was fired in 1971, in spite of his appeal a year earlier:

> This is for me an incentive to reflect on my life and Party activity from 1935, when I joined the youth movement, and the wartime, when I worked as a Communist in *Předvoj* (Vanguard). I was the link between Prague and Kladno, colporteur for Party materials. I led trainings, organised groups.... I got my Party card as a member of the *KSČ* straight after May 1945—and from that time have lived through all the Party's struggles—good times and bad, always there where I was needed and where the Party sent me... till after 1968, when the Party... summoned me to a task I resisted, but which I eventually accepted in a disciplined way and tried to perform responsibly and with integrity.... I want by my work to show my loyalty to Communism and to Marx and Lenin's teaching—and to accomplish it, whatever the outcome may be for me in the immediate situation.[287]

Kopecký was replaced by Miroslav Kouřil, whose star was on the rise again. Another member of the department, Milan Lukeš, was one of twenty-seven teachers suspended from the Faculty, but survived, pursuing a career as specialist in Elizabethan and Jacobean drama. Some theatre scholars and dramaturges (including reform Communists) expelled from universities and theatres but not thought to be an active threat to the regime found refuge in Eva Soukupová's Theatre Institute, in the archive of the National Theatre, and in the Cabinet for the Study of Czech Theatre housed in Zdeněk Nejedlý's former apartment in Smíchov. For two decades, these forgotten scholars suppressed their political animosity and worked side by side in book-lined rooms, building up a body of work, much of it at that time unpublishable.

---

* Just revealed this story at a meeting of the dramaturgy committee of the Union of Czech Dramatic Artists in May 1989.

Ludvík Kundera, a Brno scholar and translator who resigned from the Mahen Theatre in 1970 in solidarity with his colleagues, was expelled from the Party and his work no longer staged or published. In the 1960s, Kundera had been granted the Czech language rights to the works of Bertolt Brecht; as a result, his Brno colleague Evžen Sokolovský had been the first in Czechoslovakia to direct Brecht's plays. The restrictions on Kundera led to an apparently inexplicable scarcity of Czech productions of plays by Communism's most famous dramatist during Normalisation. Kundera was later allowed to publish his translations of Brecht's poems, and occasional articles in small academic journals. He began to cooperate with the Theatre on a String, which in 1983—after a long battle with the censor—staged his version of Comenius's *The Labyrinth of the World and the Paradise of the Heart*; the adaptation had won a competition at the National Theatre in Prague in 1971, but never been performed. Ludvík's cousin Milan had similarly lost his post as professor at FAMU* in 1969, and was also stripped of his Party membership in 1970. He was teaching at the University of Rennes in France when in 1979 the authorities took offence at his novel *The Book of Laughter and Forgetting*† and rescinded his citizenship. He wrote no more plays, although *Jacques and His Master* (1971), on a theme of Diderot and originally intended for the Theatre on the Balustrade (where his second play, *Cock-up*, had been premièred), was performed for many years by the Drama Studio of Ústí nad Labem under the name of Evald Schorm.

Another Brno writer, Milan Uhde (author of *King Vávra*), became an internal exile. *Host do domu*,‡ the journal he edited, was closed in 1970. In September 1972, an article in *Rudé právo* described Uhde as "politically discredited," on the pretext of having "inappropriately" adapted as a musical Jiří Mahen's pre-World War I comedy *The Lane of Courage* (about a community that wants to "live in truth").[288] Within days, his contracts were cancelled and he was unable to work in any literary field, even technical translation. For a while, his work was covered by the names of *černé duše*—ghostwriters (also known as *pokrývači*, or roofers, i.e., those who cover something).§ Uhde wrote three scripts for the Brno Theatre on a String under the name of the theatre direc-

* The Film Faculty of the Academy of Performing Arts, established in 1946.

† Completed in 1978 and published by Gallimard in 1979 as *Le Livre du rire et de l'oubli*. First published in Czech as *Kniha smíchu a zapomnění* (Atlantis) in 2017.

‡ The title translates as "The Guest in the House" and refers to Jiří Wolker's first volume of poems (1921). (The "Guest" is essentially Christ, and the reference is to the blessing a guest brings on the home.) It was adopted by a literary group in the 1950s, and then by their journal. Also related, under the name *Host*, are the 1920s literary journal, the 1980s samizdat literary journal, and the current literary journal and publishing house.

§ In a conversation in spring 1987, Uhde remembered how this seemed like a game at first, but people began to be afraid. No period of darkness had lasted longer than the present one, he said—the 1950s could not compare.

tor Zdeněk Pospíšil: *Professional Woman* (1974); *Ballad for a Bandit* (1975), a celebration of individuality in a conformist society; and *On a May Fairy Tale* (1976), a variation on Vilém Mrštík's nineteenth-century *May Fairy Tale*. (Milan Uhde, sitting in the audience, ran the risk of exposure with his tendency to speak the text along with the actors.)[289]

Pavel Kohout, once the leading exponent of Socialist Realist drama, was now accused of complicity in every "anti-state" activity, even Jan Palach's suicide. He actively resisted his exclusion and in the early 1970s established the legal principle of the author's right to negotiate his/her own foreign royalties.* In 1978, he was violently attacked in the press as one of the initiators of Charter 77. Nevertheless, he was granted permission to work for a year in Vienna's Burgtheater. Driving home in October 1979, he was turned away at the border and told he had been stripped of his Czechoslovak citizenship. It was a neat way to dispose of undesirable personalities. A few months earlier, Pavel Landovský from the Drama Club, actor and author of *Rooms by the Hour* (1969), had been treated with less consideration; his leg was broken by the secret police. He too found asylum in Vienna.

Ivan Klíma's last work for the stage, *Games*, was written in 1975 and produced in Vienna in 1978. The setting is a party that represents a microcosm of 1970s society, in which anyone might find themselves confronted with a political or moral dilemma when taking even the most mundane decision. "Life forces us to assume certain roles, to fulfil other people's expectations," Klíma wrote in the programme note for Vienna:

> In games we fake seriousness. And for a while they allow us to avoid confronting our fate. But finally our true nature glimmers through, and, for a moment, we see our real selves. Sometimes this takes us by surprise, for the nature we catch a glimpse of seems totally unknown to us. Or we notice, to our astonishment, that our true nature doesn't exist anymore; our role has absorbed us, transformed us, we have already become a function of it...[290]

In the 1960s, the theatres had grown to understand the prejudices of the censors, and evaded or challenged them, or else came to a compromise. Although the office of censorship had been abolished in June 1968, under Normalisation a more insidious form was instituted, in which a theatre director had to decide whether to risk dismissal if his theatre's programme did not conform. The planned programme had to be submitted in advance to the local authority, and was expected to include plays from the USSR and other Soviet

* After Kohout's banishment, this route to financial independence still proved beneficial to writers such as Havel and Klíma.

bloc countries; any Western authors had to be rigorously justified from the political point of view. In advance of every première, the cultural committee of the local authority attended a closed performance, with the powers to insist on changes before public performance. (A forward-thinking director would include some lines or pieces of business that were clearly unacceptable, thus saving the committee from having to take a more searching look.) In spite of official exhortations for new playwrights to produce work "worthy" of the Czech stage, few playwrights were willing to expose controversial ideas or experimental forms to the cultural committee. They chose to play safe, and directors turned to classics and adaptations. In 1978, the Institute for Research into the Arts (*Ústav pro výzkum kultury*) published the result of a survey into the popularity of dramatic art, revealing that Karel Čapek, Shakespeare, and Alois Jirásek trailed far behind the contemporary playwright Jaroslav Dietl as the nation's favourite playwright.[291] Dietl, who had dabbled in reform Communism in the 1960s, became known as the father of the Czech television series, a genre he tailored to the messages the Party wished to convey to the population.* Although he wrote several similarly oriented plays, it is probable that the survey was influenced by the popularity of his television dramas. It concluded, not unsurprisingly, that "by far the majority of the inhabitants of our country have a positive attitude towards dramatic art, and that dramatic art is therefore a sphere through which the cultural-education function of the State can be applied intensively."[292]

Plays by international writers who had publicly supported their colleagues were also banned (more precisely, "not allowed"); they included Tom Stoppard, Harold Pinter, and Samuel Beckett. Among the periodicals whose independent content caused them to be closed down in the spring of 1970 were the two professional theatre journals, the weekly *Divadelní noviny* and the monthly *Divadlo*, as well as a number of literary journals in which serious theatre criticism had appeared. (A flimsy fortnightly called *Scéna*† was launched in 1976, covering drama, ballet, opera, television, and film. It was largely a mouthpiece for the Union of Czech Dramatic Artists and its president, actress and hardline Communist Jiřina Švorcová. It was another decade before it carried articles worth reading.) In the State Library (Clementinum) issues of theatre journals dating from 1967, 1968, and 1969 were moved to the special deposits (*zvláštní fondy*) behind locked doors in the attics of the ancient building. Permission might be granted to view selected materials; how-

---

* Paulina Bren gives an account of the televised self-criticism Dietl had to undergo before being trusted by the Party, in *The Greengrocer and His TV*, pp. 131–133.

† The same name as the journal founded by František Zavřel and Arnošt Dvořák in 1914.

ever, it was impossible to obtain photocopies as the materials would have had to leave the attic, thus potentially subverting innocent library staff.

Just as unknown numbers of professors, teachers, and editors who refused to endorse the Soviet invasion were demoted, moved to minor research institutes, or thrown out of their profession entirely, so theatre directors, dramaturges, actors, and stage managers had their contracts terminated and were moved to third-rate theatres in the provinces, or prevented from working in any theatre at all (let alone film or television). Some performers continued to work in the restricted conditions allowed them: they could appear on stage but not on television, on tour but not in Prague, be mentioned in publications but not with photographs. Many emigrated. These demotions and departures led to vacancies in influential positions that were filled, not by new young talent but by opportunists and bureaucrats with little practical experience. The Ministry of Culture allocated a "worker for special purposes" to every theatre; their activities were a mystery to the rest of the company, but essentially their role was to look out for ideological lapses. In 1972, a new Union of Czech Dramatic Artists (*Svaz českých dramatických umělců, SČDU*) was created, and its members carefully vetted. The president was Jiřina Švorcová, from the Vinohrady Theatre, where the ambitious revolutionary of the postwar period, Zdeněk Míka, had since 1970 presided over the restoration of hardline ideology.

THE THEATRE ON THE BALUSTRADE AND WHAT BECAME OF JAN GROSSMAN

Václav Havel's dismissal from the Theatre on the Balustrade in 1967 had soon been rescinded, but in 1968 he resigned out of loyalty to Jan Grossman. In the insecure and emotional atmosphere of spring 1968, relationships with Vladimír Vodička had become strained, and confidential information was leaked to *Divadelní noviny*. In sorrow rather than anger, Grossman refuted errors in the article and brought his departure forward to the summer of 1968.[293] His next move should have been to the National Theatre. Milan Kundera and Miloš Macourek resigned as well, as did the actors Libíček (Ubu), Málková (by then married to Grossman), and Václav Mareš, who joined the suburban S. K. Neumann Theatre. Fourteen years later, as director of the S. K. Neumann, he was to offer Grossman his first employment in Prague since his departure from the Theatre on the Balustrade.

Even after the invasion and the internal shake-up, one play commissioned by Jan Grossman was still due to open at the Theatre on the Balustrade. He had been collaborating with Milan Kundera on his second play *Cock-up*, premièred in January 1969 at the F. X. Šalda Theatre in Liberec, and at the Theatre on the Balustrade in May, directed by Václav Hudeček. Hudeček realised that the play would make new demands on the audience of the Theatre on the Balustrade. He anticipated that its satirical objectives, expressed in exaggerated images, would arouse either disgust or spontaneous enthusiasm. *Cock-up* is set in a world of corrupt banality, where sexual mechanics and ritual humiliation substitute for valid human relationships. As in Kundera's novel *The Joke*, the action opens with a casual but harmless practical joke played by the Headmaster, who draws on the blackboard the graffito symbol for the female sex organ,* and comments:

> Apart from this thing it means much else, for example, our taste for it. And in no time this cold geometric austerity begins to show up the vanity of that taste and consequently our distaste. Obviously it doesn't only apply to the thing itself but to women in general. And because women are our life, it follows that it applies to our whole life, it represents human existence itself.[294]

Amused by the stir this causes among the prurient staff, the next day the Headmaster adds an equals sign and his own name. But the joke turns serious when a school pupil confesses to the insult. Kundera later said: "In every man's life there are moments when man is joking. But then the joke dominates and makes a joke of Man."[295] The Headmaster is forced by the sadistic Chairman of the Town Council to cut off the boy's ears, while the boy's teacher (who is also the Headmaster's mistress) is caned by the Chairman.

At its Liberec première, *Cock-up* (as *Two Ears, Two Weddings*) had been likened by the *Divadelní noviny* critic to a distorted reflection of the world of Kundera's first play, *The Owners of the Keys*.[296] Both plays deal with a microcosm where people voluntarily choose an unfree existence, subjecting themselves to humiliations for the sake of being masters of their own small territory of home comforts. But whereas *The Owners of the Keys* delivers a pseudo-heroic drama of life and death, self-sacrifice, and tragedy, the anti-heroic *Cock-up* is a heartless farce triggered by an image of male exploitation of women.

After leaving the Theatre on the Balustrade, Grossman survived fourteen years of mainly internal exile. At first he was allowed to accept invitations to direct in Finland, the Netherlands, Switzerland, and Austria. In June 1975, he directed *Oedipus* in Zurich. The following November he attended the performance of Václav Havel's *The Beggar's Opera* in the village of Horní Počer-

---

* In the programme to the Drama Club revival of 2008 (directed by Ladislav Smoček), Kundera notes regretfully that this symbol—a vertical line enclosed in a diamond—seems to be peculiar to Czech culture and renders the play impossible to perform anywhere else.

nice;* his presence was noted by the secret police and he was believed to be complicit. In spring 1976, he was due to direct his own adaptation of *Švejk* in West Berlin. (Grossman's Švejk was not the traditional homely figure of Josef Lada's illustrations but representative of the bleak world that Europe entered after World War I.) Permission to travel to Berlin for casting was refused, so the German actors presented themselves at Grossman's apartment on the Gottwald Embankment† overlooking the Vltava. His passport was to be released in time for him to travel to Berlin for the rehearsals. The day before his departure, while Jan packed his bag, Marie Málková went to collect the passport from the Interior Ministry, but returned without it. It was 1990 before Grossman saw Berlin again.

From 1973 to the end of 1980, most of Jan Grossman's work could be seen only in the Theatre of West Bohemia in Cheb, and that only because the authorities assumed that four hours in an unheated train would dissuade anyone from making the 150-kilometre journey from Prague. The invitation had been mediated by Grossman's young colleague from Brno, František Hromada; also involved were the dramaturge Miloslav Klíma and the director Miroslav Krobot. The theatre led by Mikuláš Krotký turned out to be an island of freedom; others invited to work there included Vlasta Chramostová and Evald Schorm. Cheb's population numbered only thirty thousand, so the turnover of productions was rapid. Grossman directed at first two—later four—a year, mainly the classics: Chekhov, *King Lear*, Molière's *The School for Wives*. The ideologues insisted on at least one Soviet play every season; Grossman's production of Alexander Kopkov's *Golden Elephant* (1979), however, was swiftly banned. For seven years he commuted from Prague, sleeping during the week in a store cupboard defined by the curve of the theatre's circle.‡

In late 1980, Grossman was invited to direct in Hradec Králové, almost as far to the east of Prague as Cheb had been to the west. (Nevertheless, Cheb and Hradec came to form an important theatrical axis.) He completed four productions: Gogol's *The Government Inspector* (1980), the Mrštík brothers' *Maryša* (1981), Brecht's *Mr. Puntila and His Man Matti* (1981) and Molière's *Don Juan* (1982). The stylised *Puntila*, although well reviewed, only lasted a year in the repertoire—it was not appreciated in the villages to which the company toured. *Don Juan*, on the other hand, featured a set by Jaroslav Malina covered with psychedelic graffiti—a phenomenon still rare behind the Iron Curtain. Grossman's reason for staging *Don Juan* lay in Juan's speech on hypocrisy—this was not a hero but a destroyer and outsider, a gang leader whose death lay

* See p. 220.

† In 1990 Gottwald's name was replaced by that of the embankment's earlier dedicatee, Tomáš Masaryk.

‡ Legend has it that during the evening performance he would sometimes slip into the back of the circle to watch in his dressing gown and slippers.

in the love-hate relationship inside him. A production of Karel Steigerwald's *The Tartar Feast* was planned but not allowed. The theatre's director, an embittered collaborator with the secret police, brought Grossman's activities in Hradec Králové to an end in the spring of 1982. His influence, however, remained strong, particularly among the group that had created Studio Beseda; he himself was inspired by the work of the puppet company *DRAK*.*

In 1983, Václav Mareš invited Grossman back to Prague, the outlying S. K. Neumann Theatre, to direct Chekhov's *Uncle Vanya*. It had taken Mareš two years to persuade the local authority to give permission.† The rehearsal atmosphere was intensely charged, the actors conscious of the historic moment. Vanya was played by Zdeněk Ornest, younger brother of Jiří Orten and Ota Ornest, who had survived Terezín, Auschwitz, and Dachau.‡ Grossman's penultimate production at the S. K. Neumann was Shakespeare's *Measure for Measure* (1987). He was attracted to it by its ambiguity, in which the Duke seems to be presented as heavenly justice, while in reality he is a manipulative voyeur. The play was set in a Vienna that teemed with braggarts, whores, and hypocrites. Not only the characterisations but also the costumes (by Ludmila Pavlousková) were many-layered, swaggering leather held together by structures of loops and bands. Nuns turned a pretty ankle, monks wore lacy underwear, their habits literally a cloak for appetite and scandal. Isabella was conceived as a blindly hypocritical temptress, while Froth nibbled his sweets as all hell broke loose around him. Grossman was able to lead the audience's gaze through the sweep of stage action to focus on a tiny, precise gesture. He exposed a world devoid of justice, truth, or purity—the corruption stemming from the Duke himself, an affable, vicious jester as quick with a blow as a slap on the back. But only local audiences and alert theatre goers found their way to the S. K. Neumann. Any thought of Grossman directing again at the Balustrade was remote.

---

* On Studio Beseda and *DRAK*, see p. 227.

† After Mareš's death, the actress Zdena Hadrbolcová remembered: "He was a boy from a working-class family. We never talked about his Party membership. He was my friend, and maybe the only person whose partisanship didn't matter to me" (*Lidové noviny*, 11 August 2010).

‡ Visiting the Kafka exhibition in the Pompidou Centre in Paris the same year, I was haunted by a quiet voice reading Kafka in Czech. I eventually identified the recorded reader; it was Zdeněk Ornest. Ornest was killed by a train in 1990. It was the line through Stromovka Park—the wartime route to Terezín.

THE THEATRE BEYOND THE GATE AND WHAT BECAME OF OTOMAR KREJČA

In January 1969, the Theatre Beyond the Gate was transferred from the State Theatre Studio to the direct control of the Ministry of Culture. In March 1971, shortly after the première of *Oedipus–Antigone*,* the ministry dismissed Otomar Krejča as director of the company, allowing him to remain as a subordinate employee. In April the company was scheduled to return to the World Theatre Season in London, with the more recent *Ivanov* accompanying the previously successful *Three Sisters*. Four days before the visit, the Communist authorities banned the company from performing *Three Sisters*. The festival director Peter Daubeny refused to be held hostage, writing in *The Times* that:

> Faced with this last-minute breach of contract… I was left with no alternative but to cancel the company's visit. This I did with the greatest reluctance, having spent many months preparing for this particular production of *Three Sisters*. […] A formal protest has already been lodged with the Czechoslovak Government by Her Majesty's ambassador in Prague but this does not alter the fact that London has been denied the opportunity of seeing once again a masterpiece such as Otomar Krejca's *Three Sisters*.[297]

At the end of June 1972, the Theatre Beyond the Gate was officially closed down on the grounds that its building contravened fire regulations (although the *Laterna magika* company continued to play in the same theatre). The company was forced to disband.† For a brief period, Krejča was allowed to work at the S. K. Neumann Theatre (including productions of Chekhov's *Platonov* [1974] and Preissová's *The Farmer's Woman* [1975]), but was then forbidden to direct in Czechoslovakia at all. From 1976, he was allowed to travel abroad as long as his productions were not reviewed nor his name mentioned in his homeland, a unique arrangement backed by the promise that after two years' or so penance, Krejča could return to the mainstream of Czech theatre. Meanwhile, Marie Tomášová, one of Czechoslovakia's leading actresses but guilty of being Krejča's wife, was banned from permanent theatre employment and took such freelance work as was offered to her, mainly with the poetry theatre Lyra Pragensis. Krejča's associate director, Helena Glancová, could similarly work only with Lyra Pragensis.‡ Jan Tříska—who, with his friend Václav

---

* Krejca's own adaptation of Sophocles's trilogy.

† Among those who protested was the British director Peter Brook. Consequently, the Czechoslovak authorities refused to invite his iconic *A Midsummer Night's Dream* to Prague when it toured Europe in 1972.

‡ A loosely structured, peripatetic poetry theatre that functioned within the State Theatre Studio 1967–1972 and was then adopted by Supraphon. It did not overdramatise its material, relying on continuity with the past, restrained performance, and an atmosphere of something unsaid.

Havel, had spent the week following the August invasion broadcasting on Liberec radio—lived hand to mouth for several years. In 1977, after signing Charter 77, he emigrated to the USA, where Jiří Voskovec helped him make a new career. Karel Kraus was banned from any cultural occupation, even that of sales assistant in a secondhand bookshop, for fear he should damage Socialist culture. Josef Topol made a living as translator and proofreader until he signed Charter 77. After that, he was forced to become a labourer on the restoration of Charles Bridge, until disabled by an industrial accident. From then on, he lived in seclusion on an invalidity pension, writing poetry and meeting only close friends. All their names were excised from the history books.

Krejča described theatre as "a political arena," but an arena that is at its most powerful when it fulfils its purely artistic intentions to the utmost. The theatre's productions were political in the broad sense, because they gave people a context in which to think about actions and their consequences, about suffering and rebellion, about freedom and compromise. Karel Kraus believed that it was by making people think that the Theatre Beyond the Gate attracted hostility. Other theatres were jealous of Krejča's success, claiming that he was too demanding; he worked his ensemble too hard, rehearsed too long, expected too much of his actors, took theatre too seriously, and wanted other people to take it seriously too. In the 1970s, official artistic policy guided companies towards a levelling of standards. In 1971, an English theatre magazine quoted Krejča as saying that: "We believe in a theatre of free choice, even though we fully realise the danger which inevitably accompanies the desire for a freedom of choice."[298]

On 28 September 1988, Krejča reminded Minister of Culture Milan Kymlička of his promises:

> Thirteen years ago, representatives from West Germany requested that I be allowed to work in their country. The deputy minister of culture of that time informed me of this request. I replied that I would only accept the offer on the condition that I would not, as a consequence, be permanently banned from working in the Czech theatre. The deputy minister indicated that I would not be allowed to work at home while I accepted work abroad, but that after two years I would have the choice of re-entering Prague theatrical life. This has still not happened. And in all this long time I have never for a moment given up hope that I would once again be able to put my theatrical experience at the service of Czech actors, Czech audiences, Czech culture.[299]

THE FATES OF MACHÁČEK, RADOK, AND SCHORM

Miroslav Macháček

The actor and director Miroslav Macháček, who had survived charges of espionage in the 1950s to become one of Krejča's team, was first purged from the Party and then expelled from it as well. His 1971 production of Shakespeare's *Henry V* at the National Theatre was condemned by *Rudé právo* as deliberately antisocialist.[300] In 1975, he was persuaded to enter a psychiatric hospital.[301] Complex, stubborn, and self-questioning, Macháček returned to the National Theatre to struggle in 1979 with the National Theatre's head of drama, Václav Švorc,* over his unconventional casting of Stroupežnický's *Our Proud Peasants*. One member of the cast, Jaroslava Šiktancová (who had also been involved as Macháček's unofficial assistant), was definitively banned from the National Theatre on the grounds of having signed Charter 77. The production of *Our Proud Peasants* became a legend, but was bitterly criticised for focusing on the contemporary relevance of the classic, with its portraits of petty jealousies and self-important authorities.[302]

Alfréd Radok

Alfréd Radok did not hesitate in his reading of the 1968 invasion. He had suffered more than one heart attack. In two days he was out of Czechoslovakia forever. He had a contract to direct Molière's *The Misanthrope* in Göteborg and so, with his wife Marie and children,† set out by car for Sweden. They took with them only winter clothing and the bare necessities. Work could be found in the European theatre for such an internationally known director, but psychologically, emigration was hard to bear. Radok had lived in fear of his life during the occupation, ending it in a concentration camp; the fear persisted under Stalinism, when he felt betrayed even by such a close colleague as Svoboda. At the same time, he passed his knowledge on to the next generation, especially Václav Havel, who recognised Radok as his first teacher and corresponded with him to the end of his life. According to the photographer Jaroslav Krejčí, it was Radok who taught Grossman how to find the inherent meaning and rhythm of a text: "There are 648 ways to approach this text. I'm down to 38 and eventually I've got to decide on one." Radok, Krejčí said, saw rhythm as present in everything: a tree, tramlines, engraving on glass. (He also, Krejčí claimed, had a tendency to appear suddenly from nowhere, neat and precise.)[303]

---

* The brother of Jiřina Švorcová.

† Radok's son David followed his father's profession in Sweden, and after 1989 returned to direct some major productions in the Czech Republic.

On 1 July 1970, Radok was notified that he was abroad without permission from the Czechoslovak authorities. On 10 September 1971, the government stripped him of the titles and honours awarded by the state. On 27 December 1974, he, his wife, and his daughter were sentenced in absentia to fifteen months' imprisonment. In 1976, Radok was invited to direct Havel's Vaněk plays *Audience* and *The Unveiling* at the Vienna Burgtheater. He was hospitalised shortly after his arrival in Vienna and died in exile of a heart attack on 22 April 1976, at the age of sixty-one.

Evald Schorm

After the upheavals of 1968, the Theatre on the Balustrade continued on its way under the directorship of Vladimír Vodička, seemingly unshakeable even after the "illegal" emigrations of three directors of the drama company in a row.* The only director of Grossman's stature was a man who could not be offered permanent employment, the former film director Evald Schorm. A farmer's son, Schorm had spent his childhood in the South Bohemian countryside, still following the centuries-old pattern of life. He was a teenager when the Communists drove the "*kulak*"† family out of their home. Disgraced and expelled from school, he was twenty-five before, during the brief thaw of 1956, FAMU accepted him as a student. Between 1964 and 1971 he created some of the most ethically searching feature films of the Czech New Wave (*Everyday Courage*, *The Return of the Prodigal Son*); after 1971, he was only allowed to direct in the theatre, and only as a guest. He grasped at invitations when and where they were offered—travelling to Olomouc, Brno, Cheb, and Gottwaldov, or negotiating occasional productions with the Drama Club, Ypsilon, Theatre on the Fringe, Semafor, Balustrade, and *Laterna magika*. Schorm was aware that Miroslav Müller, head of the Communist Party's cultural department in Prague, was playing cat and mouse, but was unable to come face to face with him. One probable reason for his persecution was his role in Jan Němec's film *The Party and the Guests* (1966), officially denounced in 1967 as having "nothing in common with our republic, Socialism, and the ideals of Communism." Schorm played himself, the guest who refuses to join in the forced merriment imposed by the host (Ivan Vyskočil, looking very like Lenin) and is left to be hunted down by dogs.

Two of Schorm's memorable productions at the Theatre on the Balustrade were Shakespeare tragedies translated by Milan Lukeš, who attended rehearsals and worked on the productions with Schorm. They were the First

* In this farewell waltz, Grossman's former assistant Jaroslav Gillar fled to the West in 1974, Jaroslav Chundela in 1978, and Karel Vondrášek in 1982.

† A term derived from Russian, used indiscriminately for any hardworking farmer opposed to collectivisation.

Quarto *Hamlet* (1978) and *Macbeth* (1981). *Macbeth* was an example of how a director's insights into Shakespeare's text could cause the authorities to put pressure on dramaturges at the Ministry of Culture to condemn a production of a classic play as "anti-state". Schorm laid open the techniques of tyranny through Macbeth's dealings with the three murderers; in the character of Macduff, he brought home the trauma of exile. In the sleepwalking scene the Nurse and the Doctor connived at the murder of Lady Macbeth, indicating the way in which corruption is fostered by complicity. In the final scene, Macduff realises the futility of all his efforts; by securing Malcolm's return to the throne he has not achieved the restoration of order, but enthroned a tyrant even more ruthless than Macbeth.

In 1984, the Theatre on the Balustrade obtained permission for Schorm to direct his dramatisation of Bohumil Hrabal's *Too Loud a Solitude*. The work was largely unknown to most of the audience; heavily censored extracts had been published in 1981, but the original novel (1976) circulated only in *samizdat*.* Hrabal's text comprises the reminiscences of a waste-paper worker (one of Hrabal's own trades), in which sorting and recycling emerges as an image of the manipulation and destruction of memory. In the theatre, the closing image of a grotesque ogre was deleted on the demands of the local authority, who claimed it showed disrespect to the Soviet Union. "But it has nothing to do with the Soviet Union," protested Schorm. "No, but the audience may think it has," replied the authority, notifying the Balustrade Theatre that Schorm should not be re-engaged. By May 1985, Schorm was prepared to go through any channel, even Švorcová, to reach the elusive Müller.

Closest to Evald Schorm's heart was his work at the *Laterna magika*, where he directed (but only as a guest director) eight productions during Normalisation. Of these, it was the least spectacular, *Night Rehearsal* (1981), which drew the largest and most intent audience. Antonín Máša's script has at its heart a theatre director, Jonah (Radovan Lukavský), who has returned from treatment for alcoholism to direct Shakespeare's *Othello* with actors who long ago sold out to routine, easy effects and cheap compromise. In the course of this unusual "night rehearsal", the relationships in the play start to be mirrored in the company and Jonah begins to fight "for the brutality of truth and the vindictive terrorism of love."[304] The issues at stake are the stewardship of one's talent and the moral responsibility for one's own life. In *Night Rehearsal*, Schorm used *Laterna magika* techniques in a totally new way. The theatre in which Jonah is rehearsing—and in which we are sitting—is

* When, after 1968, hundreds of writers were banned from publishing, they shared their work by means of "self-publishing," or *samizdat*—entire books laboriously typed through up to fourteen layers of carbon paper, the operation and its products kept hidden for fear of police raids that could end in long prison sentences.

fitted with an extensive CCTV system. The stage is full of TV equipment and a mixture of chairs, rostra, ropes. The monitors are banked on the stage; the images screened (in black and white) may have been recorded within the last two hours, or they may be live. Actors used the front row of seats and behaved as though the rest of the auditorium was empty. Jonah rehearsed each actor one by one, until the explosive culmination when together they took over the theatre. Every performance became an immensely personal experience for the actors, whose tension drew the audience into the urgency of the theme; urgent not only for those actors rehearsing *Othello* but for those performing *Night Rehearsal*—all of whom had faced the moral dilemma of the Anti-Charter a few years earlier.*

The theatre in this country, Schorm once told me, was impossible to understand unless you understood the way things happened here. "*Divadlo je těžké*," he repeated, "Theatre is difficult/hard/heavy"—he had known it, but it was worse than he had expected. Life in this country was a mystery (*záhada*) and making plans impossible.[305] Suffering from a long-drawn-out vascular disease, Evald Schorm collapsed and died at the age of fifty-six, eleven months before the Velvet Revolution.

SEMAFOR, DRAMA CLUB, AND THE END OF THE STATE THEATRE STUDIO

For Semafor, the 1970s had opened in crisis; on St. Stephen's Day 1969, the bodies of Jiří Šlitr and a girlfriend, suffocated by carbon monoxide, were found in Šlitr's studio. The post mortem concluded that the deaths were accidental. While dealing with this tragedy, Suchý was resisting the authorities' attempts to oust him from Semafor. At the end of the season, he was replaced as artistic head by his colleague, the bandmaster Ferdinand Havlík; but Suchý's nationwide popularity combined with his openness about the problems made it difficult for the authorities to take direct action. Without Šlitr, Suchý moved away from literary cabaret towards more lyrical productions inspired by Nezval and by Poetism. The content was innocuous, and the audiences kept coming. The authorities attempted to curb Semafor's popularity by restricting Suchý in other ways, preventing him from appearing on radio or television, making films, publishing, or recording his new work. Three LPs of earlier recordings were issued in a brief relaxation in 1978; another three remained on the publisher's shelf. "Semi-official" publications were brought out by the *Jonášklub*, a circle of supporters. As with all "members-only" publications, they were of

* See p. 220–222.

limited circulation and served to emphasise the system's method of granting someone a "half-life." Suchý had never engaged in political activity; the punishment was founded on resentment and jealousy of his unaffected sincerity and consistent record of integrity.

At the Drama Club, Jaroslav Vostrý was replaced as artistic director in January 1973; Kačer had to leave in 1975, to be remembered for a series of Russian classics (Chekhov and Gorky, translated by Suchařípa and Topol). His work at the National Theatre similarly came to an end in 1975, but not before he had directed Ludvík Kundera's translation of Brecht's *Mother Courage* (1970) with Dana Medřičká in the lead; his interpretation was widely seen as a protest. The text was censored, and on the first night the actors drew attention to the cuts by pausing at the appropriate places. Vostrý and Kačer spent years working in other fields, until they were permitted to accept positions in provincial theatres—Vostrý in Ústí nad Labem, Kladno, and Pardubice; and Kačer in Ostrava. In 1981, with the dissolution of the State Theatre Studio, the Drama Club was handed to the Vinohrady Theatre—under its current leader, Zdeněk Míka, who had replaced František Pavlíček, too closely identified with the reform movement. In spite of the changes, the Drama Club kept something of its old quality, and its audience. Ladislav Smoček's *Cosmic Spring* opened in March 1970. After that, he wrote no more plays (or none that were performed) but remained at the Drama Club as a director—mainly of classics, with a renewed emphasis on the psychology of the characters and the virtuosity of the performers: O'Neill's *Long Day's Journey into Night* (1978, with Josef Somr as James Tyrone), von Horvath's *Tales from the Vienna Woods* (1981), and Gogol's *Gamblers* (1982).* In 1981, Ivo Krobot directed a dramatisation of Bohumil Hrabal's *The Gentle Barbarian*, about the artist Vladimír Boudník, which until then had circulated only in *samizdat*. Under Normalisation, the Drama Club continued to shelter artists belonging to the "unofficial culture," including Joska Skalník, Libor Fára, and the Surrealist artist and filmmaker, Jan Švankmajer.†

Miloš Hercík remained as director of the State Theatre Studio until 1973;‡ the Studio survived another seven years. On 1 July 1978, the Theatre Act came into operation, laying down the exact conditions under which a new theatre group could originate, or an exhausted one close down. (Even if members

---

* As was customary, theatre people were invited to the November 11 morning dress rehearsal. A gleeful rumour spread down the rows that Leonid Brezhnev had died. When we came out, the flags were at half-mast.

† Luboš Hrůza emigrated to Norway after the invasion, where he became head of Design of the National Theatre in Oslo. The reputation of Czechoslovak theatre workers in Europe was such that most of those who emigrated were ensured a career.

‡ Hercík subsequently held a sinecure in the megalomaniacal Palace of Culture (after 1989, renamed the Prague Congress Centre) but was rarely seen there.

of a group unanimously decided to disband, their name and activities had to be continued by someone else.) As a result, no new professional theatre company was created between 1978 and 1990. This was part of official policy to centralise decision-making and control the activities of the small theatres. Although some people had seen the State Theatre Studio as another form of control, for others it stood for artistic independence, the encouragement of new talent, and the opportunity to take responsibility for failure. The Studio was closed down on 31 December 1980. Companies still under its patronage were allotted to the jurisdiction of larger theatres: Semafor to the Music Theatre of Karlín (home of operetta), and Ypsilon to the Jiří Wolker Theatre for Youth. In this way, companies that had pursued an independent policy and programme under the State Theatre Studio were obliged to compromise with the dogmatic managements of their "mother" theatres.

VÁCLAV HAVEL, CHARTER 77, AND THE ANTI-CHARTER

In January 1969, Václav Havel sent a telegram to President Svoboda, protesting against the censorship being reimposed by Gustáv Husák. From that date, DILIA, the state monopoly literary agency, refused to handle his work. Among his unperformed plays was an adaptation of *The Beggar's Opera*, originally written for the Drama Club. In 1973, at his country cottage Hradeček,* Havel showed it to his friend and neighbour Andrej Krob, who had been the stage manager of the Theatre on the Balustrade, responsible *inter alia* for *The Garden Party* and *The Memorandum*. Krob got his colleagues together and began to rehearse *The Beggar's Opera*. Havel enthusiastically joined in, and the group was named the *Divadlo na tahu* (Theatre on the Road). The manager of a pub in the village of Horní Počernice was persuaded to allow the unaccredited group to perform there, provided there was no advertising and no admission charge. The première and only performance took place on 1 November 1975, after which the secret police interrogated not only the company but also audience members, for some of whom (Jan Grossman) it proved catastrophic. Havel wrote to the authorities:

> Does not the fact that the mayor of our capital city... has to spend his time at various meetings discussing an amateur theatrical performance in a small village on the out-

* In normalised Czechoslovakia, a country cottage was not a privilege but a necessity; first, because it was impossible to holiday abroad; and secondly, because it was the only place where you were not (usually) watched.

skirts of the city demonstrate with grotesque explicitness the abnormality of conditions in our culture?[306]

During this time, Havel wrote other satirical plays—*Conspirators* (1970–71), *Mountain Hotel* (1970–76)—which were performed only abroad.* His miniature "Vaněk plays"—*Audience* (1975), *Private View* (also translated as *The Unveiling*, 1975), and *Protest* (1978)—had a more active life. With the unassuming, apologetic "dissident" Ferdinand Vaněk as the catalyst, they poignantly analysed the moral contortions of those who try to accommodate themselves to an absurd regime. Vaněk was never a self-portrait of Havel, and became "common property" when Kohout, Landovský, and the former foreign correspondent Jiří Dienstbier made him the central character of their own plays. Marketa Goetz-Stankiewicz, who published all the Vaněk plays in English translation in 1987, wrote in the preface that:

It is important to realise that these eight plays are related to each other not merely by the figure of Vaněk but by the whole surrounding social context. The audience... is made to feel that there are real lives being lived.[307]

She quotes Havel as saying that their success taught him that he must focus on his own "concrete living background" as the means by which he could "provide a more general comment as witness of a certain period."[308]

In January 1977, Havel was one of the initiators and spokesmen of Charter 77, an appeal to the Czechoslovak government to observe the international treaties it had signed in Helsinki in 1975; the other two spokesmen were the former Foreign Minister Jiří Hajek and the philosopher Jan Patočka. Apart from the accident that another of the initiators (Pavel Kohout) was also a playwright, Charter 77 had nothing to with the theatre. The first signatories to Charter 77 included doctors, art critics, electricians, sociologists, housewives, students, pensioners, newspaper reporters, priests, and ambulancemen.

It is perhaps strange that one of the first actions the Communist authorities took against against the charter was to invite the country's leading performers and artists to a meeting (carried live on television) on 28 January 1977 in the National Theatre—the *zlatá kaplička* (golden chapel). Here they unveiled a cloyingly sentimental riposte drafted (it was claimed) by the unions of writers, visual artists, composers, dramatic artists, and architects, with the title "For New Creative Deeds in the Name of Socialism and Peace," but known

* *Conspirators* at the Theatre der Stadt in Baden-Baden in 1974, *Mountain Hotel* at the Akademietheater in Vienna in 1981.

to history as the "Anti-Charter." The declaration was flowery propaganda; the sting appeared in a paragraph midway:

> ...those who, in the unbridled pride of their narcissistic haughtiness, for selfish interests, or even for filthy lucre in various places all over the world—even in our land a small group of such backsliders and traitors can be found—divorce and isolate themselves from their own people and its life and real interests and, with inexorable logic, become instruments of the antihumanistic forces of imperialism and, in its service, the heralds of disruption and discord among nations.[309]

It was presented in the National Theatre by the president of the Union of Czech Dramatic Artists', Jiřina Švorcová, who urged (or rather, ordered) all artists to sign it. A week later, the same document was presented to a meeting of popular artists in the Theatre of Music (*Divadlo hudby*) by the singer Karel Gott. Even those who avoided the meetings were confronted with the document in their own theatre. When employees such as Lída Engelová in the J. K. Tyl Theatre in Pilsen asked to read the charter itself, they were told: "Everything you need to know is in this document!"[310] For weeks, the front page of *Rudé právo* was filled with the names of signatories. Only four members of the Vinohrady company did not sign, and in the whole country, there was only one theatre where no one signed at all: the Theatre on a String in Brno. Jan Werich, who had not grasped the implications, asked Švorcová two days later to remove his signature; she did not do so. The Theatre on the Balustrade was under especial pressure. Havel was denounced on television by Vladimír Vodička and Václav Sloup (Hugo Pludek in *The Garden Party*).* The theatre secretary Milena Tomíšková vainly tried to help Jan Přeučil (Josef K in *The Trial*) escape the police pursuit that he knew would lead to the betrayal of his colleague. In fact, few reprisals were taken against those who did not sign—which only intensified the humiliation of those who did. Interviewed in 2010, Švorcová disclaimed responsibility for coercing the artists into an act which most of them regretted the rest of their lives. She claimed that she had merely agreed, as an actress, to read the declaration to the audience; in any case, she argued in the same breath that it was the Chartists themselves who were to blame:

> The process of relaxation in society and the creative field had already started, and it was only a question of time before it reached a generally satisfactory form, when it would be capable of reacting to criticism and purging itself of dogmatism of any kind. This process was naturally upset by the Chartists' intervention.[311]

---

* See *Divadelní revue*, no. 3, 2018, p. 42, for the transcript.

Soon afterwards came the death of Jan Patočka, and Havel's first experience of prison. Nevertheless, in that turbulent, tragic year, there was at least one event he could cherish. On 18 June the British playwright Tom Stoppard returned to Czechoslovakia for the first time since his family had fled from the Nazis in 1938. For the "dissidents" it was a deeply symbolic occasion. More than four years later, in August 1981, the philosopher Ladislav Hejdánek briefed his Western colleagues on the kind of visitor they would like for the "underground university": "Those who would be most appreciated would be writers… Tom Stoppard's visit provided inspiration that lasted for two years." On arriving in Prague, Stoppard was led through a complex procedure designed to throw off the secret police. They embarked on a trip that remains hazy in the minds of those involved. It seems that there was a meeting with Ludvík Vaculík at "his home in Všenory"; to converse more freely, Vaculík took them to the "railway buffet at Řevnice."* Petr Pithart (historian and future prime minister) was at some point a part of the group, as was Pavel Landovský (in "a battered white Saab"). Stoppard met Hejdánek "in a cheap 'fish grill' just off Wenceslaus Square," as well as Pavel Kohout and Karol Sidon (writer and future chief rabbi). Karel Bartošek accompanied him to a rather dishevelled debate and press conference in a stylish Constructivist villa. He had just, according to Jan Patočka Jr., taken Stoppard on a lightning tour of Prague hotspots from which Stoppard had emerged in better shape than Bartošek. Above all, there was his first—and for many years, only—meeting with Václav Havel (who had been released a month earlier) at Hradeček. Over the next two months, Stoppard wove out of his material a long article.[312] With an almost uncanny awareness of what it meant to live under a totalitarian regime, he seamlessly combined his own experiences with what he had learnt about the Charter, Jan Patočka, and the rock band Plastic People of the Universe.

IRREGULAR DRAMATURGY

The Communist Anti-Charter bears a clear resemblance to the methods used by the Nazis in 1942, when they forced theatre artists to take the Pledge of Allegiance in the National Theatre.[313] No other profession was so closely identified with the quality of "being Czech." It was an effective stroke against Charter 77 to use those historically relied on to uphold the truth and honour of the nation. At the same time it was an opportunity for the authorities to impose a

* This account of Stoppard's odyssey is reconstructed from unreliable memories from various sources. Vaculík's home was actually in neighbouring Dobřichovice and there is no railway buffet on Řevnice station, although on another occasion Vaculík wrote that "the best food and service […] was opposite the station at Řevnice" (*Český snář*, Toronto 1983, p. 336).

uniform subjugation on theatres countrywide. Signing the Anti-Charter was a particular kind of individualised humiliation.

Another part of the strategy was the Theatre Act of 1978, already mentioned in connection with the demise of the State Theatre Studio. Under the new act, administration of the theatres was concentrated in the hands of the local authorities; for example, whereas several theatre companies had been operating under different "sponsors" in an industrial city like Ostrava in Northern Moravia, these were now reassigned to the municipal cultural department and their programmes adjusted to "complement" each other. This rationalisation satisfied the bureaucrat, but extinguished vital contrast and competition. Official policy was to produce on the established stages what was called "good" theatre (i.e., professionally presented and acted) as a model towards which other companies could be gently guided.

Morale was at its lowest at the end of the 1970s; yet in retrospect, it was the turn of a tide. A new term was needed for theatres reflecting the time. "Small theatres" belonged to the past but the term "studio theatre" took hold. The name fitted the ambiguity of the time, being applicable not only to an actual theatre company but also to part of a theatre company or even to a tendency within a theatre company. The first reference to "studio-type theatres" as a genre seems to have been the second issue of the Theatre Institute's low-profile (but essential) series *České divadlo* (*Czech Theatre*),* *Divadla studiového typu* (1980). The theatres it referred to were Theatre on a String, Ypsilon, and others described later. Yet the concept of "studio theatres" *inside* established "stone" theatres was emerging; for example, Studio Forum attached to the State Theatre of Oldřich Štíbor in Olomouc, and Studio Beseda attached to the Theatre of Victorious February in Hradec Králové. In a largely moribund and centralised theatre, the studios provided writers and directors like Daniela Fischerová, Přemysl Rut, and Lída Engelová with opportunities to experiment and work with like-minded colleagues. In the 1980s, much that was original and creative in Czech theatre took place in the provinces. One reason was that scores of theatre workers, some of them household names, had been banned from working in Prague. It would be impossible to produce a definitive list; actors, dramaturges, etc. would simply be dismissed and unable to find another job in Prague. Their cadre file would be consulted alongside their applications, until they would be happy with a foothold in negligent Šumperk (for example). At the same time, the local authorities who ran the theatres were not under the same pressure as the Prague municipality and the Ministry of Culture; if they were in a good mood, they could permit a cer-

* Semi-official publications in small editions (750–800 copies) intended for academic use only.

tain amount of experimentation. One of the most dynamic regional centres was Liberec, where in the 1960s the drama company of the F. X. Šalda Theatre* had its most successful era under Ivan Glanc, dismissed in 1971. In the decade that followed, director Karel Kříž and dramaturge Vlasta Gallerová worked within the limits of Normalisation to find new ways of communicating with audiences. An important role was played by "action scenography," in which a flexible and versatile stage environment provided new ideas and possibilities for the performers—the Constructivist "playground" enjoyed by the avant-garde performers between the wars. In 1964, the Surrealist Libor Fára had created a "dunghill" for Grossman's production of *Ubu Roi*, where the elements of the set had countless possibilities according to the actors' needs. In Liberec in the 1970s the designer Jaroslav Malina, who had coined the term "action scenography," made use of its versatility in a series of productions.

Liberec also rejuvenated the Czech tradition of puppetry for adult audiences, in 1968 changing the name of its North Bohemian Puppet Theatre to the Naïve Theatre. It had already given birth to an experimental offspring, Studio Y, soon known as Ypsilon, founded in 1963 and led by Jan Schmid. Schmid was an artist gifted with a complex of skills; he had studied stage design in Bratislava, theatre direction with Radok, and was now a designer with the puppet theatre. Ivan Vyskočil, however, saw Schmid's early training as a glassworker as crucial.[314] In Vyskočil's eyes, everyone working in the ancient, elite crafts was a performing artist, never more so than when working with the living substance of liquid glass, reacting to temperature and subtle play with breath and movement—physical, dramatic, kinaesthetic, and fragile. Working with glass involved teamwork, improvisation, and split-second timing. The deep forests of North Bohemia had been home for centuries to glass foundries independently run by generations of glassmakers. With this behind him, Schmid created an *auteur théâtre* of creator-performers who deliberately retained features of their amateur style even after the group turned professional; that is, the actors' personal characteristics were allowed to exceed the parameters of the parts they were playing. (One detail: the actress Jana Synková wore her large tinted spectacles for every role.) It could be argued that they were in any case not actors, but puppet handlers, in a setting where the puppets (sometimes recognisable as such, at other times not) formed a parallel resource rather than being the main participants. The performers / puppet handlers, some of them musicians or designers by training, resembled Schmid in their versatility. The company worked on the principle of montage,

* F. X. Šalda (1867–1937), a native of Liberec, was an influential literary figure of the early twentieth century.

sometimes in the relatively conventional form of cabaret based on text-appeals and jokes. At other times they created a production out of episodes which were invented and prepared by members of the company and then tried out before the rest of the ensemble. This collective, improvisational approach was often extended into the actual performances, encouraging the audience to feel they were all in the same space. (There were some audience members who felt alienated by this collaborative atmosphere.)

One outcome of Ypsilon's working method was that, in the course of the actual performance, different actors would play the same roles—even title parts such as that in *Michelangelo Buonarroti* (1974). A situation that might have led to fragmentation was held together by Schmid, demonstrably the director not only in rehearsal but also onstage in performance, where a certain amount of negotiation was necessary. It did mean that the presentation the audience was watching was not so much a story or event but a web of analytical reflections on that story or event, controlled by a Prospero figure—although "controlled" gives a wrong impression, as the performance appeared to progress under its own volition.

After years of building up an audience for their Prague appearances, Studio Ypsilon moved to the capital permanently under the patronage of the State Theatre Studio—ironically in 1978, the year of the new Theatre Act designed to extinguish the State Theatre Studio. It was in Prague that Ypsilon premièred one of its key productions, *Outsider, or Biography of a Famous Man* (1981). Based on dialectical philosophy but featuring song and dance (and Ljuba Hermanová), it examined the problem of understanding a single personality through the use of a "Cubist portrait" of an artist. Among the "restricted" directors engaged as guests by Studio Ypsilon were Evald Schorm (in 1973 and 1975), Jan Kačer (1976), and Jan Grossman (1977). In 1984, it was one of five studio-type theatres involved in the analytical project *Cesty*.*

Liberec is not far from Ústí nad Labem, where the members of the former Kladivadlo, disbanded in 1971 for political reasons, reformed as the Drama Studio of Youth (*Činoherní Studio mladých*), after 1972 just "Drama Studio." Jaroslav Chundela, before leaving for the Theatre on the Balustrade, was the first artistic director to invite Evald Schorm as guest director. Ivan Rajmont, who followed Chundela, directed Milan Kundera's third play *Jacques and His Master* (1975)—the authorship ascribed not to Kundera, but to Schorm. In repertoire and on tour, the production played 223 performances over fourteen years. Rajmont engaged not only Schorm and Grossman but also Vostrý as guest directors at the Ústí Drama Studio.

---

* See p. 250.

Rajmont also cooperated with one of the few dramatists to emerge during this period, Karel Steigerwald. Steigerwald had been one of Milan Kundera's students at FAMU and worked as a dramaturge at Barrandov Film Studio until he was dismissed for political reasons. Two of the plays on which he worked with Rajmont were staged at the Drama Studio: *Period Dances* (1980), set in the mid-nineteenth century, and *Foxtrot* (1982), set in the First Republic. Two others were not passed for performance: *The Tartar Feast* (1979, staged 1988), set in the 1950s and *The Neapolitan Disease* (1984, staged 1988), set in the future. All four plays dealt with the psychology of the Normalisation period, reflecting the moral confusion of the time.

The architecturally innovative east Bohemian city of Hradec Králové was home to not only the Studio Beseda initiative, but also the innovative puppet theatre *DRAK* (Dragon), founded on a fully professional basis in 1958 and from 1971 led by Josef Krofta.* In 1977, *DRAK* brought eight productions directed by Krofta to Prague, "each better than the one before." Then and subsequently the same production was played in the morning for children and, unchanged, in the evening for adults. One of these eight scripts, *Cinderella*, was by the Charter 77 signatory Jan Vladislav; it was quickly banned by the authorities. In 1986, *DRAK* appeared at the Wrocław Open Theatre Festival with *The Dragon* by the Russian writer Evgeny Schwartz. The audience reacted spontaneously to the scene where the (puppet) Archivist used live fire to destroy the archives—his country's "memory." *DRAK*'s particular quality was in its combination of puppets with live actors—neither was in in any way diminished, and the often silent communication between them was strangely moving. The manipulated puppet became the image of a life spent under the control of an unseen power.

By the early 1980s, small groups of performers were circumventing the restrictions and appearing in clubs, halls, and galleries all over the country. (According to one count, 127 such groups were recorded in Moravia.) They were also under surveillance, but as long as they kept a low profile they were not as tightly controlled as the better-known theatres (such as the Balustrade, Semafor, and Drama Club). Some of the venues for these peripatetic groups were clubs belonging to the Socialist Youth Union, set up to ensure young people's energies were controlled in a suitable environment. The managers of the clubs had a certain amount of autonomy in choosing entertainments that would attract a young audience; some managers had a genuine inter-

* One of *DRAK*'s performers, Matěj Kopecký, was the seventh generation of a line of strolling folk puppeteers. At the turn of the eighteenth and nineteenth centuries, his forebear (likewise Matěj Kopecký) scraped a living by travelling from town to village performing his plays with his carved wooden figures. After his son published his plays in 1862, Kopecký became celebrated as a hero of the National Awakening and the founder of a dynasty.

est in alternative movements and cautiously tried to promote them. Some clubs, such as Futurum in the Ironworkers House in Smíchov, were run by the Trades Unions, ostensibly for their younger workers but open to all. Other venues were the multipurpose halls in Culture Houses to be found in every town and larger village. As this kind of entertainment grew in popularity, local authorities refurbished disused halls and theatres, such as those in the Prague districts of Žižkov and Kobylisy. Venues whose programmes were eagerly followed in the monthly *Kulturní přehled* (*Culture Guide*)* included the *Malostranská beseda*, the *Baráčnická rychta*† (both in the Lessser Quarter), and the sports hall of the *Junior klub Na Chmelnici*. (The last named, twenty minutes from Wenceslas Square on the number nine tram, probably hosted the largest number of risk-taking productions of the 1980s, many of them visiting Prague from the provinces.)

With audiences of a hundred or fewer, a performer could risk departing from the approved script. Nevertheless, it could be dangerous. Each venue had to obtain advance approval from the local authority for the touring shows it booked. A freelance group or partnership might find itself no longer welcome in its own district (usually Prague) and face months or years travelling to the far-flung regions. It often turned out that approval had been withheld for an irrational or personal reason—a single official offended by some song or sketch (which they had possibly even misunderstood). The small stages were also criticised for neglecting the spoken language and verbal expression. In the context of European theatre, the greatest value is usually placed on the dramatic text, a tangible property that can be adapted for other stages. "Drama" is understood as meaning dramatic literature. Czechoslovak theatre has not been rich in internationally recognised texts. It has tended to seek a "stage language" dependent not on words on their own but on nonspecific aural and visual material, on juxtaposition and contrast. The word was too often "bound," and alternative expression had to be found.

An alternative school of mime began to evolve in the 1960s through the collaboration, initially on an amateur basis, of Boris Hybner and Ctibor Turba. Ladislav Fialka had recognised Hybner's talent and engaged him on a year's contract (1964) at the Theatre on the Balustrade, but Hybner rebelled against Fialka's playful Romanticism. He was more attracted by the roughness and vitality of Jan Grossman's stagings in the same theatre, especially Jarry's *Ubu Roi* in May that year. Turba's path to mime led through puppetry and animat-

---

* It was produced to a plan that ensured copies sold out early in the morning of the day of issue. For a new subscriber to be accepted, I was told, "Someone has to die."

† The *Baráčnická rychta* originated at the end of the nineteenth century as one of the patriotic charitable associations. Under Communism, its premises figured among the informal and low-profile venues that sheltered subversive performances.

ed film. In tune with their time, they were doubtful, questioning, impatient with optimism. Their lifestyle was bohemian, involving cabaret appearances at venues like the Alhambra nightclub, the wine-cellar Viola and a Vyšehrad squat. In 1966, the *Pantomima Alfreda Jarryho* (Alfred Jarry Mime Company) was born. The name demonstrated Turba and Hybner's impatience with Fialka's imaginative form of mime, which they called "Pierrot pantomime"—why spend time describing in detail imaginary objects? Why not just assume they exist, and describe *what* happens, the relationships between people? They saw the cruelty in life, its absurdities and weaknesses, but were not deeply serious about them, employing the kind of black humour they found in French popular papers.[315] Their originality was acknowledged with an invitation to appear with the *Laterna magika* at Expo 67 in Montreal, where (among other things) they discovered the satirical magazine, *Hara-Kiri*, predecessor of *Charlie Hebdo*.

This led, at the end of 1968, to *Harakiri*—anti-positivist, existential, absurd—a production that put *Pantomima Alfreda Jarryho* on the international circuit. The actors began the performance still wearing the clowns' costumes and white faces of traditional pantomime, but gradually removed them in the course of the evening. In one scene, "Jubilee," two spirited old actors run through the classic gags of silent film, their cruelty exaggerated by the actors' age. Buster Keaton observes them from a poster on the wall. It was after the success of *Harakiri* that, from March 1969, *Pantomima Alfreda Jarryho* became part of the State Theatre Studio. Turba was at this time studying in the theatre department of Charles University, where he came under the influence of Milan Lukeš and Jan Kopecký.

There were close links between the Surrealists and the *Pantomima Alfreda Jarryho*, not only through the name (a reminder of Prokop Voskovec's 1960 Surrealist production of *Ubu Roi*). Hybner and others from the *Pantomima Alfreda Jarryho* participated in meetings of the UDS (the pseudo-abbreviation by which the Surrealists were known from the mid-1960s); and both Voskovec and Libor Fára contributed to Hybner's 1970 production, *Idiots*. Turba devised the one-man programme *Turba tacet* (premièred in Orfeus), an exploration on the theme of suicide. In November 1971, the *Pantomima Alfreda Jarryho* premièred *P.A.R. 3441*, on the theme of man in the machine.* In this they worked with naturalistic objects, turning the Absurd into Naturalism. But the authorities had lost patience, and at the beginning of 1972 the *Pantomima Alfreda Jarryho* was closed down without explanation.

Turba and Hybner continued independently—for some time Turba worked with the Joker Teatret in Denmark. Cooperating with international compa-

---

* It was revived in 1977 in the Théâtre de l'Est Parisien.

nies such as Mummenschanz, he learnt how to use unconventional space and spaces. In 1974, Turba founded the *Cirkus Alfred*, a genuine circus in a big top with perfectionist jugglers and a ringmaster ruling over all—circus as a microcosm of the world. The clowns were the anarchistic element in a fallible society—for Turba, *Cirkus Alfred* was about "outsiderism" and the will to live. *Cirkus Alfred* first raised its tent in the open spaces of Prague, but after 1975 was allowed to perform only abroad.* It lasted until 1979. Boris Hybner, meanwhile, founded the peripatetic group Gag (from 1978), reviving his 1975 production *At the End of a Garden Named Hollywood*, based on silent movies. A fantasy about a film producer, an out-of-work journalist, and a fortune-seeking girl, it did not have the stark immediacy of the *Pantomima Alfreda Jarryho*.

There was a diversity on the fringe which was largely tolerated because, as Ivan Vyskočil once said, "The thing that costs too much money can influence the whole nation." Some of the groups which performed were professional, some entirely amateur, others "semi-amateur"—performers who received a fee but earned their living elsewhere. They were not listed under "theatre" in the monthly cultural guides, but under "programmes for culture and entertainment." Some of the performing groups had turned professional before 1978; others came together on an amateur or agency basis after the passing of the Theatre Act. They had no consistent pattern to their existence, which was part of their attraction on that borderline between "official" and "independent" culture, a feature of the 1970s. The main thing they shared was an "irregular dramaturgy," a concept articulated by the Brno Theatre [Goose] on a String (*Divadlo [Husa] na provázku*).

THEATRE [GOOSE] ON A STRING

The Mahen Theatre in Brno, like the other regional theatres, had to serve both the needs of the broad local population and centralised ideological aims. The selection of plays had to be approved by the cultural committee of the local authority, and was bound to include new plays from the Soviet Union and other Warsaw Pact countries, as well as Czech and Eastern European classics. In the mid-1960s, a frustrated dramaturge (Bořivoj Srba) and director (Evžen Sokolovský) made an unsuccessful attempt to introduce productions inspired by E. F. Burian's pre-war "poetic theatre." The Janáček Academy of Music and Performing Arts was more receptive. Srba and Sokolovský seized

---

* The regime had few problems about allowing artists prohibited from exhibiting and performing at home to do so abroad, as long as they could earn foreign currency that was then taxed at a rate of 46 per cent.

The *Dům umění* (House of Art) in Brno, originally built as the Kaiser Franz-Josefs-Jubiläums Künstlerhaus, was for decades the home of the Theatre [Goose] on a String. Ironically, the propaganda banner, typical of those on public buildings during Communist times, reads "With Soviet Union to Eternity." (Photograph from the City of Brno Archives)

the moment; it was a short opportunity when conditions had relaxed enough for students to be admitted to higher education based on their ability rather than on political grounds. A close-knit collective evolved, calling itself "Goose on a String,"* the title taken from a set of six "ideas for film" by Jiří Mahen, published in 1925 with graphic design by Karel Teige. Mahen's brief preface describes an earnest young theatre group vainly trying to interest postwar audiences in performances of Ibsen and Chekhov. Better by far, reflects Mahen, to use the new medium of cinema; or "cinema and theatre, theatre and circus, circus and cinema, libretti both readymade and improvised, ideas in poems and prose, megaphones and lights, the audience pulled on stage and made to play with us, amphitheatres with people emerging and disappear-

* The word *husa* (goose) had to be removed after Gustáv Husák replaced Alexander Dubček as First Secretary of the Communist Party. The same night (17 April 1969), the theatre's posters in the Brno streets were "adapted" by graffiti amending "Husa" to "Husák" and adding a little figure dangling from a rope.

ing." And the goose? Mahen recalls his friends' merriment when, on a country walk, they met "a perfectly ordinary goose, a beautiful big white goose" striding ahead of its owner: "A man took a goose and tied a string to it. The goose strode out and took the man for a walk. Let's go!"[316]

The group performed in a space loaned by the municipal art gallery, the House of Arts (*Dům umění*). Claiming an affinity with Honzl's wartime Little Theatre for 99, in the same spirit they set up the acting area and audience seating for every performance. Three students of directing—Petr Scherhaufer, Zdeněk Pospíšil and Eva Tálská—were crucial to the group's development. In the spring of 1968, still as students, they showed their first productions: in March, Pospíšil's staging of a montage and a one-act play—*Panta Rei, or the History of the Czech Nation in a Nutshell*—by Milan Uhde (author of *King Vávra*), and the absurd drama *Collector*; and two days later, Tálská's adaptation of Christian Morgenstern's *Gallows Songs*. Scherhaufer's productions opened in May: Chekhov's *Three Sisters* and an adaptation from Balzac, *The Art of Paying Your Debts*.

> THE THEATRE COLLECTIVE OF THE HOUSE OF ARTS IN BRNO
> is a free association of professional theatre people and theatre students, together with young writers, musicians, artists, and other interested persons who want [...] to uncover previously unused possibilities of theatre. [...] As is clear from the use of Mahen's title to head the venture, its productions will be based not so much on theatre plays as on poetry and prose. Its members believe that they will find here the inspiration for a new lyrical expression on stage that would reveal the living springs of our human existence, the poesie within us and outside. [...] [But] the programme should not limit the further development of the venture, which intends above all to make room for the ascent of a new theatre generation.[317]

With no financial support—Srba contrasted their situation with that of groups in Prague under the wing of the State Theatre Studio—the company rehearsed and performed as amateurs, as and when they could, until in January 1971 they were formally adopted by the House of Arts and turned professional. One of the collective's aims was to create a new and more appropriate method of theatre management. Peter Scherhaufer's diploma work (a substantial part of which was published in the penultimate issue of *Divadlo*)[318] analysed the wasteful systems and hierarchical structures of traditional theatres that had led, in the example of the Workers' Theatre (*Divadlo pracujících*) in Gottwaldov, to the employment of two hundred administrative staff as against forty-five artists. Scherhaufer proposed, in place of a rigid chain of command and a set timetable of productions, a flexible model that consisted of four phases for each production: preparation, realisation, reproduction, and feedback. The term "irregular dramaturgy" was used for the first time.

"Feedback," the final stage of Scherhaufer's model, was an unfamiliar concept in a totalitarian state where theatres were heavily subsidised and free tickets distributed to factory workers, and where it had already been decided what audiences should think. The Theatre on a String focused on the preparation of the audience and an analysis of its response. Publicity material, in other theatres a conventional product with low priority, was reconceived for every production.* Activities were thought up to catch the attention of the potential audience, and over the next twenty years a community life evolved in Brno unmatched in Prague or other towns and cities. Similarly, performances outside Brno were not treated as a tiresome duty, but rather an opportunity to be inspired by new sites and audiences. Simple questionnaires were distributed, politely asking the age and educational background of audience members, what appealed to them, and what they found boring. Discussions were arranged between company and audience, in an age when it was unusual to encourage questions in any environment. A children's studio was created. Although theatre *for* children was an established feature of Czech theatre, the principles behind drama in education had been slow to take root. The studio of Theatre on a String (led by Tálská) introduced children to drama games, improvisation, and methods of devising their own productions.

The working principle that evolved at the Theatre on a String was known in the small theatres of the 1970s and 1980s as *autorské divadlo*, or *auteur théâtre*, indicating a stage work created by the director, or by the performers under the guidance of the director. It increased the responsibility of the performer, who had to be capable of creative improvisation with the director and dramaturge. In Scherhaufer's model, company members were expected to know their responsibilities at each phase of the production, and to carry them out on their own initiative. In 1972, the season was for the first time preceded by a three-week "training camp" which enabled the company to focus on working together and preparing potential productions.

The same year, the art and theatre historian Petr Oslzlý joined the company as *"dramaturge-élève."* Although he was from a family that openly opposed Communism, Oslzlý had caught the brief moment of the Prague Spring, registering in the theatre department of the Jan Evangelista Purkyně University in Brno.† Previously an apprentice steelworker, he had worked with an experimental amateur theatre group, Quidam. After 1968, he and his fellow

* The Theatre on the Balustrade and the Drama Club also attached importance to the design of programmes and posters, but were not thinking so strategically.

† After 1989, the university returned to its original name of the Masaryk University.

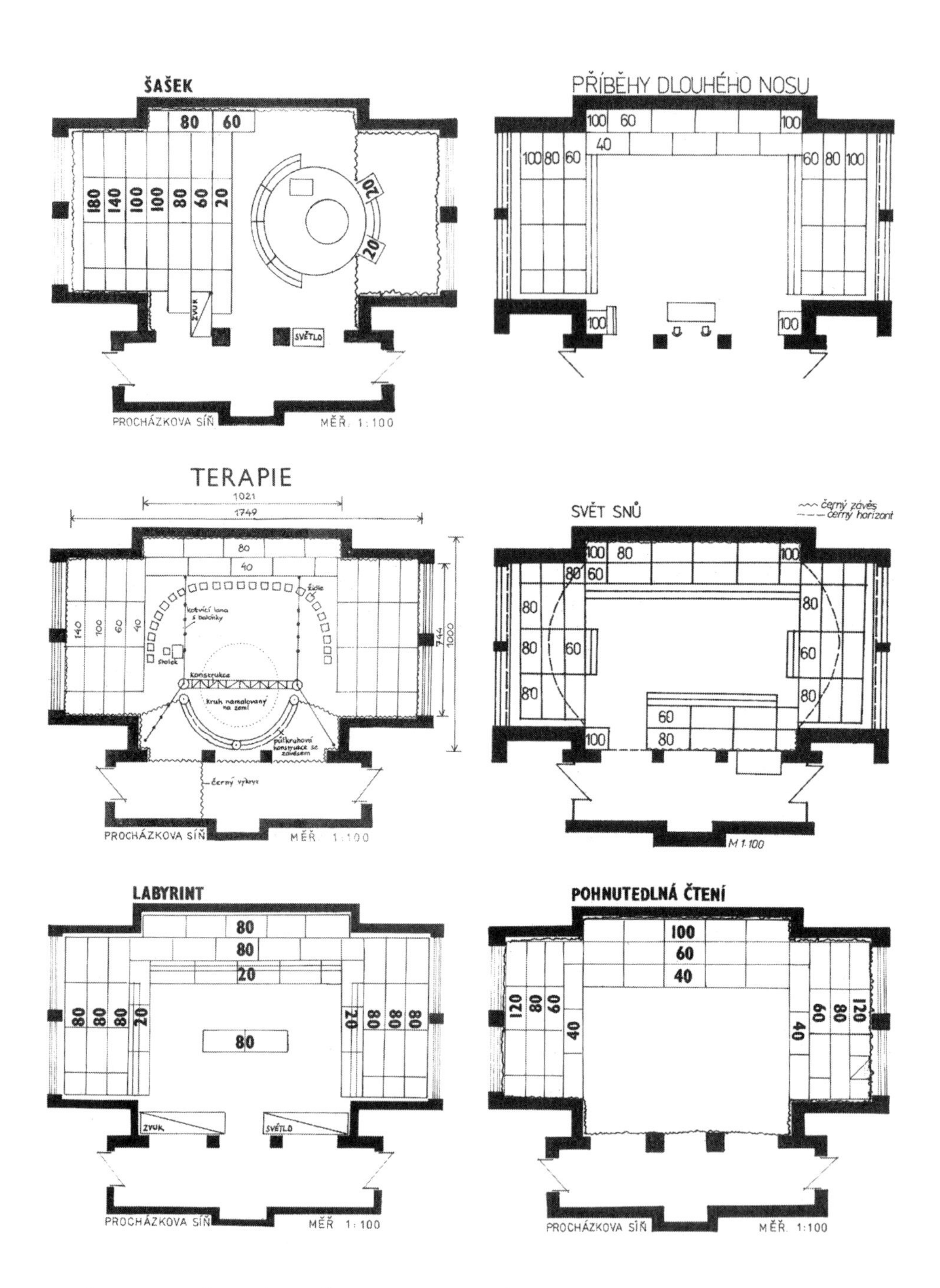

students were branded a "lost generation," but allowed to finish their studies. In a short time he became head of Theatre on a String, and its intellectual and moral compass. Under Oslzlý, the dramaturgy focused on questions of private and public morality, presented in ways that delighted and entertained audiences. The "irregular dramaturgy" was an important element; the company could choose from a range of materials—non-dramatic texts such as Dante's

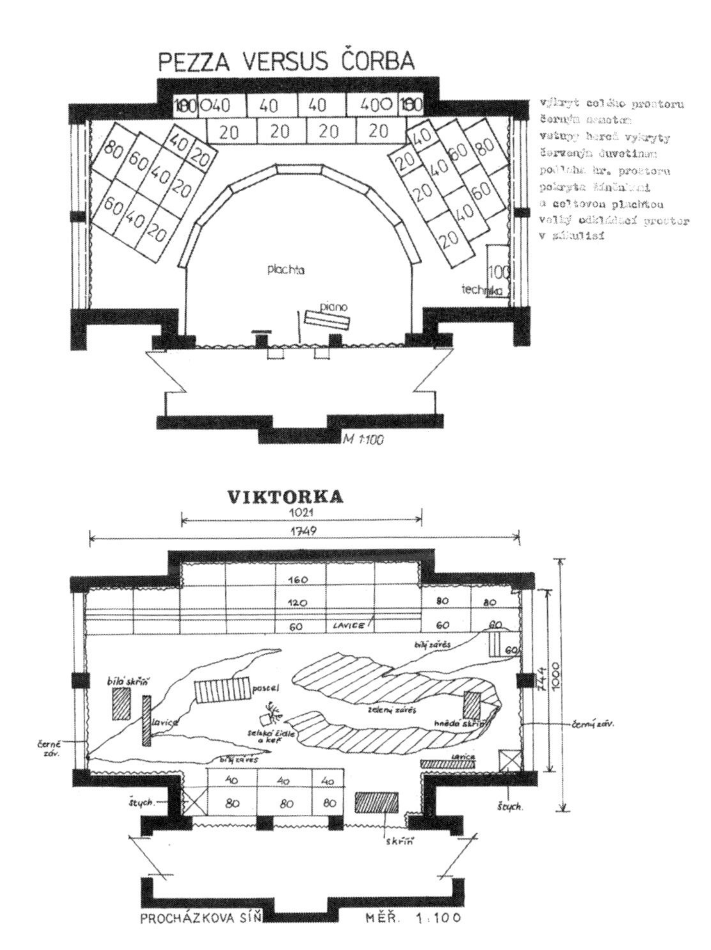

The ground plans for Theatre on a String productions show the versatility of the Theatre on a String's stagings in a gallery of the House of Art. Actors, technicians, and audience members all used the single entrance. The backstage area, with offices, dressing rooms, wardrobe, and workshops, was two floors down in the basement. (Courtesy of the Theatre on a String archives)

Divine Comedy and Lewis Carroll's *Alice in Wonderland*, a storyboard adaptation of Brecht's *Arturo Ui* (*Ballet Macabre*), dramatisations of novels, stagings of poetry and songs, new versions of the classics, mime, puppetry, and cabaret. The company felt itself part of a movement that included the Living Theatre of New York, the British director Peter Brook and the Polish Jerzy Grotowski. In the closed world of normalised Czechoslovakia, international sources and networks represented both a window on a "normal" world and, on occasion, a lifeline. In 1978, the company was involved in a joint project in Wrocław on the theme of "Hope"; out of this, a lasting relationship develped with Teater 77 of Łódź. Meanwhile, Theatre on a String had initiated a Brno festival, Theatre on the Move (*Divadlo v Pohybu*); the first took place in 1973; the third, in 1987, although officially banned, involved international participation.

The variety and interrelatedness of the source material used by Theatre on a String was one of the great strengths of its work. Working on Burian's principles of selection and juxtaposition, the company engaged in a search for a "stage language" composed from the elements of movement, words, music, costume, light, and space. Film was a strong influence, especially in the use of montage—in this case, a montage of sequences created in the course of rehearsal studies. Music played a major role; where possible it was live, and Scherhaufer relied on his actors having an elementary knowledge of at least one instrument.

As the company performed in a gallery and other free spaces, they were free to fashion the stage according to the needs of the theme. The arrangement defined not only the performing space but also the audience space. In *Pezza Versus Čorba* (1975), two warring families built a barrier across the arena in which they performed, so that half the audience saw the action on one side of the wall, half on the other side. When audiences arrived for Ludvík Kundera's adaptation of Comenius's *The Labyrinth of the World* they were squeezed into a narrow space and found themselves fighting for seats when, at the last minute, covers were whipped from the stands. Each performance was an encounter, with the audience being active partners rather than mere spectators. In some cases this was literally so, as in Eva Tálská's staging of Edward Lear's limericks, *Tales of the Long Nose* (1982), where the actors closely observed the audience—especially latecomers—and gleefully identified Lear's Old Men and Young Ladies, drawing them into the action and consoling them with beer and cream cake in the interval.

On 1 January 1978, in accordance with the new Theatre Act, Theatre on a String became administratively the fifth stage of the State Theatre in Brno. The authorities now had more direct control and appointed a new head, a reliable Party member from the State Theatre, over Petr Oslzlý.* Theatre on a String, like other theatres, was now obliged to produce an annual dramaturgical plan that delineated its ideological and artistic tasks. The result could appear schizophrenic, as in the plan for 1981–1982:

> The season's busy programme will culminate with the action "Theatre on a String—Theatre on the Move (II)" [...] with international participation, if possible, to celebrate the fifteenth anniversary of the DNP [Theatre on a String]. It will also celebrate a century of Czech-language theatre in Brno. The DNP thus intends to link itself to the tradition of endeavours for experimental theatre in Brno connected with such names as J. Honzl, E. F. Burian, J. Mahen, and others, to a tradition that requires endless searching, reviving, and renewing of attempts at an exclusively contemporary Socialist theatrical expression.[319]

That season, another (unsuccessful) attempt was made to get *The Labyrinth of the World* past the censors, in the context of the Theatre on the Move. It

* A note in the margin of history should be reserved for Jaroslav Tuček, State Theatre actor and Party member charged with the task of bringing the Theatre on the String into line. Won over by the company's open and creative atmosphere, he quietly resolved to preserve it in its original form.

defined its "ideological dramaturgical intention" using the appropriate terminology:

> [T]hrough a specific creative act in the artistic field of theatre, to show the possibility of the international peace cooperation for which the governments of the lands of the Socialist camp strive in international politics. It was completely logical that the initiative should come from the theatres of the Socialist lands because the joint production will also be a manifestation of the creative development of the Socialist theatre, an expression of Socialist internationalism in a theatre work, and an attempt at multilingual cooperation.

The flexible structure of the Theatre on a String provided each director with the autonomy to develop their own artistic programme. Zdeněk Pospíšil (who emigrated in 1980) collaborated closely with the playwright Milan Uhde and composer Miloš Štědroň; in the mid-1970s they created the musicals *Ballad for a Bandit* (1975) and *On a May Fairy Tale* (1976). *Ballad for a Bandit* is based on Ivan Olbracht's 1933 novel about the Ruthenian* bandit Nikola Šuhaj. The original is a paeon in praise of the "natural man," who spurns conventional rules, seeking only justice and freedom. The role of Šuhaj's girlfriend Eržika was played by Iva Bittová, a longtime member of the company whose musical talent strongly influenced its work.

In June 1971 a former JAMU student, Boleslav Polívka, had joined Theatre on a String. Author, director, and above all performer, he was to play an important role in securing its international reputation—thus helping the theatre to survive political harassment at home. A mime actor and a clown, Polívka was in a very different tradition from Fialka. His gangling frame could stretch and distort itself into impossible postures; his face (rarely painted white) twisted itself into bizarre masks. His comedy issued from the logical consequences of absurd situations: two incompatible clans inhabit the same space (*Pezza Versus Čorba*); an isolated individual tries to establish a "normal" routine (*Castaway*, 1977); a ruler tries to govern a country without knowing its language (*The Fool and the Queen*, 1983). In 1979, Polívka revived Ladislav Smoček's black farce from 1966, *The Strange Afternoon of Dr. Zvonek Burke*, interpreting Vladimír Pucholt's old role. The physical energy of Polívka's performances gave him command over audiences in the largest halls. He did not avoid speech altogether, but it was an irrelevant, primitive tool compared with his physical expression. This was an important element of his international success; however, Czechoslovak audiences interpreted Polívka's aban-

* Ruthenia was a part of Czechoslovakia during the First Republic. It was annexed by the Soviet Union in 1945 in contravention of international agreements and is now a part of Ukraine.

donment of spoken language on another level. The 1970s and 1980s were a time when the Czech language, as used in public, had ceased to have dignity, eloquence, or meaning. It was not surprising that one of the best actors of his generation should express himself through inarticulacy.

Eva Tálská also experimented with communication without verbal language. She conveyed her ideas through images, contrasted and juxtaposed, and transformations. *World of Dreams* (1981), a production for children based on fairy tales by Božena Němcová, was without dialogue. It was arranged as a traverse production, using simple contrasts and transformations—green and red for the actors as apple trees, black cloaks when they changed into ravens. The actors communicated with the children and each other through single words shaped and twisted into distorted syllables, and the rhythmic use of vowels and consonants. The nonverbal vocalisation employed techniques reminiscent of Burian's Voiceband: guttural noises, hissing, tutting, whistling, fluttering. Tálská also experimented with clapping, stamping, clicking, and other uses of the body as a resonating instrument.

It was as though, under Normalisation, only nonsense could make sense. Eva Tálská's *Tales of the Long Nose* (1982), a dramatisation of Edward Lear's verse translated by Antonín Přidal, remained in the repertoire for fifteen years. The visual foundation was Lear's pen drawings, with their dapper, fleet-footed gentlemen with tangled beards and pointed toes. Their particular energetic and flighty quality was best caught by Miroslav Donutil, one of the key actors of the company. Although the characters announce they are setting out on an expedition, nothing actually happens except for a constant stream of deviations and the production of quantities of documents—possibly owing to the background presence of two shady bureaucrats. There is no identifiable satire, just a sense of a great deal of energy being expended on futilities. Yet, like Scherhaufer's *Labyrinth of the World*, Tálská's *Tales of the Long Nose* was blocked by the censors for several years.

On other occasions Tálská used the finest verse and prose of the past. The story of Viktorka originated in Božena Němcová's classic novel *Grandmother* (Babička, 1855). Viktorka falls in love with a soldier whose language she does not share, is seduced, goes mad, and drowns the child born of the relationship. In 1949, Jaroslav Seifert was inspired by Němcová's story to write *The Song of Viktorka* (*Píseň o Viktorce*), condemned by the Communist critics as pessimistic and reactionary. Tálská based her version of *The Song of Viktorka* (1984) on Seifert's poem, which—or a long time unavailable—was published in full in the programme.* Seifert's melancholy and nostalgic text set the mood for Tálská's production; her aim was to create a "musically scenographic

* An action that anticipated the Nobel Prize for Literature awarded to Seifert later that year.

Tales of the Long Nose by Edward Lear, dramatised and directed by Eva Tálská for Theatre on a String in Brno, 1982. (Courtesy of the photographer: Jaroslav Krejčí)

space."[320] As the story was seen through Viktorka's eyes, it was set in her room, where the flowing white curtains represented a river and waterfall, the green carpet a meadow... Miloš Štědroň's music was based on balladic folk song, with elements of the Voiceband in the chorus of villagers. Iva Bittová's vocal improvisation intensified the atmosphere of loss and grief.

Peter Scherhaufer used broader, more drastic effects. *Commedia del'Arte* (1974) with Boleslav Polivka was a fast-moving, semi-improvised show that demonstrated the company's skills as acrobats and circus artists.* In 1978, Scherhaufer directed *The Wedding* (1978), an early (1926) play by Brecht written in cabaret style. It was presented (in Ludvík Kundera's translation) as circus knockabout, with the deceptions and role-playing in grotesque caricature. The 1984 production *Chameleon* was described as an opera, with music by Miloš Štědroň (Bittová again played a key role), libretto by Petr Oslzlý† and Ludvík Kundera, and directed by Scherhaufer. It was based on the life of the Abbe Fouché, who retained control of the French secret police during the power shifts of the French Revolution. Both the subject and the setting evoked Radok's great production of Rolland's *Le Jeu de l'amour et de la mort* twenty years earlier. The Revolution surged from end to end of the gallery; the aristocracy paraded in exaggerated costume on a white stage cloth which was ripped away to reveal red floorboards, as the costumes were torn from

* In 1985, *Commedia del'Arte* was the centrepiece of a festival based at Bristol University.

† It was after a performance of *Chameleon* in Prague in 1984 that Václav Havel contacted Petr Oslzlý and their collaboration began.

the actors to reveal peasant smocks; palisades were stripped from the walls while the court orchestra calmly moved aside; women's bodies, identified as France and as Revolution suffered torture and manipulation, were bound with ropes: "Revolution is betrayed" exclaims the Chorus "by those who should defend her!" The "Marseillaise" was the key theme of Štědroň's score, which in operatic parody traced the development of the music of the time. The performance, however, appears to run out of energy; at what seems to be the end, Scherhaufer or Oszlý comes forward as though to answer questions. At this point, a number of television monitors are uncovered. While the fictitious "questions" are being "answered," the restlessness of the actors (their irritable reactions replicated on the screens) sets the action going once more. The Abbe Fouché has arrived in Prague, and the costumes and heraldic symbols are those of the Habsburg Empire. Without a word being said, the audience realises that the world of *Chameleon* is that in which they are living themselves, and that this regime too is drawing near its end.

In the mid-1980s, a new director joined the Theatre on a String, bringing the number back to four. Ivo Krobot had also studied at JAMU but joined the Drama Club in Prague. He and Petr Oslzlý dramatised Bohumil Hrabal's novel *I Served the King of England* (*Obsluhoval jsem anglického krále*), a novel that had been officially published only in censored form. It had been published in full in samizdat and by the exile press, and in 1982 the Jazz Section took the risk of publishing the uncensored version "for members only."* Oslzlý and Krobot succeeded in including it in the repertoire under the blameless title *Recollections* (1985). Hrabal recorded a voiceover that opens the play:

> I couldn't so much as look at the blinding white squares of paper. I had no control over what I wrote. I wrote in a luminous state of intoxication, automatic writing. The light of the sun blinded me so much that I saw only the outlines of the shimmering typewriter. The metal roof was so scorched for several hours that the typewritten sheets of paper rolled into cylinders with the heat. And because the events of the past year had swept me on so much that I hadn't even had time to register my mother's death, so these events force me on, to leave the text as in the first take and hope someday I'll have the time and the courage to tamper with the text and rework it... And if I'm no longer in this world, let it be done by one of my friends. Let him cut a short novel out of it or a longer short story. There we are.[321]

* The Jazz Section originated inconspicuously in the post-invasion years as the Jazz Section of the Prague Branch of the Union of Czech Musicians. It grew to be a cultural and intellectual force, dangerously independent, and was only (partially) quelled by the imprisonment of its committee in 1986.

This luminous intensity pervaded the whole performance, which followed the career of the little commis waiter Jan Dítě to the peak of his ambition as a millionaire hotel owner. Having achieved it, he is philosophical when he loses everything under Communism, and as a road mender in the depopulated Sudetenland, reflects on the years under Austria-Hungary, the First Republic, and the Protectorate. Three actors played the role of Jan Dítě and another fifteen shared more than eighty roles—wholesalers, waiters, train dispatchers, whores, wounded soldiers, gestapo, wandering friars, militiamen, professors of French, villagers, gypsies, and Emperor Haile Selassie. The storytelling wove a spell over audiences brought up on quite a different interpretation of history. Theatre Goose on a String revived the production after Hrabal's death in 1997, when the story "of how the unbelievable came true" ended in a whirl of birds' wings and the cooing of pigeons.

HADIVADLO (THEATRE OF THE HANÁ REGION)*

The Haná region, rich in archaeology and agriculture, folk customs and rustic Baroque, lies in the middle of Moravia. One of its towns is Prostějov, from 1957 home to a festival named after the poet Jiří Wolker. "Wolker's Prostějov" was (and is) a festival of poetry, recited and staged. It was here that, in 1974, the teacher and theatre director Svatopluk Vála and dramaturge Josef Kovalčuk restructured the theatre studio of the local art school (*Lidová škola umění*) into the *Hanácké divadlo*, or Theatre of the Haná Region. Kovalčuk described HaTheatre's programme as "theatre of poetic emotion" and Vála's work was largely lyrical. In 1977, he inaugurated a "poetic triptych" inspired by the inter-war avant-garde—not only Czech: the first part (*Ekkykléma*) focused on Jiří Mahen and Alexander Blok, and the third on Charlie Chaplin (*Chapliniáda*). The centrepiece of the triptych was a version of Vítězslav Nezval's *Telegrams on Wheels* (1978), an acknowledgement of the legacy of Frejka and Honzl, but freely adapted by Vála with the addition of other texts.

In 1978, Arnošt Goldflam—who had studied at JAMU and worked with Radim Vašinka's X-ka, Theatre on a String, and Evening Brno—joined HaTheatre as actor, author, and director. He was a former member of the Surrealist group, and his productions were not based on lyrical narrative but on unexpected juxtapositions, often accompanied by nonverbal or inconsequential language. Like Václav Havel, Goldflam played with the linguistic manipulation that corrupted everyday life in Communist Czechoslovakia. Some of his scripts are autobiographical, such as the trilogy ending with his best-known

* Known as *HaDivadlo*, or *HaDi* for short.

work *Sand (So long ago...)* (1988), based on motifs of growing up in a bohemian Jewish family in Brno after World War II.

By 1980, while still keeping a base in Prostějov, HaTheatre had expanded to Brno. Under the new Theatre Act it was, like Theatre on a String, incorporated into the State Theatre. In some circumstances, the two avant-garde companies could have been rivals, but their leaders saw the need for a common resistance to Normalisation policies, in the State Theatre and in society. During the 1980s there was close cooperation, particularly between the dramaturges Oslzlý and Kovalčuk.

BETWEEN DOG AND WOLF

In 1980, Karel Kříž and Vlasta Gallerová moved from Liberec to Smíchov in Prague, to the former Švanda Theatre, which under Communism was renamed the Realist Theatre of Zdeněk Nejedlý. As early as 1979, the Realist Theatre had premièred a promising new playwright, Daniela Fischerová. Already an accomplished writer for children, she attempted something different in her first play for adults (so different, that the authorities suspected she was covering for a banned author). The title, literally translated as *The Hour Between Dog and Wolf* (1979), has a double meaning: the hour between dog and wolf is the twilight hour, a time of change and transience, of mutability between one state and another. In the context of the play it also refers to François Villon's choice between the antisocial, lawless existence of the artist and conformity with the establishment. Fischerová weaves several different timelines into a single "now" so that at Villon's trial we are faced with both the murdered victim as the counsel for the prosecution, and present-day reporters with all their technological apparatus. Towards the end of the final scene, Regnier de Montigny laughs quietly. "Freedom? There is no freedom. I thought you knew that. Freedom is only a mask for necessity, and our task is to serve that necessity." At the end the trial is not terminated but adjourned. "Here and now!" exclaims Montigny, adding the date in real time. "I summon the jury!"[322]

After four performances, the local authority intervened to ban the play, on the grounds that it was unsuitable for public performance. It was five years before Fischerová's next play, *Princess T* (1986), based on the Turandot story, could open in Ostrava, followed by *Legend* (1987), on the Pied Piper story, also in Ostrava. The three plays belong to a genre typical of the theatre of the 1980s: the historical allegory, the adaptation of familiar stories to deal with contemporary moral problems. The action is set against a mythical background—seventeenth century France, ancient China, mediaeval Hamelin—overlaid with transparent layers of Central European metaphor. However, the themes that run through all three plays—themes of betrayal and of free will—are presented in realistic terms. The characters are faced with specific situations that they have to resolve by their own judgement.

It was another ten years before *Dog and Wolf* could reopen in Prague, and then only at the tiny but courageous *Klub v* Řeznické (Club on Řeznická Street),* under the directorship of Doubravka Svobodová. At this time, no professional theatre in Prague was comparable with the Brno Theatre on a String. Studio Ypsilon had its followers, but had become an "established" theatre, where individual productions might shock or delight, but there was no consistent force in the dramaturgy, nor was any serious risk taken. Prague's "small theatres" had become smaller than ever—some of them just one-man shows or partnerships, others engaging performers on an amateur basis. Most of them were peripatetic, appearing on occasional nights at such venues as the *Malostranská beseda*, the Club Futurum in the Ironworkers House in Smíchov, or the *Junior klub Na Chmelnici*. Companies such as Vangeli's, or the puppet company *Paraple*—which told stories by using inflexible objects moved into position by visible operators—relied on visual expression. Other performers did without props and depended on quick-witted wordplay, often taking the chance that there could not be an informer at every performance, and if there were, he or she may not be bright enough to catch on. Among such were the partnerships of the Brothers Just, of Jan Burian and Jiří Dedeček, and of Jan Vodňanský and Petr Skoumal. All of them had periods when they were banned from performing, a ban that was never formally announced; the performers merely found it impossible to get bookings. In 1988, *Scéna*, which from being a mouthpiece of the union was finding its own voice, interviewed Jan Vodňanský on the subject.[323] Vodňanský described frankly the interruptions to their engagements in the mid-1970s, usually unexplained or put down to "technical reasons." A complete gap in Prague bookings followed, until in 1978 they were permitted to perform on Tuesday evenings in a classroom in Prague 3. It was a brief idyll that ended in January 1980. Then they were back on the road, travelling the provinces like the old strolling players. Ivan Vyskočil's current performances came into this category too; some of his projects were more theatrical than others, but always within his own definition of *Nedivadlo*—"Non-theatre." One was *Haprdáns* (1980), standing for *Hamlet, Prince of Denmark*. With the help of two fellow performers and a collection of kitchen instruments transformed into puppets, Vyskočil retold the story of *Hamlet*, reaching some unexpected but entirely logical deductions.

The most ambitious of these loosely structured groups was the Theatre on the Fringe, a group of freelance actors (including Zdena Hadrbolcová

* As noted earlier, a "club" did not require membership; it was just a reference to the intimacy of the space.

and Sergej Machonin's daughter, Lenka Machoninová). Led by the director Zdeněk Potužil, they performed mainly in *Rubín*, Orfeus's old home on Lesser Quarter Square. Working in a space which held an audience of less than a hundred, Theatre on the Fringe used a different form of staging for every production: traverse stage for Jiří Šotola's *Kuře on Fire* (1979); end stage for dramatised readings of Jaroslav Hašek's letters, *Švejks* (1980); and a thrust stage measuring barely two by three metres for *Romeo and Juliet* (1981). This production, cut to fit seven performers, was fast and dangerous, the verse speaking rehearsed to a metronome.

This was in the tradition of the *auteur théâtre* described earlier. Between the dramatic extremes of the Theatre Beyond the Gate, created by Krejca's powerful personality, and simple cellar performances, lay a range of possibilities: dramatisations and adaptations of novels and prose works, stagings of poetry and songs, rewritten versions of Shakespeare and other classics, mime, puppetry, and cabaret. At the beginning of the 1980s these were joined by another kind of theatre. The harassment of rock musicians, beginning with the Plastic People of the Universe in the mid-1970s, had made it increasingly difficult to present the popular unofficial entertainment enjoyed by young people. Students and young workers, looking round for alternative entertainment, discovered the "Postmodern" groups with short, aggressive names like *Sklep* (Cellar), *Vpřed* (Forward), and *Křeč* (Spasm). Their performances were put together from short sketches, often poetic or absurd, sometimes using film, mime, or unusual vocal effects. In the early days their creators denied that the productions had any intellectual or dramaturgical content, but in the political climate of the time, any independent initiative marked its perpetrators as being dangerously subversive. In 1988, five groups collaborated on the film *The Prague Five*,* some of its parts directly satirical. That such a film could be made was a sign of the times, of the hidden war being waged between different factions of the Communist Party, secret police, and government during the last few years of the totalitarian regime. As the ferocity of individual attacks on artists increased, so too did the solidarity of the opposition.

Another territory "between dog and wolf" was the amateur theatre. Ironically, "Normalisation" was a golden age for amateur theatre. It was of inestimable importance not only in the big cities but countrywide. Creative individuals, deprived of their rightful place in politics, business, culture, and education, and condemned to routine employment, used their free time to express their ideas and ambitions through theatre. The greatest surge in amateur theatre occurred in the 1970s; at the turn of the decade many of the most

* An oblique allusion to President Masaryk's "Pražská Pětka" of political parties through which he governed the First Republic.

dynamic participants were looking for ways to leave a country in which they had no prospects. The amateur stage also made an important contribution to theatre studies; its publication, *Amatérská scéna*, provided a platform for scholars, critics, and journalists forbidden to publish in more prestigious periodicals. Amateur companies were also allowed more freedom in their choice of authors—Kafka, for example, or the Polish author Sławomir Mrożek. In the mid-1980s the group Lampa had four plays in its repertoire, including those of Mrożek and Stanisław Lem. They performed once a week in the *Baráčnická rychta*, a punishing schedule for an amateur group, but a necessary condition to maintain a concession dating back to 1870.

In a totalitarian society it was not possible to create an amateur theatre by putting on a show in a barn or a garage, or even by opening a bank account in the group's name. Every organisation had to be part of a structure ultimately under the control of the Central Committee of the Communist Party of the Czechoslovak Socialist Republic. Amateur groups were therefore affiliated to the local authority or a major employer such as a factory. In the 1980s one of the most successful was DOPRAPO, short for *Dopravní podník*, which translates as "transport authority" (the name was later changed to *Jak se Vám jelo* ["How was your ride"] and then shortened to JELO). In 1982, a seventeen-year-old graphics student and member of the group, Petr Lébl, tried his hand at an experimental production of a work by the American author Kurt Vonnegut. Three years later, after Vonnegut met Lébl on a visit to Prague, Lébl's work was taken up by the American Embassy, and word spread. A brilliant talent both intellectually and in the visual arts, Lébl staged Morgenstern, Kafka, Genet, Wyspiański, and other European masters in venues like the *Malostranská beseda* and Letná Park. Lébl turned professional after 1989, became director of the Theatre on the Balustrade, and was hailed as one of the talents of the century.

Among the amateur companies was the Studio of Movement Theatre (*Studio pohybového divadlo*)* led by Nina Vangeli, a student of Jan Kopecký (the once-powerful critic and dramaturge) and an admirer of Grotowski and the Living Theatre of New York. Her productions included a version of *The Tempest* (1982) performed with irresistible energy—climbing, struggling, dancing, wriggling—in a central space filled with brightly painted stepladders, artificial flowers, joss sticks, swords, children, and a whirling mass of brilliant fabrics. Simple black costumes were elaborated with crepe-paper ruffs, tophats, wings, and mermaid tails. By contrast, *Requiem* (1987) was played against dark draperies, with costumes—baggy suits and sleek 1940s skirts—in grey and black, a single swathe of gold lamé striking the eye like sunlight in a

* Preceded by the White Theatre (*Bílé divadlo*) and Flint (*Křesadlo*).

tomb. A child with a still, solemn face moved through a lapidarium of mocking baroque statues. Vangeli knew how to create effective theatre by setting limited tasks within the scope of the actors' abilities–most of them students and young workers.

One of the most important amateur groups was the Brno initiative. *Ochotnický kroužek* (Amateur Circle) or OCHKR. It had been preceded by *Tak, tak* (Only Just), created by members of Theatre on a String's Youth Studio who had invited the stage manager Zdeněk Petrželka to work with them. In 1979, *Tak, tak* staged an evening of Russian and Soviet poetry including Voznesensky, Yevtushenko, and Joseph Brodsky. The next poetry programme was to have been *Hamletiana*, which included excerpts from Vladimír Holan and Tom Stoppard. Before it could take place, *Tak, tak* was forcibly disbanded by the authorities following the scandal of Petrželka's unauthorised street theatre tribute to Dostoyevsky on the centenary of his death. Petrželka was banned from working in the theatre and became a librarian; however, under the pseudonym J. A. Pitínský, he was to become one of the country's most creative theatre directors. In 1985, he cofounded OCHKR with the philosopher and aesthetician Petr Osolsobě under the wing of the Cultural and Educational Centre for the Brno V district, whose wooden cabin of a culture house, Šelepka, it made its home. They began by adapting Kafka's *America*–the first staging of Kafka's work in Czechoslovakia since Jan Grossman's dramatisation of *The Trial* nineteen years earlier. The script incorporated excerpts from Kafka's letters to Felicia Bauer and from Božena Němcová's *Grandmother*. For each character Pitínský prepared a technique of isolated, highly stylised gestures. "*America* was prepared with great hesitancy, even embarrassment," he wrote later, "and for all that we took shortcuts of vertiginous proportions..."[324]

The following year, OCHKR staged Comenius's *Abrahamus Patriarcha*, an allegory about the exile's love for his homeland. Comenius's play, however, was camouflage for a more controversial text, *The Abraham Case: A Question of Faith*, based on Søren Kierkegaard, Helmuth Heissenbüttel, and the Old and New Testaments by the medical student Luboš Malinovský (who had written the music for *America*). Another source of inspiration was the American theatre *auteur* Robert Wilson and his theatre of synthesis, in which the formal design of the whole is more important than psychological interpretation.* As an amateur company, OCHKR had access to only the most rudimentary equipment: old-fashioned lanterns cast stark shadows; a crudely built staircase dominated the performing space. Costumes were simple in style

* Malinovský's knowledge of Robert Wilson (and American composer Philip Glass) came from the semi-official publications of the Jazz Section, which under Normalisation were virtually the only source of information on modern art movements.

and colour (black, white, khaki, and terracotta), the actors' faces lightly whitened, their hair sculpted with white china clay (orange for the Lord God). The Conductor alone (Martin Dohnal, who also composed the music) wore meticulous evening dress without sculpted hair or makeup. Movement was precisely choreographed, down to the exact placing of the hands; actors who were not performing remained straight and still onstage, eyes fixed on the middle distance.

The focus of the script is on the "here and now" of theatrical performance—the paradox that an event can take place only once in history, and yet, in the theatre, that one and only time happens before the present audience. The context is the question of faith in an age of conformity and calculation, expressed through Abraham, a man at odds with his time, who consciously accepts responsibility. What amazed Kierkegaard was Abraham's faith in God:

> All along he had faith, he believed that God would not demand Isaac of him, while still he was willing to offer him if that was indeed what was demanded. He believed in the strength of the absurd, for there could be no question of human calculation, and it was indeed absurd that God, who demanded this of him, would in the next instant withdraw the demand.[325]

At the climax of the action, shortly before Isaac is to be sacrificed the Conductor observes: "We do not feel in ourselves the courage to want to be contemporaries of such events. Our audience simply cannot understand, nor let its gaze rest on this without a troubled mind."[326]

In September 1987, OCHKR was invited to perform *Abrahamus Patriarcha* in Utrecht, and at an international conference in Comenius's home town of Uherský Brod—to the secret embarrassment of the authors, who knew how little their text had in common with Comenius. Subsequent productions by OCHKR included Oscar Wilde's *Salome*, the thriller *Pineapple Medium-Fox*, the social drama *Mother* (both by J. A. Pitínský, both from 1987), and Goethe's *Elective Affinities*; the last of these being a series of staged "home seminars" held in the apartment of the (future) political scientist Pavel Barša.

Even more confined was Vlasta Chramostová's initiative, the Living Room Theatre (*Bytové divadlo*, literally Apartment Theatre). This began in the apartment she shared with her husband Stanislav Milota at the top of Wenceslas Square. Chramostová had been one of the most popular Prague actresses until in 1970 she supported the director František Pavlíček as head of the Vinohrady Theatre against his replacement, Zdeněk Míka. From then on, and especially after signing the Charter, she could not be employed in any theatre even as a guest. Between 1976 and 1980, four productions were prepared for her living room. The first, *All the Beauties of the World*, was created from the poetry of Jaroslav Seifert; the second, *Apelplatz II* was a collage based on the Polish author Jerzy Andrzejewski and including excerpts from silenced authors such as Havel, Vaculík, Kohout, and Klíma. In 1978, Pavel Kohout adapted *Macbeth*—called *Play Makbeth*—for five actors (thus inspiring *Cahoot's Macbeth*, as imagined by Tom Stoppard). An audience member later wrote that:

> Their evident refusal to set the performance in a contemporary context made it all the more topical… The theatre is not a place we attend to grumble at our condition. It is an arena where we go to assert our freedom.[327]

Play Makbeth was also performed at Václav Havel's cottage and in the apartments of Ivan Havel and Daňa Horáková—both venues for underground seminars.

František Pavlíček, former head of the Vinohrady Theatre, in 1968 a member of the Central Committee of the Communist Party, but also one of Krejča's writers, had been imprisoned for seventeen months after signing Charter 77. In 1979, while working as a labourer, he wrote a monodrama for Chramostová. *Long, Long Ago, or A Report about Burying in Bohemia*, was based on Božena Němcová's reflections on the death of Karel Havlíček Borovský. In Pavlíček's dramatisation, Němcová's thoughts on the failed revolution of 1848, on absolutism and on the difficult relationships between patriots echoed the contemporary world of Normalisation. It was written as gift from one Chartist to another. Ironically, the performances of the Living Room Theatre reached a wider audience than most official theatre groups. Milota, a professional cameraman, filmed them and smuggled the tapes into Vienna. Broadcast on Austrian television, the performances were watched by households in South Bohemia and Moravia with aerials angled to the border with the West. The recording of *Long, Long Ago* was broadcast to coincide with the centenary of the National Theatre.

VII THE THEATRE AND THE VELVET REVOLUTION

The Velvet (or Gentle) Revolution in Czechoslovakia was largely prepared by theatre workers, which was why it came as a surprise to Western experts who had been diligently following political trends. It was the culmination of two centuries of theatre tradition—an environment and a community where ethical and patriotic principles were combined with the practical experience needed for handling unpredictable situations.

From the early 1980s, a secret alliance had been shaping within the theatre community. In December 1980, a working meeting in Hradec Králové discussed cooperation between the studio-type theatres. In a Communist society, interested parties could not simply decide to hold a meeting for themselves; it had to take place within an existing structure, in this case the Union of Czech Dramatic Artists. The meeting was held under the auspices of the union's Committee of Theatre for Young Audiences (*Komise divadla mladého diváka*, KDMD), chaired by the historian and dramaturge Bohumil Nekolný. At a seminar on "team theatre work," the committee appointed a working group and planned seminars, workshops, a magazine,* and a festival of young people's theatre.

In 1981, a seminar was held on "issues of staging in relation to the younger generation, directed towards the collective and teamwork methodology of theatre work" (the terminology had to be correctly formulated to obtain union approval). The working group was concerned with the long interruption in critical thinking during Normalisation, and hoped to restore it through

* These aims were eventually achieved, albeit that the magazine remained only in a "semiofficial" form, as the cyclostyled bulletin of the KDMD.

an analysis of theatre in practice. Vlasta Gallerová, still at the F. X. Šalda Theatre in Liberec, opened the seminar; her theme was theatre as a process, not a fixed state—its dynamic development through the interaction of its different elements. When the working group tried to release its proceedings, it met with resistance from the union, which objected that the opinions were outdated, the theory weak, the terminology unclear, and moreover, there was no evidence of the influence of the Soviet theatre... Nevertheless, the Hradec Králové seminar insisted on the principle that practice should not be subordinated to theory, as it was in the Socialist Realist theatre—that, on the contrary, theatre practice was the material from which theory was derived. Five companies agreed to participate in a joint project: Theatre on a String, Studio Ypsilon, HaTheatre, Theatre on the Fringe, and the Drama Studio. As Petr Oslzlý of the Theatre on a String observed, the critical shift was that theatre was being talked about not as an artefact but as a process.

Another principle became evident in the joint workshops—the ethical and artistic responsibility of the members of the group for the meaning of their theatre work. The five companies agreed to work on a joint theme, and ideas were discussed throughout 1983; the concept of "timetables" emerged, giving them the title *Cesty* (travels/journeys/ways/paths). In October 1984, the five companies rehearsed together in Brno. A dress rehearsal of *Cesty* was held for representatives of the local authority and of the State Theatre. Each part of the performance had to be approved separately. The cooperative work was also performed in Bratislava and Prague; Bohumil Nekolný noted that the production acquired a dynamic of its own.

In 1985, discussions began for a project based on the life of Karel Sabina, the nineteenth-century Czech writer and patriot, and librettist of Smetana's *The Bartered Bride*. Imprisoned by the Austrian authorities for his nationalism, he submitted to becoming an informer for the secret police. Three of the studio-type theatres performed their versions at the *Junior klub Na Chmelnici* at the end of January 1988: *The Bartered and the Bought* by Theatre on a String,* *The Bartered Bride* by *DRAK* from Hradec Králové, and *Mysterious Natures* by HaTheatre. The other groups were to present the results of their research at an open symposium to which theatre workers from dissident circles had been invited. The authorities granted permission for the discussion—provided the script was submitted for prior approval, and no one departed from it. The event was cancelled.

As the 1980s progressed, more initiatives were planned and executed. One of the activists' main allies was the theatre newspaper *Scéna*. After Jan

---

* Although *The Bartered and the Bought* was attributed to collective authorship, the author was Milan Uhde.

Dvořák had been appointed editor in 1987, articles critical of official cultural policies had begun to appear (largely unnoticed by the general public, and completely overlooked by Western experts). There was pressure, resisted by the hardliners, to shift the barriers. Dvořák remembers that every issue of the newspaper was a struggle, a fight to keep the content. At the same time, the activist could sense the barriers beginning to give way.[328] In the expectant atmosphere that preceded Gorbachev's visit to Prague in spring 1987, a group of theatre workers published a manifesto in *Scéna*. It was a call for artistic independence and freedom from bureaucracy:

> Most energy is taken up with trying to secure things which ought to be a matter of course if you are involved in creative work... instead of a naturally operating theatre we have an economically demanding self-devouring administrative machine apparently capable of functioning even without any artistic company and moreover led by people from outside the theatre with no understanding of stage practice and who certainly do not understand the creative side.[329]

The twenty-five signatories—theatre directors, performers, and playwrights—claimed that the established theatre was run with both eyes on directives coming from above and mediated through bureaucrats who themselves would neither take nor give responsibility. The article continued:

> Numbers of contemporary socially relevant plays... and productions have become victims of administrative intervention. In a similar way, many names have disappeared from Czech theatrical life, and for a number of years we have been pretending that these people and their works never existed.[330]

The manifesto was published in *Scéna* in anticipation of the May conference of the Union of Czech Dramatic Artists, which turned into a battle of wills. For the first time elections to the committees were held by secret ballot. Those elected included Petr Oslzlý from Theatre on a String, Arnošt Goldflam of HaTheatre, Ivan Rajmont of the Drama Studio of Ústí nad Labem, and the playwright Karel Steigerwald.

Petr Oslzlý was one of the chief authors of the manifesto.* In September 1987, he organised the third Theatre on the Move festival. Its importance lay in its choice of "unofficial" material, in its reference to Czechoslovakia's past culture, and in its relationship to the international context. There were exhibitions of sculptures and paintings by artists without state licences (includ-

* At the same time the net was closing in on Oslzlý. From 1985, he was forbidden to travel abroad with the Theatre on a String (or in any other way).

ing the performance artist Tomáš Ruller); readings by unpublished authors; videos of theatre groups such as the Living Theatre; talks about the work of, for example, the postwar Czech Surrealist group Skupina Ra. It was also a popular festival with children's workshops, jazz concerts, and a balloon flight. It culminated in a joint performance in the open spaces of the town with Theatre on a String, the Polish Teatr 77 and the Dutch Den Bla Hest.

The following May, at the conference of the Union of Czech Dramatic Artists, Oslzlý asked:

> Why is the culture of our own society so far behind that of our neighbouring Socialist countries? [...] Why do we go on uselessly mistreating both our spiritual heritage and the potential of our contemporary artists?
>
> We need to renew the memory and continuity of our culture, to return to our society its cultural inheritance, to allow formerly banned books and magazines to be freely borrowed from our libraries, to readmit to our encyclopaedias and specialist publications every suppressed name and subject, and to make circumscribed works freely available to the public.
>
> In the theatre we must be allowed to perform plays by Josef Topol, Ivan Klíma, Václav Havel, František Pavlíček, and Milan Uhde, as well as foreign plays, whose existence our audiences don't even know about. Normal working conditions would be restored to our directors, dramaturges, and actors, so that they can have a free choice of repertoire and work at a level corresponding to their artistic abilities. Theatres which have suffered from administrative interference should be allowed to return to their normal pattern of development.[331]

The speech provoked an outburst from the representative of the cultural department of the Central Committee of the Communist Party, Jaroslav Pernica:

> If we're naming names, let's mention the activities that go with them. No one has ever been thrown out of our cultural life! I'll emphasise that—no one!... But since the names of Havel and others have already been mentioned, then we can tell you openly that these people are and were militant antisocialists... We've always said and we'll say it again, that the way is open to each and every one of us, even Mr. Havel himself has tried several times to make contact with us, but these people only want one thing, to spit in the face of Socialism, and for us to wipe our faces and thank them for having spat on us. I mean to say—what kind of morality is that?... And on top of that we're expected to start re-evaluating this that and the other from the 1960s. This kind of trend tries to make out that everything from the last twenty years has been the total ruination of our culture. And that what's more, that what went before those twenty years was the wonderful flowering of that culture! But I'm telling you, my friends, that these propagators, these

preachers, are spitting in your face, because for these twenty years you've been doing good honest theatre... And the more our intellectual mouths this trendiness, the more he's convinced that he's some kind of revolutionary. Please forgive me for having got so worked up about this, but I had to speak up for myself as a Communist, a Communist who today and every day looks out for every available opportunity to bear witness to the truth of history.[332]

Many of the theatre reformers were friends of Václav Havel and his circle: the theatre critic Sergej Machonin, dramaturge Karel Kraus, actress Vlasta Chramostová. The circle included younger people such as Andrej Krob (director of the amateur Theatre on the Road) and his wife Anna Freimanová. Krob became involved in the production of the *Original Videojournal*—a samizdat video news service—that began to circulate during the late 1980s, while Freimanová was responsible for the production of the samizdat journal *O divadle* (About Theatre). This was one of the weightiest samizdat journals, each of the five issues* consisting of approximately four hundred pages of erudite articles by authors who, in the 1960s, had been stars of the theatre and academic worlds. The carefully structured editions covered archival issues and memoirs as well as translated articles and contemporary topics such as the uninspiring management of the National Theatre's "experimental" stage. There were book reviews and reviews of new productions. As a whole, the samizdat periodical completely outclassed any official publication in breadth and depth. The editor-in-chief was Krejča's former dramaturge, Karel Kraus; the editorial board consisted of the banned critic Sergej Machonin, banned playwright František Pavlíček, and Přemysl Rut, still working on the borderline between the official and the unofficial.†

In summer 1988, another initiative was launched. Nine activists, including Karel Steigerwald and Petr Oslzlý from the theatre, the philosopher Petr Rezek, poet Petr Kabeš, artist Joska Skalník (from the Drama Club), translator Jaroslav Kořán, and sculptor Jan Šimek, signed the manifesto "Open Dialogue" (*Otevřený dialog*). "Open Dialogue" was intended to break down the barriers between writers, artists, filmmakers, and critics, confined by the Communists to their own professional disciplines, and often subdivided into age groups. "Open Dialogue" emphasised that it was not a formal organisation (because that would require registration with the Communist authorities) but a "free association" which anyone could join by signing the manifesto:

* July 1986, Feb 1987, Nov 1987, Oct 1989. A selection of articles was published officially in 1990.

† A seminar to celebrate twenty-five years from the foundation of *O divadle* was held on the Kolowrat stage of the National Theatre on 31 October 2011. One of those present was Václav Havel, fragile but still focused. It was the last time many of his friends saw him.

> The association will hold informal meetings where different opinions, styles, ideas, and trends, in art as well as in daily life, can be discussed. This dialogue will be conducted in an entirely free and democratic spirit, in keeping with cultural traditions which still remain alive in this country... We wish to re-establish the continuity of our culture, to make contact with artists abroad, and invite them to take part in our dialogue.[333]

The day of 28 October 1988 was a significant anniversary in the history of Czechoslovakia: seventy years since the founding of the First Republic. Two theatres were working on special productions for the anniversary. Theatre on a String had prepared a joint production with HaTheatre—a "staged magazine" with the name *Rozrazil* (in translation, the flower known as speedwell or veronica, but also with the meaning of "breaking open").* Successive issues were planned—this first one, *Rozrazil 1/88 (On Democracy)*, opened in Brno on 21 October 1988. After the crushing of two attempts by the company to start its own publication, this was a "living newspaper" in an era when the official newspapers published mainly lies and distortions.

Meanwhile, the Realist Theatre in Prague had thought up *Res Publica*, the first version subtitled *How We Did Not Experience the Twenties*. It was a collective project, created by two directors, two dramaturges and the head of the theatre, Jiří Fréhar. The programme was shaped from recollection of favourite passages, songs, and poems popular in the First Republic: Čapek, Hašler, Teige, and Seifert, but also Ježek, Janáček, and Martinů, and even the Seven of Hearts parody of a detective story, *Harry's Case*. The actors were joined by guests whose names had been missing from public life for the last twenty years. First played on 27 October 1988, it was an immediate hit with the general public.

Unknown to most of the co-workers on these two productions, there was another dramaturgical team behind the scenes, one that met by night in the temporary office of architects involved in restoration work on Vyšehrad. It was a mixed group of dissidents who could no longer work in the theatre—including Václav Havel and Vlasta Chramostová—and those who still could, including Petr Oslzlý, Karel Kříž, and Vlasta Gallerová. Gallerová remembers that these discussions were largely about ethics and values and how to help build a free and open society, but that very often they covered practical aspects of staging.

There was an expectant tension in Prague on the morning of 28 October. It was the seventieth anniversary of founding of the First Republic, and the government had, perhaps rashly, restored the state holiday that had marked

---

* There are also echoes of Nezval's poetry and of the ambiguity of *Devětsil* Poetism. In a sense, this too provided "cover."

Res Publica in the Realist Theatre of Zdeněk Nejedlý in Prague. *From left to right*: Zdeněk Urbánek (*standing*), Elmar Klos, Svatopluk Beneš, Marie Rosůlková, Rudolf Hrušinský, Milan Machovec, 1988. (Photographer: Jaroslav Kořán; from the author's personal archive)

the anniversary in pre-Communist days. All the dissidents the police could lay hands on had been interned for forty-eight hours. Crowds gathered in Wenceslas Square. Well-trained security worked to seal off the centre of the square. A line of riot police in helmets and shields blocked side entrances to the square, such as the Kino Blaník passage. Tourists were addressed politely, and asked to leave the square by the nearest exit. Women with prams tried to convince young policeman that their apartment was within the cordoned-off zone.

Meanwhile, crowds were being forced out of Old Town Square, still chanting: "Masaryk!" "Dubček!" "Democracy!" and "This is our perestroika!" as well as "You're not Czechs!" and "Shame!" (directed at the police). The police had also surrounded the *Junior klub Na Chmelnici*, where the Theatre on a String and HaTheatre were due to give the Prague première of *Rozrazil*. The audience was allowed in and the performance went ahead. Its magazine format included "reports," "reviews," and "original prose" interspersed with poems by Viktor Dyk. An item headed "study" turned out to be a short play called *Tomorrow!*, a dramatisation of the founding of the First Republic in 1918, when a group of untried politicians hurriedly improvised a revolution. Many of the events in this lightly didactic piece uncannily foreshadowed the Velvet Revolution of 1989. No one but Petr Oslzlý knew (although some suspected) that the author was Václav Havel.*

Another of *Rozrazil*'s items, the "discussion" *The Philosophers' Feast* (by the Brno philosopher Vladimír Čermák), brought an intake of breath as the dinner lady demanded "Patočka! Where's Patočka?" and Pericles answered "*Patočka už není*" ("Patočka's dead"). When the audience stood to sing *Kde domov můj?* ("Where is my home?" – the national anthem) many were in tears. It was suggested that no Prague company would have dared to stage such a piece, which was widely reviewed; within a short time, an official committee attended a closed performance, and the production was "interrupted" (*přerušená*); not technically banned, but put on hold while the State Theatre looked for a convincing reason to shut it down permanently.

Meanwhile, other barriers in the theatre began to give way; in January 1989, Josef Topol's play from the early 1960s, *The End of Shrovetide*, was revived at the Theatre of West Bohemia in Cheb (where Jan Grossman had spent much of his exile).† A long review appeared in *Scéna*,[334] dealing as much with the significance of its revival as with the production itself. The first paragraphs were devoted in detail to Topol's career, not overlooking his years as a labourer, and including as many "forbidden" names as possible.

In May, Jan Grossman returned to the Theatre on the Balustrade as a guest director, with Molière's *Don Juan*.‡ Eight years had passed since his Hradec Králové production; this version was fiercer and more pointed in the intensity of its social and political thrusts. The setting was a vast and hollow monument, vandalised and insecure, grossly large for the small stage. The characters balance dangerously on the edge of precipitous steps; no one, as Don Juan bleakly realises, believes in the Omnipotent in whose honour the monument was erected. Jiří Bartoška as Juan delivered his speech on hypocrisy on a breath as sharp as a dagger; it was interrupted by bursts of applause from the audience. At the première, Miroslav Štěpán, Communist Party boss for Prague, congratulated Grossman familiarly with the words "We need more such productions." Grossman wondered whether the price of his return to Prague was to spend time with people like Štěpán.§

---

* Havel, hospitalised and under the supervision of the secret police, missed the performance. His brother Ivan was there.

† In 1988, the idea of a play by a "Chartist" being publicly performed was still beyond belief for most.

‡ Jiří Bartoška, Grossman's Don Juan, openly signed the petition "A Few Sentences" (*Několik vět*) issued on 29 June 1989.

§ Conversation with Jan Grossman, 12 June 1989. Half a year later, Štěpán was sentenced to two and a half years imprisonment for abuse of power in ordering the police action during Palach week in February 1989.

Václav Havel was the focal point of another action that brought together the official and unofficial activists: One sleepy afternoon in June 1989 the agency DILIA held a *beseda* in the bookshop *Československý spisovatel* for the public to meet their playwrights. A handful of audience and participants were hanging out on the mezzanine when, in a military-style operation, Přemysl Rut and Karel Steigerwald escorted Havel into this most official of venues to be introduced by DILIA's moderator Jitka Sloupová alongside the approved playwrights Oldřich Daněk and Jiří Hubač, as though he were not a banned writer and enemy of the state. Such small victories began to accumulate.

Jan Kačer had been directing some exceptional productions at the Vinohrady Theatre since 1986. In January 1988, the ideologue Zdeněk Míka was replaced as head of the theatre, and in June 1989 Kačer directed Topol's previously unstaged *The Voices of Birds*. A subtle and poetic play examining the continuity of a man's life and the legacy of his work, it did not carry any political message. Nevertheless, the first night was an emotional occasion,* attended by other "banned playwrights" for whom the possibility of production was now opening up. The theatres, including the Theatre on the Balustrade, were now taking concerted action, scheduling such authors in the autumn programmes now being submitted to the local authorities. On 10 October, Marta Kubišová was invited to appear as a guest at Studio Ypsilon, her first time onstage for twenty years. As winner of the Golden Nightingale† in 1968 and 1969 and spokesperson for Charter 77, the popular singer had been silenced for her refusal to renounce the ideals of the Prague Spring. *Mladá fronta* even reviewed the performance on 12 October. Fifteen days later, the Realist Theatre premièred *Res Publica II*—focusing on the 1960s and including excerpts from Václav Havel's *The Garden Party* and Josef Škvorecký's *Tank Battalion*. It was banned immediately.

This was the tense autumn leading up to the students' demonstration of 17 November, the fiftieth anniversary of the day on which the Nazis had executed nine Czech students and closed the universities. After the war, 17 November had been declared International Students' Day and a commemorative procession was held annually in Prague. That night, the Brno theatres had been newly allowed to play *Rozrazil* at the *Junior klub Na Chmelnici*. As they rehearsed, they could hear the transport trucks lining up in front of the neighbouring barracks and wondered whether the audience would not be frightened away. Meanwhile, the students processed along the Engels and

* One of the leading roles was taken by Jiřina Švorcová. When the author and Charter signatory came onstage for the curtain calls at the end of the première, he took his bow alongside the instigator of the Anti-Charter.

† At that time, an annual award given to one male and one female singer who gained the highest number of votes in a popular poll.

Gottwald Embankments, turning right at the National Theatre down Národní třída. A line of riot police blocked their way ahead. A second line closed in behind. The cordon drew tighter; the students stretched their empty hands in the air. Radio Prague estimated that six hundred people were treated for injuries that night, some of them serious.

One of the students trapped in the procession, Roman Ráček from Brno University, made for the *Junior klub*, where the *Rozrazil* company cancelled the last part of the performance and interviewed him onstage: "Twice tonight, I thought I was going to die," he told the audience. "Once, when I faced the armoured cars, and the second time when the police cordon squeezed us until I thought we would suffocate." Meanwhile, students from DAMU and other schools had made their way to other theatres with the news, including the fact that the students were planning a protest strike. At the Realist Theatre, where a new production of the Mrštíks' *Maryša* had premièred that evening, Jan Grossman, Jan Kačer, Ivan Rajmont, and Karel Steigerwald were already sitting with Kříž and Gallerová in the theatre offices. They decided to call theatre representatives to a meeting at two o'clock the next afternoon. Gallerová was on the phone to her colleagues in the provinces until the early hours.

When Petr Oslzlý arrived on Saturday afternoon he automatically turned into the offices where the conspirational group normally held their meetings. The stage doorkeeper directed him to the auditorium, which was packed with three hundred people. Among those onstage were the dramatist Karel Steigerwald, the actors Tomáš Töpfer and Jiří Ornest,* the head of the National Theatre drama company Milan Lukeš, and the director of the Realist Theatre Jiří Fréhar. It was agreed that the theatres would strike in sympathy with the students. Those appointed to the strike committee and the coordination committee included Karel Král, Bohumil Nekolný, Arnošt Goldflam, Ivan Rajmont, Karel Steigerwald, Karel Kříž, and Miroslav Macháček. It was also agreed that a nationwide general strike should be called for 27 November—Monday week. The question was, when to start the theatre strike? It was now after three o'clock and two companies—Semafor and Theatre on a String / HaTheatre—had matinees starting at four.

It was decided that the strike would begin immediately. At the *Junior klub Na Chmelnici*, the actors in *Rozrazil* assembled in front of the audience in civilian dress. The audience was told that instead of a performance there would be an announcement and a discussion, and that if they wished, they could collect their money at the box office and leave. No one stirred. The story of the previous day's events was told calmly and without exaggeration.

---

* Son of Ota Ornest and nephew of Jiří Orten and Zdeněk Ornest.

How the Velvet Revolution began: the founding of Civic Forum in the Drama Club (*centre stage*, Václav Havel) on 19 November 1989. (Photographer: Petr Mazanec; photograph from the Czech News Agency)

Over the next few days, this pattern was taken up by almost every town in the country. The public filled auditoriums, not for a play or an opera, but to hear what was happening in the rest of the country, especially in Prague. The theatres became forums, and in many cases the model was the Realist Theatre's *Res Publica*. For the first week, there was virtually no other source of news, except for the telephone; radio, television, and newspapers were still in the hands of the Communists. However, those filling the theatres were still only a small part of the population, and it was vital to reach people to prepare them for the general strike. In many cases, the actors were invited to speak at institutes, factories, and offices. Sometimes their contacts secretly gathered workers together; sometimes they tricked their way into official meetings and spoke out before they were thrown out. In one town, a car chase ended in an arrest; in another an actor was chased on foot to the railway station. They travelled across Bohemia, Moravia, and Slovakia by any means they could find; in twos and threes, or singly. In some remote districts, they stayed overnight and found themselves unofficial counsellors for local problems. Other villagers drove them away: "We have a pig in the sty and potatoes in the cellar. What do we need with you?" Industrial areas, particularly North Moravia, were difficult to penetrate. On 8 December, a car returning from the mines of Ostrava crashed as it approached Prague. The passengers included the director Jan Kačer and the young actor Jan Potměšil, who had created the role of Robert in Topol's *The Voices of Birds* that summer. Kačer was unhurt; Potměšil was paralysed for life.*

Meanwhile, Civic Forum† had been coming into existence. Havel had avoided preventive detention by staying at his country cottage, returning on 18 November with the intention of catching the second première of *Maryša* at the Realist Theatre. He was active in preparations for the gathering on 19 November held in the Drama Club. (The actor Petr Čepek had negotiated use of the theatre with the caretaker, who had set a time limit on the meeting.) Those summoned to the small underground theatre wondered whether they would not emerge under arrest. On Monday 20 November, Civic Forum set up its headquarters in the gallery *U Řečických* on Vodičkova Street, moving on Thursday to the larger premises of the *Laterna magika* in the basement of the Adria Palace. The students, meanwhile, established their headquarters in DAMU, and the theatre people in the Theatre Institute. Many of them were engaged in planning the manifestations, first in Wenceslas Square and then on the plain of Letná. Foreign observers noted the relaxed humour and good manners of the crowds; no calls for vengeance, no mob behaviour. Havel and his stage managers had forestalled such risks; a sound system was quickly in place, points of entry and exit were monitored, the voices had to be varied, the speeches short and not seeking to incite the crowd, there was relief in the form of songs and popular personalities, and release of emotion in the jingling of keys and the mass singing of the national anthem. Havel exercised his theatre skills in his negotiations with the Communist government; the photographer Jaroslav Krejčí remembered that he worked out in advance the potential variations of the Communists' approach, and rehearsed his optimal response to each variation.[335] He was thus ready to move smoothly into "variation 2) b)" when the moment came.

After the success of the general strike, the pattern changed. Actors and students still travelled the country, but now the aim was to help to organise branches of Civic Forum. The programmes for the "strike evenings" became more structured and wider in content, as the audiences' appetites for information increased. Experts in different fields were invited to speak: economists, clergy, metro workers, samizdat publishers, historians. At the Jiří Wolker

---

* Potměšil nevertheless continued his career from a wheelchair and became a popular and successful actor, mainly with the company Kašpar.

† A citizens' initiative that negotiated the transfer of power from the Communists.

Theatre for Youth, the evenings were called "What's Not in the Text Books." The actors found that young people, unlike older audiences, did not ask what was happening—they knew already. They wanted to understand *why* it was happening; to find out what had happened in the past.

The theatres remained "on strike" for three weeks before returning to their normal repertoire. After the drama of the preceding weeks, it was not easy to repeat performances rehearsed in the days before the revolution, in front of audiences more concerned with what was happening in the streets and on the television news. On the other hand, there were new productions to rehearse: plays by Milan Uhde, Ivan Klíma, and above all Václav Havel. Theatres competed to be the first to present Havel's plays.* Jan Grossman's wife Marie Malková reflected as she returned to rehearsals in the S. K. Neumann Theatre in Libeň, "Only three weeks have passed, but it seems like a hundred years." No one knew what would come next. As Petr Oslzlý wrote:

> In Czechoslovakia in the last twenty years the theatres had taken over those activities which were absent from ordinary life—free speech, free discussion, political debate. And now the theatres had become again only theatres and no more. The activities that the theatres had taken over returned where they belonged: to parliament, to the press, to television, to political conferences, to the privatisation auctions. It is in these arenas that the great dramas are being played out which will transform our society from totalitarianism to democracy. These have become the *Theatrum mundi*, the setting for the great dramatic contest between totalitarianism and humanity.[336]

Say what you will—there are few more climactic moments in modern history than the inauguration of Václav Havel as president of Czechoslovakia in Prague Castle on 29 December 1989.

Approximately thirty years ago as I write, the theatre took the lead in bringing down a political system based on hypocrisy and lies. But in spite of the euphoria of the time, it could not establish a perfect society. The moment of glory was naturally followed by disappointment. Nevertheless, this "theatre that is always at the beginning" is also theatre that is never at an end; a stage where "all the Adams, Eves, Clowns, Cains, Eurydices, Hamlets, and Ophelias patiently perform their somersaults… beat their drums, and repeat a hundred times the same motion, often merely for one purpose: not to do it at all." The theatre we have been following is a theatre that emphasises, not how the political and social system affects people, but "how the way [they]

* In the end he himself decided, arranging simultaneous productions by four theatres: *The Garden Party* by Theatre Goose on a String; *Redevelopment* at the Realist Theatre; the Vaněk plays by the underground Brno group Theatre at the Table; and *Largo desolato* at the Theatre on the Balustrade, directed by Jan Grossman.

behave creates the system." It is a theatre where we face again the question of faith in an age of conformity and calculation expressed through Abraham, "a man at odds with his time who consciously accepts responsibility." It is in the theatre that we experience the paradox of the "here and now," of the event that can take place only once in history, and yet that one time is in front of the present audience. It is the "Here and now!" of Regnier de Montigny, as he summons the jury.

"Freedom is not something we're waiting for, some gift, but our task. We create our freedom by thinking and working freely, by wresting it out through our own specific actions."

DRAMATIS PERSONAE

(Certain characters, not always major figures in themselves, recur in different sections of the book and form threads connecting the changing periods. This cast list may help in following these connections. The order of names follows the English alphabet. With some borderline exceptions, only Czechs and Slovaks are listed.)

Mikoláš Aleš (1852–1913) *prolific artist and illustrator, at first in the Romantic style, later Secession; his scenes from Bohemian history and legends (early 1880s) still decorate the National Theatre.*

Ludvík Aškenazy (1921–1986) *a writer with strong Communist beliefs in the 1950s, he wrote text-appeals in the 1960s. Remained abroad after the 1968 invasion, and wrote in German. A banned writer under Normalisation.*

Lída Baarová (1914–2000) *a film actress who was fatefully talent-spotted by a German film studio, leading to a relationship with Goebbels. After WWII, spent eighteen months in custody accused of collaboration. A witness in the Vlasta Burian case.*

Zdenka Baldová (1885–1958) *an actress at the Vinohrady and National Theatres and in film; wife of the director K. H. Hilar. Supportive of Otomar Krejča in his struggle with the old guard.*

Pavel Barša (*1960) *studied in Brno under Normalisation but decided not to be a part of Communist academia. Became a stoker, devoting his time to underground music and seminars. After 1989, a leading political scientist.*

Jan Bartoš (1893–1946) *theatre critic, dramatist, and historian; head of the theatre department of the National Museum.*

Karel Bartošek (1930–2004) *historian, and a fervent Communist when young. After 1968, expelled from the Party and imprisoned for six months. Signed Charter 77 but after persecution emigrated to France (1982).*

Jiří Bartoška (*1947) *trained as an actor at JAMU in Brno and began his career with Theatre on a String. Grossman's Don Juan at the Balustrade Theatre. In 1989, led the petition to get Havel out of prison and was a founder member of Civic Forum.*

Eduard Bass (1887–1946) *an erudite and elegant personality, and a great performer of Czech cabaret, about which he wrote a guide; the author of several popular novels (e.g.,* Klapzuba's Eleven*); in the 1930s, editor of the thinking person's daily,* Lidové noviny.

Edvard Beneš (1884–1948) *Masaryk's foreign minister, subsequently president, 1935–1938; 1945–1948.*

Božena Benešová (1873–1936) *author of novels, poetry, short stories, and plays dealing with inner psychological conflicts. Her last novel* Don Pablo, Don Pedro, and Věra Lukášová *was dramatised by E. F. Burian, who later turned it into a film.*

Petr Bezruč (1867–1958) *a Silesian poet passionate about the social conditions of the exploited workers. Hostile to all authority, whether Austrian or Czech.*

Konstantin Biebl (1898–1951) *poet and friend of Wolker. An active member of the Surrealist Group in the 1930s but enthusiastic about Communism in the 1940s. It is unclear why he committed suicide.*

Iva Bittová (*1958) *raised in a musical family and studied at JAMU in Brno. Spent several years as an actress, mainly with Theatre on a String, where she left her unique mark on the theatre's music. From the late 1980s, an independent artist (composer/singer/violinist).*

Vratislav Blažek (1925–1973) *playwright and scriptwriter, critical of the Communist regime; his work was banned and he emigrated after the invasion of 1968.*

Petr Bogatyrev (1893–1971) *an internationally important Russian semiotician who lived in Czechoslovakia from 1921–1939 and was a leading member of the Prague Linguistic Circle. His work on folklore was a major influence on Czech avant-garde theatre in the 1940s, 1960s, and 1980s.*

František Borový (1874–1936) *the owner of a publishing house in Národní třída (*U Topičů*) that concentrated on original Czech writing; in 1928 it was bought by Jaroslav Stránský (publisher of* Lidové noviny*), who kept the original name of the publishing house, and Borový as director.*

Pavel Bošek (1932–1980) *writer, actor, and theatre director; a close colleague of Ivan Vyskočil and exponent of the text-appeal.*

Vladimír Boudník (1924–1968) *an artist traumatised by forced labour in Germany. His plates for printmaking "suffered" through burial for long periods. He chose a working-class existence and was the inspiration for Hrabal's novel,* The Gentle Barbarian *(dramatised for the Drama Club).*

Vlastimil Brodský (1920–2002) *studied acting with E. F. Burian from 1939 until the school was closed by the Nazis. During WWII, worked at the Windmill, afterwards at the Theatre of Satire, with Burian again, then with Frejka, remaining at the Vinohrady Theatre.*

Ludmila Brožová-Polednová (1921–2015) *a would-be actress who failed the entrance exams and so trained for one year at the Workers' Law School. As state procurator at Milada Horáková's show trial in 1950 she was (after 1989) considered to be complicit in Horáková's illegal death sentence. In 2008 Brožová-Polednová was sentenced to six years in prison, part of which she served.*

Johann Joseph von Brunian (1733–1781) *director of the leading German-language theatre company in Prague, for some years based in the Kotzen Theatre below Wenceslas Square; one of the first to experiment with Czech-language performances.*

Aleš Březina (*1965) *composer, mainly for the cinema and stage, including the opera* Tomorrow There Will Be... *(2008) about Milada Horáková, in which Soňa Červená played a major role.*

Emil František Burian (1904–1959) *musician, rebel, and theatre director of international stature, creator of "synthetic" theatre, the Theatregraph technique, and other innovations in his theatre D34; a convinced Communist, he struggled to conform to the dictates of Socialist Realism, which destroyed him.*

Jan Burian (*1952) *son of E. F. Burian and his third wife Zuzana Kočová, a popular satirical songwriter and performer; heavily restricted under Communism.*

Vlasta Burian (1891–1962) *a hugely popular comic performer in the First Republic, in both theatre and film; after the war accused and condemned by the Communists of collaboration with the Nazis; his name was not cleared until the 1990s (through the work of Vladimír Just).*

Zuzana Burianová (*1947) *actress and singer, joined Semafor in 1966 and remained there until the 1990s.*

Vojtěch Cach (1914–1980) *Vienna-born Socialist Realist playwright who suffered unemployment in the 1930s and joined the Communist partisans in WWII. From 1956–1960, editor-in-chief of* Divadlo.

Cajlajs (real name Jiří Süssland, 1920–1945) *Jewish actor and member of E. F. Burian's company, eventually transported to Terezín. A kind and gentle man and superb actor. Survived internment but died of exhaustion in first days of freedom.*

Josef Čapek (1887–1945) *writer, caricaturist, and avant-garde artist; arrested by the Nazis for his political activities and died of typhoid fever in Bergen-Belsen. Invented the word "robot" for his brother Karel's play* R.U.R.*; wrote* The Insect Play *and other plays with Karel.*

Karel Čapek (1890–1938) *prolific and popular writer, internationally known for* The Insect Play, The Makropolous Case, R.U.R., *etc. Brother of Josef and friend of President Masaryk. Fiercely anti-Hitler, his bad health was exacerbated by Munich and attacks on him in the press. Died just before the German occupation.*

František Čech (1928–1995) *imprisoned in April 1950 when the Communists closed the seminary where he was studying to be a priest. Forced to spend the 1950s in the "Black Brigade." On his release studied theatre and directed at the Balustrade Theatre, but was forced out of Prague.*

Petr Čepek (1940–1994) *studied at DAMU under Miloš Nedbal, then worked in Ostrava and the Drama Club. Active in the Velvet Revolution (secured the Drama Club as the venue for the founding meeting of Civic Forum on 19 November 1989).*

Vladimír Čermák (1929–2004) *philosopher and political scientist; in 1990 cofounded the department of political science in the Masaryk University in Brno. Contributor to the work of the Theatre on a String (e.g.,* Rozrazil*) in the 1980s.*

Emma Černá (1937–2018) *trained as an actress at DAMU, worked at the Theatre on the Balustrade, in Most, and at the S. K. Neumann Theatre in Prague.*

František Černý (1926–2010) *theatre historian. Founder of the Cabinet for the Study of Czech Theatre (1956). Taught at Charles University as a non-Party member throughout Normalisation but the professorship he was to have been awarded in 1968 was witheld until 1989.*

Jindřich Černý (*1930) *theatre historian convicted of anti-state activity as a student, only at intervals able to publish and work in his field; from 1977 allowed to work in National Theatre archive. Director of the National Theatre from 1990–1993.*

Ondřej Černý (*1962) *son of Jindřich Černý, studied librarianship but also obtained a theatre qualification from Charles University. Worked at the Theatre Institute, where he was director from 1996–2007. Director of the National Theatre from 2007–2012.*

Soňa Červená (*1925) *daughter of Jiří Červený; a singer who worked with Jiří Frejka but emigrated after harassment by the Communists; returned after the Velvet Revolution to star in productions by Robert Wilson (e.g., Čapek's* The Makropulos Case*) and operas about Milada Horáková and Fr. Toufar.*

Jiří Červený (1887–1962) *a law student who with his school friends formed the influential cabaret, the Červená sedma (Seven of Hearts), at the beginning of the twentieth century.*

Jindřich Chalupecký (1910–1990) *a literary and art historian and critic, his 1939 essay "The World in Which We live" (about art in urban life) was the impulse for the foundation of Group 42. During Normalisation he published only in samizdat. A major art award is named after him.*

Vlasta Chramostová (1926–2019) *an actress at the Czechoslovak Army (Vinohrady) Theatre but protested against the director Pavlíček's removal. Joined Krejča's Theatre Beyond the Gate. Banned from public life after signing Charter 77. Created Living Room Theatre, 1976–1980. Member of the National Theatre after 1989.*

Jaroslav Chundela (1939–1995) *first artistic director of the Drama Studio in Ústí nad Labem in 1972, where he developed an outstanding acting company and invited Grossman, Schorm, and Kačer as guest directors. Head of the drama company at the Balustrade Theatre, 1975–1978, when he emigrated.*

Josef Chvalina (1920–1982) *trained at the Conservatoire and performed at a succession of theatres, from 1964–1965 and 1969–1979 at the Balustrade Theatre. Largely cast in roles of the petty bourgeoisie.*

Věra Chytilová (1929–2014) *a New Wave film director, best known for the controversial* Daisies *(1966).*

Jan Císař (*1932) *a theatre critic and historian, editor-in-chief of* Divadelní noviny *from 1963–1970. Author of the key text* Theatres That Found Their Time *(Divadla, která našla svou dobu, 1966).*

Vladimír Clementis (1902–1952) *a Slovak intellectual and politician involved in the Communist coup of 1948; foreign minister after the death of Jan Masaryk. In 1950, accused of treachery and hanged.*

Jiří Daněk (1949–1998) *a theatre critic and dramaturge. Head of the Drama Club in the 1980s, when he helped to stabilise the company after a critical period.*

Jean-Gaspard Deburau (1796–1846) *a Bohemian-born French clown fictionalised by Tyl as Jan Kašpar Dvořák. Pierrot in the Parisian Funambules; immortalised by Jean-Louis Barrault in Marcel Carné's 1945 film* Les Enfants du Paradis. *An inspiration for Fialka and his company at the Balustrade.*

Jiří Dědeček (*1953) *poet and songwriter, from 1973–1985 collaborated with Jan Burian as Burian & Dědeček; they were banned from TV appearances or performing in Prague.*

František Derfler (1942–2019) *trained as an actor at JAMU in Brno, member of Theatre on a String, later State Theatre. Signatory of Charter 77; involved in samizdat and underground seminars, founder of underground* Divadlo u stolu *(Theatre at the Table).*

Jiří Dienstbier (1937–2011) *in his youth a star Communist foreign correspondent, but as a reform Communist fell from grace and became a boiler man and dissident, writing (i.a.) a play on Havel's "Vaněk" character. In 1979, as a member of the Committee for the Defence of the Unjustly Prosecuted, he was sentenced to 3 years imprisonment. After 1989, foreign minister of Czechoslovakia.*

Jaroslav Dietl (1929–1985) *a prolific author, mainly of television serials which underpinned the passive and consumerist values of Normalisation society; the most political is* A District Up North *(1981,* Okres na severu*) which unintentionally exposes the Communist Party's manipulation of the judiciary.*

Nina Divíšková (*1936) *leading actress at the Drama Club (and in films); wife of theatre director Jan Kačer.*

Josef Dobrovský (1753–1829) *a historian and philologist, key figure in the Czech National Awakening. Although his first language was German, he became a scholar of the Czech language.*

Martin Dohnal (*1959) *Brno musician and actor, involved in performance from an early age. In 1984 cofounded the Amateur Circle and was co-creator of* Abrahamus Patriarcha *and other noteworthy productions. Became a key member of HaTheatre when Amateur Circle merged with it in 1990.*

Miroslav Donutil (*1951) *studied acting at JAMU and joined Theatre on a String in 1973. Played leading roles in* Ballad for a Bandit, Tales of the Long Nose, *and other long-running productions. After 1990 became a star of the National Theatre in Prague.*

Jan Drda (1915–1970) *a Communist novelist, journalist, scriptwriter, and playwright (*Games with the Devil*), from 1949–1957 chairman of the Union of Czechoslovak Writers. Led a campaign* *against non-Communist writers which led to long prison sentences for many of them; he opposed the invasion of 1968.*

Alexander Dubček (1921–1992) *Slovak politician who became First Secretary of the Czechoslovak Communist Party in April 1968 and a key figure of the Prague Spring ("Socialism with a human face").*

Antonín Dvořák (1841–1904) *Bohemian musician who became an international composer, worked closely with Jaroslav Kvapil, director of the National Theatre and author of the libretto for* Rusalka. *In the twentieth century his music was vilified politically by Zdeněk Nejedlý.*

Antonín Dvořák (1920–1997) *theatre director and critic, a strong Communist from his youth; in 1939 he was rounded up and sent to Dachau by the Nazis but released after some months. Assistant to Jindřich Honzl, later director in various theatre companies and a writer on the avant-garde theatre. Longtime dean of DAMU.*

Arnošt Dvořák (1881–1933) *a writer and medical doctor who spent WWI on the battlefields.*

Jan Dvořák (*1951) *son of the art historian František Dvořák (1920-2015) and brother of the stage designer Daniel Dvořák (*1954). In 1987 took over the editorship of the periodical* Scéna *and was one of the group fighting to eliminate the barriers between what was banned and what was allowed.*

Viktor Dyk (1877–1931) *poet, playwright, and nationalist politician, worked with Jiří Karásek on the Intimate Free Stage; imprisoned by the Austrians during WWI; politically opposed to President Masaryk.*

Vratislav Effenberger (1923–1986) *a writer, theoretician, and artist; member of the Surrealist Group from 1947, later its leader. Persecuted by the Communists in the 1950s, 1970s, and 1980s, could publish only in samizdat.*

Pavel Eisner (1889–1958) *from a German-speaking Bohemian Jewish family, Eisner was fascinated by the Czech language and wrote,* inter alia, *the enchanting book of essays* Chrám i tvrz *(*Temple and Fortress*).*

Lída Engelová (*1944), *one of the most popular directors in the Czech theatre, although prevented for political reasons from holding a permanent position in Prague. Began her career with Jan Grossman and spent many years in Pilsen and Ostrava - the most difficult region at the time of the Velvet Revolution.*

Karel Jaromír Erben (1811–1870) *an ethnographer and poet, whose* Nosegay *(1853) is a classic work of Czech literature.*

Vlasta Fabianová (1912–1991) *studied and worked as an actress in Prague and Brno, from 1941 at the National Theatre. Excelled especially in aristocratic roles.*

Josef Fajta (*1931) *a dancer with the National Theatre until he joined Fialka's mime company at the Theatre on the Balustrade, making his first appearance in* Pantomime on the Balustrade.

Libor Fára (1925–1988) *Surrealist artist who studied with Emil Filla at the School of Applied Arts in late 1940s. Joined Burian's Art Theatre of the Army but was closer to Grossman than to Burian. Set and costume designer for the Balustrade Theatre in 1960s. Husband of Anna Fárová, close friend of Havel and witness at his wedding.*

Otakar Fencl (1920–2008) *dramaturge, after WWII worked at Barrandov Film Studio and then in the Ministry of Culture. From 1950–1961 dramaturge for Krejča at the National Theatre alongside Karel Kraus.*

Ladislav Fialka (1931–1991) *internationally successful mime artist who established a permanent company at the Theatre on the Balustrade; in the 1960s created productions acclaimed around the world. After 1968 he became caught in the web of Normalisation politics.*

Drahomíra Fialková (1923–2010) *actress and cofounder of Viola. In the 1980s able to work only freelance because of her "unsuitable" friends.*

František Filipovský (1907–1993) *between the wars, a member of E. F. Burian's Voiceband and the Liberated Theatre. Member of the National Theatre 1945–1992; also performed with Semafor.*
Emil Filla (1882–1953) *internationally known avant-garde artist, founder member of the* Eight. *Like Josef Čapek, spent WWII in German concentration camps, but survived.*
Daniela Fischerová (*1948) *writer mainly in the field of children's literature, but in the 1980s author of plays on legendary themes alluding to contemporary life. Frequently banned.*
Theo Herkeľ Florin (1908–1973) *Slovak poet and diplomat. During WWII worked for the exile government in London. Private secretary to Foreign Minister Clementis, imprisoned when Clementis was executed. Partner of the dancer and choreographer Saša Machov.*
Josef Bohuslav Foerster (1859–1951) *Bohemian German composer who adapted to Czech-language culture and society. Based his opera* Eva *on Gabriela Preissová's* The Farmer's Woman.
Miloš Forman (1932–2018) *a major figure of the Czech New Wave in cinema in the 1960s (*Loves of a Blonde*), he became after his emigration one of America's leading directors (*Amadeus*).*
Jiří Fréhar (*1938) *worked in many theatres throughout Bohemia and Moravia. Best known as a director, but also wrote scripts. In 1989 head of the Realist Theatre of Zdeněk Nejedlý.*
Anna Freimanová (*1951) *under Normalisation worked in the library of the National Museum, but devoted her energy to samizdat; secretary for the samizdat journal* About Theatre; *wife of Andrej Krob.*
Jiří Frejka (1904–1952) *brilliant young member of the interwar avant-garde, cofounder of the Liberated Theatre, Theatre Dada, and Modern Studio; directed at the National Theatre during the occupation; after the Communist coup joined the Party, but under pressure committed suicide.*
Aleš Fuchs (*1932) *Communist theatre and film critic.*
Julius Fučík (1903–1943) *a Communist journalist active in the resistance; captured and executed by the Nazis but before his death wrote and smuggled from prison notes that were published as* Report from the Gallows; *throughout Communism held up as a hero and example for young people but has since been discredited.*
Ferenc Futurista (1891–1947) *pseudonym of František Fiala; comic actor, popular during the First Republic; praised by Marinetti during the latter's visit to Prague.*
Vladimír Fux (1928 - 2015) *a Moravian playwright and translator, originally from Ostrava, later house dramatist of the Satirical Theatre in Brno.*
Vlasta Gallerová (*1942) *a dramaturge who, with her husband the director Karel Kříž, transformed the F. X. Šalda Theatre, Liberec, into a dynamic centre; later did the same thing for the Realist Theatre of Zdeněk Nejedlý, Prague, a venue for meetings of the theatre underground network in the 1980s.*
Vladimír Gamza (1902–1929) *a Czech avant-garde theatre director born and educated in St. Petersburg; influenced by Vakhtangov, introduced Constructivism to the Czech theatre. Founded experimental theatre studios first in Brno (Czech Studio), later in Prague; worked with Jiří Mahen and E. A. Longen.*
Jaroslav Gillar (*1942) *from 1964, Grossman's assistant at the Balustrade Theatre; from 1968–1974 head of the drama company, until his emigration.*
Ivan Glanc (1923–1991) *director of the F. X. Šalda Theatre in Liberec from 1958–1971, at the Realist Theatre in Prague from 1971–1987.*
Helena Glancová (*1938) *the niece of Gustav Schorsch, she survived two years in Terezín during the war; actress and director, invited by Otomar Krejča to work at Theatre Beyond the Gate; under Normalisation banned from working in the theatre except for Lyra Pragensis.*
Marie Glázrová (1911–2000) *a popular dramatic actress who joined the National Thatre in 1940.*
Josef Gočár (1880–1945) *a leading architect who built in the Rondocubist and Functionalist styles.*

Arnošt Goldflam (*1946) *Brno actor, playwright, director, and in 1974 cofounder of HaTheatre, where he worked for most of the 1980s; since then with numerous other theatres (and in film).*

Karel Gott (1939–2019) *singer who received state awards from Communist and post-Communist governments. Winner of the thirty-eight Golden Nightingales/Czech Nightingales between 1963 and 2014. In 1977, propagated the Anti-Charter—but also wrote a song believed to be in memory of Jan Palach.*

Klement Gottwald (1896–1953) *the first Communist president, 1948–1953.*

Jan Grossman (1925–1993) *involved in the resistance during the occupation, then started on a literary career but was banned by the Communists; changed to theatre and worked with E. F. Burian; from 1962–1968, artistic director of Balustrade Theatre, where he created an extraordinary series of productions; punished by the Communists under Normalisation; after 1989, returned to lead Balustrade Theatre.*

Otto Gutfreund (1889–1927) *leading Cubist-Expressionist sculptor.*

Zdena Hadrbolcová (*1937) *an actress associated with the S. K. Neumann Theatre and the Theatre on the Fringe. Played Sonya in Jan Grossman's 1982 production of* Uncle Vanya.

Jiří Hájek (1913–1993) *foreign minister in the Prague Spring, one of the first spokesmen for Charter 77.*

Jiří Hájek (1919–1994) *theatre critic who tended to reflect the political opinions of any given time; cf. his attack on the reforms of 1968, which he had originally endorsed, in his book* Mýtus a realita ledna *(The Myth and Reality of January,1968). Father of Petr Hájek.*

Petr Hájek (*1951) *son of theatre critic Jiří Hájek; deputy head of President Klaus's office. In* Smrt v sametu *(Death in Velvet, 2012) he described Václav Havel as the "servant of the Antichrist."*

František Halas (1901–1949) *lyric poet, translator, essayist, and politician. His poetry expressed his feelings of impotence with regard to the events in his country. A fervent Communist postwar parliamentary deputy, he became disillusioned and died of heart failure.*

Jaroslav Hašek (1883–1923) *the author of* The Adventures of the Good Soldier Švejk, *enjoyed bohemian life, Anarchism, and practical jokes; however, after serving in the Czechoslovak Legion he joined the Red Army, not returning to Czechoslovakia until 1920, where he died of obesity.*

Karel Hašler (1879–1941) *a greatly loved patriotic actor, singer, and songwriter in a range of genres. Director of Lucerna and other cabarets. In WWI, imprisoned for defying the Austrians; in WWII, murdered in Mauthausen when left to freeze under an ice-cold shower.*

Ivan Havel (*1938) *mathematician and philosopher. With his brother Václav, he spent his childhood in a wealthy family of developers and property owners which had everything confiscated after the Communist coup. Invented the artificial languages Ptydepe and Chorukor for his brother's play* The Memorandum.

Václav Havel (1936–2011) *had three careers: as playwright, dissident activist, and president of Czechoslovakia 1989–1992; of the Czech Republic 1993–2003. As a playwright, his most important years were 1962–1968 with Jan Grossman at the Theatre on the Balustrade.*

Vácslav Havel (1861–1921) *a builder and entrepreneur, he was responsible for Lucerna Palace and the Barrandov Terraces in Prague. Grandfather of Václav and Ivan.*

Karel Havlíček Borovský (1821–1856) *writer, patriot, and politician; one of the leading members of the National Awakening, he was a member of the 1848 parliament but was exiled by the Austrians and died of TB. Always insisted that only the highest standards were worthy of the nation.*

Ferdinand Havlík (1928–2013) *clarinettist and jazz musician who cofounded Semafor with Suchý and Šlitr. Under Normalisation took over the official leadership when Suchý was demoted.*

Jakub Hejna (*1976) *film editor; grandson of the stage designer Josef Svoboda and author and director of the documentary* Theatre Svoboda.

Miloš Hercík (1929–1991) *a bureaucrat at the Ministry of Culture who in 1962 created—out of the funds for outdated companies touring the countryside—the State Theatre Studio, which sheltered such innovatory small stages as Semafor and the Drama Club. He lost his position in 1973.*

Iva Hercíková (1935–2007) *a novelist and scriptwriter, married to Miloš Hercík, later to Jiří R. Pick. Wrote the first book on the small theatre movement,* Začinalo to Redutou *(It Began at Reduta, 1964). Emigrated in 1986.*

Ljuba Hermanová (1913–1996) *an effervescent chansonnière who sang with the Liberated Theatre. Under Communism she was considered an unsuitable person, rarely appearing onstage. The Theatre on the Balustrade revived her fortunes and she remained a popular performer until her death.*

Antonín Heythum (1901–1954) *an avant-garde stage designer and architect, created sets for the Liberated Theatre; at the start of WWII was in the USA, where he worked with the German director Erwin Piscator. Although he returned to Europe, he never lived in Czechoslovakia again.*

Karel Hugo Hilar (1885–1935) *a writer and theatre director of immense energy and ambition. Head of the drama company at the National Theatre from 1921 until his early death from a stroke. Criticised for taking over others' ideas and changing authors' work. Inventor of "Civilism."*

Jaroslav Hilbert (1871–1930) *a writer and dramatist, whose first play,* Guilt *(1896), had an immediate success at the National Theatre. Wrote more than a dozen more plays and many theatre criticisms.*

Adolf Hoffmeister (1902–1973) *a wealthy and multi-talented member of the left-wing avant-garde, known for his prolific cartoons but also a playwright and set designer; in the USA during the occupation, he lost his privileged position in the Communist hierarchy after 1968.*

Vlastislav Hofman (1884–1964) *an autocratic and influential architect, artist, author, and theatre designer who worked closely with the theatre director K. H. Hilar during the First Republic*

Karel Höger (1909–1977) *from a poor working-class family in Brno, spent a childhood involved with puppetry; quickly became a leading actor with the National Theatre in Prague and played many leading roles on stage and in film. Involved in the underground resistance during the occupation.*

Vladimír Holan (1905–1980) *published his first poetry (often dark and introverted) in the 1920s. Briefly a member of the Communist Party after the Liberation, but later became a recluse. An influence on Václav Havel. Best known for his long poem* A Night with Hamlet.

Václav Holzknecht (1904–1988) *a musician and musicologist, wrote about Jaroslav Ježek.*

Jindřich Honzl (1894–1953) *a science teacher who became the driving force of the left-wing theatrical avant-garde; theatre director and cofounder of Liberated Theatre; founder of Little Theatre for 99 during WWII and afterwards of Studio of the National Theatre, briefly led the drama company there; died bitter and frustrated.*

Daňa Horáková (*1947) *philosopher whose apartment was the venue for underground seminars and the Living Room Theatre. Married to the filmmaker Pavel Juráček (1935-1989); emigrated at the end of the 1970s.*

Jarmila Horáková (1904–1928) *an actress whose vivacity and energy embodied the spirit of the 1920s and whose death from a brain tumour affected many. Jiří Frejka edited and published her diary in 1940.*

Milada Horáková (1901–1950) *outstanding politician and activist, imprisoned and condemned to death by the Nazis but reprieved; after the war she renewed her work but was targeted by the Communists for a show trial and executed for treason on trumped-up charges.*

Miroslav Horníček (1918–2003) *multi-talented writer and performer mainly on the small stages, including the Windmill, Theatre of Satire, and Semafor; in the 1950s partnered Jan Werich in place of Voskovec.*

Zdeněk Hořínek (1931–2014) *theatre historian, critic, and dramaturge. Unable to work in his profession in the 1950s, or as a teacher in the 1970s and the first half of the 1980s. Closely associated with Ypsilon.*

Ondřej Hrab (*1952) *in the 1970s and 1980s, one of the most energetic members of the semi-official Jazz Section; in 1980 organised a performance in Prague by the Living Theatre on a twenty-four-hour transit visa. After 1989 turned the moribund E. F. Burian Theatre into the Archa.*

Bohumil Hrabal (1914–1997) *one of the greatest Czech writers, he recorded the turbulent history through which he lived in remarkable fiction; some works appeared in samizdat and some were seen in stage adaptations while still banned from publication. He fell to his death from a fifth-floor hospital window while feeding the birds.*

Laurette Hrdinová (1907–1958) *a dancer and choreographer who performed internationally before WWII; taught at the Conservatoire, where she was the main influence on the postwar development of Czech dance and encouraged the creation of Ladislav Fialka's mime company.*

Bohumil Hrdlička (1919–2006) *leading opera director, first in Ostrava, later in Prague. His 1957 "Surrealist"* The Magic Flute *for the National Theatre caused a storm that drove him to emigrate to Germany, where, working under the name Bohumil Herlischka, he popularised Janáček's operas.*

František Hromada (*1941) *actor and director, in the 1960s involved with the small theatres in Brno; in 1970, joined the theatre in Cheb, where he mediated Jan Grossman's employment.*

František Hrubín (1910–1971) *a poet who joined Krejča's stable of writers at the National Theatre. Krejča and Kraus worked closely with him on his two plays (in 1958 and 1961) which helped to initiate a new era of theatre. Although a Communist, in 1956 he joined Seifert in condemning abuses in the past.*

Lubomír (Luboš) Hrůza (1933–2008) *theatre designer who studied with František Tröster. Worked with Jan Kačer in Ostrava and moved with him to the Drama Club. After 1968, emigrated to Norway, where he became head of design at the National Theatre in Oslo.*

Jiří Hubač (1929–2011) *originally an electrician, after illness became editor, dramaturge, and eventually scriptwriter mainly of TV serials. Worked with Antonín Moskalyk and also wrote plays for the theatre.*

Václav Hudeček (1929–1991) *theatre director who worked with Radok, then in provincial theatres and from 1960 in Prague. Invited by Grossman to direct at the Balustrade because of his unusual (for the time) engagement with modern Western drama. His later work was more routine.*

Luděk Hulan (1929–1979) *performed jazz in Czechoslovakia from 1948 onwards, when it was ideologically condemned. Involved in the "Jazz and Poetry" movement. In the 1960s the leading jazzman in Czechoslovakia; remained active after 1968 although "politically undesirable."*

Gustáv Husák (1913–1991) *president of Czechoslovakia from 1975–1989: the "President of Forgetting"*

Edmund Husserl (1859–1938) *a German-speaking Moravian philosopher, founded the study of phenomenology.*

Boris Hybner (1941–2016) *one of Fialka's most talented mime pupils, who distanced himself from Fialka's more classical style and created his own school of mime. A founder of the* Pantomima Alfreda Jarryho *and the* Cirkus Alfred, *he provided a chaotic foil to Ctibor Turba's more systematic approach.*

Roman Jakobson (1896–1982) *a Russian linguist who came to Prague in 1920 as a Soviet diplomat. A professor at Masaryk University in Brno, cofounder of the Prague Linguistic Circle.*

Leoš Janáček (1854–1928) *a Brno musician who became one of the twentieth century's leading composers. Innovatory in his use of the natural rhythms of speech and everyday life in his music, especially operas. Specific and down-to-earth in his choice of characters and subject matter.*

Milan Jariš (1913–1986) *editor of* Rudé právo *in 1935. Spent 1942–1945 in Mauthausen for his underground Communist activities. Journalist and Socialist Realist playwright postwar but as a reform Communist not published or performed under Normalisation.*

Jaroslav Jakoubek (1927–1993) *studied chemistry but his real love was music; started writing songs at the beginning of the 1950s. In 1960s, excelled in the chanson, some of his best work was for the Balustrade Theatre, but also wrote for Reduta, Paravan, Rokoko.*

Joe (Josef) Jenčík (1893–1945) *a left-wing avant-garde dancer and choreographer who after WWI worked in cabaret (including the Seven of Hearts and Lucerna). Also choreographed mass displays. Choreographed Liberated Theatre revues in which his six highly professional "Girls" also performed.*

Jaroslav Ježek (1906–1942) *a classical composer with an instinct for jazz and improvisation; although chronically ill and almost blind, he was an immensely popular personality. His compositions were largely responsible for the success of the Liberated Theatre's jazz revues. He died in exile in the USA.*

Alois Jirásek (1851–1930) *author of many patriotic historical novels and stories, and six plays. Three are about the historical figures Hus, Žižka, and Roháč; two belong to the village drama genre (*Vojnarka *and* The Father*) and the sixth (*The Lantern*) is a fairy tale allegory.*

Jiří Jirásek (*1932) *originally an architect, he devoted himself to satirical drawings, caricatures, poems, and stories. His work used in* The Demented Dove *(Balustrade Theatre, 1963). After 1968, forbidden to publish. Worked with Havel on production of samizdat Expedice edition.*

Nina Jirsíková (1910–1978) *a dancer and choreographer who became one of Joe Jenčík's "Girls" at Lucerna and the Liberated Theatre; in 1935 joined E. F. Burian's Déčko. 1941–1945 in Ravensbrück concentration camp, where she improvised theatre performances with other inmates.*

Jiří Just (*1941) *an actor, scriptwriter, journalist, and playwright; one half of the Brothers Just, a cabaret-style act which in the 1980s pushed the boundaries of what could be said (and sung) in public.*

Vladimír Just (*1946) *a theatre historian, critic, performer, and second half of the Brothers Just; rehabilitator of Vlasta Burian. Focused especially on possibilities of small form and studio theatre.*

Vladimír Justl (1928–2010) *a literary and theatre critic and editor who took over Viola in 1965, when its founders were considered to be too unruly; established it on a well-organised basis but criticised for having sacrificed Viola's spontaneity and originality.*

Petr Kabeš (1941–2005) *a poet and editor of* Sešity (Notebooks*) until banned in 1969. Night watchman and signatory of Charter 77.*

Jan Kačer (*1936) *actor and theatre director, husband of the actress Nina Divíšková; cofounder of the Drama Club; during Normalisation banned from major activity in film or theatre.*

Franz Kafka (1883–1924) *this writer's works were banned by the Nazis and for most of the Communist period; nevertheless, with his Jewish-German-Czech cultural background he was inspirational for the Czech theatre of the 1960s and 1980s.*

Jiří Kaftan (1935–2011) *studied modern dance at the Conservatoire with Laurette Hrdinová, cofounder and key performer of Fialka's mime company at the Balustrade Theatre (especially in naïve and innocent roles). Also appeared in films of the 1960s.*

František Kahuda (1911–1987) *a natural scientist and politician. Minister of education from 1954–1963; Member of the Central Committee of the Communist Party from 1964. Considered the most successful and innovative culture minister of the Communist era; largely responsible for Czech success at Expo 58.*

Josef Kainar (1917–1971) *a poet, dramatist, musician, and artist; member of Group 42 and dramaturge of the Theatre of Satire. Played jazz with poetry, wrote the first Czech absurd drama (*The Return of Ubu*).*

Ján L. Kalina (né Schwarz, 1913–1981) *a Slovak writer working in radio, of Jewish origin but survived the war under various aliases. In 1972, sentenced to two years imprisonment; in 1978, emigrated. Rehabilitated 1990. Author of* Svet kabaretu *(*The World of Cabaret; *Bratislava, 1966).*

Jiří Karásek ze Lvovic (1871–1951) *a poet, critic, and collector; cofounder of the "decadent"* Moderní revue *(1894–1925) and of the* Intimní volné jeviště *(1896–1899).*

Jiří Karnet (1920–2011) *a law student who joined E. F. Burian when Nazis closed universities, then worked with other companies until taken for forced labour in Germany. Emigrated after the Communist putsch, cofounded the* Svědectví émigré *journal in Paris; became a cultural journalist in New York.*

Peter Karvaš (1920–1999) *a Slovak theatre historian and playwright whose works were widely performed in the 1960s but proscribed under Normalisation.*

Peter Kien (1919–1944) *a German-speaking Jewish artist and poet, in Terezín from 1941–1944. Wrote plays and libretto for Viktor Ullmann's* Der Kaiser von Atlantis. *Worked with Gideon Klein and Gustav Schorsch. Died in Auschwitz.*

Egon Erwin Kisch (1885–1948) *known as the "raging reporter," a German-speaking journalist, writer, anti-Fascist campaigner and lifelong Communist. Imprisoned by the Nazis in Berlin in the early 1930s, he moved to Paris, Spain, the USA, and Mexico, returning to Czechoslovakia after WWII.*

Jaroslav Kladiva (1919–1987) *a historian, at Charles University head of the department of Communist history, vice rector from 1956–1966 and dean of the Arts Faculty in 1960s; presided over the funeral of Jan Palach in 1969. Subsequently purged; in 1982 his book on E. F. Burian was published through the Jazz Section.*

Ladislav Klepal (1938–2002) *a stagehand and actor at the Balustrade Theatre and Krob's Theatre on the Road.*

Václav Kliment Klicpera (1792–1859) *arguably the first modern Czech playwright, his comedies (*Hadrian of Rheum, The Wondrous Jug*) and historical dramas are still popular in Czech theatres. When a schoolmaster in Hradec Králové, he taught Josef Kajetán Tyl; he later moved to Prague.*

Ivan Klíma (*1931) *internationally famous as a novelist, in the 1960s wrote plays reflecting the conflicts of Communist society. Subsequently banned; his work published in samizdat.*

Ladislav Klíma (1878-1928) *a philosopher who rejected the culture and institutions of his day. His main opus was* Svět jako vědomí a nic *(World as Consciousness and Nothing, 1904); otherwise, little of his work was published. He tried to put his philosophy into practice, living without money, and died of TB. Influenced the alternative culture of Normalisation.*

Miloslav Klíma (*1941) *a dramaturge in Cheb and Hradec Králové at the time when Jan Grossman was working there in exile. In 1990 joined Grossman at the Theatre on the Balustrade; in 1991 dean of DAMU, in 2005 vice rector of AMU.*

Jan Klusák (*1934) *a classical composer whose work was premièred by Libor Pešek at the Balustrade Theatre. Worked with Krejča. Compositions banned under Normalisation because of his work on New Wave films. Allowed to work for Jára da Cimrman until 1975.*

Jan Koblasa (1932–2017) *a multi-talented artist who studied at Academy of Fine Arts and DAMU (under Tröster); resisted Socialist Realism and formed avant-garde group. Worked with Krejca at Theatre Beyond the Gate but after the 1968 invasion emigrated and became professor of sculpture at Kiel University.*

Zuzana Kočová (1922–1988) *an actress, writer, and theatre director; student and third wife of E. F. Burian; mother of Jan Burian; founder of the experimental theatre Maringotka.*

Pavel Kohout (*1928) *a novelist and playwright, initially "shockworker-poet" who glorified Stalin. In the mid-1950s he opposed censorship and in 1968 was among the "reform Communists" expelled from the Party under Normalisation. An initiator of Charter 77, he was forced into exile in Austria.*

Josef Jiří Kolár (1812–1896) *a well-travelled scholar and tutor who took the name "Jiří" (George) in homage to Lord Byron. Introduced to the theatre by his less scholarly rival Tyl. Became an actor (also in German) and married into an acting family. In 1866, he was made director of the Provisional Theatre.*

Jan Kopecký (1919–1992) *a theatre historian, critic, dramaturge, and professor at DAMU and FF UK; in 1968 deputy culture minister. An enthusiastic Communist in the 1950s, but remembered for adaptations of religious folk plays in the 1960s. Expelled from teaching in 1970, he became an employee of the Water Board.*

Matěj Kopecký (1775–1847) *the son of a puppeteer, he continued the tradition, passing it down through his children to the present day. He travelled throughout the Bohemian Lands with his own puppets and plays, and was part of the National Awakening.*

Matěj Kopecký (1923–2001) *great-great-grandson of the above-mentioned Matěj Kopecký, in a continuous line of puppeteers. From 1959, a leading actor with the company* DRAK *in Hradec Králové.*

Miloš Kopecký (1922–1996) *son of a Jewish milliner who died in Auschwitz; suffered from depression. Originally an amateur actor, he joined Windmill Theatre in 1945, eventually becoming hugely popular on stage and screen. In 1987, he made a speech criticising Communist policies.*

Václav Kopecký (1897–1961) *born a thirteenth child, Communist journalist and ideologist involved in the show trials, the cult of Julius Fučík, and the propagation of Socialist Realism. Minister of information from 1948, of culture from 1953. His joviality hid a vicious nature.*

Pavel Kopta (1930–1988) *a translator and songwriter, especially for Ljuba Hermanová.*

Jaroslav Kořán (1940–2017) *studied dramaturgy and scriptwriting, worked at Barrandov Film Studio until 1973, when imprisoned for a year for singing anti-Soviet songs. In 1980s leading translator of American literature. First post-Communist mayor of Prague, subsequently editor of Czech* Playboy *and publisher of art books.*

Václav Kotva (1922–2004) *originally a teacher, he became an actor and founding member of the Drama Club.*

Miroslav Kouřil (1911–1984) *a highly skilled theatre designer, originally assistant to E. F. Burian and inventor (with Burian) of the Theatregraph technique. He used the occupation (and Burian's imprisonment) to consolidate his position and establish his power in the postwar Communist system (and later under Normalisation).*

Josef Kovalčuk (1948–2018) *a historian who in 1974 cofounded HaTheatre in Prostějov and was its dramaturge until 1996. Author of works on modern Czech theatre history; after 1989 was successively parliamentary deputy, dean of the Drama Faculty of JAMU, and head of drama at the National Theatre.*

Lída (Ludmila) Kovářová (also Fialková *and* Bílková) (*1937) *studied modern dance at the Conservatoire with Laurette Hrdinová, member of Ladislav Fialka's original mime group, cofounder and key performer of the pantomime company at the Theatre on the Balustrade.*

Karel Král (*1953) *a student of Milan Lukeš who involved himself in the official and unofficial sides of theatre; one of those responsible for the stage management of the Velvet Revolution. After 1989, founder and editor until today of* Svět a divadlo *(*World and Theatre*).*

Jiří Krampol (*1938) *trained as a metalworker but switched to acting. Worked at the Balustrade from 1962–1971 and 1979–1983, after which he began his most successful career at Semafor.*

Zdenka Kratochvílová (also Fialková) (*1936) *student of Laurette Hrdinová and cofounder of Fialka's mime company at the Balustrade. Excelled in comedy (as Columbine) but also performed* *with pathos. Later formed her own company,* Kapesní divadlo *(Pocket Theatre) with Lída Engelová.*

Karel Kraus (1920–2014) *possibly the most significant postwar theatre scholar and dramaturge. Studies interrupted by wartime closure of universities, afterwards invited by Frejka to Vinohrady Theatre, then by Krejča to the National Theatre and Theatre Beyond the Gate. Constantly harassed by the Communists.*

Otomar Krejča (1921–2009) *an actor and theatre director; from 1958–1972, created some of the most remarkable productions of European theatre at the National Theatre and the Theatre Beyond the Gate. After 1972, created productions around Europe, but banned from working in Czechoslovakia.*

Jaroslav Krejčí (1929–2006) *photographer extraordinaire whose photographs captured the essence of the theatre of the 1960s; he worked especially on productions by Radok and Grossman. His studio was at water level on Kampa Island, and his archive was lost in the floods of 2002.*

Karel Kříž (*1941) *a theatre director; with his wife the dramaturge Vlasta Gallerová transformed the Liberec F. X. Šalda Theatre into an innovative centre; later repeated the feat at the Realist Theatre of Zdeněk Nejedlý, Prague, a venue for meetings of the theatre underground network in the 1980s.*

Andrej Krob (*1938) *a scene-shifter at the Balustrade Theatre who created the amateur Theatre on the Road to perform Václav Havel's work, including the historic single performance of* The Beggar's Opera*; cofounder of the samizdat* Original Videojournal. *Husband of Anna Freimanová.*

Ivo Krobot (*1948) *studied at JAMU in Brno, in the 1980s director at the Drama Club, but worked with other theatres, especially Theatre on a String. With Petr Oslzlý dramatised Hrabal's* I Served the King of England.

Miroslav Krobot (*1951) *studied at JAMU in Brno, director in Cheb and Hradec Králové, in the 1980s at the Realist Theatre and after 1990 at the National Theatre. In 1996, created a new company at the Dejvice Theatre.*

Josef Krofta (1943–2015) *studied puppetry at DAMU in the 1960s, from 1971 director of the DRAK puppet theatre in Hradec Králové.*

Jarmila Kröschlová (1893–1983) *studied modern dance in the Jaques-Dalcroze school; worked with Hilar, Frejka, Honzl, and Burian.*

Mikuláš Krotký (1928–2007) *director of the Theatre of West Bohemia in Cheb (1970–1977) and Tyl Theatre in Pilsen (1977–1984), where he had the courage to offer work to Jan Grossman and other "undesirables."*

Josef Štefan Kubín (1864–1965) *a writer, teacher, ethnographer, and internationally celebrated folklorist. An inspiration for Josef Šmída at the Windmill Theatre during the occupation.*

Otakar Kubín (1881–1969) *member of* Osma; *emigrated to France but retained his Czech contacts.*

Marta Kubišová (*1942) *1960s pop star banned for twenty years because of her resistance to the Soviet invasion; her song "Marta's Prayer" became a key symbol of the period.*

Bohumil Kubišta (1884–1918) *in spite of having a difficult start in life, became a leading member of* Osma. *Died in the Spanish flu epidemic.*

Josef Kulda (†1920) *worker shot dead during antigovernment riots.*

Ludvík Kundera (1920–2010) *Brno-based historian, poet, playwright, and Surrealist; cousin of Milan. Under Normalisation, heavily restricted and rarely able to publish under his own name. Worked closely with Theatre on a String, e.g., Comenius's* The Labyrinth of the World *and the opera* Chameleon.

Milan Kundera (*1929) *best known as a novelist forced into exile in France in the 1970s. His first play (1962) was directed by Krejča at the National Theatre; his second at the Balustrade in 1969;*

his third (based on Diderot) at Ustí nad Labem theatre with authorship ascribed to Evald Schorm (1975).

Miroslav Kůra (*1924) *leading dancer and choreographer, joined National Theatre in 1949; Saša Machov created many roles for him. At a Gala Matinée in 1951 he received more applause than the Soviet guest dancer and was immediately banished to Košice. Returned in 1954 and retired in 1991.*

Jaroslav Kvapil (1868–1950) *historian, critic, dramaturge, playwright, politician; as director from 1900 brought National Theatre into European mainstream; member of Masaryk's "*Maffie*" during WWI; first Czechoslovak minister of education; withstood Communist pressures after 1948.*

Hana Kvapilová (née Kubešová, 1860–1907) *an actress at the National Theatre, married Jaroslav Kvapil in 1894. Played Ophelia to Eduard Vojan's Hamlet, and other leading roles especially in contemporary dramas.*

Marián Labuda (1944–2018) *one of the most popular Slovak actors, working at the National Theatre and the* Divadlo na Korze *(Theatre on the Main Street) in Bratislava.*

Josef Lada (1887–1957) *eternally popular artist and illustrator of traditional Czech themes.*

Pavel Landovský (1936–2014) *actor and playwright;* Rooms by the Hour *(1969) premièred at Drama Club. Acted with Chramostová's Living Room Theatre. Involved in Charter 77; seriously injured by the secret police and expelled, he accepted a contract at the Vienna Burgtheater arranged by Kohout.*

František Langer (1888–1965) *Jewish doctor and playwright, in WWI served with Czechoslovak Legions in Russia. Member of the avant-garde. His best-known play is* On the Periphery *(1925). Escaped to England during WWII; after the Communist takeover his work was not published or performed.*

Karel Laštovka (1938–1986) *although Laštovka performed in small theatres (Balustrade, Paravan) in the early part of his career, as a trained artist he made his name with naked but veiled portraits of celebrity performers. His lifestyle was considered "inappropriate" by the Communist regime.*

Petr Lébl (1965–1999) *in the 1980s, as a dynamic young director in amateur theatre (DOPRAPO and Jak se Vám jelo), he was given encouragement by the American Embassy. In the 1990s, artistic director of the Theatre on the Balustrade, where he created some legendary productions.*

Helena Lehká (*1929) *actress, mainly known for her work at the Balustrade Theatre 1961–1989. Created roles in e.g., Grossman's* The Trial *(1966) and Havel's plays, e.g., the role of Helena in* The Memorandum *(1964).*

Paul Leppin (1878–1945) *a German-speaking writer, editor, and translator, best known for his decadent lifestyle and Expressionist novel* Daniel Jesus.

Jan Libíček (1931–1974) *performed with the Village Theatre and in Zlín before joining the Balustrade Theatre 1963–1968). Jan Grossman's* King Ubu.

Lubomír Lipský (1923–2015) *actor, at first in cabaret, from 1950–1990 with Prague Municipal Theatres. Originally from Pelhřimov, cofounder of Theatre of Satire, which moved to Prague at end of WWII. Brother of Oldřich.*

Oldřich Lipský (1924–1986) *theatre and film director and scriptwriter. Originally from Pelhřimov, cofounder of Theatre of Satire, which moved to Prague at end of WWII. Brother of Lubomír.*

Emil Artur Longen (Pittermann, 1885–1936) *a brilliant talent of the early twentieth century, crippled by alcoholism. As an artist a founder member of the* Eight. *A member of the left-wing avant-garde, he founded the Revolutionary Stage at prices the poor could afford, but it accumulated debts. Influenced E. F. Burian.*

Polyxena (Xena) Longenová (1891–1928) *actress and first wife of E. A. Longen, travelling with him around Europe. After she killed herself, he wrote the novel* Actress *based on her life.*

Radovan Lukavský (1919–2008) *a popular and highly respected actor in theatre and film, although as a non-Communist kept subordinate. With Frejka at the Vinohrady Theatre, then spent fifty years at the National Theatre. Famous for his* Hamlet *in 1959, directed by Pleskot. From 1947, teacher of acting, mainly at DAMU.*

Ivan Lukeš (1927–2010) *an actor who became a founding member of Ladislav Fialka's mime company at the Theatre on the Balustrade. He excelled in roles of cruel and cold characters.*

Milan Lukeš (1933–2007) *a historian, critic, translator, and professor; a specialist on English-language drama. Editor-in-chief of* Divadlo *1964–1970. In the 1970s almost expelled from Charles University. Head of National Theatre Drama Company 1985–89, minister of culture from 1989.*

Miroslav Macháček (1922–1991) *trained as an actor under Nedbal; in 1951 accused of espionage. Began to direct in 1952; joined the National Theatre in 1959. His opposition to Normalisation put him into a psychiatric hospital in 1975. One of his most famous productions was* Our Proud Peasants *(1979).*

Sergej Machonin (1918–1995) *born in Moscow, he came to Prague as a child. Multilingual. Spent WWII in Sachsenhausen; afterwards studied at Charles University and became theatre critic and editor of* Literarní noviny. *After 1968 forbidden to publish; situation worsened after he signed Charter 77.*

Lenka Machoninová (*1951) *daughter of Sergej Machonin, worked with the Theatre of South Bohemia, Theatre on the Fringe, and* Laterna magika, *and on the 1983–1984* Cesty *project.*

Saša Machov (né František Alexander Maťha, 1903–1951) *dancer and choreographer, worked with E. F. Burian and the Liberated Theatre. During WWII directed at Sadler's Wells in London. On his return became head of the ballet company at National Theatre; killed himself after political and personal persecution.*

Harry Macourek (1923–1992) *a pianist, singer, and composer. During WWII he operated an illegal cabaret in Ostrava; in 1945 he joined the Theatre of Satire. Later he worked mainly in film.*

Miloš Macourek (1926–2002) *best known as a writer of children's books (*Mach and Šebestová*). First worked at the Balustrade Theatre in 1959; in 1962 worked with Havel on a play for Hermanová; in 1964 helped Grossman adapt* Ubu Roi; *in 1967 wrote* Playing at Susie *for the Balustrade.*

Jiří Mahen (1882–1939) *novelist, playwright, and journalist based in Brno; of an aristocratic family, he was an Anarchist in his youth. He killed himself when Hitler invaded. Post-WWII the Deutsches Stadttheather was renamed after him. The title of his book* Goose on a String *was used for the Brno theatre founded in the 1960s.*

Gustav Mahler (1860–1911) *born and raised in Kaliště (Kalischt) in the Bohemian-Moravian Highlands. Briefly attended school in Prague but studied in Vienna. In 1885, assistant conductor at the Königlich Deutsches Landestheater (Royal Estates Theatre) and in 1908 returned to Prague for the première of his* Seventh Symphony.

Zdeněk Mahler (1923–2018) *in the 1950s taught Marxism-Leninism and worked as an editor and journalist in Czechoslovak Radio. Involved in Expo 58 and the* Laterna magika. *In the 1960s, a freelance writer, one of Krejča's stable. Expelled from Communist Party after 1968.*

Marie Málková (*1941) *actress and the wife of Jan Grossman, created many roles at the Balustrade Theatre in the 1960s, including Mère Ubu in* Ubu Roi, *Lenka in* The Trial, *and Marie in Havel's* The Memorandum. *Subsequently (until 1983) was able to find work only on a freelance basis.*

Václav Mareš (1940–2009) *an ambitious and intelligent actor chosen by Grossman for the Balustrade company in the 1960s. Later joined the Communist Party to become director of the S. K. Neumann Theatre in Libeň, and in the 1980s made it possible for Grossman to return to Prague.*

Jiří Martínek *cofounder of Viola; later emigrated to Canada, where he founded Viola II.*

Bohuslav Martinů (1890–1959) *composer whose work included operas and ballets. Lived abroad from 1930s; in the 1950s, he wrote a series of cantatas including* The Opening of the Wells *(1955), which Alfréd Radok prepared for the* Laterna magika *in 1960 but which was banned by the authorities.*

Antonín Máša (1935–2001) *dramatist, scriptwriter, and film director who worked closely with Evald Schorm, and particularly at the* Laterna magika *in the 1980s.*

Charlotte Garrigue Masaryk (1850–1923) *an American of Hugenot origin who met Tomáš Masaryk in Germany, and married him in 1878 in the USA. The war years broke her health.*

Jan Masaryk (1886–1948) *son of Tomáš and Charlotte, ambassador to the UK (1925-138), foreign minister of Czechoslovakia from 1940 until his defenestration.*

Tomáš Garrigue Masaryk (1850–1937) *president from 1918–1935, the "Philosopher President"*

Waldemar Matuška (1932–2009) *the son of an operetta singer, began to make recordings after joining Semafor, then Rokoko. His 1968 song "My Small Country" became iconic (but was banned). Emigrated in 1986, but at last was buried under a guitar-shaped gravestone on Vyšehrad.*

Milča Mayerová (1901–1977) *studied modern dance (Laban) abroad and returned to become a dancer, choreographer, and member of Devětsil. The model for the alphabet in Nezval's* Abeceda *(1926).*

Dana Medřická (1920–1983) *a talented and greatly loved actress, married to the actor Václav Vydra, from 1959 engaged by the National Theatre.*

Jiří Menzel (*1938) *best known as a New Wave film director (*Closely Watched Trains*) and actor, Menzel is also closely associated with the Drama Club.*

Zdeněk Míka (1919–2000) *a student of E. F. Burian, postwar he became an ambitious and ruthless left-wing director. Falling out of favour in the 1960s, he recovered under Normalisation and became director of the Vinohrady Theatre (which at that time controlled the Drama Club).*

Ladislav Mňačko (1919–1994) *Slovak writer and journalist, originally a Communist but began to be critical in the late 1960s and emigrated in 1968.*

Antonín Moskalyk (1930–2006) *a pupil of Alfréd Radok, directed in the small theatres in the 1960s but is best known for his TV films.*

Jindřich Mošna (1837–1911) *a member of the Provisional and National Theatres who also excelled in farce and comedy in the arenas. Famous for creating characters totally dissimilar in appearance without the use of external aids, and for acrobatic feats which stunned his audience.*

Vladimír Mráček (1945–1990) *theatre historian who wrote his diploma work on the works of Václav Havel on the eve of the Russian invasion. Became a dramaturge in regional theatres and radio and died soon after the Velvet Revolution.*

Alois Mrštík (1861–1925) *a writer from Moravia who with his younger brother Vilém wrote the drama* Maryša, *a harsh critique of contemporary village society, still popular in the theatre today.*

Vilém Mrštík (1863–1912) *the younger brother of Alois, with whom he wrote* Maryša. *He also wrote the autobiographical novel* Pohádka máje *(May Fairy Tale, filmed 1926).*

Jan Mukařovský (1891–1975) *a member of the interwar avant-garde and cofounder of the Prague Linguistic Circle, one of the earliest and most important movements of Structuralism. As a postwar Communist, he renounced his errors and propagated Marxism-Leninism.*

Miroslav Müller (1926–1997) *head of the cultural dept. of the Central Committee of the Czechoslovak Communist Party 1972–1989 (i.e., the Normalisation period). Nicknamed Müller Thurgau, he was ambitious as a writer, publishing under pseudonyms. Capriciously controlled the lives and careers of others.*

Luděk Munzar (1939–2019) *actor with the National Theatre from 1957. Played Mercutio in Krejča's* Romeo and Juliet, *Jiří in* The Owners of the Keys *and Jindřich in* The End of Shrovetide.

Lída Myšáková (1915–2007) *studied modern dance in Paris; on return worked with Milča Mayerová's company and independently. In 1945, joined Jindřich Honzl's Studio of the National Theatre, and also worked with him and Radok at the National Theatre itself.*

Václav Neckář (*1943) *pop singer and actor in the small theatres of the 1960s, played the leading role of in Menzel's Oscar-winning film version of Hrabal's* Closely Watched Trains. *In 1968, a member of the Golden Kids with Kubišová and Vondráčková.*

Miloš Nedbal (1906–1982) *legendary actor who was a member of the Liberated Theatre and later of the National Theatre. His stage presence was used by Jan Grossman and Otomar Krejča. From 1942, a teacher of acting mainly at DAMU; students appreciated his discipline.*

Zdeněk Nejedlý (1878–1962) *authoritarian musicologist who was a major influence on cultural life from the 1920s to 1950s. Believed in the social necessity of art. Condemned Dvořák (especially* Rusalka*) and Janáček while lauding Smetana. After 1945, held ministerial posts and dictated cultural policy.*

Bohumil Nekolný (*1944) *theatre historian and dramaturge; one of the forces for change in the theatre in the late 1980s.*

Božena Němcová (1820–1862) *author of the classic novel* Grandmother *(1855), dramatised many times. Possibly the illegitimate daughter of aristocrats, she lived the life of an emancipated woman, marked by poverty and illness, but wrote about an idealised Bohemia which endeared her to her readers.*

Jan Němec (1936–2016) *film director of the mid-1960s New Wave (*The Party and the Guests*). Married first to screenwriter and costume designer Esther Krumbachová, subsequently to Kubišová. After the Soviet invasion emigrated to the USA.*

Jan Neruda (1834–1891) *a native of Prague's Lesser Quarter who became a poet, journalist, theatre critic, and belletrist. Valued in the twentieth century for the clarity of his ideals and his literary expression.*

Jiří Nesvadba (1921–2004) *theatre director and designer who belonged to Honzl's Studio from 1945–1948. Later worked in the provinces and for television. His brother Miloš was also an actor in the studio.*

Angelo Neumann (1838–1910) *singer, theatre director, and impresario, moving in the German-speaking world; successfully presented Wagner's* Ring *in Leipzig. In 1885, appointed director of the Estates Theatre in Prague; instrumental in building the New German Theatre (now the State Opera), of which he became director in 1888.*

Stanislav Kostka Neumann (1875–1947) *an avant-garde anarchist critic, poet, and journalist, founder member of the Czechoslovak Communist Party. The* Divadlo pod Palmovkou *in Prague's working-class Libeň was called after him during the years under Communism.*

Stanislav Neumann (1902–1975) *actor son of S. K. Neumann; in the 1920s worked at the Liberated Theatre with Frejka; in 1925 Hilar asked him to join the National Theatre, where he remained until his death. His grandson Julius (Julek, 1953–2019) was a member of Studio Ypsilon from 1973–1985.*

Vítězslav Nezval (1900–1958) *avant-garde poet and a founder member of Devětsil; Poetist and (in the early days) Surrealist. Author of plays and scenarios. A Communist who in the 1950s glorified Stalin and Gottwald (but was nevertheless regarded affectionately).*

Franz Anton Josef Graf von Nostitz-Rieneck (1725–1794) *patriotic German-speaking Bohemian nobleman who in 1781 built the theatre now known as the Estates, where in 1784 Mozart's* Don Giovanni *was premièred.*

Antonín Novotný (1904–1975) *president from 1957–1968; unseated during the Prague Spring.*

Oldřich Nový (1899-1983) *possibly the most popular actor of the early twentieth century; founded his own theatre in 1935 for musical comedy and similar genres. During the occupation refused to divorce his Jewish wife and was imprisoned. Lost his theatre again under the Communists.*

Vladimír Nývlt (1927–1995) *after studying applied art, worked for E. F. Burian and became his head of design. Also cooperated with Grossman. First worked at the National Theatre in the 1960s, joined the company in 1983.*

Milan Obst (1926–1980) *an academic intensely interested in theatre practice, wrote about the interwar avant-garde even during the Stalinist years.*

Ivan Olbracht (1882–1952) *writer and translator of German texts, joined Communist Party in 1921 and wrote for* Rude právo *but protested against 1929 bolshevisation of the Party. Author of* Nikola Šuhaj *(1933), dramatised by Theatre on a String as* Ballad for a Bandit.

Eva Olmerová (1934–1993) *a legendary jazz and country singer who was furnished with a criminal record as the niece of an émigré who had served in the Royal Air Force. It limited her performing career, but in the mid-1960s she could sing with Semafor and the Balustrade.*

Jiří Ornest (1946–2017) *son of Ota Ornest, actor with E. F. Burian Theatre from 1968 until its closure in 1990.*

Ota Ornest (1913–2002) *eldest of three Jewish Ohrenstein brothers; escaped to England in 1939. On his return, he continued as a theatre director, introducing Western authors to the Czech public. Imprisoned in 1977 for the import of "forbidden literature", he was broken by the secret police and made a television "confession."*

Zdeněk Ornest (1929–1990) *the youngest of the Ohrenstein brothers; arrested by the Nazis, he nevertheless survived the death camps and after WWII became an actor, including working with Jan Grossman in 1980s. He was known for his voice work, particularly recitals of his brother's poetry.*

Jiří Orten (1919–1941) *the middle Ohrenstein brother, a poet. Studied at the Conservatoire but as a Jew was forced to leave; joined in student productions, especially with Gustav Schorsch. Published under pseudonyms. Refused to emigrate and leave his mother alone; killed in the blackout by a German ambulance.*

Petr Oslzlý (*1945) *apprenticed as a steelworker for political reasons; during Prague Spring studied dramaturgy and in 1972 joined Theatre on a String, becoming its de facto head. Under Normalisation a leader of the theatre resistance and of an underground seminar. In 1989 a founder of Civic Forum.*

Jiří Ostermann (1935–1990) *involved from early age in recitation and cabaret; created the Poetic Cabaret and in 1963 was the main founder of the Viola café theatre, but was forced out in 1965. Emigrated to Toronto in 1968 and earned his living as a waiter.*

Jan Palach (1948–1969) *a student who set fire to himself in Wenceslas Square to protest against the Czechs' and Slovaks' increasing apathy in the face of the Soviet invasion. An iconic national figure.*

František Palacký (1798–1876) *author of* The History of the Czech Nation in Bohemia and Moravia, *the most influential work of the National Awakening. After being involved in the revolutionary politics of 1848, he headed the Committee to Build a Czech National Theatre for quarter of a century.*

Ivan Palec (1933–2010) *worked with Grossman at the Balustrade, playing Josef K in* The Trial. *Studying in France at the time of the August 1968 invasion, he decided to stay. In the 1980s translated Havel's* The Beggar's Opera *into French and presented it at the Avignon Festival. After 1989, performed with the Forman Brothers.*

Ivan Passer (*1933) *film director of the mid-1960s New Wave (e.g.,* Intimate Lighting*); emigrated to the USA after the Soviet invasion.*

Jan Patočka (1907–1977) *philosopher of phenomenology who studied under Martin Heidegger and Edmund Husserl. Banned from teaching except briefly in late 1940s and late 1960s. Held underground seminars and became one of three spokesmen for Charter 77. Died during police interrogation. Major influence on Havel.*

Jiří Pauer (1919–2007) *prolific composer; from 1979–1989 overall director of the National Theatre. Consistently loyal to the Communist regime, he is notorious for having locked the performers out of the National Theatre during the Velvet Revolution.*

František Pavlíček (1923–2004) *originally a strong Communist, in 1965 director of Vinohrady Theatre, where he directed some major productions of the 1960s. One of Krejča's writers. After 1968 forced to work in menial occupations. Signatory of Charter 77, tried for subversion in 1978.*

Josef Pehr (1918–1986) *an actor; when the Nazis closed the theatres, started a puppet company with his wife Luba Skořepová and with Miloš Nesvadba. After the war joined Honzl's Studio and then the National Theatre but continued with puppetry.*

Jaroslav Pernica *hardline Communist, represented the cultural department of the Central Committee of the CP in the late 1980s.*

Libor Pešek (*1933) *known originally as a jazz trombonist and founder of the Prague Chamber Harmony, which performed at the Balustrade Theatre; was married to mime performer Jana Pešková. Music director of the Royal Liverpool Philharmonic Orchestra from 1987–1998; in 1996 awarded the KBE by Queen Elizabeth II.*

Jana Pešková (*1937) *a dancer in the Pilsen Tyl Theatre ballet company until joining Fialka's mime group at the Balustrade Theatre in 1959. Performed in the major productions of the 1960s. Married Libor Pešek.*

Helena Philippová (1919–1986) *writer and radio producer; cofounded both the Balustrade Theatre and the Theatre of Jára Cimrman, but in each case left because of irreconcilable differences with the other founders.*

Jiří R. Pick (1925–1983) *spent WWII in Terezín because of his Jewish origin; afterwards joined Honzl's Studio. As a writer involved in cabaret and "small form" theatre. Founded Paravan, first within Reduta and then the State Theatre Studio. After 1969 banned from publishing or performing.*

Eva Pilarová (*1939) *a popular singer, especially with the early days of Semafor.*

Antonín Matěj Píša (1902–1966) *intellectual, and early member of Devětsil, which he left in disagreement with Poetism; like his friend Wolker, he tended towards proletarian poetry. Interested in theatre and was dramaturge at National Theatre 1945–1946.*

Petr Pithart (*1941) *a lawyer and reform Communist who became an underground historian and, after 1989, Czech prime minister.*

J. A. Pitínský (*1955, Zdeněk Petrželka) *a Brno librarian who became a writer and theatre director after having been involved with amateur theatre and Theatre on a String.*

Jaromír Pleskot (1922–2009) *an actor with the wartime Windmill Theatre, who joined Frejka at the Vinohrady Theatre as a director; invited by Krejča to direct at the National Theatre from 1957.*

Sofie Podlipská (1833–1937) *sister of Karolína Světla and mother-in-law of Jaroslav Vrchlický. Author of journalism, short stories, and novels.*

Jaroslav Pokorný (1920–1983) *member of Déčko when it was closed by the Gestapo; unable to study until after WWII. Energetic and ambitious Communist, talented writer and translator, but less successful as dramaturge at National Theatre (1948–1953), where he was associated with Honzl and Dvořák.*

Boleslav Polívka (*1949) *internationally known as a mime artist and clown; trained at JAMU in Brno and was one of the leaders of the Brno Theatre on a String until the early 1990s. More recently popular as a film actor.*

Zdeněk Pospíšil (1944–1993) *cofounder of the Brno Theatre Goose on a String and director of some of its most important productions (*Ballad for a Bandit*). Emigrated to Switzerland in 1980; returned after the Velvet Revolution, but killed himself.*

Jan Potměšil (*1966) *studied at DAMU in the 1980s, creating role of Robert in Josef Topol's* The Voices of Birds. *Critically injured in car accident while active in the Velvet Revolution; became popular and successful actor although wheelchair-bound.*

Zdeněk Potužil (*1947) *theatre director who in 1969 founded the experimental group Theatre on the Fringe; using actors employed elsewhere, he created original and high-quality performances mainly in the small space of Rubin.*

Gabriela Preissová (1862–1946) *writer of the late period of the National Awakening; her two plays set on the borders of Moravia and Slovakia at the turn of the 1880s and 1890s,* The Farmer's Woman *and* Her Stepdaughter *(Janáček's* Jenůfa*), about the changing society, caused a critical uproar in Prague.*

Zbyněk Přecechtěl (1916–1996) *musician colleague of E. F. Burian who was arrested with him by the Gestapo but released; after Burian's return continued to work with him, although his compositions were mainly politically focused.*

Jan Přeučil (*1937) *actor son of František Přeučil, sentenced in the 1950s to life imprisonment. Jan Přeučil's roles at the Balustrade Theatre included Josef K in Grossman's production of Kafka's* The Trial; *he led the Balustrade drama company from 1982–1987.*

Antonín Přidal (1935–2017) *Brno writer and translator who worked closely with Theatre on a String.*

Arnošt Procházka (1869–1925) *poet, critic, translator, and collector, cofounder of the "Decadent"* Moderní revue *(1894–1925) and of the* Intimní volné jeviště *(1896–1899). Best-known work* Bawdyhouse of the Soul.

Zdeněk Procházka (1924–1967) *actor with the Balustrade Theatre; his sudden death resulted in Miloš Nedbal playing the part of the Lawyer in* The Trial.

Ivo Váňa Psota (1908–1952) *appointed head of the National Theatre ballet company in Brno at the age of twenty, but left to join the Ballets Russes. Returned, but in 1938 left again for New York, where he became head of the Metropolitan Opera ballet company. Died in Brno following fierce political criticism.*

Vladimír Pucholt (*1942) *starred in Miloš Forman's films while still studying at DAMU; also acted at the Drama Club; in 1967 he emigrated to Britain, where, with the help of John le Carré, he studied medicine and became a pediatrician in Canada.*

Radko Pytlík (1928–2019) *literary historian who studied under Jan Patočka. Expert on Jaroslav Hašek.*

Roman Ráček (*1965) *in the late 1980s a student of the Purkyně University in Brno; led an unofficial drama group called VáHa (Czech for Scales, but a kryptogram of "Václav Havel") that staged Havel's* The Unveiling. *On 17 November 1989 brought the news of the police intervention from Národní třída to the Junior klub Na Chmelnici.*

Alfréd Radok (1914–1976) *theatre director whose work was limited by the Communists, but had a major influence on Grossman, Havel, and others. A student of E. F. Burian, he was sacked from the National Theatre in the 1950s as a Formalist, but went on to create the* Laterna magika. *In 1968 he chose exile in Sweden but was still persecuted by the Communists and died in Vienna of a heart attack.*

David Radok (*1954) *son of Alfréd who grew up in Sweden and continued in his father's profession; created some remarkable productions in Prague in the post-1989 period.*

Emil Radok (1918–1994) *brother of Alfréd and close collaborator with him; cofounder of* Laterna magika. *From 1968 in exile in Canada.*

Marie Radoková-Tesařová (1922–2003) *actress, theatre director, and playwright; in 1945 married Alfréd Radok and went with him into exile in 1968.*

Ivan Rajmont (1945–2015) *director of the Drama Studio in Ústí for a decade under Normalisation, where he helped directors such as Grossman and Schorm. Came to Prague in mid-1980s and directed at Balustrade and National Theatres. Was married to E. F. Burian's daughter Kateřina.*

Miloš Rejnuš (1932–1964) *a Brno mediaevalist who also wrote theatre criticism and plays for radio and the theatre that were widely performed and translated. He died in a car crash, and after 1969 his work was banned.*

Petr Rezek (*1948) *graduated in philosophy from Charles University and worked as a clinical psychologist; in the 1980s worked as a boiler man and organised underground seminars. After 1989, university professor and publisher. Winner of the Tom Stoppard Prize in 2010.*

Tomáš Ruller (*1957) *artist who became involved in body art and action art in the 1970s. Took part in art events in neighbouring countries by crossing borders on foot without documents. In the 1980s, became involved in social movements such as Open Dialogue.*

Přemysl Rut (*1954) *one of the multi-talented artists who moved fluidly between worlds under Normalisation– director, performer, composer, writer, editor, teacher–working in the "official" theatre and with the dissidents.*

Karel Sabina (1813–1877) *ardent Czech nationalist who manned the barricades in 1848; sentenced to death in 1851 but amnestied in 1857. His writings included the libretto for Smetana's* The Bartered Bride. *From 1859, an informer for the Austrian state, a subject dramatised by the small theatres of the 1980s.*

Josef Šafařík (1907–1992) *Brno philosopher who wrote about the theatre but could not publish officially. Most of his work appeared in samizdat. Critical regarding Charter 77.*

František Xaver Šalda (1867–1937) *prominent and powerful as a literary critic, but also a poet, novelist, and dramatist. In 1928 founded a journal,* Šaldův zápisník *(*Šalda's Notebook*) written entirely by himself.*

Zdena Salivarová (*1933) *a performer in the small form theatres of the 1960s, where she met and married the writer, Josef Škvorecký. Emigrated with him to Toronto, where they founded 68 Publishers, which published banned Czech writing; she was responsible for the practical running of the press.*

Jiří Šašek (1930–1996) *trained at DAMU but met Darek Vostřel on military service and formed a comedy duo at Rokoko. Best known as Robot Emil on children's TV in the 1960s; banned in the 1970s.*

Erik Adolf Saudek (1904–1963) *Jewish translator of Shakespeare who survived WWII. As dramaturge of the National Theatre after the war he was uninspiring, and opposed Krejča's appointment.*

Olga Scheinpflugová (1902–1968) *actress and writer, whose career was considerably influenced by meeting Karel Čapek in 1920; she married him in 1935, but continued her acting career after his death in 1938.*

Peter Scherhaufer (1942–1999) *a native of Bratislava who studied at JAMU and was a cofounder of Brno's Theatre Goose on a String, where he directed some of its most famous productions (*Commedia del'Arte, The Bartered and the Bought*). A true Czechoslovak, devastated by the division of Czechoslovakia.*

Adolf Scherl (1925 - 2017) *theatre scholar who specialised, insofar as possible in the 1950s, on the interwar avant-garde. Worked in the Cabinet for the Study of Czech Theatre from 1957–1990.*

Jan Schmid (*1936) *originally a glass designer, he began his theatre career in Liberec with puppets at the Naïve Theatre; in 1961 he founded the experimental Studio Ypsilon and in 1978 moved it to Prague, where it became part of the theatre moment working to overcome Normalisation.*

Evald Schorm (1931–1988) *actor, film and theatre director unable to compromise with the Communists. Created major films of the Czech New Wave (*The Return of the Prodigal Son*) but banned after 1969. Under Normalisation worked as guest director, particularly at the Balustrade Theatre and* Laterna Magika.

Gustav Schorsch (1918–1945) *theatre director of Jewish origin, with Jiří Orten involved with Honzl's Little Theatre for 99. Transported to Terezín, where he directed (e.g., Gogol) and lectured on the theatre. Believed to have been shot during the liquidation of Fürstengrube in the last months of WWII.*

Josef Schulz (1840-1917) *an architect who had a share in many of the nineteenth-century buildings in Prague, especially the rebuilding of the National Theatre after the fire of 1881.*

Karel Schulz (1899–1943) *Roman Catholic writer, some of whose stories were dramatised by Josef Šmída at the Windmill during the occupation. Father-in-law of Josef Topol.*

Milan Schulz (1930–2014) *author of short stories and cabaret sketches, particularly for Semafor and Paravan in the 1960s. Emigrated in 1969 and worked for Radio Free Europe.*

Vincy (Vinzenz, Vincenc) Schwarz (1902–1942) *Czech patriot, writer, translator, and literary scholar of German origin. Collaborated with Honzl at the Little Theatre for 99. Shot by the Nazis because of his anti-Fascist propaganda.*

Anna (Andula) Sedláčková (1887–1967) *a popular actress pre-WWII; during the occupation, established her own company in the Mozarteum and presented a spirited programme including works by Karel Čapek. In 1945, expelled by Antonín Dvořák on the grounds of her "bourgeois repertoire."*

Jaroslav Seifert (1901–1986) *working-class poet and journalist, cofounder of Devětsil and exponent of Poetism. Left the Communist Party in 1930 but was welcomed back postwar until he opposed 1968 invasion and signed Charter 77. In 1984, awarded Nobel Prize, which was patronisingly tolerated by the Communist authorities.*

Zdeněk Seydl (1916–1978) *painter, graphic artist, and stage designer. He worked for E. F. Burian in the 1950s and then for the National Theatre; best known for his book covers for the new writing of the 1960s.*

Karol Sidon (*1942) *studied at FAMU while working backstage in theatres. In 1968, dramaturge for Trnka. Wrote several plays published only in samizdat, of which the best-known is* Shapira *(1972). Emigrated in 1983; appointed chief rabbi of Prague in 1992.*

Zdeněk Šikola (1937–1997) *composer who worked on most of the Balustrade productions in the 1960s, both drama and mime. Also composed the music for Jan Švankmajer's first film, and later for TV.*

Jaroslava Šiktancová (*1956) *studied at DAMU but expelled because she signed Charter 77. Survived by menial employment and occasional work in the theatre, secretly assisting Miroslav Macháček at the National Theatre. In 1990, the same DAMU professor who had expelled her presented her with her graduation certificate.*

Jan Šimek (*1941) *Brno sculptor, son of a political prisoner. Creator of both small-scale and massive objects, some of landscape size. Harrassed by police and denied a licence. Active in collective events in Moravia.*

Joska Skalník (*1948) *artist who made his living as a graphic designer in the theatre; involved with the State Theatre Studio and the Drama Club. In 1986, imprisoned as a committee member of the Jazz Section.*

Aloys Skoumal (1904–1988) *critic and translator mostly from English, including G. B. Shaw's plays.*

Petr Skoumal (1938–2014) *son of Aloys; composer for theatre and film; from 1966 music dramaturge at the Drama Club, where he performed with Jan Vodňanský. Frequently banned or limited during Normalisation.*

Josef Škvorecký (1924–2012) *writer whose first novel was banned and his second (*The Cowards, 1958*) withdrawn; involved in small theatres and active in Prague Spring. After 1968, emigrated to Canada, where he founded 68 Publishers for works banned in normalised Czechoslovakia.*

Milan Sládek (*1938) *Slovak mime artist who studied in Bratislava and then with E. F. Burian in Prague. Created his own company but after 1968 emigrated to Sweden and from there to Germany.*

Rudolf Slánský (1901–1952) *founding member of the Czechoslovak Communist Party, quickly rose to high position. Spent WWII in Moscow. On his return was made general secretary of the CP, but in an internal power struggle was charged with treason and executed after a show trial.*

Jiří Šlitr (1924–1969) *trained as a lawyer but earned his living as a graphic artist and musician; in 1948 founded the Czechoslovak Dixieland Jazz Band. Involved in the origin of the* Laterna magika*; formed a famous partnership with Jiří Suchý at Semafor.*

Václav Sloup (1936–2014) *as an actor at the Theatre on the Balustrade, created the role of Hugo in Havel's* The Garden Party, *among other leading roles. At the Vinohrady Theatre with Zdeněk Míka in the 1980s he proved to be a ruthless implementer of Communist Party discipline.*

Jitka Sloupová (*1953) *theatre critic and translator; in the 1980s was working for the official agency DILIA while one of the circle around Václav Havel.*

Vladimír Šmeral (1906–1982) *E. F. Burian's leading actor; showed courage in the war in refusing to divorce his Jewish wife; a Communist and later chairman of the theatre artists' branch of the Revolutionary Trade Union Movement, where he demonstrated his power over his former director.*

Bedřich Smetana (1824–1884) *patriotic composer involved in the National Awakening and in creating the first Czech opera company at the National Theatre. Extolled in the twentieth century by Zdeněk Nejedlý over other Czech composers.*

František Leopold Šmíd (1848–1915) *a popular singer in Prague arenas,* šantány, *and cabarets; in the early twentieth century, became the owner of one of the first cinemas. Author of sketches and short plays.*

Josef Šmída (1919–1969) *student of E. F. Burian, assistant to Honzl; actor, playwright, and founder and director of the Windmill during the occupation. After it was closed in 1946, found occasional work but suffered increasing problems. Died from physical and mental exhaustion.*

Ladislav Smoček (*1932) *director, playwright, and founder of the Drama Club; his first play,* Picnic, *opened there in 1965. His most successful play has been* The Strange Afternoon of Dr. Zvonek Burke.

Ladislav Smoljak (1931–2010) *director, scriptwriter, and actor; co-creator with Zdeněk Svěrák of the fictional Czech genius Jára (da) Cimrman, who first appeared in 1966 in a radio broadcast from the (fictional) non-alcoholic wine bar "At the Spider."*

Hana Smrčková (*1940) *actress who joined the Balustrade Theatre under Jan Grossman; played the Laundress in* The Trial *and created the role of Hana in Havel's* The Memorandum.

Viktor Sodoma (the elder; 1917–1997) *with his wife Vlasta, Sodoma formed the group* Akord Club, *which played rock 'n' roll from 1955–1958 at Reduta, where they were joined by Jiří Suchý.*

Evžen Sokolovský (1925–1998) *theatre director and scholar, in the late 1960s part of the Brno avant-garde in the Studio of the State Theatre and Večerní Brno. As a teacher, influenced students who founded Goose on a String. In the 1970s, succumbed to Normalisation, especially as a director of TV serials.*

Josef Somr (*1934) *intended to be a railwayman but studied acting at JAMU. In 1965, a founder member of the Drama Club; later joined the National Theatre. Starred in the 1960s New Wave films.*

Jiří Šotola (1924–1989) *a writer who studied theatre direction with Jiří Frejka; banned from publishing from 1970 until his recantation in 1975. His novel* Kuře on Fire *(samizdat 1974, officially published 1976) was dramatised by Zdeněk Potužil at the Theatre on the Fringe in 1979.*

Eva Soukupová (1918–2006) *studied medicine before WWII, theatre afterwards; head of theatre dept. at the Ministry of Information and Enlightenment; cultural commissioner for Czech pavilion at Expo 58; founder of the Theatre Institute. Helped and supported many including Krejča's circle, but criticised for closeness to regime.*

Franz Anton Reichsgraf von Sporck (1662–1738) *son of German nobleman granted land in Bohemia confiscated from original Czech aristocracy after defeat in 1620. Patron of music, opened first theatre in Prague, but subsequently lost interest.*

Fraňa Šrámek (1877–1952) *Romanticist and anti-militaristic poet remembered for the impressionistic simplicity, sentimentality, and erotic lyricism of the poetry he wrote in WWI and between the wars (parodied by Václav Havel). The play* Moon Over the River *(1922) established him with the public.*

Bořivoj Srba (1931–2014) *a Brno dramaturge who also taught at JAMU in the 1950s and 1960s and was a cofounder of Theatre Goose on a String. Dismissed and persecuted under Normalisation but pursued his academic research, although little of it could be published.*

Jiří Srnec (*1931) *studied puppetry and in 1961 founded the Black (later Black Light) Theatre. Originally based at the Balustrade Theatre, it was one of the innovative small form theatres of the 1960s but although commercially successful to the present day, was and is limited in its artistic development.*

Miloš Štědroň (*1942) *Brno composer whose music for the stage including key productions by the Theatre on a String (*Ballad for a Bandit, Chameleon*).*

Miloslav Stehlík (1916–1994) *theatre director, dramaturge, and playwright; his plays were based on the contest between capitalism and (triumphant) Socialism. In 1945, a founder member of the Realist Theatre (later of "Zdeněk Nejedlý").*

Karel Steigerwald (*1945) *worked in TV and film but became one of the few playwrights under Normalisation to address contemporary issues using allegorical themes. His work was often banned. Worked closely with Ivan Rajmont and Jan Grossman.*

Miroslav Štěpán (1945–2015) *member of the* Central Committee of the Communist Party of Czechoslovakia *and head of the Prague Municipal Committee of the CP. Responsible for ordering brutal attacks on students in 1988 and 1989, for which he was sentenced to gaol in the 1990s.*

Jan Nepomuk Štěpánek (1783–1844) *from a working-class family, Štěpánek studied philosophy and theology at Charles University. First involved in the theatre as a translator, then playwright and eventually director of the Royal Estates Theatre. A leading member of the National Awakening.*

Zdeněk Štěpánek (1896–1968) *a descendant of Jan Nepomuk Štěpánek. During WWI he joined the Czechoslovak Legionnaires, who held the Trans-Siberian Railway; afterwards became a popular member of the National Theatre. Cleared after WWII of collaboration with the Nazis, he led the NT Drama Company from 1953–1956.*

Jiří Štěpnička (*1947) *son of Jiřina Štěpničková, actor in theatre, film, and TV. From 1974 member of National Theatre; in 1986 played role of President Gottwald in TV series.*

Jiřina Štěpničková (1912–1985) *theatre and film actress (played Maryša in film version of the play). In 1951, was arrested when trying to leave the country, was put on trial, and served ten years' hard labour.*

Jiří Stivín (*1942) *iconic jazz musician.*

Zuzana Stivínová (*1940) *sister of the jazz musician Jiří Stivín, played Zuzana in Semafor's series of "Zuzana" entertainments. She emigrated to France in 1964.*

Ladislav Štoll (1902–1981) *hardline literary critic, involved in "bolshevisation" of the Communist Party; minister of education in 1953, of culture in 1954. Responsible for the banning and imprisonment of many writers, especially Christians, and suppression of theatre initiatives.*

Jiřina Stránská (1912–1999) *actress who played leading roles for E. F. Burian at Déčko. Moved to the Vinohrady Theatre when Déčko was closed by the Nazis, but in 1949 gave up the theatre.*

Adolf Stránský (1855–1931) *journalist and politician, founder of* Lidové noviny.

Jaroslav Stránský (1884–1973) *son of Adolf and inheritor of* Lidové noviny. *Became a parliamentary deputy in 1918. Member of government-in-exile during the war, on his return became first minister of justice and then minister of education. After the Communist takeover went into exile.*

Zdeněk Stránský (1921–1945) *actor/writer son of the director of the National Theatre, Rudolf Stránský. Member of Little Theatre for 99 and Windmill, involved in Communist resistance to Nazis. Shot and killed during the Prague Uprising while on guard on the terrace of National Theatre. Honzl's Studio gave him a memorial performance.*

Ladislav Stroupežnický (1850–1892) *did not gain a full education, but as an insurance clerk in Prague wrote humorous pieces and then plays. Became chief dramaturge and mainstay of the National Theatre after its rebuilding. Best known for* Our Proud Peasants, *constantly successful up to today.*

Jan Štursa (1880–1925) *a leading sculptor, much affected by WWI.*

Jindřich Štyrský (1899–1942) *leading member of Devětsil, artistic partner of Toyen and a Surrealist. At the end of the 1920s, designer for the Liberated Theatre (*Ubu Roi*).*

František Adolf Šubert (1849–1915) *a distinguished writer (also of plays) involved from his youth in amateur theatre, and a member of the board of the National Theatre; head of the theatre from 1883–1900.*

Leoš Suchařípa (1932–2005) *theatre critic, historian, and translator from Russian, especially Chekhov. Dramaturge of Drama Club in the 1960s, forced to leave under Normalisation; unofficial dramaturge of the Drama Studio in the 1970s and 1980s. Frequently an actor, especially at the Balustrade in the 1990s.*

Jiří Suchý (*1931) *graphic artist and early exponent of rock 'n' roll, cofounder of the Balustrade Theatre, founder of Semafor, where he formed a legendary partnership with Jiří Šlitr and subsequently with Jitka Molavcová. Until 1989, constantly harassed by the Communists.*

Josef Suk (1874–1935) *major composer; a strong influence on his students in the interwar years.*

Josef Šváb-Malostranský (1860–1932) *entrepreneur and comic actor on stage and screen.*

Pavel Švanda ze Semčic (1825–1891) *studied as a priest but followed a varied career until he became head of drama at the Provisional Theatre. Founded his own company in 1865 and a permanent theatre in Smíchov in 1881. A major innovator in Czech theatre, not only in Prague.*

Jan Švankmajer (*1934) *Surrealist filmmaker and artist. Born into a German Bohemian family, he graduated in puppetry and worked with Emil Radok, then Semafor and* Laterna magika. *Strongly influenced by Effenberger and the Surrealist Group of Prague, becoming a leading member. His films could not appear in the 1970s.*

Karel Švenk/Schwenk (1917–1945) *before WWII, an actor, director, writer, and composer; held in Terezín, where he initiated many of the cabarets; died on a death march a month before the Liberation.*

Zdeněk Svěrák (*1936) *playwright, scriptwriter, and actor, and in 1967 with Ladislav Smoljak founder of the Theatre of Jára Cimrman.*

Karolína Světlá (1830–1899) *born into a German Bohemian family, she became a promoter of Czech language and literature and women's writing. Wrote stories and novels about Bohemia and Moravia. In love with Jan Neruda, but the affair ended with a lost letter.*

Ivan Sviták (1925–1994) *a Marxist philosopher with a strong affinity with Surrealism. Emigrated after 1968; in 1971 sentenced in absentia to eight years for "damaging the important interests of the ČSSR."*

Jiří Svoboda (1924–1990) *theatre director working with Míka in Gottwaldov from 1948, head of the drama company in Olomouc from 1960–1974, with Krejča directed the première of Topol's* The End of Shrovetide.

Josef Svoboda (1920–2002) *possibly the most sought-after international stage designer of the postwar period. A superb technical ability and invention enabled him to achieve the extraordinary visual effects desired by theatre directors in opera, ballet, and drama worldwide.*

Ludvík Svoboda (1895–1979) *WWII hero, and president from 1965–1978.*

Doubravka Svobodová (*1956) *joined* Laterna Magika *(as an usherette, received the bronze badge of the Brigade of Socialist Labour) before studying at DAMU and Charles University. In 1982, director of the* Řeznická *Theatre; in 1993, of the Balustrade Theatre; in 2014, dean of DAMU.*

Václav Švorc (1919–2013) *from a Silesian working class family, brother of Jiřina Švorcová; studied acting at the Conservatoire during the war and joined the National Theatre in 1944, where he became head of the drama company. Hardline Communist who helped to implement Normalisation.*

Jiřina Švorcová (1928–2011) *actress for forty years at the Vinohrady Theatre but best known for the Normalisation TV soap opera* The Woman Behind the Counter. *Loyal Party member; in 1976 voted onto the Central Committee of the CP and was chair of the Theatre Union. Figurehead of the Anti-Charter; great power over the lives of others.*

Jana Synková (*1944) *actress, and wife of Jan Schmid of Studio Ypsilon. Began her career with Kočová's Maringotka.*

Václav Talich (1883–1961) *violinist, conductor, and teacher; from 1935–1944 head of opera at National Theatre, where he promoted Janáček. Falsely accused by the Communists of collaboration with the Nazis.*

Eva Tálská (*1944) *founding member of the Theatre Goose on a String and one of its key directors. Exceptionally successful in her work with and for children and young people.*

Ore Tarraco (also Carratera; real name František Kulhánek) (1889–1934) *oriental dancer (originally a music student and bank clerk) performing under pseudonyms in cabaret; travelled Europe and beyond. Best known for his portrait by the avant-garde photographer Jaromír Rössler.*

Karel Teige (1900–1951) *multi-talented avant-garde artist who was the driving force behind Devětsil. Energetic correspondent with international avant-garde. Defined Poetism, later became a Surrealist. After 1948 denounced as a Trotskyite and hounded to death.*

Karel Ignác Thám (Karel Hynek Thám) (1763–1816) *the elder and more academic of the Thám brothers, one of the earliest of the "national revivalists"; earned his living as a librarian and teacher, but was above all a translator into Czech, especially of Shakespeare (from German).*

Václav Thám (1765–c.1816) *the younger and more active of the Thám brothers; after being dismissed from the police he entered the theatre, for which he wrote around fifty plays, encouraging other "national revivalists" to do likewise. A founder of the* Bouda; *date and place of his death is unknown.*

Marie Tomášová (*1929) *a leading actress at the National Theatre and the Theatre Beyond the Gate until Normalisation ended her career. Otomar Krejča's wife, and his Juliet.*

Zdena Tominová (née Holubová, *1941) *expelled from DAMU when she refused to join Communist Party. Married to the philosopher Julius Tomin, ran underground seminars under Normalisation, for which they were severely persecuted.*

Tomáš Töpfer (*1951) *actor and theatre director involved in the Velvet Revolution while working at the Vinohrady Theatre. In the 1990s, founded the theatre Fidlovačka.*

Josef Topol (1935–2015) *wrote his first play for E. F. Burian's theatre; Krejča and Kraus then involved him in their inner group at the National Theatre where he wrote two major plays. He became the dramatist of Krejča's Theatre Beyond the Gate but was a forbidden writer from 1972–1989. Persecuted as a signatory of Charter 77.*

Toyen (Marie Červenková) (1902–1980) *with Jindřich Štyrský a leading member of the interwar avant-garde. A founder member of the Czech Surrealist Group, she went into exile in France in 1948.*

Paul (Pavel) Trensky (1929–2013) *theatre historian, in 1956 emigrated to Austria and later settled in the USA.*

Jan Tříska (1936–2017) *appeared at the National Theatre as student in 1956. Part of Krejča's circle, playing key roles and joining him at the Theatre Beyond the Gate. With the National Theatre until he attended the "illegal" Krob/Havel* The Beggar's Opera. *Emigrated to North America in 1977, when pressured to inform on Václav Havel.*

Jiří Trnka (1912–1969) *illustrator, puppet maker, and filmmaker, Trnka did groundbreaking work in puppet film in the 1950s and 1960s. His film* The Hand *(1966) made with Ladislav Fialka expressed his trauma as an artist at being manipulated by the Communists.*

Alois Pravoslav Trojan (1815–1893) *a lawyer and politician, he was disappointed by the outcome of the 1848 revolution, joined those who sought other means to assert Czech identity and in 1850 became chairman of the Committee to Build a Czech National Theatre.*

František Tröster (1904–1968) *architect who from 1935 worked with Frejka at the National Theatre, later with Radok and Krejča. Fought in the resistance until captured by the Nazis. After the war, tension arose between him and the more assertive Svoboda. Known for his creative use of light and space; awarded Grand Prix at Expo 58.*

Jaroslav Tuček (*1938) *actor with the State Theatre in Brno, considered by the Communists to be "a safe pair of hands" when in 1979 he took over the leadership of the Theatre on a String and HaTheatre together. Instead, he pursued a policy that enabled the theatres to survive the remaining years of Normalisation.*

Ctibor Turba (*1944) *multi-talented mime artist, co-creator of the legendary* Pantomima Alfreda Jarryho *and the* Cirkus Alfred. *Tacitly resisted the anti-values of Normalisation. Worked internationally but did not emigrate.*

Svatopluk Turek (also T. Svatopluk, 1900–1972) *graphic designer who wrote a novel* The Shoe Factory *(1933, later a play and film) full of hatred of the Baťa enterprise.*

Josef Kajetán Tyl (1808–1856) *a pupil of Klicpera in Hradec Králové, he left his university studies to join the theatre. Hugely active in theatre, journalism, and politics, he encouraged others to write in Czech. Often in conflict with Havlíček over standards. Marginalised, he died as a touring actor.*

Milan Uhde (*1936) *a Brno academic and writer, Uhde wrote several satirical plays in the late 1960s. His works were banned during Normalisation, but he secretly cooperated with the Theatre on a String. Entered politics after 1989 and i.a. became minister of culture.*

Dalibor Cyril Vačkář (pseudonyms Faltys/Faltis, 1906–1984) *classical and popular composer, violinist (played in the orchestra of the Liberated Theatre); protégé of Josef Suk. Also a playwright, scriptwriter, and dramaturge.*

Ludvík Vaculík (1926–2015) *Communist writer who spoke out at the 1967 Writers' Congress and in June 1968 became famous as the author of "Two Thousand Words" (which may have provoked the Soviet invasion). Under Normalisation became a dissident and the first systematic publisher of samizdat.*

Svatopluk Vála (*1943) *after involvement in student theatres, in 1974 founded Haná Theatre (HaTheatre) in Prostějov and was its artistic director until it moved to Brno.*

Vladislav Vančura (1891–1942) *leading writer of the interwar period, cofounder of Devětsil and member of the Communist Party. Arrested by the Gestapo in reprisals following the assassination of Heydrich; tortured and executed on the killing fields of Kobylisy.*

Nina Vangeli (*1946) *graduated in theatre studies from Charles University, where her teacher was Jan Kopecký. Specialised in dance and ritual theatre. In the 1970s and 1980s, ran the unofficial Studio of Movement Theatre.*

Emília Vášáryová (*1942) *Slovak actress working mainly in the Slovak National Theatre in Bratislava. Sister of the actress and diplomat Magda Vášáryová (*1948).*

Radim Vašinka (1935–2016) *in 1959 founded the poetry theatre Xka in Brno; in 1962 coauthored* The Demented Dove *at the Balustrade Theatre but preferred to work independently and in 1967 founded the poetry theatre Orfeus in a cellar in the Prague's Lesser Quarter (later a travelling group).*

Božena Věchetová (*1943) *graduated from the Conservatoire in 1962, joining Fialka's mime company at the Balustrade Theatre soon after its foundation and performed in the major productions, including* Fools. *Third wife of Ladislav Fialka.*

Vítězslav Vejražka (1915–1973) *a powerful actor and theatre director, especially at the National Theatre. Also entered politics and became a member of the Central Committee of the Communist Party.*

Jan Vladislav (1923–2009) *a Slovak-born poet and translator. Allowed to complete his doctorate during the Prague Spring, he was persecuted under Normalisation, signed Charter 77, and emigrated in 1981. He settled in France and continued to write and publish.*

Jindřich Vodák (1867–1940) *teacher, editor, translator, and fervent theatregoer and drama critic.*

Vladimír Vodička (1925–2015) *songwriter and Communist Party member whose admiration for Vyskočil and Suchý at Reduta led him to facilitate the creation of the Theatre on the Balustrade, where he was general manager from 1958–1991.*

Jan Vodňanský (*1941) *an actor and singer who first partnered Petr Skoumal in 1963 at Reduta, and especially at the Drama Club from 1969; from 1973 only at smaller venues. Signatory of Charter 77.*

Eduard Vojan (1853–1920) *actor of great psychological insight. Played the major Shakespearean characters at the National Theatre—most notably in Kvapil's Shakespeare cycle during WWI.*

Jaromír Vomáčka (1923–1978) *musician who cofounded Theatre on the Balustrade and later worked with* Laterna magika. *Wrote many popular songs, especially in 1968 with the anti-Soviet "Home With You, Ivan."*

Helena Vondráčková (*1947) *1960s pop star; originally a singing partner of Kubišová, Vondráčková conformed after 1968 and retained her popularity with the public, whereas Kubišová was outlawed.*

Karel Vondrášek (*1943) *head of the drama company at the Balustrade Theatre from 1978–1982, when he emigrated.*

Jiří Voskovec (1905–1981) *cofounder of the comedy duo V+W and of the Liberated Theatre; during Communism in exile in the USA. A Czech icon, but a little less supreme than his partner Werich.*

Prokop Voskovec (1893–1977) *brother of Jiří, a translator.*

Prokop Voskovec (1942–2011) *son of the translator Prokop Voskovec and nephew of Jiří. Writer and Surrealist; failed to complete his theatre studies. Rebelled against Normalisation, signed Charter 77, and emigrated to France in 1979.*

Darek Vostřel (1929–1992) *at the end of the 1950s founder and leader of the Rokoko cabaret, where his partner in a comedy duo was Jiří Šašek. Forced to leave under Normalisation; forbidden to publish or perform and did so only under a pseudonym; later allowed to perform.*

Alena Vostrá (1938–1992) *wife of Jaroslav Vostrý, cofounder, dramaturge, and key playwright at the Drama Club in the 1960s.*

Jaroslav Vostrý (*1931) *theatre critic, dramaturge and director; cofounder of the Drama Club; harassed by the Communists and forced to leave the Drama Club. In 1987, allowed to accept a teaching position at DAMU; in 1993 appointed rector of AMU.*

Eva Vrchlická (1888–1969) *daughter of Jaroslav Vrchlický; writer and actress, once married to the playwright František Zavřel, and longtime member of the National Theatre; opposed to Krejča.*

Jaroslav Vrchlický (1853–1912) *prolific and influential poet, dramatist, critic, translator, and politician; helped Czech literature to turn towards French, Italian, and English models and fought for the independence of the writer.*

Václav Vydra (1876–1953) *an actor who played leading roles not only at the National and Vinohrady Theatres but also in politics. A member of the Communist Party from the 1930s and director of the National Theatre from 1945, he was arguably the most powerful personality in the theatre post WWII.*

Josef Vyleťal (1948–1989) *a native of Brno who studied art and architecture in Slovakia and later inclined to Surrealism and magic realism. From 1962, set designer at the Theatre on the Balustrade.*

Ivan Vyskočil (*1929) *writer, psychologist, theatre director, pedagogue; with Jiří Suchý created the concept of the text-appeal; cofounder and first director of the Theatre on the Balustrade; creator of Non-Theatre. One of the most influential figures in theatre and film in the 1960s and later.*

Stanislav Vyskočil (1920–2004) *during the occupation acted with the Little Theatre for 99. Joined Honzl's Studio as a director but left after a year and became head of provincial theatres (Pilsen, etc.). Political hardliner.*

Blanka Waleská (1910–1986) *began her career in avant-garde theatres and joined the National Theatre in 1948, where she played leading roles for Krejča. Close friend of the founder of the Theatre Institute, Eva Soukupová.*

Josef Waltner (1883–1961) *a corpulent cabaretier who from 1911–1922 ran the Cabaret Montmartre (during the war, Cabaret Montwaltner) on Řetězová Street in the Old Town. Vlasta Burian, Eduard Bass, Jiří Červený, Jaroslav Hašek, E. A. Longen, Xena Longenová, and E. E. Kisch appeared here.*

Richard Weber (1932–2017) *denied higher education, so entered the theatre as a wigmaker's apprentice. Trained himself as a mime and became a key member of Fialka's company at the Balustrade. In 1975 cofounded and for over three decades co-directed the Scuola Teatro Dimitri in Switzerland.*

Josef Wenig (1815–1939) *a prolific stage designer of the early twentieth century, working mainly at the National and Vinohrady Theatres and with all the leading directors. Nephew of F. A. Šubert.*

Jan Werich (1905–1980) *cofounder of the comedy duo V+W and the Liberated Theatre; his activities were drastically curtailed during the Communist period but in the late 1950s he was allowed to manage a theatre and perform; a supreme Czech icon.*

Jiří Wolker (1900–1924) *born into a provincial middle-class family, credited with having initiated the Proletarian Poetry movement. A founder member of Devětsil and the Communist Party, under Communism he became a cult figure (a Prague theatre was named after him).*

Jan Zajíc (1950–1969) *a student from Šumperk who became the second torch of protest after Palach.*

Antonín Zápotocký (1884–1957) *president from 1953–1957; author of a number of novels, including* Red Glow over Kladno, *(1951), later filmed.*

František Zavřel (1879–1915) *a theatre director who spent most of his career in Germany, where he learnt the techniques of Expressionism, bringing them to Prague in 1914 when he directed* Lulu *and* The Mikado. *Not to be confused with his cousin, the playwright František Zavřel.*

František Zavřel (1885–1947) *a lawyer and successful playwright in the period between the wars, he became a supporter of the Protectorate regime, which brought him a post as dramaturge at the National Theatre. He died a homeless outcast in 1947. Not to be confused with his cousin, the theatre director František Zavřel.*

František Zelenka (1904–1944) *a native of Kutná Hora; his first designs were for a Jewish drama group of which Ota Ohrenstein (Ornest) was a child member. An architect by profession, he was one of the most energetic and talented members of the interwar avant-garde but died in a concentration camp.*

Julius Zeyer (1841–1901) *a writer who, in spite of his mixed ancestry and wide travels, passionately loved the mystic background and legends of his country. A strong influence on historical drama.*

Otakar Zich (1879–1934) *professor of aesthetics at Charles University and one of Zdeněk Nejedlý's circle, Zich was author of* Aesthetics of the Art of Drama *(1931), a significant influence on Structuralism.*

Josef Zítek (1832–1909) *in 1865 architect of the winning designs for the National Theatre. He did not, however, take part in the rebuilding after the fire in 1881, owing to political struggles. Also designed the Rudolfinum concert hall and art gallery.*

Josef Zora (1894–1971) *teacher and organist who became involved with the professional theatre, including the Revolutionary Stage, but especially group projects such as Dědrasbor and Voiceband, and mass spectacles. He was also involved in film, including Gustav Machatý's* Ecstasy.

TITLES OF CZECH AND SLOVAK PLAYS, OPERAS AND FILMS

About My Murder : Jak jsem byl zavražděn
Abraham Affair, The : Případ Abraháma
Act : Akt
**Adventures of the Good Soldier Švejk, The* : Osudy dobrého vojáka Švejka
**Agathamania* : Agatománie
**All My Good Countrymen* : Všichni dobří rodáci
All My Granddads : Všichni moji dědové
All the Beauties of the World : Všecky krásy světa
Armoured Circus, The : Cirkus plechový
Ass and Its Shadow, The : Osel a stín
At the Crossroads : Na rozcestí
At the End of a Garden Named Hollywood : Na konci zahrady jménem Hollywood
**Audition* : Konkurs
August Sunday : Srpnová neděle
Ballad for a Bandit : Balada pro banditu
Ballad of Rags, The : Balada z hadrů
Ballet Macabre : Balet makábr
Bandits at Chlum, The : Loupežníci na Chlumu
Bartered and the Bought, The : Prodaný a prodaná
**Bartered Bride, The* : Prodaná nevěsta
Battalion Inn : Batalion
**Beggar's Opera, The* : Žebrácká opera
Behold the City! : Aj, hle město!
Best Rock/Years of Mrs. Hermanová, The : Nejlepší rocky paní Hermanové
Brandenburgers in Bohemia, The : Braniboři v Čechách
Břetislav and Judith, or Abduction from the Cloister : Břetislav a Jitka anebo Únos z kláštera
Bring them Back Alive, or Hunting : Přivezte je živé čili Lovy
Broken Trilogy, The : Rozbitá trilogie
Burning Souls : Hořící duše
Cassander and Pierrot: Castaways : Cassander a Pierrot—Trosečníci
Castaway : Trosečník
**Cat on the Rails* : Kočka na kolejích
Cimrman in the Realm of Music : Cimrman v říši hudby
Cinderella : O Popelce
Circus of Hope : Cirkus nadeje
**Closely Watched Trains* : Ostře sledované vlaky
Clowns : Cesta
Cock-up : Ptákovina (Dvě uši, dvě svatby)
Come to Stay! : Přiďte pobejt!
Conspirators : Spiklenci
Cosmic Spring : Kosmické jaro
Count Johnnie : Kníže Honzík
Crystal Night : Křišťálová noc
**Cunning Little Vixen, The* : Liška bystrouška

Love, Defiance and Death : Láska, vzdor a smrt
Lovers from the Kiosk : Milenci z kiosku
**Loves of a Blonde* : Lásky jedné plavovlásky
Magic Circus : Kouzelný cirkus
**Makropulos Case, The* : Věc Makropulos
Man from the Attic, The : Člověk z půdy
Man and His Pint, A : Muž s pivem
May Fairy Tale, A : Pohádka máje
Maze, The : Bludiště
**Memorandum, The* : Vyrozumění
Midnight Wind : Půlnoční vítr
Miners of Kutná Hora, The : Kutnohorští havíři
Missing : Nezvěstná
Murder in the Saloon Car : Vražda v salonním coupé
Moon Over the River : Měsíc nad řekou
**Mother, The* : Matka
**Mountain Hotel* : Horský hotel
Mrs. Hermanová's Best Rocks : Nejlepší rocky paní Hermanové
Much too Merry Christmas, A : Příliš štědrý večer
Mysterious Natures : Záhadné povahy
Neapolitan Disease, The : Neapolská choroba
Night Rehearsal : Noční zkouška
Night with Hamlet, A : Noc s Hmaletem
Nightingale for Supper : Slavík k večeři
Nine Hats on Prague : Devět klobouků nad Prahou
No Heroes Live in Thebes : (*Die Stunde der Antigone*) : Hrdinové v Thébách nebydlí
Of Dreams and Follies : O snech a bláznivinách
Of Human Troubles, or Moody Blues : O lidském tráblu čili Nálady blues
On a Knife's Edge : Na ostří nože
On A May Fairy Tale : Na Pohádku máje
**On the Periphery* : Periférie
Our Proud Peasants : Naši furianti
Outsider, or Biography of a Famous Man : Outsider anebo Životopis slavného muže
**Owners of the Keys, The* : Majitelé klíčů
Pantomime on the Balustrade : Pantomima na zábradlí
Paper Blues : Papírový Blues
Parrot's Got All the As, The : Papoušek má jedničky
**Party and the Guests, The* : O slavnosti a hostech
Pearls from the Depths : Perličky na dne
Period Dances : Dobové tance
Philosophers' Feast, The : Hostina filosofů
Picnic : Piknik
Pied Piper, The : Krysař
Pierrot the Baker : Pierot pekařem
Playing at Susie : Hra na Zuzanku
Portrait of Antonín Dvořák, A : Portrét Antonína Dvořáka
**Power and Glory* (*The White Disease*) : Bílá nemoc
Princess Dandelion : Princezna Pampeliška
Princess T : Princezna T
Prague Five, The : Pražská pětka
**Private View* (*The Unveiling*) : Vernisáž
Pseudolos the Fox : Lišák Pseudolos
Professional Woman : Profesionální žena
Ransacked : Vykradeno
Recollections : Rozvzpomínání
Redevelopment : Asanace
**Report from the Gallows* : Reportáž psaná na oprátce
Requiem : Rekviem
Res Publica, or How We Did Not Experience the Twenties: Res publica aneb jak jsme nezažili 20. léta
Res Publica II, or How We Experienced It: Res publica II aneb tak jsme to zažili
**Return of the Prodigal Son, The* : Návrat ztraceného syna
Revenge : Pomsta
Roaming : Bloudění
Robber, The : Loupežník
Romance of Oldřich and Božena, The : Romance o Oldřichu a Boženě
Romeo and Juliet, The Dream of One Prisoner : Romeo a Julie, sen jednoho vězně
Rooms by the Hour : Hodinový hotelier
Rozrazil 1/88 (On Democracy) : Rozrazil 1/88 (O Demokracii)
Sad Christmas : Smutné vánoce
Sand (So long ago…) : Písek (Tak dávno…)
Second Folk Suite : Druhá lidová suita
Sentimental Romance, A : Sentimentální romance
Ship of the Living, The : Loď živých
Shoe Factory, The : Botostroj
**Shop on the Main Street* : Obchod na korze

Six Wives : Šest žen
Song for Hamlet : Píseň pro Hamleta
Songs of the Czech Pedlars : České písně kramářské
Story of Love and Honour, A : Román lásky a cti
Strange Afternoon of Dr. Zvonek Burke, The : Podivné odpoledne dr. Zvonka Burkeho
Such a Waste of Blood : Taková ztráta krve
Švanda the Bagpiper : Strakonický dudák
Švejks : Švejci
Tales of the Long Nose : Příběhy dlouhého nosu
Tank Battalion : Tankový prapor
Tartar Feast, The : Tatarská pouť
Teacher and Pupil : Učitel a žák
Telegrams on Wheels : Depeše na kolečkách
Their Day : Jejich den
Third Wish, The : Třetí přání
Thrift : Šetrnost
Today the Sun Still Sets over Atlantis : Dnes ještě zapadá slunce nad Atlantidou
**Tomorrow!* : Zítra to spustíme
**Tomorrow There Will Be... or Playing at Trials* : Zítra se bude aneb Hra na proces
Tomorrow There Will Be Dancing Everywhere : Zítra se bude tančit všude
Tonka the Gallows : Tonka Šibenice
**Too Loud a Solitude* : Příliš hlučná samota
**Trial, The* : Proces
Two Briefcases/One-Act Plays and a Dispatch Case/Female Diplomat : Dvě aktovky a diplomatka
Two Loves of Mikoláš Aleš, The : Dvě lásky Mikoláše Aleše
Two Nights with a Girl : Dvě noci s dívkou
Unveiling : Vernisáž
Up We Go the Rio Botičo : Vzhůru po Rio Botičo
Victory of the Revolution, The : Vítězství revoluce
Voices of Birds, The : Hlasy ptáků
War : Vojna
Was the Wolf Here? : Byl tady vlk?
Wedding Feast : Svatební hostina
Where is Kuťak? : Kde je Kuťak?
White Disease, The : Bílá nemoc
Whose is Jazz : Komu patří jazz
Whose Turn Next? : Na koho to slovo padne
Witch, The : Bosorka
World Behind Bars, The : Svět za mřížemi
World of Dreams : Svět snů
Zuzana is Alone at Home : Zuzana je sama doma
Zuzana is Alone at Home Again : Zuzana je zase sama doma
Zuzana is Everywhere at Home : Zuzana je všude jako doma
Zuzana is at Home for No-one : Zuzana není pro nikoho doma

* English translation known to exist, although it may not be easily obtainable. In the case of an adaptation, the asterisk may refer to the original work. In the case of an opera, it will usually refer to the libretto (or possibly the work from which the opera was adapted). In the case of a film, it will usually refer to a subtitled version.

SELECT BIBLIOGRAPHY

PUBLICATION IN CZECH/ENGLISH

Koubská, Vlasta et al. *František Tröster: Basník světla a prostoru / Artist of Light and Space* (exhibition catalogue). Prague: Obecní dům; Národní muzeum; Divadelní ústav, 2007.

PUBLICATIONS IN ENGLISH (BY AUTHOR ACCORDING TO THE ENGLISH ALPHABET)

Albertová, Helena. *Josef Svoboda: Scenographer*. Translated by Barbara Day. Prague: Art and Theatre Institute, 2008.

Beck, Dennis C. "The Czech Authorial Studio Theatres, 1968–1989: Twenty Years of Rehearsing the Revolution." PhD diss., University of Texas, 1998.

Beck, Dennis C. "Divadlo Husa na Provazku and the "Absence" of Czech Community." *Theatre Journal*, 48/4 (Dec 1996).

Beck, Dennis C. "Setting the Stage for Revolution: The Efficacy of Czech Theatre, 1975–1989." *Theatre Survey*, 44/2 (Nov 2003).

Brandesky, Joseph. *Czech Theatre Design in the Twentieth Century: Metaphor & Irony Revisited*. Iowa City: University of Iowa Press, 2007.

Brock, Peter, and Gordon H. Skilling, eds. *The Czech Renaissance of the Nineteenth Century*. Toronto: University of Toronto Press, 1970.

Brod, Max, ed. *The Diaries of Franz Kafka 1910–1923*. Translated by Joseph Kresh and Martin Greenberg with Hannah Arendt. Harmondsworth: Penguin Books, 1964.

Brook, Peter. *The Empty Space*. London: MacGibbon & Kee, 1968.

Burian, Jarka. *The Scenography of Josef Svoboda*. Middletown, CT: Wesleyan University Press, 1971.

Burian, Jarka M. *Modern Czech Theatre*. Iowa: University of Iowa Press, 2000.

Burian, Jarka M. *Leading Creators of Twentieth-Century Czech Theatre*. London & New York: Routledge, 2002.

Chamberlain, Lesley. *The Philosophy Steamer: Lenin and the Exile of the Intelligentsia*. London: Atlantic Books, 2006.

Císař, Jan. *The History of the Czech Theatre*. Translated by Andrew Philip Fisher and Julius Neumann. Prague: AMU Press, 2010.

Czech Theatre Review 1989–2009. Translated by Robin Cassling and Julius Neumann. Prague: Arts and Theatre Institute, 2011.
Day, Barbara. "The Theatre on the Balustrade in Prague and the Small Stage Tradition in Czechoslovakia." PhD diss., University of Bristol, 1986.
Day, Barbara, ed. *Czech Plays*. London: Nick Hern Books, 1991.
Dubská, Alice. *Czech Puppet Theatre over the Centuries*. Prague: The International Institute of Puppet Arts.
Dvořák, Arnošt, and Ladislav Klíma. *Matthew Honest*. Translated by Robert Russell. In *Visegrad Drama II: Escape*, edited by Andrea Tomba. Budapest: Hungarian Theatre Museum and Institute, 2009.
Elam, Keir. *The Semiotics of Theatre and Drama*. London: Methuen, 1980.
Esslin, Martin. *The Theatre of the Absurd*. Revised & enlarged edition. Harmondsworth: Penguin, 1967.
Gibian, George, ed. *The Poetry of Jaroslav Seifert*. Translated by Ewald Osers and George Gibian. North Haven: Catbird Press, 1998.
Goetz-Stankiewicz, Marketa. *The Silenced Theatre: Czech Playwrights without a Stage*. Toronto: University of Toronto Press, 1978.
Goetz-Stankiewicz, Marketa, ed. *The Vaněk Plays*. Vancouver: University of British Columbia Press, 1987.
Goetz-Stankiewicz, Marketa, ed. *DramaContemporary: Czechoslovakia*. New York: Performing Arts Journal Publications, 1985.
Grunzke, Adam Robert. "Models of Aesthetic Subversion: Ideas, Spaces, and Objects in Czech Theatre and Drama of the 1950s and 1960s." PhD diss., University of Toronto, 2011.
Hames, Peter. *The Czechoslovak New Wave*. Berkeley–Los Angeles–London: University of California, 1985.
Hamšík, Dušan. *Writers Against Rulers*. Translated by D. Orpington. London: Hutchinson, 1971.
Hards, Peter. "The Concept of Revolution in Czech Writing 1918–1938." PhD diss., University of Cambridge, 1974.
Havel, Václav. *Disturbing the Peace*. Translated by Paul Wilson. New York: Random House, 1990.
Hayman, Ronald, ed. *The German Theatre*. London: Oswald Wolff, 1975.
Honzl, Jindřich. *The Czechoslovak Theatre*. Anonymous translator. Prague: Orbis, 1948.
Howey, Nicholas. *Who's Afraid of Franz Kafka?* Detroit: Wayne State University, 1970
Janáček, Leoš. *Janáček's Uncollected Essays on Music*. Edited and translated by Mirka Zemanová. London: Marion Boyars, 1989.
Kusin, V. V. *The Intellectual Origins of the Prague Spring*. Cambridge: Cambridge University Press, 1971.
László, Péter, and Robert B. Pynsent, eds. *Intellectuals and the Future in the Habsburg Monarchy 1890–1914*. London: Macmillan Press, 1988.
Kazda, Jaromír. *Czech Theatre*. Translated by Anna Bryson. Prague: DAMU, 1994.
Kimball, Stanley Buchholz. *Czech Nationalism: A Study of the National Theatre Movement*. Urbana: University of Illinois Press, 1964
Klíma, Ivan. *My Crazy Century*. Translated by Craig Cravens. New York, Grove Press, 2013.
Kriseová. Edá. *Václav Havel*. Translated by Caleb Crain. New York: St Martin's Press, 1993.
Kundera, Milan. *The Book of Laughter and Forgetting*. Translated by Michael Henry Heim. London: Faber & Faber, 1982.
Locke, Brian S. *Opera and Ideology in Prague: Polemics and Practice at the National Theater 1900–1938*. Rochester, NY: University of Rochester Press, 2006.

Matejka, Ladislav & Irwin R Titunik, eds. *Semiotics of Art: Prague School Contributions*. Cambridge: MIT Press, 1976.
Mňačko, Ladislav. *The Seventh Night*. Anonymous translator. New York: J. M. Dent & Sons, 1969.
Mrštík, Alois, and Vilém. *Maryša*. Translated by Barbara Day in *Visegrad Drama I: Weddings*, edited by Anna Grusková. Bratislava: Divadelný ústav, 2002.
Nešlehová, Mahulena, ed. *Vlastislav Hofman*. Prague: Vlastislav Hofman Society, 2005.
Pérez-Simón, Andrés, "The Theatrical Pendulum: Paths of Innovation in the Modernist Stage." PhD diss., University of Toronto, 2010.
Piscator, Erwin. *The Political Theatre*. Translated by Hugh Rorrison. London: Eyre Methuen, 1963.
Quinn, Michael L. *The Semiotic Stage*. New York: Peter Lang, 1995.
Raabe, Paul. *The Era of German Expressionism*. London: John Calder and Riverun, 1974.
Reinfeld, Barbara K. *Karel Havlíček (1821–1856): A National Liberation Leader of the Czech Renascence*. New York: Columbia University Press, 1982.
Rocamora, Carol. *Acts of Courage*. Hanover, NH: Smith and Kraus, 2004.
Rosemont, Franklin. *André Breton and the First Principles of Surrealism*. London: Pluto Press, 1978.
Rothkirchen, Livia. *The Jews of Bohemia and Moravia*. Lincoln: University of Nebraska Press, 2005.
Salter, Chris. *Entangled: Technology and the Transformation of Performance*. Cambridge: MIT Press, 2010.
Sayer, Derek. *The Coasts of Bohemia*. Princeton: Princeton University Press, 1998.
Sayer, Derek. *Prague, Capital of the Twentieth Century*. Princeton: Princeton University Press, 2013.
Senelick, Laurence, ed. *National Theatre in Northern and Eastern Europe, 1746–1900*. Cambridge: Cambridge University Press, 1991.
Švácha, Rostislav, ed. *The Czech Avant-garde of the 1920s and '30s*. Oxford: Museum of Modern Art, 1990. Exhibition catalogue.
Tausky, Vilem & Margaret. *Leoš Janáček: Leaves from his Life*. Thetford: Kahn and Averill, 1982.
Theiner, George, ed. *New Writing in Czechoslovakia*. Translated by George Theiner. Harmondsworth: Penguin, 1969.
Topol, Josef. *The End of Shrovetide*. Translated by Gerald Turner in *Visegrad Drama III: The Sixties*, edited by Kamila Černá. Prague: Art and Theatre Institute, 2009.
Trensky, Paul I.. *Czech Drama Since World War II*. White Plains, NY: M.E. Sharpe, 1978.
Tynan, Kenneth. *Show People*. New York: Simon and Schuster, 1979.
Veltruský, Jiří. *An Approach to Semiotics of Theatre*. Brno: Masaryk University, 2012.
Vladislav, Jan, ed. *Václav Havel or Living in Truth*. London: Faber & Faber, 1986.
Wellek, Rene. *Essays on Czech Literature*. The Hague: Mouton, 1963.
Williams, Kieran. Václav Havel. London: Reaktion Books, 2016.
Whitton, David. *Molière: Don Juan*. Cambridge: Cambridge University Press, 1995.

PUBLICATIONS IN CZECH (BY AUTHOR ACCORDING TO THE CZECH ALPHABET)

Avantgarda bez legend a mýtů. Radio cycle in 15 parts. Cyclostyled version issued "only for the specialist needs of a narrow circle of listeners." S.l., s.n., 1967.
Barta, Petr. *Sametové rovnoběžky Černého divadla*. Prague: Mladá fronta, 1983.
Bass, Eduard. *Jak se dělá kabaret*. Prague: Springer, 1917.
Bernard, Jan. *Evald Schorm a jeho filmy*. Prague: Primus, 1994.
Bogatyrev, Petr. *Lidové divadlo české a slovenské*. Prague: František Borový, 1940.

Boková, Marie, and Miroslav Klíma. *Jan Grossman*. Vols. I, II. Prague: Pražská scéna, 1996, 1997.
Bošek, Pavel. *Redutání*. Československý spisovatel, Prague 1970.
Bošek, Pavel. *Z repertoáru malé scény*. 2 vols. Prague: DILIA, 1964, 1965.
Brabec, Jiří et al., eds. *Slovník českých spisovatelů*. Toronto: 68 Publishers, 1982.
Brůna, Otakar. *Synkopy před útokem*. Prague: Naše vojsko, 1966.
Brušák, Karel. *České drama*. S.l., s.d. Typescript lecture notes.
Burian, E. F. *Pražská dramaturgie*. Prague: private publication, 1938.
Burian, E. F. *Pojďte, lidé, na divadla s železnýma kladivama*. Prague: Českomoravský kompas, 1940.
Burian, E. F. *Zahajujeme*. Prague: Svoboda, 1938.
Burian, E. F. *O nové divadlo 1930–1940*. Prague: Ústav pro učebně pomůcky průmyslových a odborných škol, 1946.
Burian, Jan. *Nežádoucí návraty E. F. Buriana*. Prague: Galén, 2012.
Císař, Jan. *Život jeviště*. Prague: Orbis, 1962.
Císař, Jan. *Divadlo, která našla svou dobu*. Prague: Orbis, 1966.
Čapek, Karel. *Divadelníkem proti své vůli*. Prague: Orbis, 1968.
Černý, František. *Theater / Divadlo*. Prague: Orbis, 1965.
Černý, František, ed. *Dějiny českého divadlo*. 4 vols. Prague: Academia, 1968, 1969, 1977, 1983.
Černý, František. *Měnivá tvář divadla*. Prague: Mladá fronta, 1978.
Černý, František. *Divadlo v bariérách normalizace*. Prague: Divadelní ústav, 2008.
Černý, Jindřich. *Otomar Krejča*. Prague: Orbis, 1964.
Černý, Jindřich. *Jiřina Štěpničková*. Prague: Nakladatelství Brána, 1996.
Černý, Jindřich. *Osudy českého divadla po druhé světové válce*. Prague: Academia, 2007.
Černý, Jiří. *Zpěváci bez konservatoře*. Prague: Československý spisovatel, 1966.
Červený, Jiří. *Červená sedma*. Prague: Orbis, 1959.
Dvorský, Stanislav et al., eds. *Surrealistická východiska 1948–1989*. Prague: Společnost Karla Teiga, 2011.
Dvořák, Antonín. *Trojice nejodvážnějších*. Prague: Orbis, 1961.
Dvořák, Antonín. *Zápisy o divadle*. Prague: Divadelní ústav, 1979.
Dvořák, Jan, Miroslav Krovák, Jan Kolář, Vlasta Gallerová, Vladimír Just, and Milan Obst. *Divadla studiového typu*. Prague: Divadelní ústav, 1980.
Dvořák, Jan, Zuzana Jindrová, and Miloslav Klíma. *Jan Grossman*. Vols. III–V. Prague: Prazská scéna, 1998, 1999, 2000.
Dvořák, Jan, Zuzana Jindrová, Miloslav Klíma, and Miroslava Přikrylová. *Jan Grossman*. Vol. VI. Prague: Prazská scéna, 2001.
Dvořák, Milos. *Kladivadlo*. Trutnov: "PAFI," 1998.
Drozd, David. *Příběhy dlouhého nosu*. Brno: JAMU, 2011.
Graclík, Miroslav, and Václav Nekvapil. *Jiřina Švorcová osobně*. Prague: XYZ, 2010.
Effenberger, Vratislav. *Osvobozené divadlo*. Prague: 1974. Unpublished typescript, lodged in the Theatre Institute.
Fialka, Ladislav. *Umění pantomimy*. Prague: Dům armády, 1964.
Fotíková, Kateřina, Barbara Vrbová, and Petr Oslzlý. *Eva Tálská*. Prague: Prazská scéna, 2011.
Frejka, Jiří, ed. *Deník Jarmily Horákové*. Prague: Českomoravský kompas, 1940.
Frejka, Jiří. *Železná doba divadla*. Prague: Melantrich, 1945.
Frejka, Jiří. *Režie jako projev průbojného ducha*. Edited by Jiří Hajek. Prague: Divadelní ústav, 1980.
Goldstücker, Eduard, ed. *Franz Kafka*. Prague: Československé akademie věd, 1963.
Grossman, Jan. *Král Ubu, rozbor inscenace*. Prague: Divadelní ústav, 1966.

Grossman, Jan. *Analýzy*. Prague: Československý spisovatel, 1991.
Grossman, Jan. *Mezi literaturou a divadlem*. Vols I, II. Prague: Torst, 2013.
Hájková, Gabriela. "Role brněnských studentů a divadelníků v tzv. sametové revoluci 1989." Master's thesis, Masaryk University, 2008.
Havel, Václav. *Protokoly*. Prague: Mladá fronta, 1967.
Havel, Václav. *Václav Havel o divadle*. Edited by Anna Freimanová. Prague: Knihovna Václava Havla, 2012.
Hedvábný, Zdeněk. *Divadlo Větrník*. Prague: Panorama, 1988.
Hedvábný, Zdeněk. *Alfréd Rádok*. Prague: Národní Museum, 1994.
Hercíková, Iva. *Začalo to Redutou*. Prague: Orbis, 1964.
Hoffmeister, Adolf. *Předobrazy*. Prague: Československý spisovatel, 1962.
Holzknecht, Václav. *Jaroslav Ježek & Osvobozené divadlo*. Prague: SNKL, 1957.
Honzl, Jindřich. *Roztočené jeviště*. Prague: Odeon, 1925.
Honzl, Jindřich, *Sláva a bída divadel*. Prague: Vydavatelství Družstevní práce, 1937.
Honzl, Jindřich. *K novému významu umění*. Prague: Orbis, 1956.
Honzl, Jindřich. *Divadélko pro 99*. Prague: Orbis, 1964.
Chramostová, Vlasta. *Chramostová, Vlasta*. Brno: Doplněk, 1999.
Janáčková, Jaroslava. *Gabriela Preissová*. Prague: Academia, 2015.
Jirsíková, Nina. *Vzpominky tanečnice*. Prague: Národní Museum, 2013.
Just, Vladimír, *Herectví Voskovce a Wericha*, Prague: (diploma work) Charles University, 1969.
Just, Vladimír. *Proměny malých scén*. Prague: Mladá fronta, 1984.
Just, Vladimír, ed. *Česká divadelní kultura 1945–1989 v datech a souvislostech*. Prague: Divadelní ústav, 1995.
Just, Vladimír. *Divadlo v totalitním systému*. Prague: Academia, 2010.
Kazda, Jaromír, and Josef Kotek. *Smích Červené sedmy*. Prague: Československý spisovatel, 1981.
Kladiva, Jaroslav. *E. F. Burian*. Prague: Jazz Petit, 1982.
Knopp, František. "Činoherní klub 1965–1968." Master's thesis, Charles University, 1969.
Kočová, Zuzana, ed. *Kronika armádního uměleckého divadla*. Prague: Naše vojska, 1955.
Kočová, Zuzana. *Pět sešitů za začátku*. Prague: Mladá fronta, 1975.
Kočová, Zuzana. "Experiment Maringotka." Prague: Zuzana Kočová's archive (1983), c.1975. Typescript.
Kovalčuk, Josef. *Autorské divadlo 70. let*. Prague: Ústav pro kulturně výchovnou činnost, 1982.
Kovalčuk, Josef, and Petr Oslzlý. *Společný projekt Cesty*. Brno: JAMU, 2011.
Kovalčuk, Josef. *Rozrazil 1/'88 (O demokracie), Historie, analýza a rekonstukce projektu*. Brno: JAMU, 2015.
Kraus, Karel, ed. *O divadle 1986-9*. Prague: Lidové noviny, 1990.
Krejča, Otomar. *Divadlo jsou herci*. Prague: Nakladatelství AMU, 2011.
Kudělka, Viktor. *František Langer: Divadelníkem z vlastní vůle*. Prague: Divadelní ústav, 1985.
Kundera, Milan. *Majitelé klíčů*. Prague: Orbis, 1962.
Langer, František. *Byli a bylo, vzpomínky*. Prague: Československý spisovatel, 1963.
Langer, František, *Byli a bylo*. Expanded 2nd ed. Prague: Československý spisovatel, 1991.
Lazorčáková, Tatjana, and Jan Roubal. *K netradičnému divadlu*. Prague: Pražská scéna, 2003.
Longen, E. A. *Herečka*. Prague: Pokrok, 1929.
Ludvová, Jitka. *Až k hořkému konci*. Prague: Academia, 2012.
Mráček, Vladimír. "Václav Havel a ti druzi." Master's thesis, Charles University, 1969.
Nekolný, Bohumil. *Studiové divadlo a jeho české cesty*. Prague: Nakladatelství a vydavatelství Scéna, 1991.

Obst, Milan, and Adolf Scherl. *K dějinám české divadelní avantgardy*. Prague: Československé akademie věd, 1962.
Oslzlý, Petr. *Divadlo Husa na provázku 1968/7/-1998*. Brno: Centrum experimentalního divadla, 1999.
Oslzlý, Petr. *Commedia dell'arte*. Brno: JAMU, 2010.
Pelc, Jaromír. *Meziválečná avantgarda a Osvobozené divadlo*. Prague: ÚKVČ, 1981.
Pelc, Jaromír. *Zpráva o Osvobozeném divadle*. Prague: Práce, 1982.
Píša, A.M. *Divadelní avantgarda*. Prague, 1978.
Plicková, Karolina. "Pantomima Alfreda Jarryho." Master's thesis, Charles University, 2012.
Pokorný. Jaroslav, ed. *Jindřich Honzl o režii a herectví*. Prague: Divadelní ústav, 1979.
Procházka, Vladimír, ed. *Národní divadlo a jeho přechůdci*. Prague: Academia, 1988.
Ptáčková, Věra. *Česká scenografie XX. století*. Prague: Odeon, 1982.
Pytlík, Radko. *Toulavé housle: zpráva o Jaroslavu Haškovi*. Prague: Mladá fronta, 1971.
Rauchová, Jitka. *Spoutané divadlo*. České Budějovice: Společnost pro kulturní dějiny, 2011.
Rejnuš, Miloš, ed. *Kabaret Večerní Brno*. Prague: Orbis, 1965.
Schonberg, Michal. *Osvobozené*. Translated by Ivo Řezníček. Toronto: Sixty-Eight Publishers, 1988.
Srba, Bořivoj, ed. *E. F. Burian a jeho program poetického divadla*. Prague: Divadelní ústav, 1981.
Srba, Bořivoj, ed. *Inscenační tvorba E. F. Buriana 1939-1941*. Prague: Ústav pro českou a světovou literaturu ČSAV, 1980.
Srba, Bořivoj. Ř*eči světla*. Brno: JAMU, 2004.
Suchý, Jiří. *Semafor*. Prague: Československý spisovatel, 1965.
Suchý, Jiří. "Memoirs." Prague: 1984. Typescript prepared for publication in the journal "*Jonášklub*."
Šmeral, Vladimír. *Hovory o divadle*. Prague: Orbis, 1954.
Šormová, Eva. "Větrník–Divadélko pro 99." Seminar paper, Charles University, 1963/4.
Šormová, Eva, ed. *Encyklopedie divadelních souborů*. Prague: Divadelní ústav, 2000.
Šormová, Eva, ed. *Česká činohra 19. a začátek 20. století, Osobnosti, Vols. I, II*. Prague: Academia, 2015.
Teige, Karel, ed. *Revoluční sborník Devětsil*. Prague: V. Vortel, 1922.
Teige, Karel. *Svět stavby a básně*. Prague: Československý spisovatel, 1966.
Topol, Josef, *Konec masopustu*. Prague: Orbis, 1963.
Träger, Josef. *10 let Osvobozeného divadlo 1927-1937*. Prague: Borový, 1937.
Uhde, Milan. *Rozpomínky. Co na sebe vím*. Prague: Torst, 2013.
Vydra, Václav. *Prosím o slovo*. Prague: Českomoravský Kompas, 1940.
Wenig, Adolf, ed. *K základům Národního divadla*. Prague: František Topič, 1918.

WORKS IN GERMAN

Bečvová, Romana. "Beteiligt Euch: es geht um Eure Erde." Master's thesis, Masaryk University, 2007.

SELECTED PERIODICALS (ENGLISH LANGUAGE)

Czechoslovak Life, Prague: Orbis, 1947–1992.
Index on Censorship, London: Writers & Scholars Educational Trust, 1972.
New Theatre Quarterly (*Theatre Quarterly*), Cambridge: Cambridge Uuniveristy Press, 1981.
The Spectator, London: The Spectator, 1828.
TDR: The Drama Review (*Carlton/Tulane Drama Review*), Cambridge, MA: MIT Press, 1955.

The Theatre Journal (*Educational Theatre Journal*), Baltimore: Johns Hopkins University Press, 1949.
Theatre Survey, Boulder: The American Society for Theatre Research, 1960.
World and Theatre, Prague: Svět a divadlo, 2009.

SELECTED PERIODICALS (CZECH LANGUAGE)

Acta Scaenographica. Prague: Scénografická laboratoř; Scénografický ústav, 1960–1971.
Amatérská scéna. Prague: Orbis; IPOS; NIPOS, 1964.
Divadelní noviny. Prague: Svaz čs. divadelních umělců, 1957–1970.
Divadelní noviny. Prague: Společnost pro *Divadelní noviny*, 1992.
Divadelní revue. Prague: Divadelní ústav, 1989.
Divadlo. Prague: Umění lidu; Ministerstvo školství, věd a umění; Československý spisovatel; Ministerstvo školství a kultury; Svaz čs. spisovatelů; Svaz čs. divadelních a filmových umělců; Svaz českých divadelních a rozhlasových umělců, 1949–1970.
Dramatické umění. Prague: Svaz českých dramatických umělců, 1982–1990.
Literární noviny. Prague: Svaz čs. spisovatelů, 1952–1967.
Listy (*Literární listy*). Prague: Svaz čs. spisovatelů, 1968–1969.
O divadle. Prague: samizdat, 1986–1988.
Plamen. Prague: Svaz čs. Spisovatelů, 1959–1969.
Repertoár malých scén. Prague: Orbis, 1963–1971.
Scéna. Prague: Svaz českých dramatických umělců, 1976–1992.
Svět a divadlo. Prague: Svět a divadlo, 1990.

NOTES

1 The discussion was published as "ještě jednou obrození?" in *Divadlo*, January 1969. Participants included, in addition to Grossman, Havel, and Uhde, the theatre critics Zdeněk Hořínek, Jindřich Černý, and Milan Obst.

2 "Petition to the Prague Town Council for a Czech theatre company, 10 August 1784," tr. Jitka Martin, in Barbara Day (ed.) "Czech Lands (Bohemia and Moravia), 1784–1881" in Laurence Senelick (ed.), *National Theatre in Northern and Eastern Europe, 1746–1900*, pp. 232-233.

3 Jan Císař, *The History of Czech Theatre*, p. 40.

4 *Národní noviny* 18 April 1849, in Stanley Bucholz Kimball, *Czech Nationalism*, p. 32.

5 "Kolár registers a complaint against Tyl for assault in 1841," tr. Jitka Martin, in Senelick (ed.), *National Theatre in Northern and Eastern Europe*, op. cit., pp. 252–254.

6 František Adolf Šubert, *Národní divadlo v Praze: dějiny jeho i stavba dokončená*, tr. Jitka Martin, quoted in Senelick (ed.), *National Theatre in Northern and Eastern Europe*, op. cit., pp. 261–262.

7 Jan Bartoš, *Národní divadlo a jeho budovatelé*, tr. Jitka Martin, quoted in Senelick (ed.), *National Theatre in Northern and Eastern Europe*, op. cit., pp. 263.

8 Tomáš Vlček, "National Sensualism" in László Péter and Robert B. Pynsent (eds.), *Intellectuals and the Future in the Habsburg Monarchy 1890–1914*, p. 109.

9 *Upomínka na slavnostní položení základního kamene k velikému národnímu divadlu českému v Praze*, tr. Jitka Martin, quoted in Senelick (ed.), *National Theatre in Northern and Eastern Europe*, op. cit., pp. 264–265.

10 Jan Neruda, "Slavnost je skončena" in Jan Neruda (ed. Adolf Wenig), *K základům* Národního divadla (1918).

11 *Deutsche Zeitung*, 14 August 1881, quoted in *Národní listy*, 16 August 1881, quoted in Kimball, *Czech Nationalism*, op. cit., p. 142.

12 Alois and Vilém Mrštík, *Maryša*, in *Visegrad Drama I*, p. 42.

13 Jaroslav Vrchlický in *Hlas národu*, quoted in Eva Hrabalová, "Dramata *Gazdina roba* a *Její pastorkyňa* a jejich operní adaptace," diploma work, Masaryk University, Brno 2010, p. 24.

14 František Langer, *Byli a bylo, vzpomínky*, 2nd. ed. 1991. p. 288-289.

15 Císař, *The History of Czech Theatre*, op. cit., p. 207.

16 See Robert B. Pynsent, "The Decadent Nation" in Péter and Pynsent (eds.), *Intellectuals and the Future in the Habsburg Monarchy*, op. cit.

17 František Langer, *Byli a bylo, vzpomínky*, 1st. ed. 1963, p. 30.

18 Eduard Bass, *Jak se dělá kabaret*, p. 7.

19 Johannes Urzidil, "In Expressionist Prague," tr. J. M. Ritchie, in Paul Raabe, *The Era of German Expressionism*, p. 66 (original article "Im Prag des Expressionismus," *Imprimatur*, New Series Vol 3., 1961–1962, pp. 202–204).

20 Ibid., p. 63.

21 Unsigned article in *Divadelní listy*, 1883, no. 21, p.178, quoted by Veronika Ambros in "Výměny symbolů

aneb německé divadlo v Praze mezi válkami, národy a kulturami" in *Sborník prací Filozofické fakulty brněnské univerzity Studia minora Facultatis philosophicae Universitatis Brunensis* Q6 / 2003.

22 Max Brod (ed.), *The Diaries of Franz Kafka*, p.70.

23 František Langer, "Divadlo," *Umělecký měsíčník*, III, 1913-1914, no.1, quoted in Viktor Kudělka, *František Langer: Divadelníkem z vlastní vůle*.

24 Vlastislav Hofman, "The Stage Shaped Pictorially" translated by David Short in Mahulena Nešlehová (ed.), *Vlastislav Hofman*, pp. 386-387 (original article "Obrazově formovaná scena." *Scéna 1*, 1913, no. 2 pp. 4-9.

25 Věra Ptáčková, *Česká scenografie XX. století*, p. 24.

26 Jindřich Honzl, "O scénické drama," *Kmen* year III (1920), nos. 36-37 in Honzl, *K novému významu umění*, Orbis 1950, p. 44.

27 Václav Vydra, *Prosím o slovo*, p. 77.

28 Max Brod (ed.), *The Diaries of Franz Kafka*, p.57.

29 E. A. Longen, *Herečka*, p. 163.

30 Karel Teige, "Umění dnes a zítra," *Revoluční sborník Devětsil*, p. 200.

31 Václav Holzknecht, "Avantgarda s hudbou a tancem," *Divadelní noviny*, 19 April 1967, p. 6.

32 Ibid, p.7.

33 Quoted by Adolf Hoffmeister in *Předobrazy*, p. 41.

34 Quoted in the radio series *Avantgarda bez legend a mýtů*, broadcast 4, pp. 4-5.

35 Ibid, broadcast 4, pp. 5.

36 Ibid, broadcast 4, p. 19.

37 Ibid, broadcast 4, p. 18.

38 Arthur Koestler, Chapter XVIII "Infolding" in *The Act of Creation* (1964).

39 Josef Träger, *10 let Osvobozeného divadlo*, p. 55.

40 Josef Zora, quoted in *Avantgarda bez legend a mýtů*, broadcast 6, pp. 3.

41 Jindřich Honzl, *K novému významu umění*, p. 121.

42 *Večerník Rudého právo*, 1.3.26, quoted in Jiří Hajek (ed.), *Jiří Frejka*, p.14.

43 *Host*, May 1924.

44 Karel Teige, *Svět stavby a básně*, p.158.

45 Jiří Frejka (ed.), *Deník Jarmily Horákové*, 1940, p. 148.

46 Quoted in František Černý, *Měnivá tvář divadla*.

47 Hajek (ed.), *Jiří Frejka*, op. cit., p.18.

48 Ibid, p. 17.

49 Jaromír Pelc, *Meziválečná avantgarda a Osvobozené divadlo*, preface.

50 Teige, *Svět stavby a básně*, op. cit., p.162.

51 A. M. Píša, *Divadelní avantgarda*, p. 13.

52 E. F. Burian, "Maskovaný konzervatismus," *Tam-tam* 1, no. 5, December 1925.

53 Letter from Leoš Janáček to Max Brod in *Lidové Noviny*, 13 February 1927, in Mirka Zemanová (ed.), *Janáček's Uncollected Essays on Music*, p. 106.

54 Bořivoj Srba (ed.), *E. F. Burian a jeho program poetického divadla*, p. 11.

55 Ibid, p. 11.

56 From *Lidové Noviny*, 6 April 1918, in Zemanová (ed.), *Janáček's Uncollected Essays on Music*, op. cit., p. 42.

57 Srba (ed.), *E. F. Burian a jeho program poetického divadla*, op. cit., p. 25.

58 Ibid, p. 27.

59 Jarmila Kröschlová, "S Osvobozenými," *Divadelní noviny*, 19 April 1967, p.7.

60 Jiří Voskovec, *Klobouk ve křoví*, Československý spisovatel 1965, p.120.

61 Quoted in Antonín Dvořák, *Zápisy o divadle*, p. 185.

62 Letter to *ReD* I, 1928 no. 7, quoted in Jaromír Pelc, *Zpráva o Osvobozeném divadle*, p. 35

63 Vilém and Margaret Tauský (ed.), *Leoš Janáček: Leaves from his Life*, p. 48.

64 Vratislav Effenberger, *Osvobozené divadlo*, appendix.

65 Píša, *Divadelní avantgarda*, op. cit., p. 43.

66 Milan Obst and Adolf Scherl, *K dějinám české divadelní avantgardy*, p. 187.

67 Jiří Frejka, "Nezvalovi Milenci z kiosku," *Národní divadlo*, year 9, no 24, 1932, reprinted in Jiří Frejka (ed. Jiří Hájek), *Rezie jako projev průbojného ducha*, p. 100.

68 *Žijeme*, year 2, no.1, 1932, p. 22.

69 Michael L. Quinn, *The Semiotic Stage*, pp. 71-79; Luděk Ondruška, www.phil.muni.cz/udim/avantgarda/index.php?pg=o_zich accessed 11 March 2017.

70 Jindřich Honzl, "Dynamics of the Sign in the Theatre" in Ladislav Matejka and Irwin R.Titunik, *Semiotics of Art*, originally published as "Pohyb divadelního znaku" in *Slovo a slovesnost*, 6, 1940.

71 Quoted in *Avantgarda bez legend a mýtů*, broadcast 13, p. 17.
72 Lawrence Senelick, "The Accidental Evolution of the Moscow Art Theatre Prague Group," *New Theatre Quarterly*, Vol. 30 (2), May 2014, pp. 154–167.
73 Honzl, *K novému významu umění*, op. cit., p. 170.
74 Effenberger, *Osvobozené divadlo*, op. cit., p. 106.
75 Jan Werich and Jiři Voskovec, *Hry Osvobozeného divadla*, vol. 2, p. 177.
76 Quoted in Srba, *E. F. Burian a jeho program poetického divadla*, op. cit., p. 177.
77 Quoted in *Avantgarda bez legend a mýtů*, broadcast 5, pp. 1.
78 Letter to Werich and Voskovec, 29 January 1935, quoted in Zuzana Kočová (ed.), *Kronika Armádního uměleckého divadla*, pp. 138–139.
79 Quoted in Kočová (ed.), *Kronika*, op. cit., p. 205.
80 Jindřich Vodák, "České lidové písně v D35," *České slovo*, 24 January 1935, quoted in Jaroslav Kladiva, *E. F. Burian*, p. 158.
81 Kladiva, *E. F. Burian*, op. cit., p. 155.
82 E. F. Burian, "Pražská dramaturgie" in *O nové divadlo*, p.78.
83 Jan Grossman, "25. let světelného divadla," *Acta scaenographica*, April 1961, p. 178.
84 Karel Čapek, *Divadelníkem proti své vůli*, p. 92.
85 Träger, *10 let Osvobozeného divadlo*, op. cit., p. 105.
86 Pelc, *Zpráva o Osvobozeném divadle*, op. cit., p. 171.
87 Václav Holzknecht, *Jaroslav Ježek*, p. 43.
88 Zuzana Kočová, *Pět sešitů ze začátku*, p. 156.
89 E. F. Burian (ed. Jan Kopecký), *Divadlo za našich dnů*, p. 17.
90 František Halas quoted in Jan Grossman, "Halas esejista" in Grossman, *Mezi literaturou a divadlem I.*, p. 533.
91 Quoted in Kočová (ed.), *Kronika*, op. cit., p. 419
92 Jan Rocek, *My Life*, http://rocek.knowtheworld.org/memoirs.pdf retrieved 23 June 2013.
93 Kočová, *Pět sešitů ze začátku*, op. cit., p. 174.
94 Jan Burian, "Dopis o hloubce jedné tragédie / leden 2011" in Jan Burian (ed.), *nežádoucí návraty e.f. buriana*, p. 417.
95 Antonín Dvořák, "Vzpominky na Honzlovo Divadélko pro 99" in Jindřich Honzl, *Divadélko pro 99*, p. 216.
96 *Divadélko pro 99*, op. cit., p. 32.
97 Ibid, p. 27.
98 Ibid, p. 32.
99 Quoted in Helena Albertová, *Josef Svoboda Scenographer*, p. 13.
100 Conversation with Jan Kopecký, 8 February 1983.
101 Nina Jirsíková, "Pohádka o tanci" in František Černý, *Theater/Divadlo*, p. 255.
102 Milan Kundera, *The Book of Laughter and Forgetting*, p. 8.
103 R. M. Douglas, *Orderly and Humane*, Yale University Press, 2012.
104 Conversation with Zdeněk Míka, 21 April 1984.
105 Otomar Krejča, "Ještě jednou se vratíme myšlení," *Divadlo*, 1953, p. 916.
106 Conversation with Jan Grossman, 9 December 1982.
107 Jan Skoupý, "Divadlo plné komiků," *Ahoj na sobotu*, 16 February 1973.
108 Ján Kalina, "Bojová satira a malé dramatické formy," *Divadlo*, 1953, p. 476.
109 Jindřich Honzl, "Milý Voskovče a Wericha," *Otazky divadla a filmu*, October 1946, p. 42.
110 Jindřich Černý, *Osudy českého divadla po druhé světové válce*, p. 115.
111 Ladislav Mňačko, *The Seventh Night*, p. 77.
112 Kundera, *The Book of Laughter and Forgetting*, op. cit., p. 8.
113 "THE PRINCIPAL PARAGRAPHS FROM THE ACT OF MARCH 20th, 1948 *by which are established the basic provisions for the setting up of theatres and for theatrical activity (Theatre Act)*" in Jindřich Honzl (ed.), *The Czechoslovak Theatre*, pp. 11–21.
114 Otakar Šourek, quoted by Brian S. Locke, *Opera and Ideology in Prague*, pp. 129–130.
115 Jana Machalická, "Nejedlý byl žába na pramení české kultury…" *Lidové noviny*, 19 August 2004.
116 František Götz, "Vývojová logika českého dramatu v desetiletí po osvobození," *Divadlo* 1955, p. 343.
117 Ibid, p. 342.
118 Ibid, p. 343.
119 *Divadlo*, 1957, p. 104.
120 Ivan Vyskočil, "The Incredible Rise of Albert Uruk," in Theiner (ed.), *New Writing in Czechoslovakia*, p. 227.
121 Vladimír Šmeral, *Hovory o divadle*, p. 147.

122 Černý, *Osudy českého divadla*, op. cit., p. 307.
123 Dyneley Hussey, "*Hansel and Gretel* and *The Bartered Bride*," *The Spectator*, 8 November 1943.
124 Franklin Rosemont, *André Breton and the First Principles of Surealism*, p. 52.
125 Jaroslav Seifert, "On Teige: A Dance Macabre in Smíchov" in George Gibian (ed.) *The Poetry of Jaroslav Seifert*, pp. 224–232.
126 Jitka Rauchová, *Spoutané divadlo*, pp. 171.
127 Karel Kraus, "Frejka," *Divadelní noviny*, 3 June 1964, p. 5.
128 Andrei Zhdanov, "Soviet literature: The Richest in Ideas, the Most Advanced Literature" in H. F. Scott (ed.) *Problems of Soviet Literature: Reports and Speeches at the First Soviet Writers' Congress*, International Publishers, New York 1935.
129 Zdeněk Hedbávný, *Alfréd Radok*, p. 163.
130 Rauchová, *Spoutané divadlo*, op. cit., pp. 138–139.
131 Jaroslav Opavský, "Za Jindřichem Honzlem," *Divadlo* 1953, p. 687
132 Conversation with Jan Grossman, 9 December 1982.
133 Record of the plenary meeting of D50 on 20 October 1949, quoted in Burian (ed.), *nežádoucí návraty*, op. cit., pp. 206–207.
134 E. F. Burian, "Co nám řekl EFB," *Divadlo* 1957, p. 281.
135 Sergej Machonin in *Literární noviny*, quoted in František Vrba, "Vojna," *Divadlo* 1955, p. 971.
136 Pavel Kohout, "Otázka E. F. Burianovi," *Divadelní noviny*, 29 April 1959.
137 František Černý, "Bylo to v noci," *Divadelní noviny*, 17 December 1969.
138 Jana Patočková, "Pařížský festival 1956 a Krejčův nástup do vedení činohry ND" in *Divadelní revue*, 2009/2.
139 Jindřich Černý, *Otomar Krejča*, p. 12.
140 Otomar Krejča, "Co je režisérismus?," *Divadelní zapisník*, 1946, 5/6.
141 Jaroslav Opavský in *Rudé právo* 30 November 1949, quoted in Černý, *Osudy českého divadla*, op. cit., p. 215.
142 Otomar Krejča, "*Půlnoční vítr* (Úvaha nad rukopisem)," *Divadlo*, 1955, p. 482
143 Michael Alexander, "Czechs pull up the Curtain," *Picture Post*, 11 May 1957, p. 24.
144 Miroslav Horníček, "ESEJ," in Jiří Suchý (ed.), *Semafor*, p. 200.
145 Jiří Suchý, typescript memoirs, p. 23.
146 *Universita Karlova*, May 1961 (special edition).
147 Tomáš Havlín and Jan Kubíček, "Být ve vztahu je důležitý" (interview with Ivan Vyskočil) in *Nový prostor*, 26 June 2012, pp. 18–21.
148 Howey, *Who's Afraid of Franz Kafka?*, op. cit., p. 88.
149 *Universita Karlova*, May 1961, op. cit..
150 Jiří Černý, *Zpěváci bez konzervatoře*, p.7.
151 Jitka Bodláková, Ivan Vyskočil, "Pobídky Ivan Vyskočila," *Divadelní noviny*, 11 January 1967, p. 6.
152 Dagmar Cimická, "Hölderlin: 'Člověk dostal řeč, aby poznal, kým jest,'" *Zemědělské noviny*, 10 December 1968.
153 Jiří Suchý, typescript memoirs, p. 69.
154 Císař, *Divadla, která našla svou dobu*, op. cit., p. 71.
155 Iva Hercíková (ed.), *Začalo to Redutou*, p.11.
156 Bodláková, Vyskočil, op. cit., *Divadelní noviny*, 25 January 1967, p.6.
157 Conversation with Jiří Suchý, 14 December 1982.
158 Nicholas Howey, *Who's Afraid of Franz Kafka?*, p. 264.
159 Jan Císař, *Divadla, která našla svou dobu*, p. 36.
160 Ibid. p. 37.
161 Jan Grossman, review under "Inscenace 1960–61," *Acta Scaenographica*, October 1960.
162 Svoboda quoted in Albertová, *Josef Svoboda*, op. cit., p. 48.
163 Černý, *Otomar Krejča*, op. cit., p. 82.
164 Albertová, *Josef Svoboda*, op. cit., p. 62.
165 Milan Kundera, postscript in Milan Kundera, *Majitelé klíčů*, p. 83.
166 Ibid, p. 84.
167 Otomar Krejča, insert with director's notes in Kundera, *Majitelé klíčů*, op. cit., p. 7.
168 Černý, *Otomar Krejča*, op. cit., p.112.
169 Josef Topol, *The End of Shrovetide*, in *The Sixties*, p. 41.
170 Ibid., p. 21.
171 Eva Stehlíková, "Radokovo Otvírání studánek" in *Divadelní revue* 2006/2, pp. 19–33.
172 *Kdyby tisíc klarinetů...*, programme note.
173 Conversation with Antonín Moskalyk, 23 April 1984.

174 Milan Lukeš, "Když všichni dělají všechno," *Divadlo* 1959/2.
175 jk (Jan Kopecký), "Nadejná skupina divadelní," *Divadelní noviny*, 24 December 1958.
176 *Universita Karlova*, 19 October 1961.
177 Otakar Brůna, *Synkopy před útokem*, p. 48.
178 Ibid.
179 Ludvík Veselý, "Faust a Bapopo," *Literární noviny*, 27 June 1959, p. 6.
180 František Černý, "Faust na Zábradlí," *Divadelní noviny*, 10 June 1959, p. 5.
181 Ibid.
182 Veselý, "Faust a Bapopo," op. cit.
183 *Svět v obrazech*, 21 January 1967.
184 *Fools*, English-language programme note.
185 Ibid.
186 Ibid.
187 Harold Hobson, "Glory at the last minute," *The Sunday Times*, 4 June 1967.
188 Gm (Pavel Grym), "Mladí pro mladé," *Lidová demokracie*, 6 November 1959.
189 Petr Bárta, *Sametové rovnoběžky Černého divadla*, p. 56.
190 František Černý, "Papoušek a vlk," *Divadelní noviny*, 9 December 1959.
191 Marcela Pecháčková, "Prokop Voskovec: Ani hlt vína pro básníka," *Instinkt*, 24 February 2011.
192 Václav Havel, "Ubu králem," *Divadelní noviny*, 15 February 1961, republished in Václav Havel, *Eseje a jine texty z let 1953–1969*, p.408.
193 Vladimír Justl, "Kdo umí, nechť pomůže!" *Divadelní noviny*, 7 December 1960, p.4.
194 ml (Milan Lukeš), "Herci Na zábradlí," *Divadlo* 1960, p. 541.
195 Ivan Vyskočil and Václav Havel, *Autostop*, p. 69.
196 Jan Grossmann (sic), "Autostop!" *Divadelní noviny*, 24 May 1961, pp. 3–4.
197 *Universita Karlova*, 19 October 1961.
198 Ivan Vyskočil, "Nevzpominky," *Divadelní noviny*, 6 November 1968, p.5.
199 Jan Grossman, "Proměna divadlo?" *Literarní noviny*, 14 September 1963.
200 Jan Grossman, "Svět malého divadla," *Divadlo* 1963/7, pp. 13–22.
201 Jan Grossman, Ibid. p. 18.
202 Jan Grossman, programme note for *Nejlepší rocky paní Hermanové*, republished in Jan Grossman, *Mezi literaturou a divadlem II*, p. 1085.
203 Sergej Machonin, "Satira o parazitech socialism," *Literární noviny*, 10 November 1962.
204 ml (Milan Lukeš), "Léta a Rocky," *Divadlo* 1963/2, p. 53.
205 "Svět malého divadla," op. cit.
206 Vladimír Justl, "Náhoda, nebo záměr?" *Divadelní noviny*, 9 January 1962.
207 Jan Grossman, programme note for *Nejlepší rocky paní Hermanové.*
208 Jan Grossman, programme note for *Hrdinové v Thébách nebydlí*; also Jan Grossman, "Claus Hubalek, Hrdinové v Thébách nebydlí" in Grossman, *Mezi literaturou a divadlem II*, p. 1088.
209 Radim Vašinka and Jan Grossman, *Vyšinutá hrdlička* in *Repertoár malé scény*, vol. 1–4, 1963, p. 27.
210 Ibid, p. 32.
211 Ibid, p. 35.
212 Císař, *Divadla, která našla svou dobu*, op. cit., pp. 55–56.
213 Jindřich Černý, "Scenický grenóbl," *Lidová demokracie*, 13 February 1963.
214 Karel Kraus, "Zábradlí jako typ," *Divadlo* 1963/8.
215 "Svět malého divadla," op. cit..
216 Vašinka and Grossman, *Vyšinutá hrdlička*, op. cit., p. 41.
217 Ibid., p. 39.
218 Václav Havel, *The Garden Party*, in Havel, *The Garden Party and Other Plays*, p. 10.
219 Ibid, pp. 13–14. In Vera Blackwell's translation this character is renamed Maxy Falk.
220 Ibid, p. 23.
221 Ibid, p. 50.
222 Quoted in Kenneth Tynan, "Withdrawing with Style from the Chaos," *The New Yorker*, 19 December 1977.
223 Howey, *Who's Afraid of Franz Kafka?*, op. cit., p. 141.
224 Jan Grossman, "Předmluva" in Václav Havel, *Protokoly*, p. 9.
225 Pavel Grym, "Vyrozumění. Václav Havel o cestě k divadlu," *Lidová demokracie*, 18 July 1965.
226 Karel Kraus, "Zábradlí jako typ," *Divadlo*, 1963/7, p. 41.
227 Paul Trensky, "Václav Havel and the Language of the Absurd," *The Slavic and East European Journal*, Vol. 13, no. 1, Spring 1969.

228 *The Garden Party*, op. cit., p. 3.
229 Jan Grossman, *Král Ubu* (rozbor inscenace 4), p. 6.
230 Peter Brook, *The Empty Stage*, p. 78.
231 Ronald Bryden, "A Monster of Explosiveness," *The Observer*, 28 April 1968.
232 *Král Ubu*, op. cit., p. 3.
233 Zdeněk Hořínek, "Zastavení na Zabradlí," *Divadlo*, 1965/8.
234 Ibid.
235 "Předmluva" in *Protokoly*, op. cit., p. 10.
236 Sergej Machonin, "Vyrozumění," *Literarní noviny*, 2 October 1965, p.5.
237 Vojtěch Měšťan, "Chvilka s hercem (Jan Libíček)," *Divadelní noviny*, 12 May 1965.
238 Jaroslav Opavský in *Plamen*, 1962/2 (Opavský usually wrote for the Party daily, *Rudé právo*).
239 hs, "Šest postav našlo autora," *Divadlo* 1966/4, p. 72.
240 V. V. Kusin, *The Intellectual Origins of the Prague Spring*, p. 64.
241 Eduard Goldstücker et al. (eds), *Franz Kafka* (proceedings of the Liblice conference 1963), p. 7.
242 Jan Grossman, "Kafkova divadelnost?" *Divadlo* 1964/9, p. 13.
243 František Lebenhart, Jan Grossman, "Kafka's *Trial*," *Czechoslovak Life*, November 1966.
244 Jindřich Černý, "Klec vyšla hledat ptáka," *Divadelní noviny*, 29 June 1966.
245 Miloš Smetana, Jan Přeučil, "My jsme cizinou bloudili," *Divadelní noviny*, 13 March 1968.
246 Ronald Bryden, "Salute to World Beaters," *The Observer*, 4 June 1967.
247 Jan Císař, "Hra na Zuzanku," *Plamen*, May 1968.
248 Václav Havel, *The Increased Difficulty of Concentration*, in Havel, *The Garden Party*, op. cit., p. 148.
249 Josef Šafařík, "Doslov," in Václav Havel, *Ztížená možnost soustředění*, p. 73.
250 Vladimír Just, *Divadlo v totalitním systému: Příběh českého divadla (1945–1989) nejen v datech a souvislostech*, p. 74 (quoted by Karolina Plicková in "Pantomima Alfreda Jarryho," diploma work, Charles University, Prague 2012, p. 21).
251 Hercíková (ed.), *Začalo to Redutou*, op. cit., p. 124.
252 Jiří Suchý (ed.), *Semafor*, p. 188.
253 Ibid, p. 203.
254 Sleeve notes to the LP *Jiří Suchý & Jiří Šlitr & Divadlo Semafor 1959–1969*, Record 2 of 3, Supraphon 1978.
255 Jaroslav Vostrý, "Jonáš a souvislosti," *Divadlo*, 1963/7.
256 Leoš Suchařípa and Vlastimil Urban, "Mít lepší pamět" (interview with Jiří Suchý), *Divadelní noviny*, 5 September 1962.
257 Editor's reply to letter from Zora Jiráková, "Jiří Suchý a profesionalismus," *Divadelní noviny*, 31 October 1962.
258 Jiří Suchý, Vladimír Justl, "Semafor, mládež a umění," *Kulturní tvorba*, 6 August 1964.
259 Sergej Machonin, "Takové ztráty příležitostí," *Literární noviny*, 19 November 1960.
260 Suchý (ed.), *Semafor*, op. cit., p. 184.
261 Císař, *Divadla, která našla svou dobu*, op. cit., p. 96.
262 Václav Havel, "Několik slov o Paravanu," *Divadlo* 1959, p. 790.
263 Letter from Josef Škvorecký, 30 September 1984, author's archive.
264 Zdeněk Heřman, "Zábava korunovaná a zábava za koruny," *Divadlo* 1965/4.
265 Ladislav Smoček in *Mladý svět* 3.12.65, quoted in František Knopp, *Činoherní klub 1965_1968*, p. 13.
266 Jaroslav Vostrý, "Slovo bez definitivy," *Divadlo* 1964/8.
267 Knopp, Činoherní klub, op. cit., p. 9–10.
268 Jaroslav Vostrý, notes to the LP record *Pražský Činoherní klub a jeho inscenace*, Gramofonový klub 1969.
269 Zprávy SČDU, quoted in Knopp, Činoherní klub, op. cit., p. 3.
270 Alena Vostrá, Jaroslav Vostrý, dramaturges' notes to *Na koho to slovo padne, Divadlo* 1967/1.
271 Irving Wardle, "Real Comedy," *The Times*, 24 April 1970.
272 Irving Wardle, "Integrated Company," *The Times*, 15 April 1970.
273 Kenneth Tynan, "The Theatre Abroad: Prague," *The New Yorker*, 1 April 1967.
274 Valeria Sochorovská, "Láska vzdor a život," *Divadelní noviny*, 19 November 1969.
275 Milan Obst, "utěcha z cimrmanologie," *Divadlo* 1969/9–10.
276 Ibid.
277 Otomar Krejča, "Za branou přede dveřmi," *Divadelní noviny*, 17 November 1965.
278 "World Theatre Season 71—what you need to know," *Plays and Players*, March 1971.
279 Krejča, "Za branou přede dveřmi," op. cit.
280 Hilary Spurling, "Strait is the Gate," *The Spectator*, 2 May 1969.
281 Conversation with Karel Kraus, 15 May 1984.

282 Tereza Divišová, "Divadlo za branou," diploma work, Charles University, Prague 2006, p. 81.
283 Leoš Suchařípa, Otomar Krejča, "kazdá krajnost je trochu hloupá," *Divadlo* 1967/1.
284 Zdeněk Heřman, "Zábava korunovaná a zábava za koruny," *Divadlo* 1965/4.
285 Milan Uhde, *Král Vávra*, in *Divadlo* 1964/10.
286 Václav Havel, "Letter to Gustáv Husák," in Jan Vladislav (ed.), *Václav Havel or Living in Truth* (1986), p. 25.
287 Jan Kopecký, quoted in Jakob Jakeš, Matěj Spurný, Katka Volná et al., *Náměstí krasnoarmějců 2: Učitelé a studenti Filozofické fakulty UK v období normalizace*, Filozofická fakulta Karlovy univerzity, Prague 2012, pp. 129–130.
288 Milan Uhde, *Rozpomínky, co na sebe vím*, Torst/Host, Brno 2013, p. 281.
289 *iDNES.cz*, 8.8.2009, https://brno.idnes.cz/disident-milan-uhde-zazil-nejvetsi-dramata-v-zivote-vlastni-rodiny-1pg-/brno-zpravy.aspx?c=A090804_1235222_brno_krc (retrieved 7 December 2014)
290 Quoted in Barbara Day (ed.), *Czech Plays* (1991), preface, p. xiii.
291 Hana Kasalová, *Postoje české veřejnosti k dramatickému umění*, Praha 1978, p. 135.
292 Ibid., English summary, p. 232.
293 Jan Grossman, letter to *Divadelní noviny*, reproduced in Jan Grossman, *Mezi literaturou a divadlem II.* (2014), pp. 1255–1256.
294 Milan Kundera, *Ptákovina*, in *Divadlo* 1969/1.
295 Howey, *Who's Afraid of Franz Kafka?*, op. cit., p. 159.
296 Alena Slánská, "Drápkem uviz..." *Divadelní noviny*, 26 February 1969.
297 "Czech theatre visit"; letter from the artistic director of the World Theatre Season (Peter Daubeny), *The Times*, 14 April 1971.
298 "World Theatre Season 71—what you need to know," op. cit.
299 Otomar Krejča in conversation with Ladislava Petišková, "Být věrný sám sobě," *Scéna* 17, 28 August 1989. I had mislaid the source of this quotation and looked for it in materials dated after November 1989, by chance asking Ladislava Petišková for help. When I traced the reference to her article, I wrote to tell her and received the reply: "It really didn't occur to me to look for the reference to Otomar Krejča in my own article! It's news from the last century, from an age when we were getting signals of better times ahead. Jan Dvořák had arranged for me to interview O.K. and published it in instalments. I remember very well how he drove me by car for the first time, in a good mood, looking forward to the future in spite of all the hardships. That made his end in the Theatre Beyond the Gate all the more cruel (in 1990–91 he allowed me to sit in on his rehearsals for *The Cherry Orchard*), after which I wrote a criticism for *Lidové noviny* on the same theme and recorded a programme about it for Czech Radio, etc. I followed his career to the bitter end—I always valued him, whether he was the subject of adoration, or cast aside. In the 1960s he also briefly taught the theory of directing to my year group at the Arts Faculty of the Charles University, and I was always aware that it was above all his work and ideas that that stamped themselves on my view of the theatre. Your letter has recalled for me one of my happiest professional encounters. Very many thanks." —Ladislava Petišková, email to the author, 28 August 2017 (translated by the author).
300 Kateřina Macháčková, *Téma Macháček*, Nakladatelství XYZ, Prague 2010, p. 182.
301 Miroslav Macháček, *Zápisky z blázince*, Český spisovatel, Prague 1995.
302 For example, Aleš Fuchs, "Zničili režiséři divadlo?" *Scéna 18*, 29 August 1980.
303 Conversation with Jaroslav Krejčí, 13 May 2000.
304 Quoted in Radka Denemarková, *Evald Schorm: sám sobě nepřítelem*, p. 224.
305 Conversation with Evald Schorm, 31 January 1983.
306 Václav Havel, "Much ado..." *Index on Censorship*, Autumn 1976.
307 Marketa Goetz-Stankiewicz, *The Vaněk Plays*, 1987, preface, p. xxiv.
308 Ibid., p. xviii.
309 "For New Creative Deeds in the Name of Socialism and Peace," from Vilém Prečan (ed.), *Charta 77 1977-1989. Od morální k demokratické revoluci* [*Charter 77 1977-1989. From a Moral to a Democratic Revolution*], translated by Bradley F. Abrams, (Scheinfeld-Schwarzenberg: Čs. Středisko nezávislé literatury and Bratislava: ARCHA, 1990), p. 35–38.
310 Lída Engelová, *Sto růží v bidetu*, Prague, 2017, p. 119.
311 Miroslav Graclík and Václav Nekvapil, *Jiřina Švorcová osobně*, pp. 313-314.
312 Tom Stoppard, "Prague: The Story of the Chartists," *New York Review of Books*, 4 August 1977.
313 Described in Edá Kriseová, *Václav Havel*, (1993) pp. 142–143.
314 Jan Dvořák, Jaroslav Etlík, Bohumil Nuska et al., *Jan Schmid*, p.75.
315 Conversation with Ctibor Turba, 31 January 1983.
316 Jiří Mahen, *Husa na provázku*, Ot. Štorch-Marien, Prague 1925, pp. 5-7.

317 Bořivoj Srba, typed sheet distributed at early performances of Theatre on a String, reproduced in Petr Oslzlý, *Divadlo Husa na provázku 1968/6/-1998*, Brno, 1999.
318 "divadlo na provázku–model 1970" in *Divadlo* 1970/2.
319 David Drozd, *Příběhy dlouhého nosu*, DVD appendix, JAMU, Brno 2011.
320 Eva Tálská, "K metaforickému ztvárnění Viktorky," in Kateřina Fojtíková et al., *Eva Tálská*, Prague 2011.
321 Bohumil Hrabal dramatised by Ivo Krobot & Petr Oslzlý, *Rozvzpomínání*, typescript working version, s.d..
322 Daniela Fischerová, *Dog and Wolf*, in Day (ed.), *Czech Plays*, op. cit., p. 221.
323 Miloš Petana and Jan Dvořák, "Od čítanky k povinnosti nebýt blbý..." *Scéna* 8, 8 August 1988.
324 Aleš Bergman, "Pracovní portrét–J.A. Pitínský a ochotnický kroužek," *BULLETIN*, Komise pro studiovou divadelní práci Svazu ceských dramatických umělců a její Aktiv mladých divadelníků, no. 7, p. 98, 1989.
325 Søren Kierkegaard, *Fear and Trembling*, tr. Alastair Hanay, Penguin Books, Harmondsworth 1985, p. 65.
326 Søren Kierkegaard and Helmut Heissenbüttel, *Případ Abrahámův*, working typescript, p. 23. In the typescript the words belong to the *Vyvolavač* (Speaker), but in the staged version they were spoken by the Conductor.
327 Jan Pojkar (pseudonym) in *Kritický sborník*, 3/1981, quoted in Karel Kyncl, "A Censored Life," *Index on Censorship*, February 1985.
328 Conversation with Jan Dvořák, 30 May 2011.
329 František Čech, Vlasta Gallerová, Arnošt Goldflam et al., "Přispěvek do diskuse," *Scéna*, 30 March 1987.
330 Ibid.
331 An extract published as Petr Oslzlý, "O ztrátích české kultury" in the *samizdat* publication *Lidové noviny*, July/August 1988, nos 7-8.
332 An extract published as "Soumrak bohů podle Pernici" in ibid., October 1988, no 10.
333 Duplicated double-sided A4 sheet, s.d., with addresses and facsimile signatures of Petr Oslzlý, Joska Skalník, Jaroslav Kořán, Petr Kabeš, Petr Rezek, Karel Steigerwald, Petr Kofroň, Jan Šimek and Petr Váša. Issued in Czech and in English, the version here being the original (uncredited) translation.
334 Marie Boková, "Obnovit pocit odpovědnosti," *Scéna*, 13 February 1989.
335 Conversation with Jaroslav Krejčí, 13 May 2000.
336 Petr Oslzlý, typescript dated 30 March 1992, Brno, tr. Day, quoted in the preface to Day (ed.), *Czech Plays*, op. cit., p. xvi.

INDEX OF NAMES

(The order follows the English alphabet)